POLITICAL HINDUISM

POLITICAL HINDUISM

THE RELIGIOUS IMAGINATION IN PUBLIC SPHERES

EDITED BY **VINAY LAL**

OXFORD
UNIVERSITY PRESS

OXFORD
UNIVERSITY PRESS

Oxford University Press is a department of the University of Oxford.
It furthers the University's objective of excellence in research, scholarship,
and education by publishing worldwide. Oxford is a registered trademark of
Oxford University Press in the UK and in certain other countries

Published in India by
Oxford University Press
22 Workspace, 2nd Floor, 1/22 Asaf Ali Road, New Delhi 110002, India

First Edition published in 2009
14th impression 2024

ISBN-13: 978-0-19-806418-3
ISBN-10: 0-19-806418-7

Typeset in Dante MT Std 10.5/12.6
by Sai Graphic Design, New Delhi 110 055
Printed in India by Manipal Technologies Limited, Manipal

Contents

Acknowledgements

The idea for this volume stemmed from a small conference on Political Hinduism organized by myself at the University of California, Los Angeles (UCLA) over two full days in May 2005. The sessions were open to public and the conference generated much enthusiasm, as is often the case with such undertakings. The present volume draws equally upon papers that were, if in more rudimentary forms, first presented at the conference, and papers that have been written expressly at my invitation by scholars who were not present at the conference. Some of the contributors have shown considerable patience and I hope that, on reading this book, they will feel amply rewarded for their forbearance. It is a matter of regret to me that Professor Ram-Prasad Chakravarti, with whom I had an engaging exchange, was unable, for personal reasons, to attend the conference or even contribute to this volume. Several academic units at UCLA supported the conference, but I am particularly grateful to Professor Scott Bartchy, Director of the Center for the Study of Religion, for his enthusiastic support of the conference and for placing at my disposal, with the approval of the Center's board, the funds that brought the conference, and ultimately this volume, to fruition.

Vinay Lal

Religion in Politics and the Politics of Hinduism
An Introduction

The subject matter of this volume will perhaps appear to most readers who do not look beyond the title as self-evident, though, as even a cursory reading will suggest, the political in 'Political Hinduism' can be read in registers that are as uncommon as predictable. The terrain carved out by political Hinduism, it seems, is well charted, and certainly subjected to more searching analysis than most other phenomena of socio-political life in India. Scholars appear to be in very wide agreement that the rise of Hindu nationalism or 'Hindutva' (commonly rendered into English as Hinduness, or the vigorous assertion of Hindu identity as a tenet of ideological belief) in India since the mid-1980s, constitutes one of the most significant developments in the political life of the nation since the advent of Independence in 1947, appreciably altering, for instance, the landscape of political parties, the tenor of many institutions, the social fabric of relations between different religious communities, and public understandings of masculinity. Nation building may always be a tenuous, indeed one should say fractured, enterprise but the ascendancy of (militant) Hindu nationalism has rendered the enterprise even more fragile and open to assault. So long as one remains confined to a rather narrow construction of the 'political', one can also reasonably aver that the scholarship of the last decade or two has been reasonably fecund. The organization of the Rashtriya Swayamsevak Sangh (RSS), the writings and rantings of Hindutva's ideologues, from K.B. Hedgewar, Vinayak Savarkar, and M.S. Golwalkar to the commentators that appear in the pages of the RSS mouthpiece, the *Organiser*, the political machinery of the Shiv Sena, the electoral strategies of the Bharatiya Janata Party (BJP), the orchestration of terror on the streets by the Bajrang Dal, and the Vishwa Hindu Parishad's (VHP) work in reconversion and proselytization are among some of the subjects that have received considerable attention and scholarly scrutiny.[1]

The birth of a free India was accompanied by the country's vivisection and an orgy of violence. The violence that transpired, despite the incalculable enormity of its scale, at least did not reek of the particular stench that has accompanied more recent killings, such as the pogrom of 2002 directed against Muslims in Gujarat with the active complicity of leading politicians and functionaries of the state.[2] Men, women, and children were butchered wholesale in the wake of the Partition; caravans several miles in length of human beings, weighed down by memories, sorrows, and the bundles of their worldly belongings, were pounced upon; women jumped into wells to avoid the ignominy of sexual dishonour—but there was no Narendra Modi, an elected leader of a prosperous state with aspirations to ascend to national prominence, to gloat over the atrocities with the observation that 'every action meets with a reaction'.[3] Nevertheless, even if one allows that the Partition killings were not generally orchestrated, indeed that the bulk of them took place in the heat of the moment with the perpetrators blinded by intensely experienced feelings, not only of revenge but loss of ancestral lands, cultural ties, and lifestyle norms, there were people determined to inject a political Hinduism into the proceedings of those days. Having pumped three bullets into the body of Mohandas Karamchand Gandhi, his assassin, Nathuram Godse, when he had his day in court, was forthright in enunciating the doctrine that the 'Father of the Nation', for all his patriotism, had enfeebled the Hindus and emasculated a faith that would have to learn how to stand on its feet against the depredations of Muslims.[4] Godse held Gandhi primarily responsible for the butchery, violation, and abduction of their Hindu sisters, though he scarcely had anything to say about the treatment of Muslim women at the hands of Hindus and Sikhs.

Curiously, Gandhi's other political antagonist, Muhammed Ali Jinnah, had a different, if complementary, reading of the political personality of the slain Indian leader: it is not that Gandhi proved inadequate to the Hindu community, rather Gandhi could not step outside the community and genuinely claim to represent all Indians. While the rest of the world mourned the passing of the greatest architect of non-violent resistance who resolutely believed in the intrinsic humanity of each and every person, Jinnah crafted a carefully worded message to the Indian government condoling the death of 'Mr Gandhi', who he ranked among 'the greatest men produced by the Hindu community'.[5] Apparently, in death as in life, Gandhi was to be viewed as nothing more than a Hindu political leader. We may say that Jinnah and Godse, however ample their differences, were perhaps one in thinking that a certain admixture of politics and religion under Gandhi's dispensation had been fatal. Though few, if any, of Gandhi's critics would go so far as to say that Gandhi was communal-minded, many more were willing to give their assent to the argument that the panoply of ideas, metaphors, and symbols deployed by him readily lent themselves to communal interpretations. If Gandhi, it is sometimes suggested, could not altogether succeed in operating outside the communal framework, what is one to expect of others who are barely constrained by any scruples and do not hesitate to instrumentalize religion in the service of politics? Sixty years after Gandhi's assassination and the subsequent short ban placed on the RSS, the literature on communalism has proliferated, aided no doubt by the gruesome blood-letting that, at periodic intervals, continues to be witnessed in independent India. Outsiders to the world of Indian studies might even be forgiven for thinking that communalism, especially Hindu nationalism in its most overt political manifestations, constitutes the preeminent arena of inquiry for those interested in Indian affairs.

Thinking of the rise of Hindu nationalism, several other interpretive trajectories come to mind. There is the temptation to seamlessly insert its narrative into the history of the idea of the Hindu nation, and the attractions of the idea of tracing Hindu nationalism back to Bal Gangadhar Tilak or the Bengali writer Bankimchandra Chatterjee, or indeed, from the perspective of some ideologues, much further back to the Maratha chieftain Shivaji or the Rajput warrior Rana Pratap Singh, are palpable. Others who refuse to be seduced by intellectual history and argue for a pragmatic conception of the political, are more swayed by the fact that the idea of the Hindu nation could not bear fruit under conditions of alien rule. Until its defeat in the elections of 2004, the BJP occupied the seat of power for several years. However, we have to recall that it is in less than a decade that the BJP went from being a party with a handful of seats in the Lok Sabha to being, for a few years, the single largest party in Parliament. What is to be said of colonial India, even Nehruvian India may not have been too hospitable to Hindu nationalists. Subsequent to Gandhi's assassination, they were banished into the wilderness and the Nehruvian dream had not yet had time to go stale and thus pave the way for the revival of Hindu militancy.

Those scholars whose canvas is still larger, extending from considerations about the geopolitics of nationalism to the numerous ways in which narratives of modernity may impinge upon extreme forms of political religiosity, would rather inscribe the emergence of Hindutva or Hindu chauvinism within a history that is more attentive to similar trends elsewhere in the world—from such expressions of Islamic fundamentalism as the Taliban in Afghanistan and numerous other jihadi groups in Kashmir and Pakistan, to the emergence of the Christian right in the United States as an immense political force.[6] Before the simultaneous terror attacks in Mumbai, in late November 2008, turned the spotlight back on Muslim terrorists, at least some commentators had finally felt emboldened enough to speak of 'Hindu terrorists'. A spate of violence, much of it attributed to Hindu religious activists, had engulfed Christian churches and communities in Orissa in the months preceding the Mumbai attacks, and calls were being aired for a ban on the Bajrang Dal, an organization that could with justice be characterized as performing the muscle-work of Hindu nationalism. Many people might have sympathized with the observation by the BJP leader, Yashwant Sinha, that 'the term Hindu terrorists is wrong', for 'a terrorist is a terrorist irrespective of his caste or religion', but perhaps a few of them may have wondered why this sentiment is only infrequently, if at all, voiced when the terrorists in question are Muslims rather than Hindus.[7] Only weeks before the Mumbai terror attacks, Mumbai's Anti-Terrorism Squad (ATS) had taken into custody Sadhvi Pragya Singh Thakur on suspicion of having taken part in the late September 2008 bomb blasts at Malegaon in Maharashtra. 'Her speeches were mostly about saving Hindutva and fighting Islamic terrorists,' one reporter had written, and the testimony of a Bajrang Dal leader suggests that the Sadhvi's oratory is capable of bringing women to tears.[8] And, then, in the midst of these converging tales of 'Hindu terrorism', the Mumbai terror attacks appeared to return the narrative of terrorism back to the familiar terrain where it has been lodged—as a problem largely intrinsic to Islam. Whatever one's views about the singularity or otherwise of Hindu extremism, militant Islam, or the Christian right's evident appetite for power, there are genuine questions to be asked about whether globalization offers a productive intellectual template to understand what appears to be a turn towards militant religiosity in large parts of the world. Is the drift towards Hindutva and even militant

Hinduism to be explained only by conditions peculiar to India or at best the Indian subcontinent—from the exhaustion associated with the ideology of secularism and the anguish in middle-class circles over India's impotency and indeed invisibility over the course of something like four decades following Independence, to the fact that secessionist movements within India and the intractability of certain conflicts, such as that over Kashmir, whetted the Hindu middle-class appetite for a more vigorous and militant response to real or imagined threats to the nation? Or is it, conversely, the case that under conditions of global modernity, Hinduism has striven to become a world religion and has thus set on the path of emulating those faiths which, beholden to historical founders and a single supremely authoritative text, have perhaps been less tolerant of liminality, ambivalence, and plurality than Hinduism?

Even as studies of Hindu nationalism or—in the preferred terms of its detractors and protagonists alike—Hindutva have proliferated, the parameters within which such studies have been conducted have remained spectacularly narrow. A personal impression will not be out of place: in the few years leading up to the destruction of the Babri Masjid on 6 December 1992, as well as in years immediately following that calamitous event, it became clear to me as I sought to canvass the views of family members and neighbours in an area of west Delhi that was once a Congress stronghold but had slowly gravitated towards the BJP, that there was widespread if muted acceptance of the view that Hindus had, over a substantial period of India's pre-modern past, been subject to the tyranny of Muslim rule. Since then, a few studies have documented both the wide support for the BJP and VHP among large segments of the middle class, as well as the growing market for Hindutva versions of history,[9] though by far the greater bulk of the evidence is anecdotal and prodigiously encountered, not so much in the pages of English or vernacular newspapers in India as on websites and chat rooms. But even these few studies have not ventured much into the question of how Hindutva has impacted practices of Hinduism on the ground. To be sure, the serialization of the Ramayana and Mahabharata, followed in later years by television serials on Krishna and such real or alleged stalwarts of Hindu nationalism as Shivaji, did not go unnoticed in the academy.[10] L.K. Advani's *rath*—or rather Toyota—*yatra*, the masculinization of the once comparatively benign imagery of Rama, the transformations in the *Ram Lila*, the renewed emphasis on the cult of Shivaji, and other like manifestations have been seized upon as elements

of Hindutva's burgeoning empire of signs. A recent ethnography of the
RSS ritual cycle usefully points to the manner in which celebrations of
Hindu festivals, under the dispensation of the RSS, become occasions
for nationalist mobilizations.[11] Golwalkar had urged the celebration
of Hindu festivals not merely in the interest of 'public entertainment',
but also 'to strengthen national feeling': not only are changes, some
more subtle than others, wrought in the way in which such festivals
are commemorated, but new hierarchies are established. Thus the RSS
calendar elevates to prominence *Hindu Samarajya Dinotsav*, or 'Hindu
Empire Day', supposedly the day when Shivaji, rallying the Hindus
who (as Alberuni might have said) had scattered to the winds under
the onslaught of the Mughal forces, raised the banner of revolt and
proclaimed a Hindu *rashtra*.[12] Many of RSS's innovations which purport
to return Hindus to their roots or emancipate Hindus from the shackles
of European history, seem wholly derivative of European models, and
one wonders if 'Hindu Empire Day' was itself not born of the idea of
'Empire Day', first celebrated in Britain on Queen Victoria's birthday,
24 May, the year after her death in 1901?

All things considered, however, the phenomena that have fallen
under scholarly scrutiny are rather miniscule, and as a consequence
many lines of inquiry, most particularly those which furnish some insight
into the everyday life of political Hinduism, have gone unexplored. I
adverted briefly to Hindu festivals, but have Hindu modes of worship
or religious practices more broadly been considerably impacted because
of Hindutva, and if so, what kind of transformations are we able to
witness? Have the attitudes of Hindus towards syncretic practices, for
example visits to *dargahs* of Sufi saints, come under any appreciable
restraints? If the strands of Islam that go under the name of Wahhabism
and Salafism have set up a wall between themselves and what they deem
to be heretical versions of Islam, are advocates of political Hinduism
similarly more resistant than before to the patronage of Sufi shrines by
Hindus? One can also turn to another set of questions: Have certain
texts or religious practices been demoted while others have been
elevated? Much has been said about Tulsidas's *Ramacharitmanas* in this
regard, but are Hindutva's advocates really dedicated to establishing it
as the unrivalled text of Hinduism as is commonly alleged? In *Glimpses
of World History*, Jawaharlal Nehru had opined that Tulsidas was more
popular than the Mughal Emperor himself, during Akbar's reign, and
his name was 'known to every villager in the United Provinces'.[13]
Tulsidas's popularity has not diminished in north India over the

centuries, and there is certainly reason to suppose, as the controversy over 'Ram Sethu'—a bridge between India and Sri Lanka that the Archaeological Survey of India (ASI) had initially described as a natural formation, but which the VHP insists was built by Rama's allies to enable him to cross over into Lanka—in 2007 amply demonstrates, that sentiments over the historicity of the Ramayana are still easily excited.[14] Yet if there was a controversy, it was not only on account of the claims predictably advanced by the VHP and rather unusually contradicted by a government agency—a rather greater outburst was created when the Chief Minister of Tamil Nadu, M. Karunanidhi, relying on a non-Brahminical critique of the Ramayana that is well established in Tamil Nadu, averred that Rama is far from being a historical person and was described by Valmiki himself as a drunkard.[15]

The furore over this matter had scarcely died down before activists of the Akhil Bharatiya Vidyarthi Parishad (ABVP), the student wing of the BJP, went on a rampage at Delhi University, all because the university's History department prescribed an essay by the late A.K. Ramanujan titled, 'Three Hundred Ramayanas', in its course on culture in ancient India.[16] Ramanujan's essay, ABVP activists allege, demeans the Hindu faith: what it does do, more precisely, is to offer the rather unimpeachable suggestion that there is an immense plurality of Ramayana traditions, and folk Kannada and Telugu versions, where Sita appears as Ravana's daughter, have just as much claim to our attention as the grand narratives of Valmiki, Kamban, and Tulsidas.[17] Still, is this incontrovertible evidence of the increasing hegemony of the Valmiki or Tulsidas versions, or even of the assured place of the Ramayana in narratives of political Hinduism? In Fiji, as my own experience suggested and as the well-known Indo-Fijian writer Satendra Nandan has corroborated, large portions of Viti Levu, particularly the area around Lautoka, are viewed as *Manas* country,[18] but I am not aware that these devotees of the *Ramacharitmanas* ever viewed it as a text of political mobilization, even though Indians labour under such considerable political disabilities that their population has diminished by something like 20 per cent over the last two decades, or even as a text with which one could score points over one's opponents.

There are, of course, various forms of public display of religiosity other than those which have marked the conduct of ABVP activists or of those who, enraged at a book on Shivaji which made some dents into the hagiographic accounts that have defined the Maratha chieftain's life,[19] ransacked the priceless collections of the Bhandarkar Oriental Research

Institute and managed to have a ban passed over the book. Over the last decade, no one visiting north India would have failed to notice that ever-larger statues of Hanuman and Shiva, some several stories high, have been cropping up with increasing frequency. Philip Lutgendorf has captured this nicely in his aptly entitled piece, 'My Hanuman Is Bigger Than Yours'.[20] Should we attribute this competitiveness not only to the spirit of privatization and individual entrepreneurship which appears to have seized the country, but also to the advent of a class of people who neither inherited their wealth nor came by it as beneficiaries of what in India has been called the 'license Raj'? Moreover, there is no reason why religion should be immune from the pervasive culture of the Guinness Book in middle-class India. Indeed, considering the tenacity of the view that India is preeminently a land of religion, it is perhaps apposite that religion's advocates in India have been very keen that their accomplishments should be adequately reflected in the Guinness Book. But for every Hanuman or Shiva that has gotten taller, one wonders if other deities have, so to speak, gotten smaller? Once we move beyond Rama, what deities have fared well under political Hinduism, and what deities, if any, have diminished?

The masculinization of Hinduism under Hindutva is a favourite leitmotif of the scholarship of the last two decades or more and of public commentary,[21] and also informs, to a very substantial degree, the work of filmmakers such as Anand Patwardhan.[22] Vivekananda, the icon of young and resurgent India, may have set the trend when he spoke of the desirability of injecting beef, biceps, and the Bhagavadgita into Hinduism, but one can adduce many more examples of how Hindutva's ideologues and their supporters have sought to masculinize Hinduism. To take one illustration, whatever the supposed veneration of Rama—and especially Tulsidas's Rama—found in the writings, speeches, and harangues of Hindutva's advocates, it is a telling fact that the disdain for Rama as an effeminate god runs deep in the ranks of the organizations that have spearheaded Hindutva. As scholars such as Anuradha Kapur and Richard Davis have demonstrated, and as is clear to the *bhaktas* of Rama, the changing iconography of Rama points to his remarkable transmutation into the preeminent god of a dangerously awakened Hinduism.[23] The discomfort with Rama's lack of masculinity has been transformed, if the matter may be put starkly, into a strident assertion of militancy in the name of defending Rama. Yet Tulsidas rhapsodized about Rama in a language that makes it difficult to think of him as only, or even at all, a male deity. Here is how Rama and Lakshmana looked to Sita when her eyes first fell upon them:

bikata bhrkuti kaca ghugaravare, nava saroja locana ratanare
caru cibuka nasika kapola, hasa bilasa leta manu mola
mukhachabi kahi na jai mohi pahi, jo biloki bahu kama lajah
ura mani mala kambu kala giva, kama kalabha kara bhuja balasiva.

(With arched eyebrows and curly locks, eyes red as a lotus-bud and a lovely chin, nose and cheeks, their gracious smile warmed the soul. The beauty of their countenance was more than I can describe; it would put to shame a myriad lovers. They had a string of jewels on their breast, and their lovely neck resembled a conch-shell in its spiral shape; while their mighty arms vied with the trunk of a young elephant, the very incarnation of Cupid.)[24]

A more telling illustration of the ironies with which the enterprise of masculinizing Hinduism is drenched can scarcely be found. The point need not be belaboured, but can perhaps take us to uncharted territory. Might the excess virility generated by Hindutva have its counterpart in newer forms of feminine spirituality or even a politically charged hyper-femininity? If a Hindu god is appearing in a new countenance, what of the goddesses? In Thiruvananthapuram, the goddess Attukal Devi appears to have attracted a gargantuan following among working-class women in recent years, and in the ten day festival dedicated to her in late February to early March, the feast is served by women to women alone in public thoroughfares, while the Attukal Bhagavathy temple remains closed to men on the ninth day when the *Pongala Mahotsavam* takes place.[25] I am not certain which period of history this women's festival can be traced back to, but there is widespread agreement that the festival has grown enormously over the last two decades.[26] Worship of the goddess in India is, of course, widespread and the Pongala offerings at the Attukal Bhagavathy temple are perhaps no more than another instantiation of the *Devi* tradition. It is sometimes argued that Hinduism has always been more receptive to women's spaces than the comparatively stern Semitic faiths, and that the sisterhood to which Western feminism aspires has, likewise, been a marked feature of the lives of Indian women in a diverse array of social settings. Nevertheless, if the aforementioned festival, which Dalit women in particular embrace as their own, has witnessed immense growth over the last two decades—a period that has seen the emergence of not only Hindu nationalism but the rise of Dalits as a political force—then it becomes pertinent to inquire whether the creation and enlargement of women's spaces bears some relation to the advent of militant Hinduism.

The phenomena that may possibly be embraced under the rubric of political Hinduism are still more varied than religious festivals, sacred texts, statues of deities, or other palpable displays of religiosity. The new found craze for *Vastu*, for instance, may appear to have no relation to political Hinduism, though *Vastushastra*, or the ancient and medieval works that deal with city planning, architecture, and temple sculpture, is clearly grounded in Hindu myths. One might argue that Vastu bears the same relationship to the energizing of the Indian economy as Feng-shui does to the explosion of the Chinese economy, with all the concomitant signs of a new class of the wealthy given to conspicuous consumption and leisure, and exceedingly particular about how the site for their home is selected, the energies radiating from their home, the direction of air currents, and so on. But should we then view the revival of Vastu as bearing some kind of inextricable relationship to the burgeoning economy and consider its latest arrival on the Indian scene alongside a resurgent Hinduism as pure coincidence? Is it not possible to argue that vastu, ayurveda, and yoga all trumpet the confidence increasingly encountered among many middle- and upper class Hindus? The architectural writer Gautam Bhatia once famously lampooned the architectural pretensions of the nouveau riche in India,[27] but one wonders if it will be too much of a stretch to suppose that political Hinduism has given rise to new forms of modern and vernacular architecture? There is a triumphant note in the recent invocations by Indians, at home and abroad, of yoga, ayurveda, and India's other spiritual resources once again coming to the rescue of the beleaguered West, and helping to restore the balance in lives scourged by materialism. These narratives are analogous to those which postcolonial scholars made familiar when they wrote, commencing in the 1980s, of 'the empire striking back'.

One could easily multiply queries in this direction, and turn from the architecture of the city (vastu) and of the body (yoga) to the architecture of desire, that is, to cinema in the space of the nation. The films of Mani Ratnam, particularly *Roja* (1992) and *Bombay* (1995), excited much attention and alarm among scholars and commentators concerned about film as a seductive vehicle of nakedly nationalist sentiments, and every now and then scholarly scrutiny focuses on films—among others, *Border, Mission Kashmir, Gadar, Sarfarosh*, and most recently *Lagaan*— which are viewed as particularly culpable in their easy endorsement of the ideology of the nation-state. The popular Hindi film of recent years has, to a substantial extent, become a vehicle for resolute expressions of Indian patriotism, but can the same be said of the Hindi film in relation to political Hinduism—assuming that patriotism does not exhaust the meaning of political Hinduism? In the early 1990s, for example, M.S.S. Pandian in his *Image Trap* opened up a new field of inquiry by drawing attention to the complex phenomenon of MGR, the legendary star of Tamil cinema who exploited his massive cult following to create a niche for himself in Tamil politics. While MGR ran a police state, as Pandian argues, he was presented on celluloid as a figure who was one with the masses—in a mode 'very similar to the manner in which fascist propaganda projected Hitler'.[28] The intense debates over secularism are now too well known to require any elaboration, but have they been carried out in different idioms in cinematic works? Surprisingly, there is no sustained treatment of this subject at all. Though scholarly inquiry has finally turned to Bollywood in the last few years,[29] the better recognized scholarly studies have almost nothing to say on the subject of the representation of Hinduism in popular Indian cinema, whether in Hindi, Tamil, Malayalam, or any other language.[30]

It is evident, then, that the terrain of political Hinduism broadly conceived is largely uncharted, notwithstanding the sporadic efforts of scholars to bring to light certain social and cultural phenomena that have characterized the last two decades. Even in the case of somewhat older phenomena, such as the emergence of the cult of Vaishno Devi, particularly among the refugees of 1947, it appears prudent to ask how far, if at all, it has been transformed by, and is implicated in, the resurgence of Hindu militancy. Much has been written, understandably, on the marked proliferation of schools with an avowedly Hindu agenda and curricula,[31] on textbook controversies,[32] and on Hindu nationalists' firm commitment to Vedic science.[33] But just as surely as this does not exhaust the possibilities of scholarly inquiry and reflection, even in this domain the investigations have been far from complete. A new chapter is being written, to take one illustration, in the long narrative of grandiose Hindu temple architecture, nowhere more evident than in the temples, which exude an air of ostentatiousness and self-consciousness in equal parts, constructed by Gujaratis who are adherents of Swaminarayan Hinduism. Yet these are not merely temples, since they partake of modernity's museum modality—the permanent exhibitions on Hinduism not only seek to enlighten young ones about the rudiments of the faith, but seek to furnish a definitive history of the faith that dwells on the compatibility of Hinduism's ancient tenets with the findings of modern science.[34] There is, thus, also the interesting consideration, among diasporic populations, that the rise of political Hinduism has taken place alongside renewed interest in such expressions of 'Hindu' sensibility as *bharatanatyam*, grand temple architecture, and an endless round of pujas, *satsangs*, *darshans* of holy men and women, and discourses on the Hindu way of life. Countless number of *ammas* and *babajis* come and go, talking of spiritual salvation. Yet, if even a few South Asian Muslim girls and women have also embraced bharatanatyam, and so earned the wrath of their community, then it is clear that 'Hindu' cannot be read unequivocally as a religious category. To this end, some reflection on Hinduism's multi-pronged appearances in the diaspora is also necessary.

One also has the unmistakable impression that, for the most part, the study of the rise of political Hinduism has been largely the provenance of historians and political scientists, with no doubt a few cultural anthropologists and practitioners of cultural studies, media studies, and women's studies thrown into the mix. It has often been remarked that the scholarly study of Hinduism was seldom undertaken at Indian universities, and the history of religions, which is a discipline in the United States with its own scholarly paraphernalia of institutional networks, conferences, and journals, is largely unknown in India as a scholarly field. One might understand why few scholarly studies on 'political Hinduism' in the expansive sense in which it is being deployed here have been generated in the Indian academic context, but it is more difficult to understand why the 'history of religions' fraternity in the United States has not really been a party to the debates to which I have pointed attention.[35] The serialization of the Ramayana by state-owned television in India in the 1980s, first became the subject of scholarly interpretation by practitioners of cultural studies and media studies, and only later were some scholars of religion drawn into the debate. If we turn our attention to India, it is striking that the voices of Ramayana scholars, and indeed of other devout and pietistic Hindu traditions, are seldom heard in debates about the proposed Rama mandir or the serialization of the Ramayana. Have Indian philosophers, to the extent that they wish to be characterized as Hindus, or are inclined to view their engagement with Indian philosophy as informed by their Hindu beliefs and practices, reflected on political Hinduism? While one would be extremely hard pressed to make a case for something that might go under the name of 'Hindutva Philosophy', it nonetheless seems worthwhile to ask how classical Indian ideas of self, personhood, rationality, and relationality might be used to develop some general conception of political life appropriate to contemporary India. Would some Hindu essentialism result from such an exercise or, as is far more likely, would one come to the conclusion that political Hinduism, or more precisely Hindutva in this context, fails, philosophically, in relation to its own putative cultural roots?

The eight papers in this volume do not address all or even most of the aforementioned questions, but they open up other new and productive lines of inquiry, gesturing at forms of public religiosity that are not bound to the fanaticisms with which religions today are increasingly associated, exploring the relationship of Hinduism to literature and cinema, and often revisiting familiar figures to arrive at fresh and even radically new readings. Madhav Deshpande's paper on Bal Gangadhar Tilak, for a short time the most dominant figure in Indian nationalist politics, avoids the more predictable ground of Tilak's pivotal role in bringing the Ganapati festival into the public sphere, or his characterization as an 'extremist' rather than a 'moderate' in Indian politics. Deshpande places Tilak's 'Arctic Home Theory' at the centre of his investigations, and proceeds to inquire into the intellectual milieu in which Tilak operated, the debates between Tilak and other prominent Maharashtrian Brahmin intellectuals, and the deployment of Tilak's ideas about the origins of the Aryans in recent times by Hindu nationalists. Deshpande argues that Tilak was, far from being wholly representative of the Maharashtrian Brahmin elite of his times, also unusual in various respects. Tilak abided by the view, promulgated by scholars from Sir William Jones to Max Müller, that the Aryans were not indigenous to India, even though this view could not be easily reconciled with his nationalist politics. Similarly, going against the orthodox grain of thinking which held that the Vedas are eternal, not made by the hand of man, *apauruseya*, Tilak claimed, much to the chagrin of traditional Sanskrit scholars, that the Vedas have a datable origin. Even as he admired Western scholarship, he held that the philological method was insufficient to get a grip on the histories and meanings of Indian texts. Moreover, as he would later demonstrate, when put on trial on charges of sedition, it was also essential for Indians to better the English in their mastery of the courtroom and legal language.

Deshpande traces, at some length, the intellectual relationship of Tilak to Narayan Pavgee, author of the voluminous *The Bharatiya Samrajya* or *Hindu Empire*, since, in Deshpande's view, it is Pavgee who was instrumental in reworking Tilak's ideas and making them available for use by later ideologues of Hindutva such as Golwalkar, Savarkar, and Koenraad Elst. Pavgee emerges in Deshpande's account as the principal intellectual precursor of the idea, now widely disseminated in Hindutva writings, that the Aryan migrations commenced from India. Deshpande concludes with the observation that:

... while Tilak remains among the founding fathers of the modern Hindutva movement, the substance of his Arctic Home theory, closely related as it is to the hated Aryan-Invasion-Theory, is gradually eased into retirement, in favour of the various versions of the Out-of-India theories, to be found on pro-Hindutva websites and publications.

Generations of school children in India have grown up learning of Tilak as the author of the adage, 'Swaraj is my birthright'. Narayana Guru has, at least outside his native Kerala, been obscure to the same degree. Roby Rajan and R. Reghu's paper on Narayana Guru, who has begun to attract substantial English-language scholarship only in recent years, is spectacularly ambitious in its reinterpretation of the nineteenth century 'philosopher-poet' from Kerala, an 'erudite scholar of Sanskrit, Malayalam and Tamil' who, in the words of the editor of a recent compilation of his writings, 'belonged to the great Indian philosophical tradition of Advaita'.[36] Rajan and Reghu seek, in the first instance, to lay to rest the dominant readings of Narayana Guru which either assimilate him into the timeless streams of *advaita* or absorb him, as a south Indian variant, into the historical narrative of 'reform movements' that take westernization, modernization, and Sanskritization, either singly or in combination, 'as their proper *telos*'. Narayana Guru hailed from the low caste of Ezhavas, and Marxist and liberal historiography has etched him firmly as Kerala's liberator whose mission was to catapult the masses from their state of pre-historic 'caste consciousness' to a full-blown awareness of the demon of casteism.[37]

Central to the narrative portion of Rajan and Reghu's paper is an account of the *Aruvippuram Pratishta*, the unprecedented consecration by the lowly Ezhava, Narayana Guru, of a *shivalingam* on a moonless *shivaratri* night. This act of 'subaltern resistance', as the historians have admiringly described it, is 'conferred with such performative force,' write Rajan and Reghu, 'as to have triggered an unraveling of the entire social edifice of traditional Kerala'. To appreciate what is at stake in Rajan and Reghu's resistance to these attempts to normalize Narayan Guru's ethico-political intervention as an instance, albeit a cataclysmic one, of 'caste reform', the writers remind us that what is today viewed as the anomalous story of the 'Kerala model'—a reference to the fact that, notwithstanding a low rate of economic growth as well as low per-capita income, Kerala scores as high as developed countries in the human development index, insofar as one takes such measures as gender ratios and rates of infant mortality, maternal mortality, and literacy—is also often attributed to Narayana Guru's determined efforts to rid society of its casteist superstitions. Rajan and Reghu, in their unravelling of the *pratishta*, go much further in two respects. First, they suggest that the account of the historians and the sociologists, which advances an 'evolutionary scheme leading from primitive superstition/ incipient secularism to civilized worship/full-fledged rationality', is largely reductive and has found little credibility among common people. In the 'popular memory' of Narayana Guru, they argue, 'he emerges as one who ushered in the wondrous by confounding the possible and the impossible; not only were the present and future thereby transfigured, but the entirety of the past as well.' Secondly, and most significantly, they reinterpret the pratistha as a parallel to the French Revolution, arguing vociferously for a rejection of the idea that all our universalisms are to be derived from the West. Narayana Guru's ethico-political intervention in Kerala's society is most properly understood as constituting an alternative universalism, not merely as a particularism which can be absorbed into the seamless history of a sponge-like Hinduism. We have here an account of 'Backwater Universalism'— without the Jacobin Terror.

The intellectual interests of Bankimcandra Chatterjee were perhaps no less wide-ranging than those of Tilak, and they shared much in common—from an interest in history as a modern enterprise of knowledge-seeking to a passion for the Gita, on which both penned a lengthy commentary. Bankim, however, was to acquire fame principally as a novelist, and as the author of the highly controversial *Vande Mataram*, a hymn which, though it first appeared in Bankim's novel *Anandamath* (1881–2),[38] acquired an independent existence before eventually being adopted, so Lipner argues, as India's national song. The setting for the novel itself is the 'Sannyasi Rebellion' of the 1770s, when a good bit of greater Bengal was in the grip of a crushing famine. Bankim's Bengal is a rather anarchic land: Muslim authority had crumbled, and though the East India Company (EIC) had become the principal player in the region's rapidly changing fortunes, the Company's writ did not run very far. The *sannyasis*, or renouncers, also known as *santans* ('children'), take up residence in an abandoned monastery, from where they wage a battle against the alien Britishers and now subdued Muslim rulers with the help of revenue extracted from hapless villagers. The santans invoke the Goddess in their struggle to liberate the motherland from the *yavanas*, or outsiders, but the communal element resides not only in the invocation of a Hindu goddess to free Hindus from the yoke of Muslim and British rule, but even, as Lipner submits, in the Hinduization of the motherland. 'Vande Mataram', which translates as 'I revere the Mother', poses other problems of interpretation as the composition is a peculiar admixture of Sanskrit and Bengali. Lipner argues that Sanskrit was a marker of cultural and religious continuity, a mode of acquiring intellectual legitimacy and forging a sense of Hindu national unity; the use of Bengali, however, enabled Bankim to create a platform for mass mobilization and envelop the song in the cadences of current speech.

Lipner offers in his paper a searching analysis of the forms of worship implied in the song before moving, in the second half of his paper, to a discussion of the immensely rich history that *Vande Mataram* has generated over the course of a century. Two years after Bankim's death in 1894, it was apparently recited by none other than Rabindranath Tagore at the annual session of the Indian National Congress. *Vande Mataram* became the rallying cry or battle-song of the swadeshi movement, an upsurge of nationalist sentiment in strong protest against the partition of Bengal in 1905, and an English-language newspaper by the same name, which commenced publication in 1906, would soon be spearheading militant resistance to colonial rule. By the time Gandhi returned to India from South Africa, in early 1915, Muslim opposition to *Vande Mataram*, the slogan as much as the song, was beginning to crystallize, and by the 1920s the calls among Muslims to abandon *Vande Mataram* were resonating in large parts of the country. It is not Lipner's brief to trace the unusually tumultuous history of the song in the two decades before Independence,[39] but he briefly follows the exchanges that took place between prominent nationalist leaders before its adoption by the Constituent Assembly, on 24 January 1950, as the 'national song' of Independent India.

There is, arguably, a still more complex backdrop to the adoption of *Vande Mataram* and its status as the 'national song' invites further inquiry. What exactly distinguishes the 'national song' from the 'national anthem', and is there an established order of precedence or do both have equal status?[40] Not every country has both a national anthem and a national song, but India must surely be the only country in the world where neither is written in the national language. The controversies surrounding *Jana Gana Mana*, a composition by Tagore that would become the national anthem, need not detain us here,[41] but suffice to note that it is in highly Sanskritized Bengali. Both *Vande Mataram* and *Jana Gana Mana* are, moreover, matched in their popularity by *Sare Jahan Se Accha*, a composition in Urdu by Muhammad Iqbal—who would, in time, not only disown the song but also eventually become associated as the author of the intellectual idea of Pakistan. *Sare Jahan Se Accha*, which translates as 'Better than all other lands is this Hindustan of Ours', has not incorrectly been described as India's unofficial anthem, often taking precedence over both *Vande Mataram* and *Jana Gana Mana*. If a national anthem in the national language is a critical part of the paraphernalia of the modern nation-state, then it is a remarkable testament to the plurality and ecumenism of India that such ambiguity has been permitted and even enjoyed. In India, at least, there is reason for people to think that the nation-state does not represent the only embodiment of their dreams and aspirations, and perhaps the idea of India as a civilization has not been entirely suppressed by the idea of India as a nation-state. But how long will it be before the advocates of Hindu chauvinism begin to insist that, in its quest to become a proper and great nation-state, India should have a singular national anthem in the national language?

It is another variety of pluralism that furnishes the occasion for Joanne Waghorne's inquiry, in her paper 'Global Gurus and the Third Stream of American Religiosity: Between Hindu Nationalism and Liberal Pluralism', on the transmission of Hinduism to the United States and the registers in which political Hinduism may appear abroad. She identifies two broad periods, the first being from the early 1890s to 1964, and the second commencing with the passage of new immigration legislation in 1965 that reversed the ban on Asian (including Indian) migration to the United States. Hinduism's history in the US is bookended, we might say, by the rather majestic figure of Vivekananda, who on all accounts mesmerized his audience at Chicago's World's Parliament of Religions in 1893.[42] Vivekananda gathered small groups of disciples around him, star-struck in the presence of the robed Swami who very much looked the part of the sage from the East. The circle of thinkers and writers known as the American Transcendentalists, among them Ralph Waldo Emerson and Henry David Thoreau, had encountered Hinduism by 1840, but Waghorne sees the early 1890s as the true 'dawn of religious pluralism' in the US. Not only was Hinduism's entry into the US at this juncture accompanied by a living seer, who would willy-nilly become the inaugural figure in the movement of spiritual gurus from the East to the West and underscore the importance of the physicality of the guru-disciple relationship, but the academic study of comparative religion in the US was also born at this time. Hinduism was poised to become, at long last, a 'world religion', and its globalization has eventually taken three forms. In its 'liberal' mode, Hinduism takes its place alongside other religions in a multicultural milieu; in its 'conservative' mode, its advocates, what are these days sometimes described as 'heritage Hindus', hearken back to India as the Motherland; and in its 'spiritual' mode, Hinduism opens itself to the worldwide marketplace of gurus, yoga clinics, consciousness-raising workshops and retreats, and the numerous other goods hawked in the spiritual mega mall.

Vivekananda remains, in many respects, the pivotal figure in whose life and teachings are prefigured the questions that continue to animate discussions of Hinduism in a globalized world. As Waghorne's paper makes it amply clear, Hinduism's advocates in their quest for a global reach continue to be heavily invested in Vivekananda's teachings, and the VHP and RSS have both claimed him as their own. Some have objected to Hindutva's manipulation of Vivekananda, though one should not be surprised at such appropriations, considering that militant Hindu nationalists are able to embrace simultaneously a virulent hatred for Gandhi and a purported allegiance to the homilies of the 'Father of the Nation' on national unity, economic self-reliance, and *swadeshi*. Waghorne argues that Vivekananda offered one face to India, another to the West; if he pushed for some form of neo-Hinduism in India, in the West he became an advocate of *Raja Yoga*. Vivekananda sought to universalize Hinduism, and yet he was equally firm in his understanding of Hindu identity as embedded in certain cultural mores. Though Waghorne does not stress this point, in postulating 'an eternal freedom for the soul' that can never be held in subordination, Vivekananda was subscribing to the widely held nationalist view that whatever the extent of India's subjugation in the realm of worldly affairs, in spiritual matters India still reigned supreme. But Waghorne, it should be recognized, ultimately takes the discussion beyond Vivekananda, suggesting that the worldwide popularity of guru-centred movements espousing a de-territorialized and de-ethicized religious consciousness points to a nascent global civil society that is giving rise to new organizational structures and may yet transcend older universalisms.

It cannot be said of Vivekananda, whatever Hindutva's zealots may make of him, that he was ever an advocate of a Hindu Rashtra. A generation after his death, RSS leaders would speak of a Hindu Rashtra as if it were an accomplished fact, and the all-important question was what place the Muslims would occupy in this nation. Jyotirmaya Sharma, in his paper on 'Digesting the "Other": Hindu Nationalism and the Muslims in India', hones in on a particular metaphor that circulates widely in principal Hindu texts in his attempt to wrestle with this question. He adverts to a speech made by Golwalkar in Nagpur on 19 October 1949, where the RSS leader stated: 'The Muslim community was there during foreign rule. It is now demoralized and defeated. Therefore, we must make them part of ourselves. But do we still have the capacity to digest such a process of assimilation or not?' The weight of the word 'digest', Sharma notes, can be easily missed, and to reinforce its importance, he takes us to a 1954 speech by Golwalkar:

Are there only Hindus in India today, and if there are others, will they be digested? . . . Till such time that we had the belief of not allowing anyone to go out of our fold, only till such time were we able to digest outsiders. Today we are a laughing stock [after Partition] and our society has been insulted.

Sharma's unravelling of the metaphor of digesting the 'Other' perforce leads him to a consideration of the linguistic, historical, and mythic apparatus that was deployed in India to engage with the Other, but besides traversing the somewhat familiar territory of the different registers in which words such as yavanas, *mlecchas*, and Turks were used to designate foreigners, he also suggests that nationalist writers, such as Bankim, tapped mythic material to draw a parallel between stories of Vishnu slaying the *asuras* (demons) and the call to purify the nation of Muslims. One can extract from his narrative some, to my mind, intriguing puzzles that other scholars might seek to explore. Golwalkar, to take one example, used the word *parakiya* to designate what is strange, alien, remote, and foreign—the Muslim, in short; but the same word appears frequently in the poetry of Bengali Vaishnavas, where Krishna's adulterous tryst with the parakiya, his lover Radha, is rendered as the highest form of love. The parakiya is a woman other than one's wife, and '*parakiya prem*', the saint Chaitanya reminds us, '*nikaasita hem, / Kamagandha Nahi Taya*', or 'The Parakiya mode of love is very pure like gold without alloy and there is no lust in it.'[43] In the work of Kartabhaja devotees writing shortly before Golwalkar's time, parakiya love is again celebrated as 'a task requiring great skill', and one song ends on this note: 'Be a cook, make the curry—but don't touch the pot!'[44] Did the intensity of Golwalkar's animosity towards Muslims disguise his awareness of their proximity to Hindus? What sentiments of intimacy might have been disguised by his loud denunciations of the oppressiveness of the Muslim presence in India?

It may be said that an alimentary history of Indian nationalism still remains to be written, just as a socio-cultural history of vegetarianism has eluded us. Indian vegetarianism got political in the West, inspiring early critiques of the consumer society and the rapaciousness of colonialism.[45] This was long before Gandhi discovered the ethical basis of his vegetarianism in, of all places, London, and indeed it was even much before Henry David Thoreau quietly proclaimed his conviction that 'it is a part of the destiny of the human race, in its gradual improvement, to leave off eating animals, as surely as the savage tribes have left off eating each other'.[46] A different political history of vegetarianism in India may have to be etched, if the stories of vegetarian housing societies in Mumbai denying admission to meat-eaters that have been circulating have any credibility. Sharma, on his part, invites us to probe the nationalist investment in ideas about the three *gunas*, and he suggests that in practice *rajas* had already replaced *sattvas*: in evil times, the notion of purity cannot always be sustained and the order of precedence must be reversed. Savarkar, much like Gandhi, believed in cow protection, but that did not prevent him from airing the view that the Hindus' proclivity towards vegetarianism had led to their capitulation to meat-eating foreigners. Imposing the values of Brahmins upon meat-eating Hindus would not bring about Hindu unity; indeed, such a measure was calculated to further emasculate the Hindus.

However, nothing is as it seems: in the Hindu tradition, it is Brahmins rather than Kshatriyas who are the embodiment of true manliness. Into his intricate yarn Sharma weaves in mythic stories of asuras, in particular a narrative about the sage Agastya and his consumption of an asura by the name of Vatapi. Sharma argues, in conclusion, that Agastya had an easier time digesting Vatapi than Golwalkar did in digesting the Muslim. If, I am inclined to ask, the Muslim had (as the ideologues of Hindu nationalism were inclined to argue) a ravenous appetite, and the Muslim in turn had to be digested, did this demand of the Hindu that he digest the Muslim as much as expel him? Sharma's own insights can surely be extended further, nowhere more productively than by bringing into play the whole set of ideas that Gandhi generated over a lifetime of experimentation with food, nutritional therapies, enemas, care of the body, and, if I may put it this way, the disposal of human waste. As if it was not enough to steer a revolution in the body politic,

Gandhi sought to revolutionize our understanding of the body and forge a politics where the body politic could no longer be intelligently conceived independent of the body.

It is another kind of assimilation that the Mahabharata and Ramayana have wrought in India, but Paula Richman's study of C. Rajagopalachari's multiple tellings of the *Ramkatha* suggest that attentiveness to his audiences, his political life, and the emergence of mass and print culture can enrich our understanding both of Rajaji's endeavours and the various inflections that political Hinduism might take. Rajaji valued his retellings of the Ramayana more than anything else, and he brought the story of Rama to Tamil—and subsequently English—audiences in various forms, rightly holding to the view that different genres permitted him different liberties. What perhaps make Rajaji's retellings particularly instructive is the fact that he was not only the most successful popularizer of both the Ramayana and the Mahabharata, but also a politician who had risen to the highest political offices of the land, serving as the second Governor-General of India before the post was abolished. Rajaji, it is safe to say, knew a thing or two about rulership, the subtlety of dharma, the intrigues which bedevil political life, and the relationship of leaders to followers—all subjects which are the provenance of the epics. Rajaji's forays into these literary enterprises were facilitated by the literary magazine *Kalki*, which serialized his Tamil renderings of the epics and turned him into a literary star; the newly founded Sahitya Akademi, the National Academy for Literature; the Bharatiya Vidya Bhavan, an institution created with the express purpose of promoting awareness of, and admiration for, Indian culture and 'values'; and All India Radio, which gave Rajaji a venue from where he could speak to the masses. The circulation of *Kalki* rose dramatically over the course of the 18 months that his Ramkatha made its weekly entry into its pages, and the English translation of the Ramayana, with which the Bhavan's 'Book University' was launched, was 'wildly popular in middle class families'.

In the Rajaji *katha*, if we may be bold enough to call it that, state patronage, the emergence of a public sphere, print culture, and a network of cultural institutions were all to play their part. And yet, according to Richman, this is not altogether the case: the most original of his renderings of the Ramkatha, in the form of short stories, were largely outside the purview of the institutional framework that she sketches in the early part of her paper. In the short stories, Rajaji was more daring, questioning the received adulatory representations of Sita, Rama, and

Lakshmana as the model wife, husband, and brother, respectively. At the same time, Rajaji was also mindful that a new nation had come into being, and he was certain that the epics were constitutive of a 'national culture' and could be productively utilized in the service of nation formation. As Richman suggests, Rajaji sought to convey the richness of Tamil culture, but not at the expense of compromising his vision of an equally grand Indian civilization. Just how critical the conception of Hinduism was in all this is conveyed by Richman's comparison, in the last section of the paper, of Rajaji with K.M. Munshi, founder of the Bharatiya Vidya Bhavan and a major figure in Gujarati literature. Richman argues that though both privileged the Ramayana over other texts, they did so in rather different ways: Munshi 'essentialized' the narrative, oversimplified the 'Hindu tradition', and, unable to forgo his attachment to the Brahminical tradition, could not sufficiently engage with broader ethical and moral principles. In Munshi's obsessive advocacy of the project of rebuilding the Somanatha temple, his conflation of nation with Hindu would be amply on display.

The Ramayana was just as dear to Gandhi as it was to Rajaji, and it is difficult to envision a life where politics and religion were more inextricably intertwined than the life of Gandhi. Ajay Skaria writes that, 'A striking paradox marks Gandhi's arguments: he insists both that there can be "no politics without religion", and that the post-Independence Indian state should be "secular".' One cannot, Skaria rightly submits, make short work of this paradox by arguing that Gandhi's formulations belong to different periods of his life: though by the 1940s Gandhi was perhaps more insistent on separating religion and the state, his last fast, a mere two weeks before his assassination, was itself a palpable demonstration of his intent to persist with a practice of religious politics. But is the existence of religion-based parties necessarily incommensurate with a secular state? Gandhi often distinguished between nonviolence of the weak and nonviolence of the strong, arguing that the embrace of nonviolence when its practitioner had no other recourse could not be construed as a legitimate test of the practitioner's acceptance of the creed of nonviolence. What is, we may ask, a secular state that is not tested by religion-based parties, or where the adherents of strikingly different faiths do not make their presence felt across wide domains of culture, politics, and religious worship? That Gandhi was not prepared to tolerate a theocratic state cannot be doubted, but what would he have said of religion-based parties? There is yet a prior consideration about the admixture of religion and politics, a question about the status of the 'political' in Gandhi's thinking. If Gandhi resolutely militated against the normative conception of politics, refusing to abide by the rules which shape the conduct of political actors and institutions, then we can perhaps aver that he was in some ways a profoundly anti-political thinker. Is there, then, a paradox in Gandhi's formulations about politics and religion?

In his densely argued paper, Skaria maintains that there are different registers on which Gandhi could simultaneously affirm both a religious politics and secularism. We must, he argues, first attend to Gandhi's concept of dharma, and from there he leads us to an exegesis of Gandhi's idea of *dayadharma*, 'the religion of love', as well as *sarva dharma sambhavna*, suggesting that Gandhi's sense of it as 'tolerance' should be bound neither by its common limits (as in 'tolerating others') nor by the statist appropriation of the discourse of tolerance which leads to majoritarian secularism. Skaria does, in my view, a signal service in highlighting Gandhi's subversive and obsessive insistence on equality, an insight rarely encountered in the copious commentary on Gandhi. Thus *sarva dharma sambhavna* is to be understood not merely as an affirmation of the equality of all religions, but as 'an attempt to conceptualize religion itself differently, where religion always gives equality between self and other'. Skaria claims that, in the Gandhian view, equality under the sovereignty of dharma and under parliamentary politics is not the same thing, and though Gandhi recognized that religious practices might obscure equality and plurality, the resultant inequality was conceptually different from that encountered under the sign of modern civilization. I will not here attempt to follow Skaria through the intricacies of his close reading, except to say that attentiveness to his nuanced arguments requires us to jettison many certitudes and be almost counter-intuitive. What 'separates faith from superstition', Skaria explains, 'is that the former is constituted by the practice of equality, that contrary to secular thought the giving of equality to the other is possible only where there is faith, belief, religion.' The 'spectre of superstition' is internal, not to the concept of faith as one might unthinkingly imagine, but to the concept of secularism. As an analogue, it does not surprise us that, contrary to nearly every reading of Gandhi that is on offer, Skaria holds that Gandhi did not partake in the celebration of India as a syncretic culture, for (what is now) the obvious reason that 'syncreticism is a profoundly secular category'. What is certain is that, in the name of Hinduism, Gandhi and his adversaries among the Hindu nationalists created a vastly different religious politics.

In the final paper that makes up this volume, 'Popular Patriotism in Indian Film', Ronald Inden takes us, appropriately enough for a volume that takes the public sphere as one of its principal concerns, to the world of popular Hindi cinema. Inden goes well beyond the discussions of political Hinduism in the Hindi film that were circulating a decade or two ago, suggesting that questions about the representation of Muslims in, say, the films of Mani Ratnam are wholly inadequate to grasp the 'national theology' that is at work in popular cinema. Patriotism (*deshbhakti, vatanaparasti*), is the name by which this national theology, which draws upon and 'recuperates certain features of Indian theisms', is to be understood. Such patriotism, Inden argues, should not be confused with the writings or pronouncements of national leaders or the ideological platforms of the principal political parties, including the political Hinduism of the BJP. The elites, as Inden rightly argues, look down upon patriotism; their pretensions, one might say, are larger, and are captured by such terms as 'transnationalism' and 'cosmopolitanism'. The popular patriotism on display suggests that 'people of the nation have neither marginalized the conventional religions nor have they Hinduized the nation'. In delineating the grammar of this popular patriotism, as manifested in Indian films, Inden points to elements from conventional religions that are nationalized: the creation of a 'god of the nation', and the constitution of the nation both as a mother (*Bharat Mata*) and, much less frequently noted, a 'paradise on earth' (*jannat, svarg, firdaus*) that takes the form of a 'quadripartite garden of delights' (*gulistan, carbag*). A 'national hero'—drawing upon Hindu, Muslim, and Sikh ideas of the avatar (incarnation), *farishta* (angel), and *shaheed* (martyr), respectively—makes up the last element of this national theology. Further distinctions are, of course, possible, even necessary: thus one can usefully distinguish the 'martyr to passionate love' from the martyr who sacrifices himself (or herself) for the love of the nation. Inden's illustration of his argument takes him through an extended discussion of several films, principally *Jeet* ('Victory', 1996), *Ghulam-e-Mustafa* ('Slave of the Prophet', 1999), and especially *The Legend of Bhagat Singh* (2002).

As Inden argues in his paper, the martyr who acts to preserve the nation appears most often as a military or war hero; he may also be a policeman, but generally has to renounce his profession, since he is handicapped rather than liberated by it, or must at least step outside it. Inden finds the film *Indian* (2001) instructive for his purposes—all the elements constitutive of popular patriotism are present in it: 'the incarnation of the nation drawn from Vaishnava Hinduism, the angel or messenger of the nation's morality taken from Islam, and the idea of martyrdom appropriated directly from Sikhism and indirectly from Shiite Islam.'[47] Yet, as he adds, the film is also revealing in another respect, insofar as it offers a firm rejection of the idea that communalism has any intrinsic relationship to religion. The homilies in the film are steeped in the two-fold idea that communalism is a form of false consciousness, and that greed, corruption, and competition over economic resources are at the root of what appear to be religious conflicts. Popular patriotism appears not as something random, but as displaying a remarkable and consistent coherence. Indeed, it can be viewed as an 'unofficial civil religion', and it has rather more credibility than 'the official civil religion' because it takes a more nuanced or at least sensible view of secularism. The unofficial civil religion rejects the view that with modernization, the conventional religions will, or ought to, disappear or even become marginalized; on the other hand, it offers no encouragement to those who seek to prioritize one religion over another and who have set for themselves the task of the '"purification" of popular patriotism'. In looking at 'filmic patriotism' and its articulation with forms of actually existing Hinduism, Inden moves us away from the more traditional scholarly research on Hinduism that has been focused on reform movements or the concerns that have animated those coming from a background in the history of religions and, instead, importantly steers film scholarship in new directions.

In thinking of a title for this volume, I settled upon 'Political Hinduism' and by way of conclusion I would like to further reflect on this term and its wider ramifications. I suggested at the outset that many people suppose that political Hinduism generally references nothing more than the Hindu nationalism of the last two decades. One does not routinely encounter the term 'Political Hinduism' and to most people it will not resonate as strongly as 'Political Islam'. The only warrant required for the term, one might well argue, is that there is an ethical charge to assist in questioning the sinister singularity in which one speaks of 'Political Islam'. Some of the more aggressive critics of Hindu nationalism, the majority of them secular and left-leaning scholars, have long felt that the atrocities committed in the name of defending Hinduism are inadequately condemned in India and overseas alike,[48] and 'Political Hinduism' perhaps has the virtue of bringing some awareness of the fact that Hinduism is just as susceptible as any other religion to the designs and political ambitions of extremists. I would not, however, like this to be construed as an admission that 'Political Hinduism' draws its sustenance from 'Political Correctness'. We might also ask: has there ever been a time when Hinduism was not political? I have not engaged with the arguments that one has encountered in recent years about 'the invention of Hinduism' here,[49] but even if one is inclined to reject the view that Hinduism came about as a colonial construct in the eighteenth century, the debate clearly suggests that 'Political Hinduism' already has a much longer history than is commonly supposed—and certainly extends back to a time before the twentieth century ideologues of Hindutva, such as Savarkar and Golwalkar, made their appearance.

In the closing pages of his autobiography, published nearly around the time that the RSS was coming into existence, Gandhi suggested that those who were inclined to view politics and religion as distinct realms understood the possibilities of neither and were certainly ill-positioned to understand either.[50] Gandhi consequently rejected the Enlightenment tendency to separate these categories, just as he anticipated that forcing religion into the domain of the private would have the consequence of leaving the public sphere open to a rather exclusive kind of social scientific rationality. Gandhi, as we all are aware, has insistently been faulted for drawing religion into politics, and the most frequent criticisms of him point to his support of the Khilafat movement, his invocations of Ramrajya, his appeal to religious experience in political matters, and so on. While these criticisms, however just or tiresome they may be, cannot be addressed at this juncture, one can see how the spectre of Gandhi looms large even in our conceptions of what might be called a false political Hinduism. If Hindutva is this false political Hinduism, then logically we must ask, wherein lies its falsity? Moreover, in asking this question, it will not suffice to indicate merely Hindutva's departures from accepted textual interpretations, its repudiation of widely accepted syncretic pasts, or its deviations from traditional religious practices or modes of belief. One can say of Gandhi that he, too, effected a departure from conventional readings of Hindu texts, as many of his contemporaries remarked apropos his interpretation of the Gita; equally, it is a striking though seldom-noticed feature of Hindutva's corpus that it is more engaged with Western social science than it is with the religious and philosophical writings of the Hindus. We may also find, in Gandhi's interventions in the public domain, an opening to consider whether Hinduism gets political only when the Brahminical ideologues of Hindutva engage with it, or whether there has also been an appropriation of (Hindu) texts, festivals, rituals, images, and processions by the lower castes in pursuit of their political aspirations for equality and justice. Could there be, then, a political Hinduism that is properly political, a political Hinduism that carries within it the seeds of a critique of liberalism and that takes us beyond those critiques of Hindutva which point to its incompatibility with received notions of democracy, human rights, civil society discourse, and the like?

NOTES AND REFERENCES

1. See, for example, Walter K. Anderson and Shridhar D. Damle, *Brotherhood in Saffron: The Rashtriya Swayamsevak Sangh and Hindu Revivalism* (Delhi: Vishtar Publications, 1987); Bruce Graham, *Hindu Nationalism and Indian Politics: The Origins and Development of the Bharatiya Jana Sangh* (Cambridge: Cambridge University Press, 1990); Yogendra K. Malik and V.B. Singh, *Hindu Nationalists in India: The Rise of the Bharatiya Janata Party* (Boulder, Colorado: Westview Press, 1994); Tapan Basu, Pradip Datta, Sumit Sarkar, Tanika Sarkar, and Sambuddha Sen, *Khaki Shorts, Saffron Flags* (Delhi: Orient Longman, 1993); Sikata Banerjee, *Warriors in Politics: Hindu Nationalism, Violence, and the Shiv Sena in India* (Boulder, Colorado: Westview Press, 2000); Thomas Blom Hansen, *The Saffron Wave: Democracy and Hindu Nationalism in Modern India* (Princeton: Princeton University Press, 1999); A.G. Noorani, *The RSS and the BJP, A Division of Labour* (Delhi: LeftWord, 2001 [new edn.]); and Christophe Jaffrelot (ed.), *The Sangh Parivar: A Reader* (Delhi: Oxford University Press, 2005).

2. The complicity of leading politicians, state officials, and the agents of 'law and order' in the perpetration of the atrocities has been widely documented by human rights organizations, journalists, and researchers. Human Rights Watch's first report of April 2002, *We Have No Orders to Save You*, vol. 14, no. 3 (c), comes with the subtitle, 'State Participation and Complicity in Communal Violence in Gujarat'. The complicity of the state arose not only from its abject failure to stem the violence, deploy armed troops to restore order, and discipline police officers who were mute witnesses and on occasion themselves instigators of murder and arson (p. 21). The report is candid in its description of the 'state sponsorship of the attacks' in myriad other ways, and it notes that 'accounts of politicians directing the violence are also commonplace' (p. 21). The report says of the killers that they were often 'guided by computer printouts listing the addresses of Muslim families and their properties, information obtained from the Ahmedabad municipal corporation among other sources, and embarked on a murderous rampage confident that the police was protecting them. In many cases, the police led the charges, using gunfire to kill Muslims who got in the mobs' way. A key BJP state minister is reported to have taken over police control rooms in Ahmedabad on the first day of the carnage, issuing orders to disregard pleas for assistance from Muslims (p. 5). A year later, when the passage of time had furnished the organization ample time and opportunity to investigate its sources and authenticate its findings, Human Rights Watch reaffirmed its earlier conclusions and added a stringent critique of the conduct

of Gujarat's politicians: 'The Gujarat government, and in particular its chief minister, responded to severe criticism by either tacitly justifying the attacks or asserting that they were quickly brought under control. On March 1 [2002], Chief Minister Modi confidently declared that he would control the "riots resulting from the natural and justified anger of the people. Every action has an equal and opposite reaction," Modi told reporters.' See *Compounding Injustice: The Government's Failure to Redress Massacres in Gujarat* (Washington, DC: Human Rights Watch, July 2003), p. 12. Indian human rights activists have been even more forthright in issuing an indictment of the Government of Gujarat. Thus the special issue of *Communalism Combat*, 'Gujarat: Genocide 2002', nos. 77–8 (March–April 2002), openly states that 'ministers were also leading the mobs', and its enumeration of leading politicians who oversaw the violence is bold as much as it is shocking. Thus, by way of example, it states that 'Gujarat ministers Nitin Patel and Narav Laloo Patel allegedly led the violence, arson and even sexual violence against women in Kadih and Unja in Mehsana respectively' (p. 109). See also the special issue of *Tehelka* (3 November 2007) on Gujarat's pogrom of 2002.

3. The Gujarat government, perhaps taken by surprise at the widespread outrage over Modi's reported remarks, predictably denied that he had said any such thing. But his exact words may be reproduced: '*Kriya pratikriya ki chain chal rahi hai,*' which may be rendered into English as 'An action provokes reaction, and so it goes.' See Siddharth Varadarajan, 'Chronicle of a Tragedy Foretold', in Siddharth Varadarajan (ed.), *Gujarat: The Making of a Tragedy* (New Delhi: Penguin Books, 2002), p. 22. Nearly the same quote appears in *Communalism Combat*'s report (p. 109, see note 2). Modi, one suspects, will be unable to disown this remark, though it is far from clear that he has any ambition in this respect. Robert Kaplan's profile of Modi, 'India's New Face' (*The Atlantic*, April 2009), notes unambiguously that 'in the midst of the riots, Modi approvingly quoted Newton's third law: "Every action has an equal and opposite reaction."' See online at: http://www.theatlantic.com/doc/200904/india-modi (accessed 7 April 2009). One canard that is commonly circulated about critics of Modi is that they are inspired by anti-Hindu sentiments, or that secularists or non-Hindus are unable to understand that Hindus stand behind Modi and others who purport to champion the Hindu cause. This is all the more reason why the critique of someone such as Swami Agnivesh, who unflinchingly describes himself as a believer in *sanatan dharma*, is compelling. In his collection of short essays, *Hinduism in the New Age* (Gurgaon: Hope India Publications, 2005), Agnivesh writes with brutal candour that 'Hindutva is essentially religious terrorism' (p. 107). Hindutva's leaders, Agnivesh argues, are ignorant of Hindu scriptures, and he is unsparing of Narendra Modi: 'It was not according to the spirit of Lord Rama, Lord Shiva or Lord Krishna, but according to the concepts of Isaac Newton, that he responded to the Godhra riots' (p. 114). 'Who, except the most willfully biased,' asks Agnivesh, 'will give the benefit of doubt to a Chief Minister who allows frenzied mobs to riot and butcher helpless citizens and speaks occasionally only to justify the conduct of marauders in terms of Newtonian physics?' (p. 118)

4. Nathuram Godse, *May It Please Your Honor* (Delhi: Surya Prakashan, 1987).

5. Message of 30 January 1948, available online at: http://pakistanspace.tripod.com/48.htm (accessed 10 December 2008).

6. Terrorism as a worldwide phenomenon has become something of an academic industry as well, though the Fundamentalisms project at the University of Chicago, from which numerous volumes have emerged, commenced close to twenty years ago. The first volume, *Fundamentalisms Observed*, eds, Martin Marty and R. Scott Appleby (Chicago: University of Chicago Press, 1994), provides the best introduction to the subject. For another widely read overview, from someone whose initial academic work focused on India, see Mark Juergensmeyer, *Terror in the Mind of God: The Global Rise of Religious Violence* (Berkeley: University of California Press, 2000; third rev. edn., 2003).

7. See http://www.expressindia.com/latest-news/It-is-wrong-to-use-term-Hindu-terrorists-BJP/377565/ (accessed 1 April 2009).

8. Rana Ayyub, 'The fiery and fanatical Sadhvi', *Tehelka* 5, no. 45 (15 November 2008), also online at: http://www.tehelka.com/story_main40.asp?filename=Ne151108the_fiery.asp (accessed 1 April 2009).

9. On the scholarly side, see Thomas Blom Hansen, *The Saffron Wave: Democracy and Hindu Nationalism in Modern India* (Princeton: Princeton University Press, 1999) and Christophe Jaffrelot, *The Hindu Nationalist Movement and Indian Politics, 1925 to the 1990s* (Delhi: Viking Penguin, 1995); for more anecdotal histories, see Sudhir Kakar, *The Colours of Violence* (Delhi: Viking Penguin, 1995) and Harsh Mander, *Cry, My Beloved Country: Reflections on the Gujarat Carnage and Its Aftermath* (New Delhi: Rainbow Publishers, 2004).

10. Arvind Rajagopal, *Politics after Television: Hindu Nationalism and the Reshaping of the Public in India* (Cambridge: Cambridge University Press, 2001).

11. Shubh Mathur, *The Everyday Life of Hindu Nationalism: An Ethnographic Account* (Delhi: Three Essays Collective, 2008).

12. Ibid., pp. 113–19.

13. Jawaharlal Nehru, *Glimpses of World History* (Delhi: Oxford University Press, [rpt. edn.], 1985).

14. D.N. Jha, 'Digging a little deeper', *Indian Express* (20 September 2007), p. 11.

15. 'Ram a lie, Ramayana says he was a drunkard: Karunanidhi', *Indian Express* (21 September 2007), p. 3; M.S.S. Pandian, 'We Do Things Differently', *The Times of India* (24 September 2007), p. 18; and Braj Ranjan Mani, *Debrahmanising History: Dominance and Resistance in Indian Society* (Delhi: Manohar, 2005), pp. 183–7.

16. 'Indignant DU erupts over ABVP vandalism', *The Times of India* (27 February 2008), p. 4.

17. A.K. Ramanujan, 'Three Hundred Ramayanas: Five Examples and Three Thoughts on Translation', in Paula Richman (ed.), *Many Ramayanas: The Diversity of a Narrative Tradition in South Asia* (Berkeley: University of California Press, 1991), pp. 22–49.

18. Satendra Nandan, 'Return Flights to Paradise: Three Easy Pieces', *Emergences* 10, no. 2 (November 2000), pp. 345–72, special issue on 'Islands: Waterways, Flowways, Folkways', guest edited by Vinay Lal.

19. James W. Laine, *Shivaji: Hindu King in Islamic India* (New York: Oxford University Press, 2003).

20. Philip Lutgendorf, 'My Hanuman is Bigger Than Yours', *History of Religions* 33, no. 3 (1994), pp. 211-45.

21. The best-known work along these lines is that of Ashis Nandy, whose essays are scattered in various volumes. For an extended treatment of this subject, see Ashis Nandy, *The Intimate Enemy: Loss and Recovery of Self under Colonialism* (Delhi: Oxford University Press, 1983) and Ashis Nandy, Shikha Trivedy, Shail Mayaram, and Achyut Yagnik, *Creating a Nationality: The Ramjanmabhumi Movement and Fear of the Self* (Delhi: Oxford University Press, 1995).

22. Rustom Bharucha, *In the Name of the Secular: Contemporary Cultural Activism in India* (Delhi: Oxford University Press, 1998), pp. 140–60. Patwardhan's oeuvre is substantial and he has had a robust interest in exploring the manifestations of militant Hinduism in everyday life, nowhere more explicitly than in 'Father, Son and Holy War', a two-part documentary made in the wake of the communal killings in Bombay subsequent to the destruction of the Babri Masjid. I have discussed his work in 'Travails of the Nation: Some Notes on Indian Documentaries', *Third Text* 19, no. 2 (March 2005), pp. 175–85.

23. Anuradha Kapur, 'The Changing Iconography of Ram', in Gyanendra Pandey (ed.), *Hindus and Others: The Question of Identity in India Today* (Delhi: Viking, 1993), and Richard Davis, 'The Iconography of Rama's Chariot', in David Ludden (ed.), *Making India Hindu: Religion, Community, and the Politics of Democracy in India* (Delhi: Oxford India Paperbacks, 1997).

24. Tulsidas, *Ramacharitmanas* (Gorakhpur: The Gita Press [rpt. edn], 2000), 1.232. 2-4.

25. The temple's website proudly proclaims that 'Attukal Pongala' has been entered into the *Guinness Book of Records* for hosting the largest gathering of women in the world. A link takes the reader to the ultimate marker of authenticity, a certificate from Guinness World Records Ltd. which states: 'The largest annual gathering of women takes place in February or March each year, at the Attukal Bhagavathy Temple, Thiruvananthapuram, Kerala, India, for the "Pongala" offering. The women gather with their cooking pots to perform a ritual for the health and prosperity of their families. The highest attendance recorded was 1.5 million women at the festival on 23 February 1997.' See www.attukal.org/certificate.htm (accessed 10 December 2008), and 'Ponkala makes it to Guinness', *The Hindu* (15 October 2006). See also Vinay Lal, 'Indians and the *Guinness Book of Records*: Contours of a National Obsession', in idem, *Of Cricket, Guinness and Gandhi: Essays on Indian History and Culture* (Calcutta: Seagull Books, 2003; paperback reprint, New Delhi: Penguin Books, 2005), pp. 1–21.

26. See Dianne Jenett, 'A Million *Shaktis* Rising: Pongala, a Women's Festival in Kerala, India', *Journal of Feminist Studies in Religion* 21, no. 1 (2005), pp. 35–55. *The Hindu* has been reporting on the festival every year, and a local informant in a recent year described the festival, which was 'originally confined to the temple premises', as having extended 'to a 5 km radius'. See 'All roads lead

to Attukal', *The Hindu* Online, 17 February 2003 at: http://www.hinduonnet. com/thehindu/mp/2003/02/17/stories/2003021701330300.htm (accessed 10 December 2008).

27. Gautam Bhatia, *Punjabi Baroque and Other Memories of Architecture* (New Delhi: Penguin Books, 1994).

28. M.S.S. Pandian, *The Image Trap* (Delhi: Sage Publications, 1992), p. 118.

29. For a discussion of the state of film criticism in India, see the introduction to Vinay Lal and Ashis Nandy (eds), *Fingerprinting Popular Culture: The Mythic and the Iconic in Indian Cinema* (Delhi: Oxford University Press, 2006).

30. Jyotika Virdi, *The Cinematic ImagiNation: Indian Popular Films as Social History* (New Brunswick: Rutgers University Press, 2003); M. Madhava Prasad, *Ideology of the Hindi Film: A Historical Construction* (Delhi: Oxford University Press, 1998); Lalitha Gopalan, *Cinema of Interruptions: Action Genres in Contemporary Indian Cinema* (London: British Film Institute, 2002); Vijay Mishra, *Bollywood Cinema: Temples of Desire* (New York: Routledge, 2002); Rachel Dwyer and Christopher Pinney (eds), *Pleasure and the Nation: The History, Politics and Consumption of Public Culture in India* (Delhi: Oxford India Paperbacks, 2002); and Ravi S. Vasudevan (ed.), *Making Meaning in Indian Cinema* (Delhi: Oxford University Press, 2000). The one obvious exception is Rachel Dwyer's *Filming the Gods: Religion and Indian Cinema* (London: Routledge, 2006), but even its attempts to insert itself into topical debates about secularism do not yield any insights into how representations of Hinduism may have altered in conditions more propitious for the advancement of Hindutva ideology.

31. There is no systematic full-length scholarly treatment of this subject, though there are some insights in the works of Nita Kumar, Krishna Kumar, and Tanika Sarkar. Newspapers and periodical literature have provided extensive coverage over the last ten years. For a sample selection, see Venkitesh Ramakrishnan, 'Hindutva Institutions in Education: The spreading network of RSS', *Frontline* (7–20 November 1998); Sukumar Muralidharan and S.K. Pande, 'Taking Hindutva to Schools', *Frontline* (7–20 November 1998); Angana Chatterji, 'Learning in Saffron: RSS Schools Orissa', *The Asian Age* (12 November 2003); and Taran N. Khan, 'Education and Hindutva', *Ceras Newsletter* online at: http://ceras.alternatives.ca/14/educa.htm

32. For an elaboration, see Vinay Lal, *The History of History: Politics and Scholarship in Modern India* (Delhi: Oxford University Press, 2003; new edn., 2005), introduction.

33. Meera Nanda, *Prophets Facing Backward: Postmodern Critiques of Science and Hindu Nationalism in India* (New Brunswick: Rutgers University Press, 2003).

34. Writing of the Swaminarayan temple in Neasden, in outer London, Raymond Brady Williams, in *An Introduction to Swaminarayan Hinduism* (Cambridge: Cambridge University Press, 2001), notes that 'the basement contains a permanent exhibition on "Understanding Hinduism"' (p. 220), but to me he appears to miss the increasing attraction to some of Hinduism's devotees to place their faith in an exhibition complex.

35. Perhaps there is not much of a mystery here, when we consider that the

study of Indian religions, and particularly Hinduism, has been focused on texts, on the temple setting and ritual cycles, and on religion in the context of village life.

36. Narayana Guru, *Complete Works*, ed. and trans. by Muni Narayana Prasad (New Delhi: National Book Trust, 2006), Introduction.

37. Braj Ranjan Mani, *Debrahmanising History*, pp. 300–12.

38. Bankimcandra Chatterji, *Anandamath, or The Sacred Brotherhood*, trans. and ed. by Julius J. Lipner (New Delhi: Oxford University Press, 2005).

39. For this, see Sabyasachi Bhattacharya, *Vande Mataram: The Biography of a Song* (Delhi: Penguin Books, 2003).

40. Rajendra Prasad, presiding over the Constituent Assembly, had this to say on 24 January 1950: 'The composition consisting of the words and music known as *Jana Gana Mana* is the National Anthem of India, subject to such alterations in the words as the Government may authorise as occasion arises; and the song *Vande Mataram*, which has played a historic part in the struggle for Indian freedom, shall be honoured equally with *Jana Gana Mana* and shall have equal status with it.' *Constituent Assembly Debates*, vol. XII available online at: http://parliamentofindia.nic.in/ls/debates/vol12p1.htm (accessed 15 December 2008).

41. Pradip Kumar Datta, 'Are We Still Singing for the Empire' (24 September 2008), available online at; http://www.sacw.net/DC/CommunalismCollection/ArticlesArchive/pkDatta092004.html (accessed 15 November 2008).

42. For a lengthier discussion, see Vinay Lal, *The Other Indians: A Political and Cultural History of South Asians in America* (New Delhi: HarperCollins, 2008), pp. 31–76.

43. From the *Chaitanya-charitamrita*, as cited by Sunil Kumar Bhattacharya in *Krishna-cult in Indian Art* (New Delhi: M.D. Publications, 1996), p. 22.

44. 'The Secrets of Parakiya Love', in Hugh B. Urban, *Songs of Ecstasy: Tantric and Devotional Songs from Colonial Bengal* (New York: Oxford University Press, 2001), pp. 126–7.

45. Tristram Stuart, *The Bloodless Revolution: Radical Vegetarians and the Discovery of India* (London: HarperPress, 2006).

46. The quotation is from *Walden* [1854], 150 year anniversary illustrated edition (New York: Houghton Mifflin, 2004), p. 171.

47. See also J.P.S. Uberoi, *Religion, Civil Society and the State: A Study of Sikhism* (Delhi: Oxford University Press, 1996), pp. 87–94 and 112–34.

48. As a recent and well-known illustration of such work, see Martha Nussbaum, *The Clash Within: Democracy, Religious Violence, and India's Future* (Cambridge, Mass: Harvard University Press, 2008).

49. A stocktaking and critique of this argument is to be found in David Lorenzen, *Who Invented Hinduism? Essays on Religion in History* (New Delhi: Yoda Press, 2006), ch. 1.

50. M.K. Gandhi, *An Autobiography or The Story of My Experiments with Truth* (Ahmedabad: Navajivan Publishing House, 1959 [vol. I: 1927; vol. II: 1929; vol. I, edn, 1959]), p. 371.

MADHAV M. DESHPANDE

'The Arctic Home in the Vedas'
Religion, Politics, and the Colonial Context

INTRODUCTION

Ideas relating to the theme of Aryan origins as they developed in the region of Maharashtra during the nineteenth century in response to the then dominant Western theories of Indo–European philology are important both for the intellectual dimension as well as the political dimension. Among the Indian personalities of the second half of the nineteenth century and the beginning of the next, the figure of Lokmanya B.G. Tilak stands unmatched in the area of intellectual contributions to the reconstruction of the history of ancient India and Indians, a reconstruction that was significant for its political implications, if not its motivations. Tilak's ideas reflect an Indian intellectual attempt that sought a chronologically primordial place for the ancestors of Vedic Aryans, without necessarily questioning the basic foundations of the Western Indo-European philology of the time. In this paper, I plan to discuss the colonial, intellectual, and political context of B.G. Tilak's theories regarding the dating of the Vedas as presented in his *Orion* and *The Arctic Home in the Vedas*. I will also discuss how these theories deviated from the traditional Hindu beliefs of the time, how they were contested by Tilak's contemporaries, and how they were eventually superceded by the Indo-centric and Hindu-centric theories propounded by Hindu nationalist thinkers like V.D. Savarkar and M.S. Golwalkar.

Before examining in some detail the historical context of Tilak's ideas, let me briefly summarize his views, especially as found in *The*

Arctic Home in the Vedas. What distinguishes Tilak from all others is that he was not just arguing for the Arctic home of the Aryans, in the sense of Indo–Europeans. He was specifically arguing that the descriptions in the Vedic texts themselves are of such high antiquity, that the Vedas themselves may be located in the Arctic home. Here is a summary of Tilak's conclusions in his own words:

10000 or 8000 BC—The destruction of the original Arctic home by the last Ice Age and the commencement of the post-Glacial period.

8000–5000 BC—The age of migration from the original home. The survivors of the Aryan race roamed over the northern parts of Europe and Asia in search of lands suitable for new settlements. The vernal equinox was then in the constellation of Punarvasu, and as Aditi is the presiding deity of Punarvasu, ... this may, therefore, be called the Aditi or the Pre-Orion Period.

5000–3000 BC—The Orion Period, when the vernal equinox was in Orion. Many Vedic hymns can be traced to the early part of this period and the bards of the race seem to have not yet forgotten the real import or significance of the traditions of the Arctic home inherited by them. ...

3000–1400 BC—The Kṛttikā Period, when the vernal equinox was in the Pleiades. The Taittirīya Saṃhitā and the Brāhmaṇas, which begin the series of nakṣatras with the Kṛttikās, are evidently the productions of this period. ... The traditions about the original Arctic home had grown dim by this time and very often misunderstood, making the Vedic hymns more and more unintelligible. [1]

Summing up his 'historical view' of the Vedas, as opposed to the 'theological view' of the tradition, Tilak makes three significant points:

1. The Vedic or the Aryan religion can be proved to be inter-glacial; but its ultimate origin is still lost in geological antiquity.
2. Aryan religion and culture were destroyed during the last Glacial period that invaded the Arctic Aryan home.
3. The Vedic hymns were sung in post-Glacial times by poets, who had inherited the knowledge or contents thereof in an unbroken tradition from their antediluvian forefathers. [2]

SOME MODERN CRITIQUES OF TILAK

The historical context of Tilak's theories is variously understood by modern scholars. According to Stanley Wolpert,

He directed his attention first to the work of bolstering the Hindu ego while at the same time enhancing his own prestige among his orthodox compatriots. ... Despite the fact that superficially his three books appear to be devoid of political content or implications, all were actually more significant contributions to the literature of Indian nationalism than to Indology.[3]

In contrast to Wolpert's comment, we need to note that Tilak's stand on Aryan history—his agreeing to the origin of Aryans outside India—was not terribly convenient for his nationalistic politics, and many of his contemporaries, including close associates, rejected it in favour of an Indo-centric theory of Aryan origins. For the traditional Sanskrit scholars of the time any notion that the Vedas had a datable origin was sacrilegious in its very basic assumption, contrary to the traditional belief that the Vedas were uncreated and eternal texts. Tilak did not win support from any orthodox traditional Sanskrit pandits.[4]

Gail Omvedt remarks,

Originally Lokmanya Tilak and all other thinkers of the nineteenth and early twentieth centuries were quite happy to agree that Aryans came from outside India, even claiming that their original home was in the Arctic. However, since the 1930s—note that this was after Dalit movements throughout India claimed their identity as original inhabitants (Adi-Dravida, Adi-Andhra, Adi-Hindu, and so on)—Golwalkar and his followers began to say that the Aryans also originated in India.[5]

Already in Tilak's lifetime, long before 1930, Narayan Bhavanrao Pavgee claimed that the Aryans originated in the Indian heartland—Āryāvarta. As early as the 1870s, Jotiba Phule was making vocal claims calling the Brahmin-Aryans outsiders who exploited the indigenous non-Brahmin non-Aryans. Indeed, the political disadvantages of the proposed outside origin of the Aryans for the position of the Brahmins were fully evident to the Brahmin opponents of Jotiba Phule. Tilak stuck to his Arctic Home theory in spite of its evident disadvantages. The Brahmin Tilak disagreed with the Brahmin Pavgee, and both of them held views that were different from the Brahmin Bhandarkar. Eventually, the Brahmins Savarkar and Golwalkar, moved away from Tilak's theories as they recognized their political disadvantages.

TILAK AND THE DECCAN COLLEGE:
SCHOLASTIC FOUNDATIONS

Tilak's departures both from the traditional Indian Sanskrit scholarship, as well as the philologically oriented European scholarship of his times, were significant. Wolpert points to two sources of Tilak's ideas.[6] The Deccan College itself, established in 1860, must be seen as a significant departure in Pune. After the fall of the Peshwas in 1818, the English in 1860 established the Deccan College as the premier institution in Pune for modern education, similar to the Elphinstone College in Bombay. The Deccan College transformed Tilak's generation of Brahmins into modern Western-educated Indians.[7] As Wolpert notes, the person who inspired Tilak most during his college days was the professor of mathematics, astronomy, and astrology, Kerunana L. Chhatre.[8] Chhatre directed Tilak's attention to seek astronomical data from the Vedas to determine the date of the Vedas. Puranik reports that Chhatre, under the impact of Western rationalism, had become an atheist and was willing to question the religious tradition.[9] Such was the influence of this professor of mathematics and astronomy on Tilak.[10]

TILAK'S DEPARTURE FROM THE TRADITION

Tilak's theories in *The Orion* and *The Arctic Home in the Vedas* were clear departures from the traditional ideas. In his preface to *The Arctic Home in the Vedas*, Tilak cites with approval Max Müller's statement emphasizing the need to broaden the study of the Vedas to include many branches of humanistic and physical sciences.[11] It may be remembered that with his colleagues Chiplunkar, Namjoshi, Agarkar, and Gokhale, Tilak established the New English School in Pune in 1880. He did not exert to set up traditional Sanskrit *pāṭhaśālās*. Rather he preferred to open the New English School, and the Fergusson College.[12] He urged the promoters of Sanskrit *pāṭhaśālās* to introduce the study of English in their curriculum. In the 'Introduction' to his *Vedic Chronology and Vedāṅga Jyotisha*, Tilak explains his departure from the ways of the traditional pandits,

The Vedic texts collected by Weber were not unknown to our old Pandits and the rate at which the equinoctial points retrograde is also so accurately recorded in the ancient astronomical Siddhāntas ... But it was a fixed article of faith with these pandits that the Vedas were *anādi* (beginningless) being handed over orally from generation to generation, from time immemorial, and in consequence these Vedic texts were never used for any chronological purpose. The introduction of Western education, and with it the modern historical and critical methods, in our schools and colleges, have altered this state of things.[13]

TILAK AND PROFESSOR JINSIWALE:
VEDAS ARE MAN-MADE

This brings me to the second person at the Deccan College who was most influential in Tilak's intellectual development. This was Professor Shridhar Ganesh Jinsiwale.[14] When Tilak was a student of the Deccan College, Jinsiwale had already finished his MA and was a teaching fellow. The two developed a great friendship that lasted for a long time. Jinsiwale, born in 1852 in a traditional Brahmin family, completed his matriculation in 1868, and was awarded several scholarships that allowed him to join the Deccan College. Jinsiwale was an interesting combination of a very traditional religious/ritual lifestyle combined with a newly acquired rationalist mindset. With his rationalist mindset, developed at the Deccan College, Jinsiwale openly began to question the traditional doctrine of the *apauruṣeyatva* '[eternal Vedas] not created by any human author' and argue that they were indeed man-made, *pauruṣeya*. Tilak, a student of Jinsiwale, agreed with him on this issue, and in many public debates with religious figures of the time, Tilak, like Jinsiwale, would defend the man-made nature (*pauruṣeyatva*) of the Vedas. This change-over from the traditional belief in the uncreated eternal nature of the Vedas to believing that they were man-made literary works opened the door for historically dating these texts.

TILAK'S DEBATE ON APAURUṢEYATVA OF THE VEDAS

In fact, very rarely did any traditional Hindu religious teachers of high prestige agree with Tilak on this issue, and yet he held his ground. Here is a sample of the debate between Tilak and a religious teacher named Swami Dakshinamurti, during Tilak's visit to Banaras in 1900:

Tilak: What is your view regarding the dating of the Vedas? When were they produced? Even if the absolute dating of the Vedas may be uncertain, what do you think would be their estimated date?

Swami: Since the Vedas are without beginning *(anādi)* and not created by humans *(apauruṣeya)*, they simply manifest themselves with the manifestation of the universe and disappear with the disappearance of the universe, and hence there is no question of dating the Vedas.

Tilak: Since the Vedas are linguistic expressions, some people feel that they must be composed by someone. Such is the view of many scholars.

Swami: Who are these scholars?

Tilak: Modern educated people.

Swami: What is the use of modern education in the consideration of traditional śāstras? By 'educated,' do you mean English-educated?

Tilak: Yes. Do you think that English-educated people are totally thoughtless? Do you believe that no one among modern scholars has any understanding of the Vedas? ... Some such modern scholars say that since the Vedas are linguistic expressions, one can infer that they must have been produced by someone at some time. I am presenting to you the view of such scholars.

Swami: This already shows that such people are ignorant on the question of dating the Vedas. Since they have not studied the Vedas in the traditional way, they are unfamiliar with the doctrine that the Vedas have no beginning and that they are not created by any human beings.

Tilak: OK. What do we lose if we say that omniscient sages composed the Vedas using their superior knowledge?

Swami: That would make the Vedas man-made, and that would destroy the innate validity of the Vedas.

Tilak: Then do you think God produced the Vedas?

Swami: No. The Vedas are beginningless. I told you earlier that they simply become manifest when the universe becomes manifest. However, their first utterance [at the beginning of the cycle of manifestation] is dependent on God. For this reason, some authors claim that the Vedas are (simply) brought forth by God and that they are actually beginningless, and not created by God.

Tilak: I don't think this argument will satisfy common people regarding the notions of the beginningless nature of the Vedas and that they are not created by humans.

Swami: People may not be satisfied. That is true. But that is mainly because there is absence of traditional study of the Vedas among common people, loss of traditional authoritative people, the study of English and contact with the English people. You are right! People will not be convinced. [15]

There are many such conversations of Tilak with traditional authorities, where it is evident that he was not able to satisfy the ultra-orthodox Sanskrit scholars and religious authorities of his time. Here we notice the beginning of a new breed of modern Hindus who tried to find hoary history for Vedas through modern means, a history that would place the origins of Hinduism before any other religious or civilizational tradition, and yet this very quest for history placed them at odds with the religious ideology of traditional Hinduism that placed its scripture beyond time and history. We see this dilemma continuing through the works of Savarkar and Golwalkar, as well as the modern Hindutva claims of the Indus Valley being Vedic. How can the Vedas be beyond time and history and validate some form of history? This is a continuing tension.

TILAK AND INDO-EUROPEAN PHILOLOGY

Tilak accepted the basic premise of Indo–European philology that the Sanskrit language is related to the languages of the Greeks and the Romans as a member of a common family, because he, like R.G. Bhandarkar, agreed with its logic. Tilak had particular admiration for the work of Max Müller. He viewed Max Müller not only as a great scholar of the Vedas, but as someone who pointed out to the West, the importance of the spiritual contribution of India.[16] To the discomfort of later Hindu nationalists, Tilak genuinely admired and appreciated the contributions of Western scholarship, especially in the areas of comparative philology and religion. However, while Tilak admired Max Müller, he believed that the purely philological approach of scholars like Max Müller was not sufficient to yield convincing results and that the astronomical method, though generally condemned by the philologists as being indefinite and unreliable, could be refined and used to make more exact predictions.

Tilak was in general agreement with Bhandarkar on the question of Indo–European origins, and the general idea of migrations of various peoples into India, again to the discomfort of later proponents of Hindutva. Agreeing with C.V. Vaidya's writings on the Rāmāyaṇa, Tilak says,

The Aryan people entered India via Punjab, and after establishing their colonies in north India, they then slowly entered south India. This historical fact is now almost universally acknowledged. Once it is at least accepted that the Aryan people were first in north India and then they entered south India, it is necessary to assume that they must have defeated the wild populations there and established their kingdoms in that region. The only question is about the kind of wild populations there were in south India at that time.[17]

DEBATES WITH NARAYAN B. PAVGEE: FROM INDIA TO ARCTIC AND BACK?

To understand how Tilak's contemporaries disagreed with his theory of the Arctic origins of the Vedic Aryans, I will discuss Tilak's interactions with N.B. Pavgee. Pavgee was the author of a multi-volume work *The Bhāratīya Sāmrājya or Hindu Empire*. This was projected to be completed in twenty-two volumes, and eleven volumes had already appeared by 1912. Besides these volumes, he also published, in 1912, another work, *The Vedic Fathers of Geology*.[18] Pavgee's work is distinctly inspired, though not constrained by the work of B.G. Tilak, who disagreed with Pavgee's notion of the Āryāvartic home of the Aryans. Pavgee's nationalist Hindu ideology is visible throughout his writings, something that cannot be said of the careful scholarly work of Tilak. Pavgee's multi-volume work is dedicated with love and respect to all Ārya brothers (*ārya-bāndhava*) and sisters (*ārya-bhaginī*) and is intended to express his very strong affection for his dear Ārya motherland (*dayita-ārya-bhūmi*). This is clearly a precursor to Savarkar.

The second volume of his *Bhāratīya Sāmrājya* is titled, *Āryalok va tyāñce Buddhi-vaibhav* (The Āryan People and the Wealth of their Intelligence).[19] The book begins with a section dealing with the original home of the Aryas (*āryāñce mūla-nivāsa-sthāna*). Pavgee asserts at the very beginning that the Vedas are the oldest literature of mankind, and that the Vedas support the notion that northern India is the original home of not just the Aryans, but of the entire mankind.[20] In his support, he cites Elphinstone's *History of India*:

It is opposed to their foreign origin, that neither in the code (of Manu), nor, I believe, in the Vedas nor in any book that is certainly older than the code is there any allusion to a prior residence or to a knowledge of more than the name of any country out of India. Even mythology goes no further than the Himalaya chain in which is fixed the habitation of the gods.[21]

The Aryan family of languages originated in India, Pavgee asserts, and it expanded westward from India through the regions of Iran, Greece, Italy, Spain, England, Germany, and Russia. Pavgee mentions the view of Western philologists that the Aryans came into India from outside, but he attacks this view.[22] In the ninth volume of his *Bhāratīya Sāmrājya*, titled *Bharatakhaṇḍātīl Nānāvidha Bhāṣā* (Various Languages in India), Pavgee has a section on the original land of the Ārya language, that is, Sanskrit. Pavgee asserts unequivocally that Sanskrit originated in the region of Āryāvarta within India and is the mother of all Aryan languages. All languages such as Marāṭhi, Hindī, Bengalī, Gujaratī, Iranian, Greek, Latin, German, English, and Polish were born from Sanskrit. They are daughters of Sanskrit.[23] Various originally Ārya groups left their religion, castes, and the original Ārya homeland, and these eventually became the various branches of the Aryan language family. In support of this conclusion, Pavgee offers a large number of passages from Smṛtis and Purāṇas.[24]

In his 1912 book in English, *The Vedic Fathers of Geology*, Pavgee refers to another of his publications where he tries to outdo the theories of B.G. Tilak. Here are Pavgee's theories in his own words:

In my work entitled 'The Āryāvartic Home and the Aryan cradle in the Sapta Sindhus', or 'From Āryāvarta to the Arctic and from the Cradle to the Colony', and in my larger work in Marathi with still greater details, I have endeavoured to prove, by all sorts of evidences, Vedic and non-Vedic, scriptural and profane, scientific and demonstrative, historical and traditional, that we are autochthonous in India; that we were born in Āryāvarta on the banks or in the region of the reputed and the most sacred river the Sarasvatī, which was deemed by our very ancient Vedic ancestors of the Tertiary Period to be the scene where life had first commenced; that our Colony of young adventurers, having emigrated from and left Āryāvarta, had colonised distant lands of Asia, Africa, Europe, and America, and settled in the Arctic and Circum-Polar regions, during the Tertiary Epoch, at a time when the climate of the Arctic regions having been genial, these were fit for human habitation; that at the sight of the new phenomenon of everlasting Dawns, as also of the unusual long days and nights of the Arctic Regions,—to which our colonists from India were not accustomed while living in their Mother-Country-Āryāvarta, —their astonishment and fear knew no bounds; and that at the advent of the great Ice-Age; the once genial climate of the Arctic Regions having been replaced by extreme, not to say unbearable cold, and the higher latitudes having been covered with Ice-caps of enormous thickness, such our colonists as had made settlements there, were compelled to retrace their steps back to their Mother-land Āryāvarta, by the direction of the Snow-clad Himalaya, which was ever in their minds, and which they always remembered and cherished with fondness, as the northern boundary of their Beloved Bhārata-varsha.[25]

Pavgee attempted to solve riddles which Tilak was not able to solve. His theory combined Tilak's Arctic home with an even more ancient Āryāvartic home.[26] While Tilak did not explicitly say that the languages and the cultures of the Greeks and the Romans were derived from the Vedas of the Arctic home, Pavgee went ahead and made these assertions. In arguing against the theories proposed by Western philologists, Pavgee found 'convincing' evidence in the Smṛtis and Purāṇas for the 'Out of India' model. In some sense, Pavgee may be credited to be one of the first exponents of this theory, which has gradually become popular among the Hindu nationalists of the twentieth century. In his work, the nationalist ideology and historical reconstruction occupy the same space and they reinforce each other. Beginning with the work of Tilak, and also in the work of Pavgee, Bhandarkar's philology takes a back seat, and sciences like astronomy and geology appear as the primary tools for historical reconstruction. Rejecting the primacy of Comparative Philology, Tilak asserts,

Dr Schrader, in his *Pre-historic Antiquities of the Aryan Peoples*, gives us an exhaustive summary of facts and arguments regarding primitive Aryan culture and civilisation which can be deduced from Linguistic Palaeology, or Comparative Philology, and as a repertory of such facts the book stands unrivalled. But we must remember that the results of Comparative Philology, howsoever interesting and instructive they may be from the linguistic or the historical point of view, are apt to mislead us if we know not the site of the original home, or the time when it was inhabited or abandoned by the ancestors of our race.[27]

Pavgee reports that he did not know Tilak well after 1894.[28] However, when he had finished writing the first six volumes of his *Bhāratīya Sāmrājya*, he brought the manuscripts of his books to Pune to seek a publisher. A likely publisher asked Pavgee to show his manuscripts to Tilak. Tilak read these manuscripts and returned them to the author on 14 February 1894 with a positive recommendation. However, Tilak's reviews of Pavgee's works were rather critical. In his review published in *Kesari* on 21 August 1900, Tilak says, 'It is Pavgee's view that the original home of the Aryan language is India. ... It is doubtful to what extent this will hold up in view of recent discoveries.' This statement, some years before the publication of *The Arctic Home in the Vedas*, already suggested that according to Tilak the original home of the Aryan language was outside India. Pavgee continued to debate with Tilak on this topic, offering him proofs that the home of the Aryan language was India itself, but that did not satisfy Tilak. When finally *The Arctic Home in the Vedas* was completed, Tilak showed his manuscript to Pavgee, but Tilak's arguments did not convince Pavgee. Pavgee reports that on 29 May 1906 he delivered a lecture outlining his theories, when Tilak, who chaired the meeting, in his comments, discussed the difference of views between himself and Pavgee. After Tilak's return from the jail in Mandalay in Burma, Pavgee presented him with a copy of his book *Āryāvartic Home and its Arctic Colonies* and asked him to comment on it. However, Pavgee tells us that Tilak did not agree with his views. He said, 'I know that you hold that the Āryāvarta was the original home. You know that I hold the arctic region to be the original home. Both of us have offered our arguments to prove our conclusions. How can this dispute be settled?'[29] After Pavgee again reiterated his arguments and objections to Tilak's theory, Tilak calmly responded, 'Mr Pavgee, whatever I have written and argued cannot now be changed. You go ahead and publish your work.'[30] However, as seen from other reports, just before he died in 1920, Tilak was actively thinking about publishing a revised edition of *The Arctic Home in the Vedas*.

TILAK: A SCHOLAR IN THE JAIL
What is less known is how actively he was thinking of the subject of *The Arctic Home in the Vedas* during his jail term in Mandalay.[31] His letters from the Mandalay jail, that I have seen in the collection edited by M.D. Vidvans in 1966, are truly astonishing. In the midst of ill-health, raging political and legal battles, family issues and other complicated matters, in letter after letter, Tilak was requesting for a large number of books, totalling in the end to some 400 volumes by the time his sentence ended. He not only finished writing his *Gītārahasya* while in the jail, but a fair number of books he requested and read during his sentence indicate

his continuing and active interest in the subject of *The Arctic Home in the Vedas*, and attests to the fact that he was serious about revising that book. In his letter from Mandalay dated 3 July 1909, one notices how active his academic interests were, even in the jail. We first hear him say, 'What I am doing is working out a certain theory of my own regarding the fundamental principles of the Infinitesimal calculus. And if this theory is satisfactorily developed I may publish an English essay on it.'[32] Then after a few paragraphs about his health, food in the jail, and the weather, Tilak returns to an academic topic of his interest,

I have received the *Kathaka Upanishad* and Prof. Athavale's *Shrauta Bhumi* sent by you. I am glad Prof. Athavale has published his essay separately. It strengthens my view and advances some new arguments about the Arctic nature of the Vedic sacrificial calendar. ... If I ever happen to publish a second edition of the Arctic Home, I may publish Prof. Athavale's essay as an appendix to the same. He has taken great pains to work out the astronomical details. Ask him, in my name, to send the copies of his essay to Pandit Sudhakar Dwivedi of Benaras Sanskrit College and to German and American Orientalists, whose names can be ascertained from the list of persons in the office to whom Arctic Home was sent, and to Dr. Bhandarkar and others in India.[33]

On 3rd May, 1910, he wrote, 'At the last interview, I told you to send me ... Weber's *Indian Nakshatras*. ... I mean to translate Weber from German into English.'[34] Sitting in the jail in Mandalay, he had taught himself to read French and German, well enough to have the confidence to translate Weber's book on Indian *nakshatras* from German into English.

POLITICAL IMPLICATION OF THE ARCTIC HOME THEORY
This is not to say that he did not see the political/emotional/cultural dimensions of the subjects covered in books like *The Arctic Home in the Vedas* or the *Gītārahasya*. K.L. Daftari reports a conversation he had with Tilak in June 1920, just a few months before Tilak passed away.[35] They were discussing the question of whether the Hindus learned mathematics/astronomy from the Greeks, or whether the Greeks learned it from the Hindus. To prove his point, Tilak took out Emmeline M. Plunket's *Ancient Calendars and Constellations* and showed Mr Daftari the following paragraph,

Again the opinion of the Greek-writers at the beginning of our era may be quoted as showing the high estimation in which at the time of the world Indian Astronomy was held; as for instance in the life of Apollonius of Tyana (written about 210 A.D. by Philostratus) the wisdom and learning of Apollonius are set high above those of all his contemporaries, but from the sages of India, he is represented as learning many things, especially matters in astronomy.[36]

What was important for Tilak was to establish or re-establish pride in the Indian traditions, especially when India was under the colonial rule. This project was shared in common with other personalities of the time like Vivekananda and Aurobindo. N.S. Deshpande once asked Tilak why he did not write his *Arctic Home* book in Marathi. Tilak responded by saying that while he recognizes the needs of the Marathi readers, 'it is necessary to write such books in English to refute the objections raised by western scholars against Indian traditions.'[37]

While it is true that Tilak does not bring up any of the contemporary social or political issues while discussing his theory and argues purely on the basis of technical evidence as he sees it, his theory can be seen to have some interesting implications. The earlier theories of Aryan migrations as seen in the works of Bhandarkar, Kunte, and Chiplunkar, accept the notion of the Aryans coming to India from outside, and yet they seem to connect the composition of the Vedas with the region of Punjab. That makes the Vedas a relatively late product of the Indo-Aryan branch of the Indo-European language family. However, Tilak's theory of the Arctic home in the Vedas takes the descriptions given in the Vedas, if not the Vedas themselves, back to a period ranging from 10000–8000 BC. That would almost certainly place the Vedas earlier than the Greeks, the Romans, and the Mitannis. Such a hoary ancestry to the Vedas makes their inheritors, the Indian Aryans, senior brothers to the Western Aryans. At least, it suggests the possibility that the linguistic and the cultural traditions of the Western Aryans may be derived from the more ancient Vedic tradition, and that their traditions turn out to be younger than the Vedic traditions. Such implications would certainly have energizing impact on the nationalist movement rooted in the Brahmanical tradition. The possibility that the traditions of the Greeks and Romans could be derived from the Vedic tradition has not been seriously entertained in Tilak's own writings, and yet it is clear that this is the direction that would appear in the works of nationalist Indian authors during Tilak's lifetime. Stanley Wolpert has discussed the significance of Tilak's theories for his nationalistic goals. He shows that Tilak spoke differently on different occasions, more cautious on some than on others. Wolpert claims that Tilak was 'anxious to maintain the guise of scientific impartiality' in his *The Arctic Home in the Vedas* and similar publications.[38] The cautious Tilak says,

It is impossible to demonstrate historically or scientifically that Vedic religion and worship is *absolutely* without a beginning. All that we can say is that its beginning is lost in geological antiquity. ... If theologians are not satisfied with the support which this scientific view accords to their theory about the eternity of the Vedas, the scientific and the theological views must stand, as they are, distinct from each other, for the two methods of investigation are essentially different.[39]

However, on another occasion, the less cautious Tilak says: 'We may, however, still assert that for all practical purposes the Vedic religion can be shown to be beginningless even on strict scientific grounds.'[40] The political significance of Tilak's theories was not lost on his followers. In his Sanskrit biography of Tilak, K.W. Chitale claims that, in the conflict between the Eastern and the Western civilizations, Tilak accomplished the victory of the Eastern civilization over the Western civilization in his publications (*paurvātya-pāścātya-samskrtyoh sangharse paurvātya-samskrter vijayo `nena grantha-dvaya-nirmānena lokamānyaih sampāditah*).[41]

While some did see Tilak's theory as instilling a sense of pride among the Indians, most contemporary observers seem to have seen this theory more as a scholarly activity of high calibre as against a political or a politically motivated theory. In his reminiscences about Tilak, Swami Shraddhanand remarks, 'His *Orion or the Antiquity of the Vedas* endeared him to me, because he had the courage to stand up for the Antiquity of the Vedas as against European Scholars, whom no Indian had dared to give lessons in research work before.'[42] So not just the established antiquity of the Vedas was a point of pride for the Indian audiences, the fact that an Indian could write such a scholarly work was also a point of pride. P.K. Telang reports,

My friend seems to have felt that his [= Tilak's] scholarship was directed not so much to the elucidation of truth as to the bolstering up of a theory of the greatness of Indian Literature, History, and in short, all things Indian. I am inclined to believe that this is a wrong judgment. To me it seemed that, though Mr. Tilak was first and foremost a patriot and politician, his scholarship was imbued with the true spirit of the searcher after truth.[43]

The relationship between politics and scholarship was not that of either/ or for Tilak. He was pursuing both. There was indeed some seepage of ideas and interests from one domain to the other. However, all evidence points to the fact that Tilak was sincere and passionate in his scholarly pursuits. Khaparde reports visiting Tilak on the fort of Sinhagad near Pune in the June of 1901: 'He is now writing the last chapter of his book proving that *we had an original home in the Arctic regions* (italics mine).'[44] The words in italics are very telling: *we had an original home in the arctic regions.* Tilak's interlocutors were seamlessly weaving their own identities with the ancient history as it was being reconstructed in front of their eyes. It was *our history*. Though Tilak does not use such personalizing language himself in his scholarly works, it is difficult to say that he did not share in this tendency of seeing the present as being inextricably linked with the past history.

SCHOLASTIC AND NON-POLITICAL DISCOURSES

On occasions, Tilak could and did present himself in a completely depoliticized fashion. A. Ranga Swami Aiyangar remembers a voyage on the ship *Macedonia* where he was with Tilak along with a large number of European passengers,

I here desire to narrate the transformation that took place on board the ship, of the attitude of sullen suspicion with which so many European fellow-travelers at first regarded him [= Tilak] into that disposition of awe and reverence. ... We eventually persuaded the Lokamanya [to give a speech], but *he insisted upon addressing on a non-political subject and we of course asked him to tell his audience something of the epoch making researches he had made regarding the Arctic Home in the Vedas.* He readily agreed and his audience full of Europeans of quality were wondering what they were going to pick up from the abstruse discourse that would be made. Nevertheless they gathered in full strength. ... In clear, short and simple sentences he unfolded the tale of the Vedic man's Arctic Home to an audience that found the mysteries of research solved with so little effort. ... Carrying his researches further, as he did during the days of his captivity in Burma, he showed how this deductive conclusion was confirmed by the latest discovery in geology and archaeology. ... The audience by this time became intensely interested and spellbound. No wonder at the conclusion thereof the U.P.I.C.S. Commissioner that presided paid a glowing tribute to the scholar that had enlightened them with such wealth of learning and simplicity of diction.[45]

M.R. Jayakar has recorded a similar recollection of a lecture Tilak gave at the meeting of the Bombay Presidency Association on the subject of antiquity in Vedic history,

I went to the meeting with great enthusiasm, for I had heard a great deal about Mr. Tilak's scholarship. But what I actually heard was a great deal beyond my expectation. The details with which the Lokamanya marshalled his knowledge, the accuracy and profundity with which he presented his facts, showed the finished scholar. The effect on the audience was so deep that even his political opponent in the chair [= Sir Dinshaw Wacha] was moved beyond the president's usual reticence and was compelled to remark that, if the Lokamanya could be persuaded to accord to archaeology a larger measure of his time and attention, it would be a great gain. ... The greatest tragedy in a foreign governed country is that such scholars, owing to their absorption in day-to-day politics, cannot give to the world the best results of their thought. I have often felt that his proper place was in a scholastic sanctuary.[46]

Tilak's fame as a scholar had travelled far and wide. Perhaps this perception of his scholarly eminence explains why scholars like Max

Müller signed the petition in England sent to the Queen to set Tilak free from imprisonment in 1898. The petition includes the following clause,

That Mr. Tilak has served his country well as a scholar and a Sanskritist, and his services have been recognised by the best scholars of Europe. It is clear from his paper on Orion and similar topics that his real interests lie in the ancient literature of his country, and that he cares more for events that happened 3,000 or 4,000 years ago than for the question of the day.[47]

Indeed, one can understand the exaggeration in this statement that was intended as an appeal to seek Royal clemency. However, one can also see the recognition accorded to him by leading European scholars of the day, who would have been happy to see him pursue only the scholarly interests, and not get into politics of nationalism.[48]

FROM TILAK TO SAVARKAR: 'LET US FORGET THE HISTORY OF MIGRATION'

I would now like to examine how the emerging world of Hindutva ideology, beginning with Savarkar, saw Tilak. What did Savarkar think of Tilak's theory of the Arctic Home of the Aryans? Savarkar obviously respected Tilak as a senior politician of his day. In his autobiography, Savarkar says that Tilak and Chiplunkar were his gurus in the area of politics, while Ranade and Agarkar were his gurus in the area of social reform.[49] Chiplunkar, like Tilak, accepted the outside origin of the Aryans and their migration into India, but then argued that the ancient Aryans, once they came to India, made it their homeland, unlike 'our Aryan brothers', the British, who came to India just to extract profit. Chiplunkar passed away before Tilak's publications on the Vedas, but his fiery writings inspired many subsequent generations of nationalist thinkers, including Savarkar. Savarkar did not quite reject the theory of Aryan migration into India, but much like Chiplunkar, he stressed how the ancient Aryans made it their homeland, without any loyalty to any other land,

Although it would be hazardous at the present stage of oriental research to state definitely the period when the foremost band of the intrepid Aryans made it their home and lighted their first sacrificial fire on the banks of the Sindhu, the Indus, certain it is that long before the ancient Egyptians, and Babylonians had built their magnificent civilization, the holy waters of the Indus were daily witnessing the lucid and curling columns of the scented sacrificial smokes and the valleys resounding [with] the chants of Vedic hymns. ... The adventurous valor that propelled their intrepid enterprises, the sublime heights to which their thoughts rose—all these had marked them out as a people destined to lay the foundation of a great and enduring civilization. By the time they had definitely cut themselves aloof from their cognate and neighboring people, especially the Persians, the Aryans had spread out to the farthest of the seven rivers—saptasindhus—and not only had they developed a sense of nationality but had already succeeded in giving it a local habitation and a name.[50]

As for Tilak's theory of Arctic Home in the Vedas, and the notion of the Aryan as distinct from the non-Aryan, Savarkar clearly recognized the political inconvenience of such ideas, in contrast with the notion of pan-Indian Hindutva without differentiation between Aryan and non-Aryan. Savarkar points out in the introduction to his autobiography,

Memory is useful for an individual and the society. But, in fact, like memory, forgetting is also a gift of God. It is beneficial for an individual and the society to forget certain things than to remember them. ... Similar is the case of the memories of ancient history of a society. Sometimes we are pained to find that we cannot find the ancient history of some society. However, in some sense, is it not better that we have forgotten certain portions of that history. If we could point with historical accuracy where Ravana's Lanka was, the people in that place would develop a degree of hatred for us, the Aryans, and who can say that this would not spark up new fights by reminding the old ones. This is not just imagination. ... After hearing about the explanation that the Aryans came to India from the North Pole, those who considered themselves to be non-Aryan began to treat the Aryans as 'late arrived' Hindus, and started calling themselves original Dravidas or original Hindus. If the information about the ancient times leaves the confusing appearance of the Puranic materials and if it appears before us in absolutely clear form, and if peoples' ancient identities as Aryan, non-Aryan, Asura, Danuja, Hun, Scythian, and Dravida were to become known in every household, then one can only imagine the confusion it would create. Many Brahmin castes may prove to be acculturated Scythians or Magas. Many Kṣatriyas would turn out to be Huns. ... 'Whatever has happened has happened. Let us forget it.' As soon as one says this with full intent, so many broken friendships have been reconnected. ... Truly, forgetting is as much a gift of God as memory.[51]

Savarkar knows the history of ancient times, but also knows that keeping a memory of this history alive is contrary to his present-day goal of Hindu nationalism, that demands that all Hindus, irrespective of their historical differences, must stand together, against the perceived danger from the non-Hindus, that is Muslims. Any memory of sub-identities must be actively suppressed. The political necessity of such a project is clearly laid out by Savarkar, while openly admitting that a historian's history is rather inconvenient and poses problems for the current politics.

Both Tilak and Savarkar indicate a great deal of internal consistency in their ideas of who is a Hindu. Since Tilak accepted the basic notion of the Aryan migration into India, and his specific version propounded in his *The Arctic Home in the Vedas*, he could not define Hindus as those who originated in India. His definition of a Hindu makes no mention of the origin, but only of religious faith and practices:

prāmāṇyabuddhir vedeṣu sādhanānām anekatā /
upāsyānām aniyamaḥ etad dharmasya lakṣaṇam //

('Acceptance of the ultimate validity of the Vedas, multiplicity of ways of worship and lack of restriction on the divinity that one may worship, this is the definition of [Hindu] religion.')

Such a definition puts the highest value on the scriptural texts of the Vedas, while admitting a great deal of flexibility of ways of worship and the divinities worshipped. It has been rightly suggested that such a definition would exclude those Hindu low castes that never had access to the Vedas. However, it conveniently makes no reference to geographical origins of the Vedas or the Hindu people. Muslims may be differentiated from the Hindus on the ground that they do not believe in the authority of the Vedas, but one need not say that the Hindus were primordial residents of India. Such a claim would contradict the history as Tilak understood it. So the definition of a Hindu, according to Tilak, should not and could not make a reference to historical/geographic origins. On the other hand, even while admitting a history of migration of the Aryans into India, Savarkar wanted to emphasize the loyalty and the age-old devotion of the Hindus to India as the land of their ancestors. So the definition of Hindu offered by Tilak was not quite satisfactory to Savarkar. His own definition of a Hindu runs as follows:

āsindhusindhuparyantā yasya bhāratabhūmikā /
pitṛbhūḥ puṇyabhūś caiva sa vai hindur iti smṛtaḥ //

('He is said to be a Hindu who considers the entire continent of India from Indus to oceans to be the land of his ancestors as well as his holy land.')

By composing these definitions in Sanskrit verses, both Tilak and Savarkar were creating an appearance of authenticity, as if the verses were from an ancient text like the *Manusmṛti*. This is more evident in the verse of Savarkar who uses the term *smṛtaḥ*, 'traditionally known to be', that creates for this verse an appearance of the status of a Smṛti-quotation. At least, in Tilak's definition, the notion of authority of the Vedas is a straight forward importation of classical notions, and hence Tilak's definition looks like an attempt to modernize the classical notion of the centrality of the Vedas seen in Smṛti texts like *vedo 'khilo dharmamūlam*, 'the entire Veda is the basis of dharma'.[52]

On the other hand, Savarkar's definition is a calculated modernism, made to appear like a Smṛti verse, and has no parallel anywhere in the traditional *dharmaśāstric* literature in Sanskrit. It essentially drains away all substantive religious content from the term Hindu, and raises absolute loyalty to the land to the exclusive criterion for being a Hindu. This loyalty is then split into two parts: a) India as the ancestral land, and b) India as the holy land. Interestingly, the nuance that is not commonly understood is that the definition makes no reference to primordiality of the Aryans as a native population of India, since Savarkar had clearly not proposed that the Aryans were autochthonous to India. He had come to accept the history as proposed by Tilak and others, but had chosen the route of deliberately forgetting, or deleting this unpleasant history out of political consciousness. It was, therefore, sufficient for one to merely believe and vocally assert that one's ancestors were always in India, and not worry about the history as constructed by historians. By advocating the negative value of memory, or of the history of the historians, Savarkar in effect cleared the path for his Hindutva successors to produce convenient imagined histories and enabled them to become bold in rejecting the history of the historians. This is the trajectory one observes in the writings of the Hindutva ideologues who followed in the footsteps of Savarkar. For this reason, while one may not agree today with Tilak's particular reconstruction of Vedic history, one needs to recognize that Tilak, in spite of being a Hindu politician, was very much on the side of the historian's history. He would rather fit his politics as best as he could within the reconstruction of history that was justified on the basis of evidence acceptable to him, rather than reject the historian's history and promote an assertive anti-intellectual trend of convenient imagined history.

FROM SAVARKAR TO GOLWALKAR: 'ARCTIC HOME WAS IN INDIA'

Further slippage in the value of genuinely scholarly understanding of ancient history is glaringly evident between Savarkar and Golwalkar. While Savarkar was not beyond presenting an imagined history, if it were convenient for his current political goals,[53] it must be admitted that he does not deny the validity of the academician's history of ancient India. He seems to include Tilak's efforts in the same category. It is just that he does not want a memory of such a history of migrations and ethnic distinctions to be kept alive to the detriment of his current Hindutva politics.

The successors of Savarkar in the Hindutva movement are not willing to make such a distinction. They would rather create a useful imaginary history. Such is the case of M.S. Golwalkar, the Guruji of the RSS, who clearly found Tilak's theory of the Arctic Home in its original form rather inconvenient, without a significant reinterpretation. Golwalkar seems to agree with the time frame suggested by Tilak, but not with his geography, 'We Hindus, have been in undisputed and undisturbed possession of this land for over 8,000 or even 10,000 years, before this land was invaded by any foreign race, and therefore, this land came to be known as Hindustan, the land of the Hindus.'[54] But then what to do with Tilak's theory? Golwalkar's response was a reinterpretation of Tilak's theory,

Lokmanya Tilak propounded the Arctic origin of the Aryans. We may agree with him that originally the Aryans, i.e. the Hindus lived in the region of the North Pole. But he was not aware that in ancient times, the North Pole and with it the Arctic Zone was not where it is today ... North Pole is not stationary and quite long ago it was in that part of the world, which, we find, is called Bihar and Orissa at the present: that then it moved northeast and then by a sometimes westerly, sometimes northward movement, it came to its present position. ... 'The Arctic Home in the Vedas' was verily in Hindustan itself and that it was not the Hindus who migrated to that land, but the Arctic Zone which migrated and left the Hindus in Hindustan.[55]

Pavgee's theory of migration of the Aryavartic Aryans from India to the North Pole and return to India was difficult enough, but Pavgee, to his credit, did not bring the North Pole to India. That revision was proposed by Golwalkar.[56]

POST-GOLWALKAR HINDUTVA: DEMISE OF THE ARCTIC HOME THEORY

Subhash Kak, a leading pro-Hindutva writer, exhibits the same dilemma as Golwalkar,

The existence of this [astronomical] code [in the Vedas] also implies that the internal astronomical evidence in the Vedic texts first argued by Tilak and Jacobi and later by others cannot be ignored. This internal evidence compels the conclusion that the prehistory of the Vedic people in India goes back to the fourth millennium and earlier. Such a conclusion is in consonance with the new archaeological discoveries that show a continuity in the Indian tradition going as far back as 6500 B.C.E.[57]

So Kak says yes to Tilak's chronology, but then what about Tilak's geography of the Arctic Home in the Vedas?

If Kak is respectful to Tilak in accepting his theory partially where it seems in agreement with his own, and not openly rejecting the rest, such is not the case with Koenraad Elst, a pro-Hindutva European writer. His essay 'Savarkar, Hinduness and the Aryan Homeland', almost seems to be rephrasing Kak's sentiment, but with distinct lack of respect, or positive disdain, for Tilak,

Tilak's arguments in favor of an Aryan homeland outside India are anything but 'distinguished'; they are highly contrived and sometimes downright ridiculous. ... Even without going into the details, the idea of locating in the Arctic a people destined to colonize the European and Indian subcontinents is a priori very unlikely given that region's inability to support a sizable population. Tilak was under the spell of European superiority, a presupposition to which he adapted his knowledge of Vedic history; and he even accepted the then-common European view of the Aryans as a band of spectacularly unstoppable conquerors from the North.[58]

Having rejected Tilak's geography of migrations, Elst predictably seems to accept his chronology, 'The only part of Tilak's argumentation that seems to stand up to scrutiny, and that has been confirmed by more recent researchers [that is, Kak], is the part which contradicts the AIT [= Aryan–Invasion–Theory] at least in its most common version: his astronomy-based chronology dating the Rig-Veda to the 4th millennium B.C.'[59] It is no surprise that there are few current supporters of Tilak's theory in modern times.[60] What is interesting to note is that while Tilak remains among the founding fathers of the modern Hindutva movement, the substance of his Arctic Home theory, closely related as it is to the hated Aryan-Invasion theory, is gradually eased into retirement, in favour of the various versions of the Out-of-India (OIT for short) theories, to be found on pro-Hindutva websites and publications. The study of Tilak's theories as presented here, it is hoped, will provide us insight into the multiple trajectories of intellectual movements of the late nineteenth and the twentieth centuries within their own rich and varied historical context, and the connections of these trajectories to the modern political movements.[61]

NOTES AND REFERENCES

1. B.G. Tilak, *The Arctic Home in the Vedas* (Pune: The Manager, Kesari, 1903), pp. 453–4.
2. Ibid., p. 457.
3. Stanley Wolpert, *Tilak and Gokhale: Revolution and Reform in the Making of Modern India* (Berkeley: University of California Press, 1961), p. 63.
4. 'The propositions put forward by Tilak were not accepted, like some of the Western scholars, even by Indian Pandits.' N.C. Kelkar, *Life and Times of Lokmanya Tilak*, trans. D.V. Divekar (Madras: S. Ganesan, 1928), p. 457. Also: 'But what was there in this high antiquity of the Vedas, for which the old

Sanskrit scholars should feel a sense of joy and pride? Nothing. Because it was their time-honoured and indisputable belief that the Vedas were Anādi "beginningless" and Apauruṣeya "not made by man", and therefore even if a period of 8000 years may strike modern thinkers as an achievement, it would imply that the Vedas are endowed with a beginning (sādi) and are man-made (pauruṣeya); and this would, therefore, to the old pandits be possibly a matter for feeling regret rather than for feeling proud and joyful. Any fanatic Pandit could have passed the remark that, by applying the tests of a critic and the compass of time to the Vedas ... and thus by encompassing them within small limits Tilak had only blasphemed God.' Ibid., p. 468.

5. Gail Omvedt, *Letter to Bangaru Laxman*, available online at http://www.ambedkar.org/gail/openletter.htm (accessed 30 June 2009).

6. Stanley Wolpert, *Tilak and Gokhale*, p. 63ff.

7. For details, see Madhav M. Deshpande, 'Pandit and Professor: Transformations in the 19th Century Maharashtra', in Axel Michaels (ed.), *The Pandit: Traditional Scholarship in India* (Delhi: Manohar, 2001), pp. 119–53.

8. Stanley Wolpert, *Tilak and Gokhale*, pp. 16–17.

9. S.S. Puranik, 'Life and Contribution of Vishnushastri Chiplunkar' in *Viṣṇuśāstrī* [in Marathi] (Pune: Raviraj Prakashan, 1992), p. 36.

10. 'Among the professors in the Deccan College at that time, only two, namely Professor Keropant Chhatre and Prof. Schutte, are said to be popular among students. Professor Chhatre was a self-made and self-educated man. He had made Mathematics and Astronomy his own chosen subjects; and the very fact that he, though not highly qualified in English, was raised to the position of the Acting Principal, shows that Government also had respect for his learning.' N.C. Kelkar, *Life and Times*, p. 54.

11. B.G. Tilak, *The Arctic Home*, p. v.

12. I was a student of both of these institutions in Pune.

13. B.G. Tilak, *Vedic Chronology and Vedanga Jyotisha* (Pune: Messrs Tilak Bros, Gaikwar Wada, 1925), p. 11.

14. Professor S.G. Jinsiwale was my great-great-grandmother's brother, and accounts of his life and his interactions with Tilak were traditionally handed down in my family. For further details on Jinsiwale, see N.C. Kelkar, *Life and Times*, p. 44ff.

15. S.V. Bapat, *Lokamānya Ṭilakyāṃcyā āṭhavaṇī va ākhyāyikā*, vol. 3 (Pune: Published by the author, 1928), p. 93ff.

16. For Tilak on Max Müller, see N.C. Kelkar and D.V. Vidvans (eds.), *Lokmanya Ṭilakāṃce Kesarītīl Saṃkīrṇa Lekh*, vol. 4 (Pune: Kesari Maratha Samstha, 1922), p. 124ff. Also see Max Müller's obituary written by Tilak in *Kesari*, 6 November 1900. Ibid., p. 573ff.

17. Ibid., pp. 506–7.

18. N.B. Pavgee, *The Vedic Fathers of Geology* (Pune: Published by the author, 1912).

19. N.B. Pavgee, *Bhāratīya Sāmrājya*, vol. 2, [*Āryalok va tyāñce Buddhi-vaibhav*] (Pune: Published by the author, 1893).

20. Ibid., p. 2.

21. Ibid., pp. 3–4.
22. Ibid., p. 5.
23. N.B. Pavgee, *Bhāratīya Sāmrājya*, vol. 9, [*Bharatakhaṇḍātīl Nānāvidha Bhāṣā*] (Pune: Published by the author, 1900), p. 14.
24. Ibid., p. 16ff.
25. N.B. Pavgee, *The Vedic Fathers of Geology* (Pune: Published by the author, 1912), pp. 34–5.
26. In his recollections of his meetings with Tilak, N.B. Pavgee says that beginning with 1894 he had many opportunities to discuss his theories with Tilak. Pavgee says that Tilak never agreed with him on his theory of the Āryāvartic home of the Aryans, and insisted on his idea of the Arctic home of the Aryans. See S.V. Bapat, *Lokamānya Ṭiḷak yāṃcyā āṭhavaṇī va ākhyāyikā*, vol. 2 (Pune: Published by the author, 1925), p. 523ff. It is perhaps this interaction between the two that inspired Pavgee to incorporate the notion of the Arctic home as a colony of the Aryans from their Aryavartic home in his later work.
27. B.G. Tilak, *The Arctic Home*, pp. 431–2.
28. S.V. Bapat, *Lokamānya Ṭiḷak*, vol. 2, p. 523ff.
29. Ibid.
30. Ibid.
31. Even during his previous jail term, Tilak spent a substantial part of his time in scholarly reading. In an interview after he was released from jail in 1898, he described the conditions in the jail, thus: 'They had lodged me in the European section of the jail. My room had three-beamed ceiling. There was a stone bench covered with wooden planks for sleeping, and the bedding consisted of two blankets. I had the prison clothes. I was allowed to request books to read from home and was also allowed to keep a lamp burning for three hours at night. What books I had needed to be kept in the office of the jail, and I could bring a few books into my room. I spent my time mostly reading the Ṛgveda, assisted by the commentaries. From this study I have come to conclude that the ancestors of the Aryan people must have lived near the North Pole where the night was of two months duration. But later they slowly moved southward. What I say has the support of the discoveries of the geologists. However, I did not have sufficient resources in the jail. I have yet to see the books I need to consult. After I get an opportunity to see those books, it is possible that my views might change. However, at present I am fairly certain about this question.' S.V. Bapat, *Lokamānya Ṭiḷak*, vol. 3, pp. 223–4.
32. M.D. Vidvans (ed.), *Letters of Lokamanya Tilak* (Pune: Kesari Prakashan, 1966), pp. 53–4.
33. Ibid., p. 54.
34. Ibid., pp. 80–1.
35. S.V. Bapat, *Lokamānya Ṭiḷak*, vol. 2, p. 77.
36. Emmeline M. Plunket, *Ancient Calendars and Constellations*, part I (London: J. Murray, 1903), 97. This book was published the same year that Tilak's *The Arctic Home in the Vedas* appeared, and its contents are described as follows: I. The Accadian calendar. (*Proceedings of the Society of Biblical Archaeology*, January

1892); II. The constellation Aries. (*Proc. of the Soc. of Biblical Arch.*, March 1893); III. Gu, eleventh constellation of the zodiac. (*Proc. of the Soc. of Biblical Arch.*, Feb. 1896); IV. The Median calendar and the constellation Taurus. (*Proc. of the Soc. of Biblical Arch.*, June 1897); V. Astronomy in the Rig Veda. (*Report of the Acts of the Twelfth Oriental Congress* held at Rome); VI. Notes-- Ahura Mazda, etc. (*Proc. of the Soc. of Biblical Arch.*, Feb. 1900); VII. Ancient Indian Astronomy (*Proc. of the Soc. of Biblical Arch.*, Feb. 1900); VIII. The Chinese calendar, with some remarks with reference to that of the Chaldeans. (*Proc. of the Soc. of Biblical Arch.*, Dec. 1901). One should note that Plunket's book contains full chapters on 'Astronomy in the Rig Veda' and 'Ancient Indian Astronomy', indicating that Tilak's interests in these subjects were not out of line with the general trends in those days. As I have pointed out earlier, M.V. Kibe had referred this book to Tilak just a few months earlier, and it seems that he had acquired a copy to consult by this time.

37. S.V. Bapat, *Lokamānya Ṭilak*, vol. 2, p. 125. Also see the opinion of N.C. Kelkar, a close associate of Tilak and his biographer, 'By writing these works in English Tilak had wished to secure a place of respect and honour in the esteem of the English people, not for any personal glorification but only for the Triumph of the Indian Nation.' N.C. Kelkar, *Life and Times*, p. 469. Nationalist readings of Tilak's scholarly activities were always possible and readily available.

38. Stanley Wolpert, *Tilak and Gokhale*, p. 125.

39. Wolpert cites the following reference for Tilak's comment: '*Journal of the Poona Sarvajanik Sabha*, XVII: 3, July, 1894, 37-38.' Ibid., pp. 125-6.

40. Ibid., p. 126.

41. K.W. Chitale, *Lokamānya-Ṭilaka-Caritam* (Bombay: Published by the author, 1956), p. 203.

42. S.V. Bapat, *The Reminiscences and Anecdotes of Lokamanya Tilak* (Pune: Published by the author, 1924), p. 1.

43. S.V. Bapat, *Lokamānya Ṭilak*, vol. 2, pp. 568-9.

44. Ibid., pp. 582-3.

45. S.V. Bapat, *The Reminiscences*, pp. 51-2.

46. S.V. Bapat, *Lokamānya Ṭilak*, vol. 2, p. 649.

47. B.G. Tilak, *Samagra Lokmanya Tilak*, vol. 7 (Pune: Kesari Prakashan, 1975), p. 990.

48. While Tilak was himself inspired by W.F. Warren's 1885 book, *Paradise Found, the Cradle of the Human Race at the North Pole* (Boston: Houghton, Mifflin and Company), Warren came to admire Tilak's *Arctic Home*. In the September 1905 issue of *Open Court Magazine*, Chicago, Warren comments on Tilak's *Arctic Home*, 'Suffice it here to say that in the judgment of the present writer the array of the evidences set forth is far more conclusive than any ever attempted by an Indo-Iranian scholar in the interest of any earlier hypothesis. Absolute candor and respect for the strictest methods of historical and scientific investigation characterize the discussion throughout. ... Twenty years ago, in preparing my work on the broader problem of the cradle-land of the whole human race, I went through all the Vedic and Avestic texts so far as existing translations would then permit, reaching at the end the same conclusion that Mr. Tilak

has now reached. ... Especially gratifying, therefore, is it to me to find in Mr. Tilak a man in no degree dependent on translations, yet arriving not only at my main conclusion, but also at a number of minor ones of which I had never made public mention. I desire publicly to thank this far-off fellow-worker for the generosity of his frequent references to my pioneer work in the common field, and for the solidity and charm of his won, in certain respects, more authoritative contribution. Whoever will master this new work, and that of the late Mr. John O' Neill on *The Night of the Gods*, will not be likely ever again to ask, where was the earliest home of the Aryans.' For the contemporary reception of Tilak's theory, also see Joscelyn Godwin, *Arctos, the Polar Myth in Science, Symbolism and Nazi Survival* (Kempton, Illinois: Adventures Unlimited Press, 1996), pp. 31–4.

49. V.D. Savarkar, *Sāvarkar Ātmacaritra*, third edn. (Bombay: Majestic Prakashan, 1973), p. 144.

50. V.D. Savarkar, *Hindutva: Who is a Hindu*, sixth edn. (Mumbai: Veer Savarkar Prakashan, 1989 [1923]), pp. 3–4.

51. Ibid., pp. 15–7.

52. *Manusmṛti* 2.6, edited with the commentary of Kullūka, third rpt (Mumbai: Nirnayasagar Press, 1902), p. 30.

53. Y.D. Phadke, critically evaluates Savarkar's history writing and concludes, 'Yadunath Sarkar's opinion that Savarkar's history writing was of a romantic nature is accurate. Savarkar's nationalism was clear. Nationalist individuals instinctively romanticize the past. But Savarkar had used history as an arrow in his political quiver. Savarkar wrote history, not so much to discover truth, but to awaken his countrymen who were disheartened and were possessed by the inferiority complex, by enkindling their sense of identity. ... If the reader is not on his guard while reading history written by Savarkar, he can be led astray.' Y.D. Phadke, *Śodh Sāvarkarāṃcā* (Pune: Shrividya Prakashan, 1984), p. 87.

54. M.S. Golwalkar, *We and our Nationhood Defined* (Nagpur: Bharat Prakashan, 1939), p. 8.

55. Ibid., p. 8.

56. Sitaram Yechuri's remarks: 'Granting the benefit of doubt, that Golwalkar was unaware of the advances in geological sciences and plate-tectonics, we ask the simple question: Even by the logic of his own argument, if the Arctic zone moved away from Bihar-Orissa, how could it leave behind the people who were inhabiting that land mass? When the land mass moves, it moves along with everything on it. People cannot be left hanging in a vacuum only to drop down when and where Golwalkar wishes. Such ... is employed to 'establish' that the Aryans originated in India and did not immigrate from anywhere else. This is central to the political aim of establishing a ... Hindu Rashtra.' Online article, 'What is this Hindu Rashtra? On Golwalkar's Fascistic Ideology and the Saffron Brigade's Practice', http://www.sacw.net/DC/CommunalismCollection/Articles Archive/Yechuri1993.html (accessed 30 June 2009).

57. Subhash Kak, *The Astronomical Code of the Rigveda* (Delhi: Aditya Prakashan, 1994), p. 13.

58. Koenraad Elst, 'Savarkar, Hinduness and the Aryan Homeland', http://koenraadelst.voiceofdharma.org/articles/fascism/replytopv.html (accessed 30 June 2009).

59. Ibid.

60. Except occasionally by writers like Dharmapada Dasa or Dean Delucia, the author of 'Arctic Home of the Vedas Revisited', 31 January 2002 editorial on the Vaishnava News (VNN), or the websites talking about the Arctic Homeland Hyperborea etc. We need not take these views seriously.

61. While I have only discussed here the trajectory in the direction of the Hindutva movement, one also notices that the academic lineage of the Deccan College and the Bhandarkar Oriental Research Institute represented by academic stalwarts like S.K. Belvalkar, S.M. Katre, M.A. Mehendale, A.M. Ghatage, and R.N. Dandekar held on to the evidence-based standard Indo–European theory. On the other hand, with the rising star of political parties like the Bharatiya Janata Party (BJP) and its allied organizations like the Vishwa Hindu Parishad (VHP) and the Rashtriya Swayamsevak Sangh (RSS), one can trace the significant arrival of the Hindutva ideology into academic institutions, textbooks, etc., and in the emergence of a long line of Hindutva oriented academicians. For a balanced review of the OIT [Out-of-India] theories proposed in recent years, see Edwin Bryant, *The Quest for the Origins of Vedic Culture: The Indo-Aryan Migration Debate* (New York: Oxford University Press, 2001).

Roby Rajan and J. Reghu

Backwater Universalism
An Intercommunal Tale of Being and Becoming

A SEASON FOR UNIVERSALISMS

A voracious universalism holds sway today, particularizing all that crosses its path, supplying its own logic of 'resistance', and turning every challenge into fuel for self-expansion. Equipped with a fully loaded set of contra-concepts and counter-strategies, it seeks to 'give voice' to the multifarious forms of dissent it incessantly generates. Faced with a cacophony of demands—for reparations, for equality, and for justice—that emanate from the various nation-states, races, ethnicities, genders, and classes under its purview, it continuously initiates steps to redress grievances, set right inequities, apologize for past injustices. Only one thing it is not under any circumstances prepared to do: to cede its universality.

'Progress' is the banner under which it advances: for the already 'developed', it holds out the prospect of infinite expansion in living standards, aesthetic pleasures, and multiple identities; for the 'underdeveloped', it holds out the promise that they too can one day sup with the developed, if only they would abide by its canons of rationality. To be sure, there continue to be pockets of superstition and backwardness, but as one prominent theorist puts it, this only means that Enlightenment is still 'an unfinished project'[1]—a project that must be brought to full fruition through progressively greater inclusiveness. Particular groups of humanity may feel justifiably aggrieved at their exclusion, but the key concepts—freedom, equality, and justice—are themselves without blemish, and only await further elaboration and implementation.

'Politics' in this conception is the means by which various parties advance their claims in the public sphere, engaging in bargaining through the legislative, judicial, and economic processes available so as to secure for themselves the share of the social pie rightfully due to them. The specialized task of enlarging the overall pie is to be entrusted with national and international technocrats charged with oiling the wheels of trade policy, exchange-rate policy, monetary policy, and fiscal policy. Distributive struggles over pie-size are to be expected of course, but as long as these take place within established ground rules, humanity can hope to asymptotically approach the ideals of freedom and equality that lie at the core of universality. The ethnic chauvinisms and religious fundamentalisms that are hold outs from an atavistic past of tribal feuds and internecine rivalries will gradually make way for the enlightened give-and-take of strategic compromise as progress takes hold and these irrational impulses are slowly brought within the ambit of enlightened universality.

Particular ethnic and religious 'identities' will continue to survive of course but these will serve as conduits into the experience of the larger universality of humanity. Universality would after all be merely abstract without being filled out by a wealth of particular contents, while particularity would be thwarted in its self-actualization without the medium of universality through which to break out of its narrow confines. Should any particular mount a challenge to the universal—say, by refusing its ground rules—the reigning universal must regrettably resort to coercion to restore the rebelling particular to its proper place and regain the overall balance of particularity and universality.

Global market, nation-state, and other sub- and supra-national identifications can then all balance harmoniously: each particular fits in snugly within the contours of the larger universal entity, and universal and particular both realize themselves through each other in a progressive forward movement. Any contradiction between the two is a matter of contingent circumstances that need only be brought back into proper alignment for harmony to be restored.

Lately however, discontent with this universalism has been on the rise and its promises of equality, freedom, and justice for all of humanity are beginning to seem increasingly remote. Within Western philosophy, there is now increasing interest in universalism as a process rather than a stock of values (freedom, equality, etc.) and as a consequence, the Hegelian dialectic shorn now of its teleological thrust has also witnessed something of a revival. For Hegel, the universal is not a neutral frame for the multitude of particular contents within which each element is to play its part. Particulars do not simply instantiate a neutral universal notion such as 'humanity'; rather, they coexist with the universal in mutual tension. No particular succeeds in fully actualizing the universal nor is any universal able to fully contain its particulars; this discordance gives rise to a dynamic that prepares the way for a new universal.

The paradigmatic instance of this for Hegel is the French Revolution in which the *ancien régime* was dismantled and the new bourgeois order put in place. Pre-revolutionary France had been constituted into a totality with the three estates of the nobility, clergy, and commoners as its particulars, but the failure of this totality to contain the mounting tension between itself and the third estate eventually led to its unravelling. The established universality-of-being of the ancien régime came into unmanageable contradiction with the universality-in-becoming embodied in the third estate. This Hegelian understanding of the French Revolution is also reflected in the Marxian dialectic: within the totality of bourgeois society, it is in the particular of the proletariat that the established totality encounters a contending universality. Both the third estate and the proletariat are, in their respective schema, not mere particulars integrated within the universal frame: they are, rather, embodiments of the tension between universal and particular. Although the French Revolution is placed as the historical antecedent of the proletarian revolution, Hegelian and Marxian dialectics both unfold in a parallel way: a given universality-of-being, a contradictory particular within this order of being that embodies an alternative universality, the resulting movement of becoming.

Barring minor modifications, the broad outlines of this dialectic derived from the French Revolution remain unchallenged in the work of contemporary theorists of universality; 'being' is now conceived in intersubjective terms rather than as the monadic subject's sublatory movement towards its other as narrated in Hegel's *Phenomenology*, and the 'political' is what erupts within being in the form of a contradictory particular that embodies the new universality-in-becoming. This embodied contradiction has been termed the 'universal singular'[2] by Jacques Ranciere and as 'supernumerary element'[3] by Alain Badiou: the particular within the universality of being which, although it belongs to the totality, has no proper place in it. It is this out-of-joint particular within being that becomes a stand-in for the universality-in-becoming. Unlike the liberal subject of universal 'humanity' filled out by the plenitude of its particular identitarian contents, 'subject' here is strictly correlative to an 'event' such as the French Revolution which intrudes into the order of being, elevating the predicament of the 'universal singular' into the universal-to-be. A hitherto subordinate moment is raised to the level of organizing principle for the totality.

For Badiou, such a 'subject' comes to be through 'fidelity' to the event by partaking of the emergent community of those who 'answer its call'. 'Subject' emerges in and through this decision that is in no way grounded in the pre-given order of being. Its universality lies in the fact that membership of this 'new community' of those who recognize themselves in the call of the event is heedless of the lines of division of the old totality. The universality-in-becoming cuts diagonally across this division splitting the totality into two: those who do, and those who do not, respond to its call. Anyone at all can in principle join the community-in-becoming: only an act of subjective identification with the emergent call of becoming is required to join the new community, regardless of where one stands in the current order of being.

The gap between being and event is therefore bridged by the subject who perceives the truth of the given constellation not from the standpoint of established being, but from that of the community-to-be proclaimed by the event. Whereas being always appears as a complete and self-enclosed order from within—characterized only by local imperfections and deviations correctible by progress—from the vantage point of the event, it is the falsehood of the entire totality that stands revealed. The heralding of the universal-to-come is however utterly contingent and can in no way be predicted from within the terms of being. The place of the 'excessive' contradictory particular that cannot be fully contained within being therefore also marks being's constitutive incompleteness; 'event' erupts into this void in the midst of being, making it visible to all who answer its call. The event of the French Revolution, for example, could appear as such only through a subjective act of political identification with the universality of its emergence; from the standpoint of the ancien régime, it could only appear as a multiplicity of local contingent disturbances to be re-integrated within the prevailing order of being.

As much as this account is an immeasurable improvement on the liberal idea of the universal as a genus that fully contains all its particular species, it nevertheless leaves several significant questions unanswered about both being and event: If the event erupts in the void of being, how does being constitute itself around this void in the first place? If the 'supernumerary element' within being is the 'universal singular', how does the event attach itself to it and set in motion the universality of becoming? And most of all, just how universal is this universality anyway, given that it stakes all its claims on a specific historical event—the French Revolution—as its paradigmatic example? Might there be alternative universalities-of-being? Alternative conceptions of the subject? Alternative universalities-of-becoming? Our wager in this paper is that one such universality was indeed revealed in a moment of Hinduism's becoming in south India when some of its old structures fell away and a new socio-symbolic configuration came into being.

HINDUISM IN MORE THAN THREE ACTS

The mention of 'Hinduism' usually brings to mind two distinct modalities: on the one hand, a classical Hinduism consisting of the Vedas, the Upanishads, the Gita, and other canonical texts; on the other, a popular Hinduism of devotion to its myriad gods and goddesses. To these may be added a third cliché: that Hinduism is 'not just a religion but a way of life'—by which what is usually meant is that the social organization of Hindu life revolving around the 'caste system' is also interwoven with its classical and devotional aspects. Although Hinduism has witnessed occasional ruptures leading to the formation of new religions (Buddhism, Jainism, and Sikhism), these have been few and far between, and the sheer resilience of its fabulistic mythology in the face of austere monotheisms and scientisms inevitably fosters the scholarly disposition that Hinduism is the religion of continuity par excellence. Within the tripartite picture of classicism, devotion, and caste, classical Hinduism is commonly seen as reinforcing the inbuilt hierarchies of caste, whereas the devotional practices of popular Hinduism are seen as corrosive of these hierarchies, and therefore, as the principal means of bringing about change within the framework of its overwhelming continuity.

This picture has doubtless yielded many valuable insights, but it has also had the consequence that scarcely any attention has been paid to Hinduism in moments of transformation when its structures open up and afford us a glimpse into its being and becoming. It is the universalism that blooms in just such a moment of Hinduism's becoming that is here being designated 'backwater universalism'—a universalism that first sprouts when Hinduism's tectonic plates undergo a relative shift, and a new configuration comes into being. Unlike social changes that are heteronomously imposed, the changes that spring from Hinduism's internal dialectic cannot unfold without following the grain, so to speak, of its being. Contrary to the prevailing scholarly prejudice, this does not mean that there is never an interruption in its continuity; indeed, the argument to be advanced here is that fundamental change within Hinduism occurs precisely under the paradoxical conditions of 'continuity of discontinuity'.[4]

Among scholars of Hinduism inclined to view religion as an autonomous domain not wholly determined by the so-called larger forces of economy and history, it has been customary to look to the *bhakti* practices of popular Hinduism as the primary motor of social change in India. Hard-boiled historians on the other hand wish to minimize the role of any dynamic internal to religion; the historical understanding has instead centred around secular revolts such as the peasant insurgencies and worker rebellions that have become the bread and butter of the 'subaltern theorist'. Some have unkindly suggested that the very notion of 'postcoloniality' so beloved of the subaltern historian has been advanced only to consolidate the new-found power of South Asian intellectuals in a Western academia always in search of exciting new uprisings and revolts.[5] Whether or not there is any substance to such charges, it is certainly true that while the central claims of the subaltern group are directed against nationalist/colonialist historiographies, it is always insurrections and insurgencies frontally directed at power that find pride of place in their histories. This usually translates into the national anti-colonial struggle being exalted as the main unfolding drama within which the 'regional' players play but subsidiary roles. From such an elevated perspective, internal changes that occur at the micro-level of specific castes and communities get enfolded into the larger historical narrative as 'reform movements' that take modernization, Sanskritization, or some combination thereof as their proper *telos*.

In the south Indian state of Kerala, one such 'reform movement' the historians approvingly admit into their subalternity occurred in the Ezhava caste and was led by a charismatic figure who came to be known as Sri Narayana Guru. The Ezhavas had traditionally been toddy-tappers and small farmers governed by caste rules that included stipulations specifying the distance they should keep to avoid polluting the upper castes. Entry into public places such as schools was prohibited, and worship at upper-caste temples permitted only from a designated distance outside the temple precincts.

Kerala has lately acquired a reputation within India as a middle-class tourist destination for the picturesque backwaters that crisscross its countryside, but it remains a backwater metaphorically in relation to the national consciousness. There is however one accomplishment for which the state has become well known, particularly among theorists of development: despite having a low per-capita income and a low rate of economic growth, it compares favourably with far richer parts of the world in measures such as infant mortality, life expectancy, literacy, gender ratios, and birth rates. Within the discipline of economics, it is the Nobel Prize winner Amartya Sen who has been the most vocal champion of 'the Kerala experience'.[6]

This anomalous 'success' of Kerala is usually attributed to policy measures such as government investment in medical facilities, education, family planning, and other social services that were put in place by what Sen terms 'public action'. In international Left circles as well, Kerala has a certain renown for being the first place in the world to ever vote a Communist party into public office; many of the measures in land reform, food distribution, health care, and education hailed by economists like Sen were initiated by the Communist party when it formed the state government.[7] Theorists aligned with the party have also been prominent in the history-writing enterprise in Kerala, and Narayana Guru appears in these histories as a determined social reformer who took on the historically necessary task of ridding his caste of primitive superstitions—a task that had to be accomplished preparatory to full-blown secularization. In one of the best-known of such accounts, the doyen of Kerala Communism and its first Chief Minister E.M.S. Namboodiripad—after patronizingly characterizing Narayana Guru as 'the saintly leader of the Ezhavas'—describes him as 'the first inspirer and organizer of the mass democratic movement of the cultivating and landless peasant masses of Kerala'.[8] Two other Left theorists spell this out even more baldly: for them, the 'Sree Narayana Movement' was part of the groundwork that had to be laid for the evolution of Kerala society from a pre-historic 'caste consciousness' to the properly historic 'class consciousness'.[9]

From the standpoint of the nation on the other hand, this 'movement' inevitably appears as a tertiary aspect of the pan-Indian low-caste desire to Sanskritize. M.N. Srinivas, the sociologist most responsible for conferring academic respectability on the idea of 'Sanskritization', states it quite plainly: 'the Ezhavas or Tiyyas, a 'backward' caste with the traditional occupation of toddy-tapping, have Sanskritized their way of life under the leadership of their revered leader Narayana Guru.'[10] This theme is repeated by Fillippo and Caroline Osella in their painstaking ethnography of the Ezhavas: 'Narayana Guru insisted that the search for the socio-economic progress of the community as a whole should be underpinned by and could not be divorced from the adoption of Sanskritized brahmanic-oriented practices.'[11] Sumit Sarkar in his survey of modern India similarly reaches for a ready-to-hand Sanskritization to characterize Narayana Guru as the leader of a movement seeking full and unqualified entry into the Hindu fold.[12] Sometimes a template of sorts derived from the Bengal Renaissance made up in equal parts of nationalism, religious revivalism, and caste-mobility is pressed into service with Narayana Guru projected as Kerala's somewhat timid answer to the mighty Vivekananda.[13]

What is common to all such narratives is their striving to somehow normalize Narayana Guru's ethico-political intervention in Kerala by inserting it into a larger story of unfolding progress that encompasses the nationalist struggle against the colonial master at the top and the low-caste emulation of the Brahmin master at the bottom; by sharp contrast however, in the popular forms of remembrance there appears an unmistakable sense of ruptured temporality and a thoroughly non-historicizable 'evental'[14] dimension that surrounds his memory. Where the history and the sociology seek to reduce the Narayana Guru event to a stage of nascency in the course of social development, in popular remembrance it is historical temporality itself that would have been still-born without Narayana Guru. For the historicizers and sociologists, Narayana Guru is to be located within an evolutionary schema leading from primitive superstition/incipient secularism to civilized worship/full-fledged rationality. In popular memory, he emerges as one who ushered in the wondrous (*ashcharya*) by confounding the possible and the impossible; not only were the present and future thereby transfigured, but the entirety of the past as well.

CONSECRATION BY MIDNIGHT

Among the many legends that swirl around the memory of Narayana Guru, one in particular stands enshrined as a unique moment of discontinuity-in-continuity. This incident has come to be known as the *Aruvippuram Pratishta*[15] after the remote South Travancore village on the banks of the river Neyyar where it reputedly took place. When Narayana Guru was still a wandering mendicant, so the story goes, he had made a nearby mountain cave his home for a few weeks. In response to a request from the local villagers who had begun to venerate him as a *siddha*,[16] he agreed to consecrate a *shivalingam*[17] on a moonless

Shivaratri[18] night. A platform had been erected on a large rock by the river bank and decorated with flowers, mango leaves, and buntings made of coconut palm. The prescribed hour was fast approaching but no one had prepared the idol that was to be installed. Kumaran Asan, Malayalam's pre-eminent modern poet, describes what happened next: At the midnight hour, the Guru waded into the river and disappeared. For what seemed like an eternity to the villagers who had thronged the river bank, he remained under water. When his shape finally reappeared, he began walking slowly toward the shore, and in his hands was held aloft a *shivalingam*. He strode to the decorated platform and stood there, his eyes closed in meditation, his hands holding the lingam close to his chest, tears running down his cheeks, lost to the world. For a full three hours, he stood motionless while the crowd around him rent the midnight air with cries of *Om Namah Shivayah*,[19] *Om Namah Shivayah*.[20]

Some historians have cast serious doubts as to whether such an event occurred at all. Others have said that Kumaran Asan took far too many poetic liberties and unduly embellished what in reality was a rather mundane affair. Others yet have interpreted the unprecedented consecration—something that had always been the Brahmin's prerogative—by a lowly Ezhava as a first act of 'subaltern resistance'.[21] None of these disputes centering on the veracity of the event or their varying interpretations appear to matter to the ordinary Malayali however, for whom it is the poet's vision and not the historian's scepticism that has endured. In this recounting, the only record there is of how Narayana Guru himself viewed the act is his self-deprecating response when questioned by a Brahmin as to the sacerdotal validity of a consecration performed by an Ezhava. It is an answer that has become the most famous riposte in modern Kerala: 'I have only consecrated an Ezhava Shiva,' the Guru is said to have reminded the Brahmin. This act of verbal conjunction in which Shiva the Universal God is juxtaposed with the Brahmin's conception of the Ezhava's caste as a bounded particularity lacking full access to Shiva's universality is conferred such performative force as to have triggered an unravelling of the entire social edifice of traditional Kerala.

A delectable apocryphality surrounds the narration of the rejoinder as well. Some claim it occurred immediately after the *pratishta*; others place it a full twenty years later some 500 kilometres to the north of the original site of the pratishta. According to K.V. Subramanyam,[22] the incident took place in Tellicherry when, in the course of a conversation in Sanskrit between Kumaran Asan and a group of Brahmins in the presence of Narayana Guru and some local people, Narayana Guru abruptly intervened in Malayalam to enquire of the Brahmins whether there was any injunction in the Dharmashastra texts prohibiting the pratishta of an Ezhava Shiva. Others claim that it was Kumaran Asan himself who made the rejoinder.[23] When confronted with such an ensemble of inconsistent and contradictory narratives, the historian's professional impulse is to first properly apply a discount by separating the mythical chaff from the historical wheat, and to then read into it a fierce act of 'subaltern resistance' against the prevailing power structure. But what appears to have assured the indestructibility of the *Aruvippuram Pratishta* in the collective memory of the Malayali is the precise opposite: that no trace of 'defiance' is to be found anywhere in the content of its narration. In Narayana Guru's writings as well—a corpus of some sixty works in three languages (Sanskrit, Malayalam, and Tamil)—this consecration finds no mention whatsoever, nor is there anything in these writings to suggest that he would view such an act as anything resembling a heroic act of resistance. Its status in popular memory is solely that of a deed springing from the universal dharma, and it is as a purely *dharmic* act that an aura of immortality attaches to the *Aruvippuram Pratishta*.

The seismic shift brought about by the pratishta was followed by a flood of consecrations performed by the Guru in newly built temples—some thirty in all—throughout the length and breadth of Kerala, and a few even in adjoining Tamil Nadu, Karnataka, and Sri Lanka. In the older temples of the Ezhavas where village gods and nature spirits were worshipped, liquor was the standard offering to the deity and animal sacrifice was widely prevalent. At these temples, Narayana Guru 'unseated the gods, replacing them with idols of Shiva, Subramania, and Ganesha' (emphasis added) as one chronicler puts it.[24] Of the many local gods who were 'unseated', the writer K. Sreenivasan mentions Marutha, Madan, Muthappan, Yakshi, Poothathan, Vankaramadan, Chudalamadan, Isaki, Mallankankali, Karuppan, and Irulan. 'The Guru,' according to Sreenivasan, 'gave the lead in demolishing all of them.'[25] On one such occasion when he happened to walk into the middle of a drunken temple celebration and asked the revellers how exactly the slaughter of a poor fowl would appease the god, the worshippers were reportedly so overwhelmed that they turned on the very deity they had been worshipping, admonishing the god for his bloodthirstiness, and banishing him from the temple for good.[26] Sreenivasan also recounts a different occasion when not only was a prominent deity unseated, her very abode was obliterated: 'At Kulathoor, a suburb of Trivandrum, he sponsored a drastic step. He asked the existing Bhadrakali temple to be demolished. Many a devotee of the goddess was scared by this advice. They feared the wrath of the vengeful deity. Many deemed it sacrilegious. But the Guru's advice prevailed. The substitute was Lord Shiva.'[27]

In the traditional sacred landscape of Kerala dominated by high Brahmanic temples such as the Krishna temple at Guruvayur and the Shiva temple at Trichur, the new temples consecrated by the Guru stand out for their diminutive size, surrounding garden, and attached buildings housing primary schools, high schools, technical institutes, working women's hostels, and libraries. When doubters wondered if these new temples would continue to attract devotees for long considering the great antiquity and symbolic standing of the traditional Brahmanic temples, he expressed his readiness to convert the temples into schools, libraries, assembly halls, or weaving sheds, should the day arrive when they cease to draw worshippers.[28]

'The (new) Sree Narayana temples,' observes Murkot Kunhappa, 'were like and yet unlike the old temples in the land.'[29] In the majority of these new temples, the presiding deities were drawn from the Brahmanic pantheon, but some were utterly unlike the Brahmanic temples. His temple at Karamukku houses only a lighted lamp in its inner sanctum. At the Murukumpuzha temple, there is only a slab of stone with the words *satyam*, *dharmam*, *daya*, and *sneham* etched on it. At the centre of the temple at Kalavamcodam, the Guru placed a mirror with the sacred letter 'Om' at its centre formed by scratching away the mercury coating in the back. The Advaita Ashram founded by him in Alwaye on the banks of the river Periyar has neither temple nor idol; instead, there is a prayer hall for people of all faiths, a library housing the scriptures of the world's religions, a high school, and a hostel for students drawn from all castes and religions. The construction of these new 'Sri Narayana temples' caused considerable alarm among established guardians of the faith; in some quarters, it aroused fears that the new temples would eventually lead to the creation of, in the words of one Brahmin High Court judge, 'a parallel belief system within Hinduism'.[30]

Although almost all of Narayana Guru's 'concrete' actions were initiated within the Ezhava caste where his memory continues to be strongest, these actions triggered off a chain reaction across all the other communities of Kerala. Every one of the numerous biographies and hagiographies of the Guru highlights this critical feature of Kerala's social transformation. This transmission from community to community in the course of which all the major castes and religions of Kerala underwent far-reaching internal changes is usually glossed by the historians and sociologists as a kind of 'demonstration effect'; such a reduction however begs the question as to why internal change within one community should necessarily set off an avalanche of changes across the entirety of society. The predilection to view such transmission of intra-community negation as occurring purely cognitively perhaps reflects a most deep-seated scholarly prejudice: that 'caste' is a wholly socio-empirical category, with cross-caste learning to be understood as entirely an epistemological phenomenon. Once such a limitation is imposed, the 'intersubjective matrix' becomes the common ground from which different communities spring; from here, it is a short step to reducing all of politics to a form of strategic intersubjective bargaining.[31]

BEING AS INTERCOMMUNALITY

This current consensus within Western philosophy about the intersubjective structure of being still carries the stamp of its earlier obsession with monadic subjectivity. 'Intersubjectivity' emerged as a solution to some of the deadlocks of monadicity by placing the subject within an a priori relational matrix, but what such a move still cannot 'resolve' is the question of how this underlying network can itself be radically overhauled. The changes that occurred in Kerala society are an instance of just such an overhauling for which the resort to intersubjectivity alone remains hopelessly inadequate. The only way to account for the scope and depth of the transformation in Kerala is to posit *intercommunality* as prior to intersubjectivity itself, the specific socio-empirical manifestations of 'caste' being overdetermined effects of the intercommunal relation. It is, in other words, intercommunality that must first be presupposed for intersubjective relationality to be at all, and not the other way around. Or, to put the same thing in Heideggerian terms, 'caste' must be presupposed as an ontological, not an ontic, category. Contra-Heidegger however, one is 'thrown' not into the clearing of a generalized 'epochal disclosure of being' but into the specificity of a community: being is always disclosed from within the horizon of a community (or pseudo-community[32]) , the 'specificity' of any particular community being understood as purely relational and in no way pertaining to any of its positive properties. 'Difference' therefore is not only 'constitutive' of being as the contemporary theorists like to say; this difference is always already the intercommunal difference.

The intercommunal perspective also enables us to avoid the pitfalls of a persistent theme in Western philosophy deriving from nostalgia for the 'organic unity' of the Greek *polis*. From the Hegelian *Sittlichkeit* in which subject and substance are a harmonious unity exemplified by Greek sculpture down to the purificatory dreams of the contemporary 'multicultural' pseudo-communities of world-cities, nation-states, and super-states, the drive to domesticate the intercommunal difference can then be seen for the death-wish it is: the wish to erase being as such. This does not mean that the lines of intercommunal difference are ever precisely drawn; they will, on the contrary, always be displaced and blurred—not only because of historical 'hybridization' across community boundaries but because 'community' as such lacks any independent being of its own. Not only then is caste thoroughly relational; a 'primordial repression' of its substantiality also means that the intercommunal differential structure is itself built around the void of its non-representability, conditioned by the totality of all other equally non-substantial (*nihsvabhava*) communities.

In this respect, the 'emptiness' of caste and the structure of intercommunality is identical to the *Madhyamika* concept of dependent co-arising (*pratitya-samutpada*); in Gadjin Nagao's precise words, 'emptiness is not, however, simply nothingness. It is also immediately and necessarily the being of dependent co-arising ... together, emptiness and dependent co-arising constitute an emptiness in which dependent co-arising is empty and a dependent co-arising in which that which is empty dependently co-arises.'[33] The very background against which world-disclosure occurs is the web of intercommunality woven around the void of our community's primordially repressed substance. This disclosure from within the (always partial) horizon of one's community is therefore wholly conditioned by all others similarly 'thrown' into their communities. The perspectivality of this disclosure is a function of the specific mode of the community's interlacing into the web of its relations with all other communities. And the fallacy to be avoided here of course is to too hastily equate communal non-substantiality with a pure illusoriness which must then be 'transcended' in the direction of monadic subjectivity or intersubjectivity.

Although any substantiality (*svabhava*) of the communal self is a pure effect of the totality of all non-substantial others, the self's survival depends on this very substance-effect without which being as such would collapse upon itself. It is therefore not enough to declare in a 'deconstructionist' vein that all 'identity' is a futile attempt to contain the infinite slippage of *differance*; any such assertion can only be facile unless supplemented by the minimal substance-effect of the ontological disclosure. This is why a careful distinction is drawn in Madhyamika between *atma-svarupa-siddha* which connotes substance-effect, and *atmabhava* which stands for self-enclosed essence[34]; 'not standing up' (*na-kshamate*) to the test of essentialness does not imply 'total rejection' (*apakara*).[35] One significant implication of the intercommunal conception of being therefore is that politics is inscribed in being as such—as the struggle to wrench a minimum of communal substantiality from the non-substantiality that threatens to engulf it. This affords us a perspective altogether different from a standpoint that disavows the necessity of such struggle by presuming some form of universal 'communicative rationality' that is striving to realize itself (Habermas' formulation) or some asymptotic movement towards the abstract goals of 'justice' located *a venir* in the infinitely deferred future (Derrida's formulation).

Instead, we find ourselves thrown into what Ashis Nandy has called 'epic culture'—a culture populated not by formally 'equal' subjects but by friends and foes, the godly and the demonic, each needing the others for its self-definition.[36] Friend and foe, god and demon, are alike embedded in an affective field disclosed from within the horizon of one's community and within which intercommunal likes and dislikes circulate; this circulation of affects however always remains circumscribed within the limits of a moral economy in which others are also implicitly granted the right to dislike one, just as one may like or dislike the other. What is foreclosed from such a system of affective flows is what Nandy calls 'annihilatory fantasies about the other'. The entry of such annihilatory fantasies are, according to Nandy, a product of the very culture of 'globalized cosmopolitanism which has convinced us that we must pretend, even if we do not believe so, that everyone is the same'; 'yet,' adds Nandy, 'the same cosmopolitanism allows us to classify cultures according to the distance they have traversed on the time-scale of history.'[37] The space for such a classificatory schema according to a culture's degree of evolution is opened up by the very asymptotic temporality that resolutely declares 'equality', 'freedom', and 'justice' as its goals for the a venir indefinite future.

State-driven 'policy' remains the main instrument to bring about these putative aims, such policy increasingly reduced to an iron-clad framework of rules imposed from without on nation-state formations that must find their equilibrating place of 'comparative advantage' in the global regime of trade and financial flows. For the technocracy enforcing these rules, 'austerity measures' will occasionally be called for to position the nation competitively, but these will assuredly bear fruit in the asymptotic long run if only its citizens would demonstrate an unwavering commitment to policy's demands. As Ashis Nandy sardonically puts it mimicking the technocratic directive, 'If you behave well, if you obey the textbooks that I have produced on self-improvement—through economic development, technological growth, acquisition of scientific rationality or 'proper' political education—you could be like me tomorrow.'[38] This pithy injunction condenses the entirety of the message handed down to the 'underdeveloped' from the 'developed': stick to the policies we have discovered from our long experience of development and you too can hope to be developed some day. Nandy avers that this idea 'infects virtually all liberal and radical theories of social change'[39] so that the question of how different civilizations can bring about change on their own terms has today taken on an unprecedented urgency.

BACKWATER BECOMING

Seen in light of this exigency and the escalating threat to communal survival, the intercommunal conception of being holds critical lessons for modalities of becoming. To begin with, 'communities' are recognized in their specificity but never as generic 'religions'. Narayana Guru himself unequivocally rejected the notion of 'Hinduism' as a religion:

There is no religion that may be called Hinduism. Outsiders styled the people of Hindustan as Hindus. Therefore, if by 'Hinduism' one denotes the religion of 'Hindus', then the Christianity and Islam professed by thousands of inhabitants here should also be called Hinduism. ... Today 'Hinduism' covers the agglomeration of an immense variety of beliefs belonging to an entire scale of values that span customs, manners, rites, and philosophy among different groups and believers. *Veda, Mimamsa, Samkhya, Dvaita, Advaita, Vishistadvaita, Saiva, Sakteya, Vaishnava* —all these are forms of 'Hinduism', not excluding the innumerable modes of belief that differ from place to place and caste to caste ... If this entire gamut of beliefs can be called 'Hinduism', then all religions—Islam, Christianity, Buddhism, Jainism, etc. can also collectively be known as 'one religion'. ... If a religion preached by its founder, and subsequently elaborated into different branches by its followers can be called a 'religion' and given the name of the founder, the spiritual tenets preached by the different *acharyas* can also, by an extension of this principle, be termed 'religions'.[40]

'Religion', in other words, was acceptable as a unitary concept to designate a certain kind of human striving but not as a genus containing multiple 'isms' as its distinct species—Islam, Christianity, Hinduism, etc.; for Narayana Guru, the manifold castes and communities in their interlocking specificities of place, belief, and practice were the warp and woof of being, and within which becoming must find a pathway to unfold.

A major obstacle that stands in the way of a proper understanding of this mode of becoming is the pre-eminence of the French Revolution as *the* singular event of modern times. Its weighty inheritance is comprised not only of its favoured master-signifiers—'equality', 'freedom', and 'justice'—but also the very conception of being that underlies these signifiers. For generations of progressives and modernizers raised on the self-evidence of these terms, the proposition that there may be other conceptions of being, other forms of subjecthood, other modes of becoming than those bequeathed by the French Revolution remains outside the domain of the conceivable. But events *did* take place elsewhere—events that carry different lessons, events that may yet have to be recovered if we are to free ourselves from the suffocating double-embrace of liberalism and 'radicalism'.

Claude Lefort has described the French Revolution in terms of a 'disincorporation of individuals ... when the body of the king was destroyed, when the body politic was decapitated and when, at the same time, the corporeality of the social was destroyed'.[41] The destruction of the 'king's two bodies'[42]—not only his physical body but also the symbolic place that conferred on the monarch his royal authority—also destroyed the society of the ancien régime that had modelled itself as a corporeal whole in the unity of the king's two bodies. Henceforth, according to Lefort, 'power appears as an empty place and those who exercise it as mere mortals who occupy it only temporarily or who could install themselves in it only by force or cunning'.[43] For Alain Badiou, the subject proper of the French Revolution cuts diagonally across the three estates of the ancien régime and is embodied in those who answered the call of the event by joining the new community-in-becoming of citizens free and equal under the law.

The event which unfolded in Kerala cannot however be grasped within the terms set out by Lefort and Badiou. The intercommunal structure of Indian society is irreducible to the simple three-estate schema of the ancien régime and Lefort's corporeal metaphor for pre-revolutionary French society is wholly inapposite for India. The subject born out of the Kerala event will therefore have to be thought altogether differently from the subject of the French Revolution. And the first pair of oppositions that will have to be discarded is what in German idealism has been called *Gemeinschaft* and *Gesellschaft*—with Gemeinschaft conceived on the model of the Greek polis as an organic subject-substance unity and Gesellschaft exemplified by the modern nation-state held together by law. For someone like Hegel, Gesellschaft is born of the rupture from the immediate substantiality of organic community, giving rise to the universal *Moralitat* of the individual's 'infinite subjectivity' in the modern rational state freed from the mores of communal Sittlichkeit. But what would such 'rupture' mean if, as we have argued, Sittlichkeit was never the communal substance-in-itself but only the semblance of substance— the over-determined effect of the totality of (non-substantial) communal others? How would the new universality of 'infinite subjectivity' assert itself if the Sittlichkeit it was 'freeing' itself from was insubstantial to begin with? How real then is this 'infinite right of subjectivity' if there was no Sittlichkeit from which the subject could extricate himself and declare its freedom? If, as we have maintained, being is always embedded in a matrix of intercommunality, does this then mean that 'subject' itself is illusory? And if not, then how is universality to emerge from the intercommunal multiplicity?

Here once again the fallacy to be avoided is the ready equation of 'subject' with the emergent universality of individual subjectivity that has been the preeminent legacy of the French Revolution and present in one form or other in every theory of universality from Hegel to Badiou. Continuity and discontinuity are implacably opposed in such theories: a clean break from communal Sittlichkeit inaugurates the new era of Moralitat. But, to repeat, if Sittlichkeit was never a substantiality identical to itself, how is 'rupture' to proclaim itself?

Insofar as the Kerala event also cuts across the social totality it is, like the French Revolution, a universality-in-becoming; but the mode in which universality traverses the totality could not be more different— *and it is intercommunal relationality that opens up this alternative pathway.* Communal 'substance' is neither a self-enclosed essence of subject-immersion nor an illusory formation waiting to be 'deconstructed'; it is rather a substance-effect in which the subject inheres as negativity, and it is the operation of this negativity that heralds becoming into the structure of being. Being is therefore never a pre-formed whole standing outside the subject; every edifice of being is built on some prior act of negation—and the very substance-effect of communality is the residual trace of this negation without which being, as such, could not have constituted itself.

In the Kerala event, 'subject' properly speaking first manifested itself as the self-criticism of the Ezhavas, but 'self-criticism' still belongs in the realm of epistemology and is far too weak a term if we are to properly grasp the *ontological* dimensions of the event. It would be far more accurate to say that with the unseating of the old gods, the very substance-effect of Ezhava communality was suspended in a gesture of collective self-contraction. *Every attempt to historicize this contraction as a form of progressive secularization or Sanskritization must pass silently over the void that opened up between the departure of the old gods and the arrival of the new.* This moment of eclipse between two worlds is captured precisely in the Madhyamika concept of the 'excluded middle' (*anaikantikavada*): one world is already past, the other not yet present, and between them lies neither bridge nor subterranean passage. *This moment of extreme contraction which exceeds the grasp of historicization is what is memorialized in popular remembrance as the* Aruvippuram Pratishta.

That the void as such manifested itself fully here is attested to by the fact that with the expunging of the communal substance, the Ezhavas as a community found itself facing the abyssal decision as to which gods to admit so it could minimally re-substantialize itself. It was during this period that the writer and journalist C. Krishnan was using the columns of the journal *Mithavadi* to argue for a mass conversion to Buddhism. Other prominent community leaders such as Sahodaran Ayyappan and C.V. Kunjuraman were also known to favour Buddhism. A group of Ezhavas in the southern district of Neyyatinkara embraced Christianity to become a short-lived community of 'Ezhava-Christians'; around the same time, some in Alleppey district converted to Sikhism. There were also instances of individual and family conversion to Islam although there are no known cases of large-group conversion.

Narayana Guru's own views on conversion were spelt out in the course of a conversation during the famed encounter with Gandhi at his ashram in Varkala in 1925. After an exchange of pleasantries, Gandhi wanted to know what the Guru's views were regarding conversion. 'If we see people who have converted to other religions enjoying new freedoms, who can blame them?' answered Narayana Guru. 'But does Swamiji consider the Hindu religion sufficient for spiritual salvation?' enquired Gandhi. 'There are means of salvation in other religions also' was Narayana Guru's reply.[44] In a later conversation with C.V. Kunjuraman, he was even more explicit: 'If a Hindu or a Christian loses faith in Hinduism or Christianity, he should change his religion. To follow a religion in which one has no faith is both cowardly and fraudulent. For such a person to convert is not only good for him, it is also good for the religion in which he has lost his faith.'[45]

Despite being a staunch defender of conversion in principle, such a possibility was nowhere in Narayana Guru's own horizon. Indeed, in consecrating idols at the new 'Sri Narayana temples', it is Narayana Guru himself who decided which gods to admit into their inner sanctums. There were even occasions when he changed his mind midway. A Shiva idol was originally to be installed at his Shivagiri temple, but halfway through the temple construction he decided against Shiva in favour of the goddess Saraswati (Sharada).[46] He literally picked and assigned the gods to the various temples: Subramania at Kunnumpaara; Shivalingam at Vakkom; Sree Kanteswara at Kozhikode; Jagannath at Tellicherry; Gokarnath at Mangalore, and so on. In an unheard-of reversal, the very gods that had for centuries refused entry into their sacred precincts would now come knocking, seeking admission. These gods continue to live on today in temples large and small throughout Kerala—*but only as mediated by the Narayana Guru event.*

It is important however not to leap to the conclusion that the *Aruvippuram Pratishta* that 'triggered' the sequence of temple consecrations was the outcome of a deliberate decision to 'defy' the Brahmanic order. Nor should the pratishta be seen too hastily as an 'interpretive intervention' *a la* Badiou[47] in the sense that Narayana Guru was somehow able to discern in such an act a presaging of its evental possibilities. Popular remembrance serves as a better guide here than the theories of the universalists; in the collective memory, the Pratishta at Aruvippuram and all of Narayana Guru's subsequent actions are directly derived from his insight into the true dharma. And unlike the historical accounts, this form of memory retains the 'evental dimension' by enshrining the pratishta as *the* moment (*kshana*) when the entire prior hierarchical structure of being was revealed as *adharmic*. The pratishta is memorialized in the way it is *only* because its socially detonative 'effect' is seen as the entirely accidental by-product (*agantuka*) of an act performed from 'the stillest point' (*anutpattikadharmaksanti*).

It is crucial however to not read this as an 'effect' produced in the standard historical manner by a prior cause. What we are confronted with here is a case of the *effects preceding the cause,* the so-called cause being retroactively instituted as the mythical founding moment *caused by its effects.* For a proper understanding of this conundrum, it is useful to recall a number of critical details. The pratishta is said to have been conducted in Aruvippuram, a small hamlet at the foot of the Western Ghats far removed from any centre of power. The historians date it to 1888, a time when there was no print media to speak of that would have rapidly carried the news to other parts of the state. The only people said to be present were the local villagers, and Narayana Guru had not even been conferred the appellation of 'guru' then because he was just an unknown wandering mendicant. Under these conditions it is highly doubtful if such an act, even if historically accurate, managed to immediately set off shock waves all across Kerala leading to an unravelling of its ancien régime.

Plainly, the incident's historicity is a minor part of the story; regardless of how far it strains the professional historian's credulity, it would be far more productive to come to terms with the pratishta as the *mythic moment* that popular memory registers it as—a moment marking the paradoxical birth of the subject of the Kerala event *after* its effects were already being felt across the social landscape. The point here is not to deny its veracity as history but to try to understand why a relatively minor incident in an obscure village should be given a *significance nonpareil* in the collective memory. And the answer to this puzzle is to be sought not in the chain of historical causality but in *the temporal loop in which the 'historical' effects precede the 'mythical' cause*. Indeed, even to use the word 'precede' is already excessively historicist and misleading here because without the 'caused cause' of the pratishta, the 'effects' themselves would be a meaningless bric-a-brac of occurrences that could not cohere into narrative at all. The pratishta belongs to a mythical past that was never (necessarily) present-in-itself as history, yet presences itself as the ineluctable background for all historical causes and effects. It not only memorializes the subject's passage through the void; the pratishta marks the very founding of the subject of the Kerala event in myth, and is the condition of possibility of historical narrative as such. It is therefore thoroughly misleading to speak of the pratishta as having been deliberately undertaken by Narayana Guru to 'refine the spiritual condition of the people' to 'awaken the people to their own subjectivity'[48] or to otherwise instrumentalize it, no matter how elevated the motive.

For a moment such as the pratishta to be properly mythic, it is crucial that it be devoid of any telos whatsoever. Anything less would imply a substantive subject filled out by its 'existential projects' in the manner of European phenomenology, confronting a pre-formed structure of being which it must then mould to its purposes. Whereas many of Narayana Guru's later actions such as the reform of marriage rituals may conceivably be grasped in this 'projective' way, it would be wholly inapposite to apply this logic to the pratishta whose 'effects' altogether escape the chain of historical causality. For the pratishta to be memorialized as dharmic intervention, it is crucial that the void of the subject overlap with the void of being; or more precisely, that the subject find itself where it always already was—in the void of being—at its most extreme point of self-contraction. The 'renting of the midnight air' described by Kumaran Asan is a poetic evocation of this opening up of the void in which the subject finds itself drained of its entire substance—only a 'thunderous silence' (tusnimbhava) reverberates, as the Vimalakirtinirdesasutra puts it.[49]

The 'moment of decision' when the gods come knocking marks the point where this loop of mythic temporality inaugurates the new historical temporality, and the subject must now find a way to re-substantialize itself (vyavasthapana). The historians and sociologists are accustomed to using the term 'Ezhava caste' to refer to the community which first undertook 'reforms' in Kerala, overlooking a crucial detail: that there was no 'Ezhava caste' prior to the reforms. The community which was then referred to as 'Ezhava' was a miniscule part of the Ezhavas as presently constituted; in the 1911 census the population of the Ezhavas was reported at a mere half a million;[50] in the 2001 census the Ezhava population stood at 7.36 million—an increase of 1400 per cent![51] Even after rapid population growth and lower mortality rates are factored in, it is obvious that the two censuses do not refer to the 'same' community; the only possible conclusion to be drawn from this is that what is today known as the 'Ezhava caste' is entirely a retrospective construction that brings within its fold a multiplicity of previously dispersed communities (Ezhavas, Thiyyas, Thandans, Pandichons, Panickers, Ezhavathis, Channars, Chovans, etc.) not all of whom were even engaged in the same 'caste occupation'—so that there was never the 'Ezhava caste' that first existed, then reformed itself.[52]

The prominent Ezhava leader C.V. Kunjuraman is once said to have exclaimed,

Community? Oh God! The very word community was unheard among the Ezhavas. Those with and without status are to be found among all communities but that doesn't explain the way things were among us. We were fragmented into all kinds of lineages: chattans, oolans, pandas, pambilis, illams, kollakarans. ... Ezhavas belonging to one lineage were considered a separate caste and forbidden from entering into marital relations with other Ezhavas ...[53]

What Kunjuraman does not seem to sufficiently appreciate here is that the very 'fragmentation' of the Ezhavas he bemoans can only be perceived *a posteriori* after the Ezhavas had been forged into 'a community', and that the only way to properly account for the emergence of the Ezhavas as a community is as a purely performative operation of community consolidation undertaken in the void of the event. The Ezhavas as a community do not pre-exist the contraction: it is contraction that produced the community. Not only was the community that undertook the passage through negativity therefore not the community that returned from it; the paradox proper to communality is that *it is self-contraction that retroactively revealed the self that did the contracting.* The 'return' to substantiality found the Ezhavas *newly* constituted as community; it is only then that a few intrepid souls, freshly imbued with historicist fervour, sallied forth to excavate the community's ancient historical origins with roots going back to a centuries-old mass Buddhist exodus from Sri Lanka.[54]

GRACIOUS UPROOTING

What is common to both the French and Kerala events is the void: the universality of the French Revolution must also pass through the abyss that opens up between the substantiality of the ancien régime and the universality-in-becoming of the *citoyen* whose negativity undermines the former's totality. Both the French and Kerala events attest to the irreducibility of the subject to being (*bhavabhyupagama*), both are witness to a negativity that unravels the totality. But where the void of the French Revolution opened out to Jacobin Terror, the Kerala event was akin to what Nagarjuna describes in his opening salutation to the Buddha in the *Mulamadhyamikakarika* as 'gracious uprooting' (*prapancopasanam sivam*).[55] The historicist reduction of Narayana Guru to 'social reformer' seeks to efface both these dimensions of the Kerala event that must be accorded their full proper weight: the 'uprooting' (*prapancopasanam*) and its 'graciousness' (*sivam*). And here the idea of the 'life-world' of European phenomenology occasionally disturbed by 'anxiety' will have to be left far behind; Nagarjunian 'uprooting' rather connotes a wrenching away of embeddedness itself and a recasting of the very opaque background of embeddedness. The paradox of gracious uprooting however is that such a total socio-symbolic reconfiguring can never be the object of a direct choice: the negativity of self-contraction cannot be supplied with a telos in advance.

The central fallacy of those who would like to reduce the Kerala event to a set of 'caste reforms' lies in the belief that it would somehow have been possible to pass directly from the 'pre-Aruvippuram life-world' to the new 'reformed life-world' bypassing the loop of mythic temporality—a temporality in which the pratishta's entire effectivity derives from its 'looping back' as a cause paradoxically caused by its effects. The *Aruvippuram Pratishta* is not a moment within a continuously calibrated temporal scale; it is a collective retroactive condensation of the passage through negativity when the old gods were tried and expelled. As apocryphal, the pratishta will therefore always be truer than the 'real' event in all its facticity: no set of economic, political, or cultural factors in their 'complex interaction' with each other can account for the encounter with negativity that is condensed in the pratishta—an encounter that lies outside the entire chain of historical causes and effects.

This negativity is none other than the *pratisedha* of Madhyamika doctrine which, as Nagao puts it, 'is based on the absolute otherness of ultimate meaning and worldly convention. ... Emptiness without essence is a direct negation of *the very context itself* within which propositions can be opposed to one another.'[56] This was already a major *Prajnaparamita*[57] theme in Indian philosophy when it was taken up by Nagarjuna and made the centrepiece of Madhyamika. Nagao clarifies what is meant by the 'absolute otherness' (*satyadvayavibhaga*) of ultimate meaning (*paramarthasatya*), and worldly convention (*samvrtisatya*):

If the attainment of ultimate meaning were pre-established from the start, before the journey had begun, it would have to be understood as a foregone conclusion by virtue of its inner teleology. ... If both the starting point and the destination were pre-established identifiable realities and if the journey consisted only in traversing the interval, the path could be undertaken in an altogether worldly and conventional manner. ... Only a path that is dark and empty in both its beginning and its end, in its starting point and in its destination, only a path that bespeaks a journeying, can fulfill the requirements of a process that casts a bridge from initial conventional awareness to ultimate meaning.[58]

The 'path' from one life-world to another is therefore always a fraught and paradoxical path:

The true path is the path that is originally not a path. The path that is a path is not the true path. ... If the path followed a continuous route to the yonder shore, no matter how much privation it might entail and no matter how long it might take, at some point it would reach its goal. But the fact is, the path is not shown to us. Whatever is shown cannot be the true path. ... When one is on the path, one does not know whether it leads to ultimate meaning or to hell.[59]

The point of extreme self-contraction between the expulsion of the old gods and the arrival of the new is therefore not to be mistaken for a Badiouian moment of 'militancy' when being splits into two and the subject is called upon to take sides: one is either on the side of becoming or on the side of established being. Badiou's concept of 'fidelity to the event' carries with it an unspoken demand to demonstrate fidelity—and an accompanying veiled threat. In the mythic moment of the pratishta on the contrary, 'decision' is precisely what is removed from the subject's purview; this is akin to the Kierkegaardian moment when 'the ethical *is* the temptation'—but even this is far too decisionistic a characterization to apply to a 'moment' such as the pratishta. There is indeed a moment of decision in the Kerala event as well, but it is not one of having to choose sides; 'decision' as such presents itself only after the loop of mythic temporality has been traversed and multiple gods come knocking—the decision as to which gods to admit.

In the case of the French Revolution as well, it was Hegel who stressed that the violent self-destructiveness of Jacobin Terror was born of a certain necessity; its outcome in the form of the modern state that 'reconciles' social order with individual freedom was in no way predictable in advance of the Terror. In their unavoidable passage through the void of negativity, there is indeed a parallel to be drawn between the Kerala and French events: the void is the precise place of their intersection. It is in their mode of passage and subsequent 'return' to a positive social order that they stand in marked contrast to each other.

In the French case, universality is 'embodied' in the 'universal singular' (*singulier universal*) of the third estate; once mobilized, this universality cuts across all three estates addressing itself uniformly to all who recognize themselves in the community-in-becoming of citizens equal under the law. The clearest specification of this universality has come from Alain Badiou in his categorical rejection of the idea that truth can be a function of community. Every invocation of community 'works directly against truths', writes Badiou, 'I see nothing but national if not religious reaction in the use of expressions like "the Arab community", "the Jewish community", "the Protestant community". The cultural idea, the heavy sociological idea of the self-contained and respectable multiplicity of cultures ... is foreign to thought.'[60] Although presented as the unfolding of universality, it is clear that the French Revolution is the unavowed paradigm behind this insolent declaration which also condenses with clarity the limited conception of 'community' at work in the theorists of universality. 'Community' is seen as a 'self-contained' attribute pertaining to generic categories such as 'Arabs', 'Jews', and 'Protestants', which is then rejected *in toto*. From here, it is a short step to claiming that truth can only be arrived at by 'subtracting from the grip of the communal, whether it be a people, a city, an empire, a territory, or a social class'.[61] But for all their fire and brimstone, the theorists of universality have not yet dispensed with community; indeed, what we are offered is a pseudo-community of 'equals' in the indefinitely deferred future, a community that must according to Derrida always remain a venir, never made present, for to directly translate ideal into reality would be an invitation to the totalitarian *desastre*.

In this equation of all real communities with a self-enclosed particularist substance which must then be dissolved away in the solvent of the universality-to-come, we are a long way indeed from the intricate *pratityasamutpada* of interlocking castes and communities and their dialectic of transformation through mutual contraction. Not only was the 'communal substance' of the theorists never substance as such but only a substance-effect; precisely because it is neither a purely ontic entity (*asti*) nor an entirely illusory virtuality (*nasti*), this substance-effect is susceptible to periodic self-contraction and reclamation making possible an internal dialectic of transformation rather than as heteronomous imposition from an order of pure exteriority. What any community precisely *cannot* do is to suspend its dependent co-arising with other communities, either through withdrawal into self-imposed isolation or through dissolution into some neutral medium of universality—nation-state, agglomeration of states, or 'humanity'.

The intercommunal dialectic is therefore reducible neither to seamless continuity nor to utter dissolution; it is rather a continuity-in-discontinuity in the course of which what is expelled is the entire communal substance-effect, while what is retained in the passage through negativity is the pure communal form. In positing communality as a substance to be dissolved away in the ideal universality, what the theorists overlook is the very genesis of community in the primordial repression of its substance; what remains 'the same' in a community, once it has been divested of its substance-effect, is the pure communal form sustained in the passage through negativity by 'other-dependence' (*paratantra*) on all other castes and communities. What is precluded from such a dialectic is precisely what the theorists exalt as the acme of universality: the surrender of the caste-form itself for the egali-tarian promise of aggregative community—whether 'Hindu', nation-state, or 'humanity'. In the dialectic of intercommunality, continuity between the life-worlds on either side of the passage is maintained by just this link of the pure communal form, the surrender of which can only result in proto-psychotic Terror.

THE CASE OF THE MISSING MASTER

This passage through negativity sans terror is what Nagarjuna refers to as 'gracious uprooting'. The 'graciousness' (*sivam*) of the Kerala 'uprooting' is integral to its dialectical difference: the unfolding of negativity along its central core was accompanied by an unequivocal affirmation. Whereas on the devotional plane the expulsion of the old gods went hand-in-hand with the sacredotally improper consecration of a slew of temples to the new gods, on the doctrinal plane the orthodoxy of Advaita Vedanta was unyieldingly affirmed as the unsurpassable horizon: 'whatever we have to say is what Shankara has already said', Narayana Guru had famously declared.[62] While he also composed hymns to Vinayaka, Subramanya, and Vasudeva, the Guru's *ishtadevata* was Shiva for whom he reserved the most ecstatic devotion. Among the hymns composed in praise of Shiva are his *Shiva-Satakam* (Hundred Verses for Shiva), *Shiva-Prasada-Panchakam* (Five Verses to Shiva's Boundless Grace), *Ardha-Nariswara-Stavam* (Hymn to the Androgynous Lord), and *Shiva-Stavam* (Hymn to Shiva)—songs which are still sung in homes and temples across Kerala.

His interpretation of Advaita in which the phenomenal world is seen alternately as an active 'weaving and re-weaving the tapestry of the Absolute' and as an incessant 'rising forth and merging back of wave-forms in the ocean of the Absolute' is presented primarily in two works: the hundred-stanza long Sanskrit poem titled *Darshana-Mala* (Garland of Visions), and the equally long but more loved Malayalam composition *Atmopadesa-Satakam* (One Hundred Verses of Self-Conversation). Shorter works in which this vision of the One is expounded and defended include *Brahma-Vidya-Panchakam* (Five Verses on the *Brahma-Vidya* in Sanskrit), *Municharya-Panchakam* and *Nivrithi-Panchakam* (both five-verse compositions in Sanskrit paying homage to Ramana Maharshi), and in Malayalam *Advaita Deepika* (Lamp of Non-Dualism), *Jeeva-Karunya-Panchakam* (Five Verses on Extreme Tenderness), *Anukampa-Dashakam* (Ten Verses on Mercy and Compassion), *Arivu* (Self-Knowledge), *Cit-Jada-Chintanam* (Meditations on Consciousness and Inertia), *Pinda-Nanni* (Pre-Natal Gratitude), *Swanubhava-Giti* (Self-Experience Rhapsody), *Janani-Navaratna-Manjari*

(Nine-Jewelled Bouquet to the Mother), and *Kundalini-Pattu* (Song of the Coiled Serpent).[63]

This uncompromising affirmation of the highest doctrinal orthodoxy while being the bearer of the most extreme negativity has mystified commentators no end. The paradox to be fully maintained, however, is that neither affirmation nor negation was deployed instrumentally in the service of 'social reform'. Even as astute an observer of the Kerala scene as V.R. Krishna Iyer, while fully granting the 'miracle of spiritual transformation and social reformation' worked by Narayana Guru, mistakes his actions for an 'irreverent subversion of an obscurantist order which dominated and blinded the masses of Hindus'; for Krishna Iyer, 'the Guru adopted a master strategy of installing idols, a function traditionally the exclusive preserve of Brahmins ... This master-stroke of Narayana Guru was a radical challenge to the status quo ante. The entire edifice of Brahminism and the caste-structure suffered a collapse ...'[64] Such an account in terms of 'strategy', 'master-stroke', 'challenge', and 'irreverence' completely misses the central paradox of the Kerala event: that its entire performative efficacy would have dissipated, had it deliberately been pressed into service for an aggregative social telos. Unlike the French Revolution, unlike the other 'reform movements' in Hinduism such as the Brahmo Samaj, Arya Samaj, or Dravida Kazhagam, and contrary to Krishna Iyer's claims, the Kerala event is distinguished by an utter absence of reference to a Master whether in the mode of defiance or of appeal. Neither in any of Narayana Guru's own works nor in the innumerable myths and legends surrounding his memory is there any trace of defiance or appeal to either the European or the Brahmin master—a fact completely overlooked by champions of the 'subalterns' who now wish to rehabilitate the Guru as one of their own.[65]

Partisans of high Upanishadic philosophy such as Nataraja Guru often tend to devalue his *Shiva-bhakti* either as an 'early stage' in his evolution towards the Unitive Truth or as a kind of tactic he had to maintain to 'keep the masses with him'; such claims are belied by the strength of the devotional hymns which he continued composing even as he formulated his expositions of Advaita. Others such as T. Bhaskaran, compiler of Narayana Guru's complete works, emphasize the influence of the Tamil *Saiva-siddhanta* tradition and deny the centrality of Advaita to Narayana Guru.[66] The influence of the Tamil Saiva tradition on Narayana Guru has been reiterated more recently by Udaya Kumar,[67] but it is by no means clear just what purpose is served by this struggle to claim him either as primarily *advaitin* or primarily *Saiva-siddhanta*. Other more ecumenical characterizations seem closer to the point; of these, the Kerala Theosophical Society's eulogy is perhaps the most expansive: 'Narayana Guru was a Patanjali in yoga, a Shankara in *gyana*, a Manu in social law, a Buddha in *tyaga*, a Nabi in steadfastness, and a Jesus in humility.'[68]. And the most succinct is Romain Rolland's: he was 'a *gnanin* of action'[69]. Only one figure appears to have no place in either the works or the myth of Narayana Guru: that of the Master from whom recognition is sought, or at whom defiance is directed.

INTERCOMMUNAL DIALECTICS

In a perspicacious observation, K. Sreenivasan notes that although the Guru explicitly undertook many 'reforms'—devising new worship rituals at temples, simplifying wedding and funeral rites, abolishing puberty celebrations, stopping child marriages, and so on—these reforms 'also caused important side-effects'.[70] Among these 'side-effects', according to Sreenivasan, is 'the idea of a unified Kerala',[71] a cultural and linguistic region that had historically been carved up into the three separate political-administrative regions of Travancore, Cochin, and Malabar. But perhaps the far more significant 'side-effects' set off by Ezhava self-contraction were the waves that traversed the entire intercommunal body-politic of Kerala. Kunhappa describes this as an 'osmotic process' through which 'the Nairs and other castes too stopped observing these functions after the Ezhava community had carried out the reforms at the instance of the Swami'.[72] This understanding of cross-communal transmission as a form of 'osmosis' must however be given its full ontological (*abhidhana*) weight and not confined within the terms of a communal epistemology of learning.

This is perhaps what Ashis Nandy also has in mind when he speaks of 'a culturally embedded identity in which others are telescoped into the self as *inalienable* parts of the self ... (such an) internalization need not (only) be of significant individualized others; it can be of culturally significant collective others.[73] From this perspective, the 'ethical problem' is not one of how an originary self 'relates to' the other as a Levinasian ethics would have it, or of how every self is always already embedded within a matrix of intersubjectivity; rather, the very 'inner content' of the self is nothing but the over-determined substance-effect of all *other* communal selves. The communal substance therefore possesses none of the density of the Hegelian Sittlichkeit; but to render it entirely virtual as the 'deconstructionists' would have it is to deprive it of a minimal capacity for renewal through self-contraction. In the Kerala event, it is just such a communal self-contraction that culminated in a drastic reconfiguration of the entire socio-symbolic space—first by triggering changes in other communities, then through a state-centred Left movement that successfully introduced legislative reforms in land ownership, educational access, and public health.

Kunhappa uses the analogy of shock-treatment to describe the initial self-contraction:

This shock given at about the middle rung of the caste ladder (the Ezhavas) was transmitted upwards to the Nambudiri Brahmins and downwards to the lowest among the several castes below the Ezhavas. Social reformation all round was the result of this shock treatment. It produced very strong and effective movements of reform among all the castes, such as the Nambudiris, the Nairs, the Ezhavas, and the Pulayas, besides affecting other castes too.[74]

The crucial point to be borne in mind here is that (for entirely contingent reasons), it is the Ezhavas who were *first* collectively confronted with the void of non-substantiality that opened up in the course of self-contraction. For every other community that underwent convulsions after the Ezhavas, a pathway of sorts could indeed be laid out from pre- to post-reform; no such direct passage is possible for the community that first undergoes self-contraction.

Sivadas and Rao note that 'many of the socialist and communist leaders of Kerala had their early apprenticeship' in the caste-based organizations formed in the wake of the founding of the Sree Narayana Dharma Paripalana Yogam (SNDP).[75] E.M.S. Namboodiripad, who as the first Chief Minister of unified Kerala pioneered many of the initial legislative measures while in office, began his public life in the Yogakshema Sabha, a Brahmin organization set up along the lines of the SNDP to undertake internal community reform. Among the Namboodiri Brahmins of Kerala, only the eldest son was allowed to marry within the community; this resulted in the younger sons (known as *afphans*) taking concubines from the Nair community and leaving the majority of Namboodiri women unwed. Reforms in the Namboodiri community were initiated as a 'movement of afphans' for the right to marry within the community but gradually spread to encompass abolition of the purdah-like practice of *khosha* for women, permitting widow remarriage, and extension of education beyond Vedic recitation. V.T. Bhattathiripad, leader of the Namboodiri reform movement, was unabashed in his gratitude to Narayana Guru: 'the sole inspiration for Brahmin youth in their fight against decay and stagnation in the Namboodiri community was the life and philosophy of Sri Narayana Guru.'[76]

Ayyankali, leader of the 'untouchable' Pulayas, pioneered the task of community consolidation along the lines of the Ezhavas by founding the 'Sadhujana Paripalana Yogam'; the SNDP supplied the model not only for the name of the organization but also for a variety of reforms undertaken within the community.[77] Other 'untouchable' communities such as the fisher-folk caste of Arayars and the agricultural labour caste of Kuravas also followed in their wake.

The Nair Service Society (NSS), set up for similar purposes by the Nair community, directly adopted many of the ritualistic changes introduced by Narayana Guru: simplifying marriage ceremonies, conducting weddings at temples, assuring inheritance rights for women, and so on. On the subject of Narayana Guru's influence, this is what Mannath Padmanabhan, founder of the NSS, had to say: 'the spiritual teachings of Sri Narayana Guru and the activities of the SNDP had enlightened the Ezhava masses and led them up the path of progress. All other communities learned from this and organized to reform themselves.'[78] Among the customs abolished by the Nairs was that of *sambantham*, the practice of supplying concubines to afphan Namboodiris.

Reforms were undertaken within the Muslim and Christian communities as well. In his composition *Anukampa-Deshakam*, Narayana Guru had described Prophet Muhammad as 'pearl and gem in one', and one of the legends surrounding his days as a wandering mendicant was that he 'had lived for many days with Muslims, partaken of their food from the same plate. ... eaten flesh and fish ... played with their children ... carrying their babies in his arms ... feeding the hungry ones with his own hands.'[79] It was also known that Narayana Guru had high regard for Islamic philosophy—in particular the mysticism of Dara Shikoh—and that he would listen with great attentiveness to interpretations of the Holy Koran by local Islamic scholars. Vakkom Abdul Khader Maulavi, the most prominent leader of the Muslim community, was a friend of Narayana Guru's and founded the 'Islam Dharma Paripalana Yogam' to propagate reforms within the community.[80]

It was a Christian who reputedly donated the peacock image for his temple at Aruvippuram, and when a young evangelist sought to convert him to Christianity, the Guru is reported to have laughed:

'Convert? How? I am already a Christian!'[81] And the paradox to be fully maintained here is that it is precisely *because* he never interfered in the activities of other communities or even remotely hinted that they adopt similar measures, that they too followed the lead of the Ezhavas in setting up community organizations and undertaking far-reaching internal reforms.

All of these organizations have without exception now turned into reified special-interest groups pursuing narrow caste and religious interests in the public arena, but it would be a serious mistake to see them as having always been 'sectarian'. Besides serving as organs of internal critique within communities while simultaneously redefining and redrawing their boundaries, for a brief period these organizations had also transformed themselves into open structures, some even with membership from other communities. The resolution passed at the conclusion of SNDP's fifteenth annual conference held in 1918 expressly declared that its aim was not just promoting Ezhava interests but 'the advancement of all oppressed communities'.[82] Narayana Guru had tried to capture this phenomenon of intercommunal opening-up with his idiosyncratic term for caste—*samudayam*—instead of the more standard *jati*.[83]

None of this is to suggest that these changes which cumulatively transformed Kerala's intercommunal landscape beyond recognition unfolded without any hiccups. At a time of 'transvaluation of all values' in a society with a myriad tightly imbricated communities, it would be surprising indeed if such large-scale changes were not also accompanied by friction at the edges. Intercommunal tensions were greatest between the newly assertive Ezhavas and the traditionally powerful Nairs, and there were even some instances of violence. The most significant clash between the two communities was the Kollam 'Nair-Ezhava riot' of 1905 that broke out when a group of Ezhava students was prevented by the local Nairs from entering public schools.[84] The SNDP mouthpiece *Vivekodayam* editorialized at the time that the trouble had been stirred up by a handful of Nairs who were unwilling to change with the times and 'envious of the increasing success of the organizational efforts of the Ezhavas'.[85] In another editorial, the journal even rhapsodized about the invigorating effect of riots on society: 'Riots can be a great reformer of communities. Our society can learn valuable lessons from riots. ... Riots make people who could not even approach each other on a public road come to blows and touch one other, and that is indeed a great advance!'[86]

THE ONE, THE TWO, AND THE MANY

Despite the outbreak of a few scattered incidents of violence, the Kerala 'uprooting' cannot but strike us with its extreme 'graciousness'. Crucial to this graciousness was not only the reverence with which Narayana Guru was held by all the communities of Kerala, but also the 'phenomenological reduction' performed by Hinduism: all communities, no matter how doctrinally different, are 'reduced', as it were, to caste—a category which exists only in the plural, never as dyadic. The Hindu's intercommunal world is therefore always of the many, never of the two. Within the traditional phenomenological horizon of Hinduism, religions as theologically different from it as Islam or Christianity are therefore experienced as just another of the many castes that populate its life-world; what cannot be properly 'Hindu' is the aggregation of this plurality into Two.[87]

Two, on the other hand, is the crucial number for the theorists of universality. For Badiou, the eruption of the event always splits the situation into two: those prepared to join the universal community-in-becoming by demonstrating fidelity to the event, and those who do not. 'The real Two is an evental production', declares Badiou, 'the highest duty of man is to produce, together, the Two and the thought of the Two, the exercise of the Two.'[88] For the Kerala event however, no number could be more distant than Two. For Narayana Guru, it is the *One* in which the Truth must always be sought, and *the many* through which this Truth must actively find its way; no number could be more false than Two. Consequently, the entire problematic of how the One splits into Two, whether Two comes before the One or One before the Two, what the relation is between the two that comprise Two, whether a third term necessarily mediates the two, which half of the Two contains the Truth and so on that preoccupy the contemporary theorists of universality is false—as is the sophistic 'deconstructionist' dispersal of the One into plurality pure and simple. Setting itself against both these dominant strands of contemporary theorizing, the Kerala event finds its genesis in the gap between the One and the many, this 'gap' to be conceived not as lying somewhere 'in between' but as traversing each *one* in the many from within.

This is because although the 'subject' of the Kerala event first manifested itself as the self-contraction of one within the multiple, it only became properly universal upon doubling back as the de-substantialized multiple within the One: the subject is nothing but this self-contracting/redoubling. The much speculated-on 'identity' of the Void and the One[89] lies here—not in the convergence of the metaphysical claims of Madhyamika and Advaita about 'the true nature of reality' but in this reflexive looping back of multiple into One, in the redoubling of the emptied multiple into the emptiness of the One. It is crucial to bear in mind that the two emptinesses do not simply 'exist' a priori; the very emptying of the multiple synchronously reveals the One as empty and also the empty as One. This overlapping of the two emptinesses in the course of redoubling *is* the subject. The One as empty co-emerges with the de-substantialization of the one: the one's self-contraction is congruent with the emergence of the One as form and only form (*abhavasya bhavah*).

Therein also lies the truth of Narayana Guru's oft-quoted pronouncement: One Caste, One Religion, One God. The 'One' here is not to be read as a version of the humanist platitude that no matter how different in caste, religion, or belief, all human beings have as their common denominator an underlying 'humanity' and therefore belong to the same 'human family'. The One is rather the subject's discovery that what separated the One from the many in which the One was lodged was the subject's own (quasi)substance. The many are therefore not the 'manifestation' of the One in the wealth of its plenitude; on the contrary, the One's manifestation (*prabhasate*) only occurs with the evacuation of the one's entire (quasi)substance. The Oneness of the One is nothing but the one's own residual form after its de-substantialization: 'Form is Emptiness, Emptiness is Form,' says the *Prajnaparamitahrdayasutra*.[90]

It is only with the one's subsequent re-substantializing that the One also recedes and reconstitutes itself as other-than-one. The one's 'identity' with the One is therefore paradoxically to be found only when the One is deprived of its fullness as One—which is also the moment the one loses all support in its (quasi)substance and is sustained as pure form by the totality of all other ones in the multiple. *The One is none other than this form.* The re-substantialization of the one and its re-integration into the multiple as substantive is coterminous with the One's re-emergence as other-than-one.

The 'Absolute' therefore does not designate a 'merging' of the partiality of the one's content with the fullness of the One's; on the contrary, it is in the self-contraction of the entirety of the one's content and its emergence into pure form that it also realizes itself as Absolute. The one's passage through the void of negativity is what collapses the distance separating it from the Absolute. The central paradox of the One therefore is that it appears as substantially other only when refracted through the one's own substance-effect: the One loses its remoteness the moment all the content that made the one *one and not nothing* is expunged. Synchronously, the 'substantive' differences between the one's comprising the multiple make way (*antadvayarahitatva*) for the one's *difference from itself*. It is in this reflexive relating to its *self-difference* as form and content via self-contraction that the subject declares its autonomy from external determination.

The capacity for autonomous self-contraction and passage through negativity bears no correlation to the degree of 'exploitation': it is in principle available to any community, even to the pseudo-communities. But regardless of who undertakes it, the passage remains 'dark and empty in both its beginning and its end':[91] dark and empty in its beginning because of the sheer contingency of the event's eruption, dark and empty in its end because it can only be a pure dharmic wager in the dead of a mythical night. It is Narayana Guru himself who beseeches, midway into the tenth stanza of his hundred-verse *Atmopadesa-Satakam*: '*Who sits there in the dark? Reveal yourself!*'[92]

NOTES AND REFERENCES

1. J. Habermas, *The Philosophical Discourse of Modernity* (Cambridge, MA: MIT Press, 1980).
2. J. Ranciere, *Disagreement* (Minneapolis and London: University of Minnesota Press, 1999).
3. A. Badiou, *Being and Event* (London and New York: Continuum, 2005).
4. Gadjin Nagao, *The Foundational Standpoint of Madhyamika Philosophy*, trans. John P. Keenan (Albany, NY: State University of New York, 1989), p. 96.
5. Arif Dirlik, 'The Postcolonial Aura: Third World Criticism in the Age of Global Capitalism', *Critical Inquiry*, vol. 20 (Winter 1994), pp. 328–56.
6. Amartya Sen, *Development as Freedom* (New York: Anchor Books, 1999), p. 48.
7. Samir Amin, 'Four comments on Kerala', *Monthly Review* 42, no.8 (1991), p. 28.
8. E.M.S. Namboodiripad, *Kerala: Yesterday, Today, and Tomorrow* (Calcutta: National Book Agency, 1968), p.120.
9. Thomas Isaac, 'From Caste Consciousness to Class Aonsciousness: Alleppey Coir Workers during the Inter-war Period', *Economic and Political Weekly XX*, no.4 (1985), pp. 5–18; Thomas Isaac and Michael Tharakan, 'Sree Narayana Movement in Travancore 1888-1939: A Study of Social Basis and Ideological Reproduction', Working Paper No. 214, Centre for Development Studies, Trivandrum, 1986.
10. M.N. Srinivas, *Caste in Modern India and Other Essays*, (Bombay: Media Promoters & Publishers, 1988[1962]), p. 34.
11. Fillippo Osella and Caroline Osella, *Social Mobility in Kerala: Modernity and Identity in Conflict* (London: Pluto Press, 2000), p. 187.

12. Sumit Sarkar, *Modern India: 1885-1947* (Delhi: Macmillan, 1986), p.56. Sarkar appears more wary about the 'Sanskritization' idea in a later book *Writing Social History* (Delhi: Oxford University Press, 1997), p. 40.

13. See for instance Charles H. Heimsath, 'The Function of the Hindu Social Reformers with Special Reference to Kerala', *The Indian Economic and Social History Review*, vol. XV, no.1 (1978), pp. 21–39; Kenneth W. Jones, *Socio-Religious Reform Movements in British India* (Cambridge: Cambridge University Press, 1999), p. 181.

14. Badiou, *Being and Event*, p. 175.

15. A pratishta is the act of consecrating an idol in a Hindu temple.

16. A siddha is one who has attained extraordinary spiritual powers.

17. A shivalingam is the phallic symbol associated with the Hindu god Shiva and usually represented by a cylindrical stone rounded off at the top, with the bottom end inserted in a flat horizontal stone called the *yoni*.

18. Shivaratri is a night sacred to devotees of Shiva; the night culminates in the worship of the shivalingam after a day of fasting, holding vigil, and ritual bathing.

19. Om Namah Shivayah is the mantra or invocatory hymn of Shiva worshippers meaning 'Praise be to Shiva'.

20. N. Kumaran Asan, *Brahmasree Narayana Guruvinte Jeevacharitra Samgraham* (Trivandrum: Asan Memorial Committee, 1986), p. 31. This essay was originally published in 1915 in the Malayalam journal, *Vivekodayam*.

21. Dilip M. Menon, *The Blindness of Insight: Essays on Caste in Modern India* (Chennai: Navayana, 2006), p. 61.

22. K.V. Subramanyam, *Sahodaran Ayyappan Jeevacharitram* (Aluva: K.V. Subramanyam, 1973), p. 6.

23. Moyarathu Sankaran, *Ente Jeevithakatha* (Calicut: P.K.Brothers, 1965), p. 53.

24. Murkot Kunhappa, *Sree Narayana Guru* (New Delhi: National Book Trust, 1982), p. 27.

25. K. Sreenivasan, *Sree Narayana Guru* (Trivandrum: Jayasree Publications, 1989), p. 55.

26. Ibid., p. 28.

27. Ibid., p. 54.

28. Murkothu Kumaran, *Sree Narayana Guru Swamikalude Jeevacharitram* (Varkala: Sree Narayana Dharmasangham Trust, 1999 [1930]), p. 148.

29. Kunhappa, *Sree Narayana Guru*, p. 29.

30. A.S.P. Aiyer, quoted in A. Ayyappan, *Social Revolution in a Kerala Village: A Study in Culture Change* (Bombay: Asia Publishing House, 1965), p. 135.

31. Habermas's ideal of 'communicative reason' remains the exemplar of this model of politics.

32. A pseudo-community, according to Hannah Arendt, is made up of atomized individuals held together by some form of heteronomous authority. See Hannah Arendt, *The Origins of Totalitarianism* (New York: Harcourt Brace Jovanovich, 1973).

33. Nagao, *The Foundational Standpoint*, p. 49.

34. Ibid., p. 37.
35. Ibid., p. 137.
36. Ashis Nandy, 'Freud, Modernity, and Postcolonial Violence: Analytic attitude, Dissent, and the Boundaries of the Self', *The Little Magazine* (Delhi), vol. IV, nos. 5 and 6 (2006), p. 4. Also available at: http//www.littlemag.com/looking/ashisnandy4.html (accessed on 17 April 2008).
37. Ibid., p. 4.
38. Ibid., p. 4.
39. Ibid., p. 4.
40. M.K. Sanoo, *Narayana Guru Swami Jeevacharitram* (Kottayam: National Book Stall, 1986), p. 473.
41. Claude Lefort, *The Political Forms of Modern Society: Bureaucracy, Democracy, Totalitarianism* (Cambridge, Massachusetts: The MIT Press, 1986), p. 302.
42. Ibid., p. 302.
43. Ibid., p. 303.
44. M.K. Sanoo, *Narayana Guru Swami*, p. 440.
45. Ibid., p. 472.
46. Both Shiva and Sharada are currently worshipped at Shivagiri.
47. Daniel Bensaid, 'Alain Badiou and the Miracle of the Event', in Peter Hallward (ed.), *Think Again: Alain Badiou and the Future of Philosophy* (New York: Continuum, 2004), p. 96.
48. P.K. Balakrishnan, *Narayana Guru Samahara Grantham* (Kottayam: National Book Stall, 1954), p. 125.
49. Nagao, *The Foundational Standpoint*, p. 87.
50. Editorial, *Vivekodayam*, October 1913, pp. 218–19.
51. http://www.censusindia.gov.in/Census_Data_2001/Census_data_finder/C_Series/Population_by_religious_communities.htm (accessed 17 April 2008).
52. P. Bhaskarunni, *Keralam: Irupatham Noottandinte Aarambhathil* (Trichur: Kerala Sahitya Akademi, 2005), p. 9.
53. Puthuppally Raghavan (ed.), *C.V. Kunjuramante Thiranjedutha Krithikal* (Thiruvananthapuram: Kaumudi Public Relations, 2002), p. 124.
54. N.R. Krishnan, *Ezhavar Annum Innum* (Trichur: Current Books, 1967); K. Damodaran, *Ezhavarude Ithihasam* (Kollam: Sreeramavilasam, 1930); and Kampil Ananthan, *Kerala Charithra Nirupanam Athava Theeyarude Powramikathwam* (Tellicherry, 1935).
55. Kenneth Inada, *Nagarjuna: A Translation of his Mulamadhyamikakarika, With An Introductory Essay* (Tokyo: Hokuseido Press, 1970).
56. Nagao, *The Foundational Standpoint*, p. 66.
57. The *Prajnaparamita Sutras* are among the fundamental texts of Mahayana Buddhism composed in the first century BCE.
58. Nagao, *The Foundational Standpoint*, p. 78.
59. Ibid., pp. 78–80.
60. Quoted in Peter Hallward, *Badiou: A Subject to Truth* (Minneapolis and London: University of Minneapolis Press, 2003), p. 26.

94   Political Hinduism

61. Ibid., p.109.
62. Nataraja Guru, *The Word of the Guru* (Cochin: Paico Publishing, 1968), p. 61.
63. English translations of Narayana Guru's compositions are available in *Narayana Guru: Complete Works*, trans. Muni Narayana Prasad (New Delhi: National Book Trust, 2006).
64. V.R. Krishna Iyer, 'Prolegomenon to a Biography of Narayana Guru', in M.K. Sanoo, *Narayana Guru* (Bombay: Bharatiya Vidya Bhavan, 1998), p. xvii.
65. Menon, *The Blindness of Insight*, p. 61.
66. T. Bhaskaran, *Sri Narayana Guruvinte Sampoorna Krithikal* (Calicut: Mathrubhoomi Publications, 1985), pp. xxi–xxiii.
67. Udaya Kumar, 'Self, Body, Inner-sense: Some Reflections on Sree Narayana Guru and Kumaran Asan', *Studies in History* (New Delhi), vol.13, no.2 (1997).
68. Quoted in M.Kunhappa, *Sree Narayana Guru*, p. 67.
69. Romain Rolland, *The Life of Ramakrishna* (Kolkata: Advaita Ashrama, 2001), footnote, p. 111.
70. Sreenivasan, *Sree Narayana Guru*, p. 57.
71. Ibid.
72. Kunhappa, *Sree Narayana Guru*, p. 63.
73. Ashis Nandy, 'Time Travel to a Possible Self: Searching for the Alternative Cosmopolitanism of Cochin', in *Time Warps: The Insistent Politics of Silent and Evasive Pasts* (New Delhi: Permanent Black, 2002), p. 209.
74. Kunhappa, *Sree Narayana Guru*, p. 24.
75. Sathya Bai Sivadas and R. Prabhakara Rao, *Narayana Guru: The Social Philosopher of Kerala* (Mumbai: Bharatiya Vidya Bhavan, 2002), p. 48.
76. V.T. Bhattathiripad, *Veetiyude Sampoorna Krithikal* (Kottayam: D.C. Books, 1997), p. 474.
77. T.A. Paraman, 'Harijanangal', in *Kerala Charitram Vol. I* (Ernakulam: Kerala History Association, 1973), p. 1018.
78. Mannath Padmanabhan, *Jeevitha Smaranakal* (Changanacherry, 1957), pp. 337–8.
79. Kunhappa, *Sree Narayana Guru*, p. 20.
80. P.K. Gopalakrishnan, 'Samuhya Parishkarana Prasthanangal', in *Kerala Charitram Vol.I*, p. 1301.
81. Kunhappa, *Sree Narayana Guru*, p. 21.
82. Editorial, *Mithavadi* (Kozhikode), June 1918, p. 11.
83. B. Rajeevan, 'Jathiyekurichulla Veenduvicharangal', in K.N. Shaji (ed.), *Narayana Guru: Jeevitham, Krithikal, Darshanam*, (Trichur: Current Books, 2002), pp. 379–80.
84. M.K. Sanoo, *Narayana Guru Swami Jeevacharitram*, p. 151.
85. Editorial, *Vivekodayam*, May 1905.
86. Ibid., October 1916.
87. It is this feature that makes the contemporary political movement that calls itself 'Hindutva' *essentially non-Hindu* and also imposes on its ambitions a decisive limitation.
88. Quoted in Hallward, *Badiou: A Subject to Truth*, p. 45.

89. Kencho Tenzin, *Shankara: Hindu Revivalist Or Crypto-Buddhist?* (MA Thesis, Georgia State University, 2006). Available at: http://etd.gsu.edu/theses/available/etd-11302006-094652/unrestricted/Tenzin_Kencho_200612_ma.pdf (accessed on 17 April 2008).

90. Nagao, *The Foundational Standpoint*, p. 9.

91. Ibid., p. 78.

92. Sreenivasan, *Sree Narayana Guru*, p. 36.

Julius J. Lipner

'Icon and Mother'
An Inquiry into India's National Song[1]

India, which prides itself on being a 'secular' polity constitutionally, is in the extraordinary position of having both a national anthem and a national song. This is not the place to analyse the precise meaning of 'secular' with respect to the Indian Constitution. Much ink has flowed to this end. Suffice it to say that here this word is used not in the sense of 'anti-religious' but in the sense of not granting privileged status to any particular religion in the eyes of the Constitution. In other words, from the point of view of the Indian Constitution where matters of national or state policy are concerned, there should be no majoritarian or other bias towards the privileging of a particular religious faith.[2]

The title-words of the national song are *Vande Mātaram*.[3] One translation of this Sanskrit expression would be, 'I revere the Mother', from *vande*, the first person singular, present indicative of the verb *vand*, 'to praise, revere, worship, salute, pay homage to', and *mātā*, 'mother'. The meaning of both terms has proved controversial, and we shall return to this point. As we shall see, there are nine verses in all to the song or hymn with the title-words, *Vande Mātaram*, but the Indian national song comprises only the first two stanzas of this hymn.

The national daily, *The Indian Express*, carried an article in its New Delhi edition on 21 August 2006, from which we take the following extract:

[S]ources told *The Indian Express* that [Arjun Singh, the Human Resources Development (HRD)] minister had got a letter, on August 2 this year, from Culture minister Ambika Soni on the issue of centenary celebrations of pre-Independence era themes, including Vande Mataram.

Soni explained to Singh that a National Committee for Centenary Celebrations under the Chairmanship of the Prime Minister had been organising several events in this regard. Vande Mataram, she wrote, was composed by Bankim Chandra Chattopadhyay in 1876 and Rabindranath Tagore recited it for the first time at the Congress session in Bombay in 1896. Later, in 1905, it became the battle-song in the movement against Partition of Bengal [under British rule]. It was finally adopted as the national song at the Varanasi session of the Congress party on September 7 in 1905.

Having given this brief history,[4] Soni wrote the year-long celebrations had started on September 7, 2005, when the song completed 100 years of adoption as the national song. As a 'befitting grand finale' to the year-long celebration, the Culture minister asked her HRD counterpart to have the singing of Vande Mataram at 11 a.m. on September 7 in all educational institutions across the country.

The HRD minister, on August 8 this year, wrote to all chief ministers and heads of Union Territories to have this 'simultaneous countrywide singing' of the first two stanzas of the national song at 11 a.m. on September 7 in all schools, colleges and other educational institutions.

In passing, we may point out that this date seems an odd claimant for centenary celebrations of the national song, for according to the reported statement of the Culture Minister herself, the song was composed in the last quarter of the nineteenth century, and was aired officially in a nationalist context towards the end of that century. We shall see, further, that it was adopted by the Constituent Assembly of an Independent India under the chairmanship of Rajendra Prasad (India's first President) only on 24 January 1950. None of these major landmarks coincides with a centenary celebration in 2006![5]

The HRD ministry's directive caused uproar throughout the land. This agitation occurred at several levels: religious, political, community, and state. There was strong Muslim representation that the song was idolatrous, anti-Muslim, and anti-secular. Here Sunnis and Shiites were as one.[6] Even Sikhs objected on an official level to the directive:

[T]he Shiromani Gurdwara Prabandhak Committee (SGPC) ... asked the Sikh community not to sing the national song on September 7. In a statement issued [in Amritsar], SGPC chief Avtar Singh Makkar, while making an appeal to all community members not to sing the national song, said it only propagates a particular religion and does not fulfil aspirations of minorities, including Sikhs, Muslims and Christians. 'It's a conspiracy to spread communalism in the nation,' said Makkar.[7]

The national response to the directive was a classic fudge. Some states of the Union, largely those under the influence of the opposition Bharatiya Janata Party (BJP; politically identified with the right wing) professed to follow the directive; some states left their educational institutions free to make up their own minds. Some Muslim-run institutions sang the national song, others refused to comply with the directive. In many cases, local Muslim authorities advised Muslim parents to keep their children away from schools, for the time being. In general, some schools, aware of the reasons for the controversy, decided to have the hymn sung during morning assembly as part of the daily routine; in other institutions, the hymn was sung as a special event at 11 a.m. as recommended by the directive. Indeed, almost immediately after promulgating the directive, the HRD ministry itself issued a clarification stating that this was not intended to be compulsory (to the chagrin of the BJP), and it is interesting to note that on the appointed day, Mrs Sonia Gandhi, President of the Congress party (the chief party of the coalition forming the central government), absented herself from an official function where *Vande Mātaram* was to be sung; she sent a representative instead.

The point is that religious and political controversy over *Vande Mātaram* and its status as national song has been a running issue for nearly a century. The agitation Arjun Singh's directive engendered (not to mention Mrs Gandhi's politic response to a political hot potato) is but an index of a seemingly intractable problem India has had to contend with more and more urgently since becoming an independent multi-faith democracy in 1947. This situation cannot continue; it is a serious bone of contention in the body politic. Sooner or later a decision about the status of *Vande Mātaram* will have to be taken with an eye to the future. The purpose of this essay is to look into the formative literary and political history of *Vande Mātaram*, to examine *Vande Mātaram's* text and context, and to assess various objections made against it as to both content and status as national song. This task will be facilitated by referring from time to time to the broader work I have undertaken on the matter in my book, *Ānandamaṭh, or The Sacred Brotherhood by Bankimcandra Chatterji* (abbr.:*ASB*).[8]

As the previous sentence suggests, the hymn *Vande Mātaram* was given public currency through the Bengali novel entitled *Ānandamaṭh* (which I have translated as *The Sacred Brotherhood*) written by Bankimcandra Cattopadhyay (anglicized as 'Chatterji'; 1838–94). The novel was first published serially in *Baṅgadarśan*, the literary journal in Bengali which Bankim edited, from March 1881–June 1882. Thereafter, with some important revisions, the novel underwent five editions in book-form, the last of which we may call the standard version since it is this edition that appears in the various anthologies of Bankim's works including the anthology published under the aegis of the Bangiya Sahitya Parisat (The Bengal Literary Society) to mark the centenary of Bankim's birth.⁹ The standard edition appeared in November 1892.

The novel itself is set in the early 1770s, during the so-called *sannyāsī* (or 'renouncer') rebellion as it occurred in the Birbhum district of greater Bengal, and the great famine in the region at the time. These two events provided the raw data of the narrative which Bankim then refined, and also re-defined, for his purposes. Thus, while the original 'renouncers' comprised itinerant bands of ganja-smoking Hindu and Muslim sannyāsīs and fakirs, often numbering thousands, who travelled at certain periods of the year (many accompanied by their women and children) on pilgrimage routes, exacting tolls and provisions from the villages they passed, the inner core of sannyāsīs of Bankim's story are all cultured, upper-caste Hindus (mostly Brahmins) sworn to a vow of temporary celibacy. The original sannyāsīs were for the most part a rabble of considerable nuisance value because of their importunate practices, not only to the British who had the (lucrative) task of collecting the revenue for the regional Muslim rulers and imposing order for this purpose, but also to the local villagers whose livelihood in cash and kind was imperilled by the predatory behaviour of the renouncers. This compelled the British to try and disband the renouncers on a permanent basis, which led to running battles between the two sides for several years (the so-called sannyāsī-rebellion), till eventually—by the turn of the century—the British won through. The situation in the early 1770s, however, was exacerbated by a terrible famine that gripped much of the middle regions of the Bengal of the time.

Bankim converts the deprivation and general lawlessness of these circumstances to the backdrop of his novel. Bengal is now contested land: there is no clear ruling authority. The titular Muslim rulers have gone to seed and are uninterested in enforcing the requisite order for the welfare of all their subjects, both Hindu and Muslim; they are reliant on the British to whom they have given the task of collecting revenue on their behalf. The British, who perforce have negotiated very generous terms, are interested only in their dues, and not in administering the land. Historically, these are no more than half-truths, if that, but for Bankim's purposes the scene is set for his sannyāsīs to play their part.

These renouncers are called *santāns* or 'Children', and they take up residence in an abandoned monastery in the heart of a dense jungle. They are Children of the Mother whom they worship, the focus of which are three images of the Goddess enshrined in the monastery: the Goddess-as-she-was, the Goddess-as she-is (identified with an image of Kālī), and the glorious Goddess-as-she-will-be. But it is significant that the Goddess-as-she-was is described as 'the motherland in the form of the nurturing Goddess' (*jagaddhātrīrūpiṇī mātṛbhūmi*). So the matter is complicated. Bankim has iconized the land. The santāns are Children of the Goddess as also of the motherland, and the motherland is an embodiment of the Goddess in some way. Not only has Bankim iconized the land, but through the distinctive form of the Goddess he has also 'Hinduized' it in some integral sense. This is clear from a description of the Mother-as-she-will-be:

Her ten arms reach out in ten directions, adorned with various powers in the form of the different weapons she holds, the enemy crushed at her feet, while the mighty lion who has taken refuge there is engaged in destroying the foe ... [the Goddess] roams on the lordly lion's back, [and] has Lakshmi personifying good fortune on her right, and the Goddess of speech who bestows wisdom and learning on her left, with Kartikeya signifying strength and Ganesh good success, in attendance!' [10]

This description is uncannily reminiscent of the Goddess Durgā in one of her favoured representations. It would be as well to mark this here especially in the context of charges asserting the 'communal' and idolatrous nature of the novel and its song.

The santāns emerge periodically from their forest-retreat to attack those whom they regard as unacceptable representatives of failing ruling authority: the armies of the Muslim rulers and their British allies. Their aim is to free the motherland of these alien forces;[11] in this they eventually if temporarily succeed. Of course, there are a number of sub-plots—battles, transgressions of various kinds, and episodes of requited and unrequited love are described on the way. We must leave these for the reader to discover. But it is at this point in our essay that we need to make a more detailed acquaintance of *Vande Mātaram*.

The santāns take recourse to a hymn that first appears in Chapter 10 of Part I; this paean sums up their patriotic ardour to the nurturing motherland whose Children they are and which they seek to set free. Its opening words are 'vande mātaram', but it is also important to note that in the novel this expression is used as a slogan in its own right, sometimes as a password to the santāns' secret brotherhood and sometimes as a rallying-cry in battle. We shall return to this in due course. But here is the complete hymn, in the English translation I have given it. The Children have just successfully carried out a raid on a cartload of money that the British have raised as revenue, and that is on its way to the British headquarters in Calcutta, and have rescued a wealthy landowner whose name is Mahendra. One of the commanders of the successful raiding party is called Bhabananda. It will be helpful to give the context of the first appearance of the hymn in full:

[Mahendra and Bhabananda] walked silently across the plain in that moonlit night. Mahendra was silent, anguished, unbending, somewhat intrigued. Suddenly Bhabananda seemed to become a different person. No longer was he the grave, calm renouncer, the skilled, valiant figure of the battlefield, the man who had cut off the head of a [British] commanding officer! No longer the man who had just rebuked Mahendra so haughtily. It was as if seeing the radiance of plain and forest, mountain and river of a peaceful, moonlit world had invigorated his mind in a special way, like the ocean gladdened by the rising moon. He was now light-hearted, talkative, friendly, keen to make a conversation. He tried often to get Mahendra to talk, but Mahendra remained silent. Then, with no other recourse, Bhabananda began to sing softly to himself:

I revere the Mother! The Mother
Rich in waters, rich in fruit,
Cooled by the southern airs,
Verdant with the harvest fair. ...

Mahendra was a little astonished when he heard this song, and was at a loss to understand. Who was this mother 'rich in waters, rich in fruit, cooled by the southern airs, verdant with the harvest fair'?

'Who is this mother?' he asked Bhabananda.

Without answering Bhabananda began to sing:

The Mother - with nights that thrill
in the light of the moon,
Radiant with foliage and flowers in bloom,
Smiling sweetly, speaking gently,
Giving joy and gifts in plenty.

Mahendra cried, 'But that's our land, not a mother!'

Bhabananda replied, 'We recognise no other mother. One's mother and birthland are greater than heaven itself. But we say that our birthland is our mother. We've no mothers, fathers, brothers, friends, no wives, children, houses or homes. All we have is she who is rich in waters, rich in fruit, cooled by the southern airs, verdant with the harvest fair ...'.

'Then sing on,' said Mahendra, understanding at last.

And Bhabananda sang once more:

(1)　*I revere the Mother! The Mother*
　　Rich in waters, rich in fruit,

> *Cooled by the southern airs,*
> *Verdant with the harvest fair.*

(2)   *The Mother - with nights that thrill*
        in the light of the moon,
        Radiant with foliage and flowers in bloom,
        Smiling sweetly, speaking gently,
        Giving joy and gifts in plenty.

(3)   *Powerless? How so, Mother,*
        With the strength of voices fell,
        Seventy millions in their swell!
        And with sharpened swords
        By twice as many hands upheld!

(4)   *To the Mother I bow low,*
        To her who wields so great a force,
        To her who saves,
        And drives away the hostile hordes!

(5)   *You our wisdom, you our law,*
        You our heart, you our core,
        In our bodies the living force is thine!

(6)   *Mother, you're our strength of arm,*
        And in our hearts the loving balm,
        Yours the form we shape in every shrine!

(7)   *For you are Durga, bearer of the tenfold power,*
        And wealth's Goddess, dallying on the lotus-flower,
        You are Speech, to you I bow,
        To us wisdom you endow.

(8)   *I bow to the Goddess Fair,*
        Rich in waters, rich in fruit,
        To the Mother,
        Spotless - and beyond compare!

(9)   *I revere the Mother! the Mother*
        Darkly green and also true,
        Richly dressed, of joyous face,
        This ever-plenteous land of grace.[12]

The translation follows the order of stanzas given in the original; the reader will notice that there are nine stanzas in all (which I have numbered for ready reference). In any case, no one disputes the arrangement of the first two stanzas. The hymn is composed in a mixture of Bengali and Sanskrit (that is, some lines are in Sanskrit and some in Bengali). The first two stanzas are in Sanskrit, the third has both Sanskrit and Bengali, the fourth is in Sanskrit, the fifth is in both Bengali and Sanskrit, the sixth is entirely in Bengali, and the last three verses are all in Sanskrit.

Why this peculiarly admixed composition? Let us start with Sanskrit. There seems to be little doubt that Bankim had a version of the hymn in preparation before the writing of the narrative in which the completed hymn (modified slightly for subsequent editions of the novel) was inserted.[13] In elite Hindu literary tradition, of which Bankim was widely knowledgeable, Sanskrit has always been the dominant language, and its compositional forms provided (and in important respects continue to provide) paradigms for literary activity. This was specially so, for a particular reason, at the time when Bankim was writing. In the eyes of the Bengali intelligentsia of the time, Sanskrit afforded a link of continuity, culturally and religiously, with the ancestral tradition of the majority. As such, the judicious application of Sanskrit was a psychological marker of cultural ballast, of legitimizing authority for what was being said through the use of the language, and of a sense of Hindu national identity.[14] Further, as will be evident, *Vande Mātaram* is a hymn with clear religious overtones; it is a hymn of praise to a 'deity', a 'mothering icon' (exactly to *whom* or *what* we shall see), in the manner of a *stotra*.[15] It was therefore appropriate to evoke a Sanskrit paradigm for this purpose. Its Sanskritic form and content lent it gravitas; it was to be taken seriously.

But Bankim was too good an exponent of the narratival arts to leave it at that. The hymn needed to have an emotional grip on its reader, and this was accomplished in particular by the sense and sensibilities of the Bengali. Thus the staccato effect of the Bengali in the first two lines of verse 5, or the direct and familiar form of address in verse 6 (through the use of *mā* and *tomār* for 'mother' and 'your' respectively) galvanizes the Bengali reader—notwithstanding the individual commitment evoked by the first person singular of vande—to a sense of devotional solidarity. Bengali was the vernacular in which the narrative was written, and by thus 'vernacularizing' the Sanskrit of the hymn, Bankim achieves the best of both worlds—the authority of tradition and the enveloping freshness of current speech.[16]

Now to a consideration of the hymn's content. Here we can only raise specific issues, but let us start with a core concern, viz. the mode and object of worship of this stotra. To drive the point home, let us quote some objections:

Advising the Union Government to form a committee of Sanskrit scholars and intellectuals who can decide the actual meaning of Vande, [Maulana Kalbe] Sadiq [Vice-President of the All-India Muslim Personal Law Board] said if it meant salute or salaam to the nation, he is ready to sing it. ... 'We do not even worship Mecca,

Medina or Kaba, then how can one force us to worship the motherland?' asked Sadiq.[17]

And:
'We cannot compromise on Kalma-e-Tayyaba, the basic pillar of Islam where we are committed to one God and Mohammed is our Prophet,' said Moulana Mufti Mohammed Hasnuddin, a religious scholar. The main objection of Muslims to singing *Vande Mataram* is based in this belief as the song treats even land and natural resources as God which is 'Shirk' or un-Islamic to the Muslims.[18]

Christian theologians have spoken of two kinds of worship, distinguished by the Greeks terms *latria* and *dulia*. Though the original context is Christian theological discourse, the distinction itself is universalisable, and will stand us in good stead in the present discussion. Latria is the worship—the absolute, unconditional acknowledgement or submission—due to the Supreme Being or God, the one and infinite being. So there is only one object of latria. Dulia, on the other hand, is reverence or homage paid to a finite being regarded as superior to one or as deserving of respect in some way. Hence we say 'Your Worship' to the mayor, and jokingly or devotionally proclaim that we 'worship' the ground our beloved has walked on, or that we 'worship' the image of a great human being or some ancestor. Accordingly, since the object of dulia is by definition not God or the Supreme Being, and since dulia implies only veneration or respect, the objects of dulia can be indefinite in number. To revert now to the question raised above: what kind of 'worship' does the term vande imply in *Vande Mātaram*? Is it dulia or latria?

Let us begin with an inquiry into classical Hindu tradition, the basis of current usage (further, we should not forget that vande mātaram is a Sanskrit expression). There can be no doubt that the verbal root vand- has been used regularly in the sense of latria, viz. the worship or veneration due to God alone. Here are a few examples. The *Bhāgavata Purāṇa* (*circa* ninth century CE), which has played such a central and influential role in the devotional worship of many Hindu *sampradāyas* or sectarian traditions, lists the 'nine marks/characteristics' of genuine devotion (*iti bhaktir navalakṣaṇā*) to the Supreme Being (named Viṣṇu) as follows:

Hearing (the name and the deeds of the lord; *śravaṇa*), singing the praises (of the Lord; *kīrtana*), keeping in mind (the Lord and his deeds/attributes at all times; *smaraṇa*), being at the service (of the Lord; *pādasevana*), worshipping (the image of the Lord; *arcana*), greeting and paying homage (to the Lord; *vandana*), offering one's actions (to the Lord; *dāsya*), having faith and trust (in the Lord as friend; *sakhya*), and offering body and soul (to the Lord; *ātmanivedana*).[19]

Note the presence of vandana (noun from the root vand-) as one of the nine. This is paying homage to the Supreme Deity.

The great devotional theologian Rāmānuja (eleventh–twelfth century CE), takes up this idea and affirms it. Thus in his Sanskrit commentary on the Bhagavadgītā, that foundational text of devotion to the one Lord (*bhagavān, īśvara; circa* first–third century CE), which describes worship of the personal Supreme Being, he glosses as follows in words attributed to Krishna, the divine being: 'Those set on Me.... with bodies enraptured and voices tremulous with emotion....strive after Me through such deeds as worshipping my image by acts of reverent greeting, praising (*vandana-stavana-karaṇādi-*) and so on ...' (9.14). There are countless other instances of such use of the root vand-. Thus it is clear that without semantic violence, in Hindu tradition vand-can be and has been used in the sense of address or approach to the Supreme Being. Nevertheless, vand- has often been used from ancient times in the ordinary sense of greeting or salutation, that is, of showing respect to a person or thing that is not the divine being.[20] So the matter is inconclusive from the point of view of traditional usage.

Now we may ask: is there evidence to indicate what Bankim himself may have meant by the vande of the hymn he inserted into his famous novel? Let us look into this in pursuit of further clarification. It is at this point that we shall have to draw in the meaning of 'Mother' or mātā (the accusative of which is mātaram), the object of the verb vande.

We have already seen that in Bankim's description of the 'Mother-as-she-will-be', we have more or less a description of the Goddess Durgā as she appears every year during the great autumnal festival in Bengal of the Durgā Pūjā. It is no coincidence then that verse 7 of the hymn makes salient reference to Durgā by name who is identified with the 'Mother' (as well as to the Goddess of wealth and of speech, both associated with the 'Mother-as-she-will-be' in the earlier description). The point that I am making is that though the first two stanzas seem to entail a straightforward description of the 'Mother' as a nurturing motherland, the matter is certainly not that obvious, since already from stanza 6 ('Mother ... Yours the form we shape in every shrine') and then moving into stanza 7, the 'Mother' shades into a personal form of the Goddess as worshipped by Hindus. It is perhaps then disingenuous to dismiss without further consideration objections which raise the issue

of 'idolatry' as permeating the hymn as a whole. The first two stanzas
(the national song) are a part of a whole which does seem legitimately
to raise this issue.[21]

But we must still inquire further as to the precise theological force
of vande and mātaram. Can the author of the novel, who inserted the
hymn into his narrative, provide any clue? Here we turn to a controversy
Bankim entered into between the time the novel was completed in
serial form (mid-1882) and the time it was first published as a book
(end-1882). On 17 September 1882, a grandee of Calcutta, Maharaja
Harendra Krishna Deb, held an elaborate rite (śrāddh) to commemorate
the death of a close relative. A fairly detailed report appeared in the
Calcutta *Statesman*, and the attendance at this grand event (during
which an image of Krishna, the family deity, was brought into the hall)
by leading English-educated Bengali men in particular so outraged the
religious sensibilities of the Revd W. Hastie, principal of the General
Assembly's Institution of that city, that he wrote a furious letter to *The
Statesman*, decrying the bad example of the male attendees, especially,
for appearing to countenance the idolatrous rites and thus misleading
their (less-educated) womenfolk. Hastie wrote arrogantly and rudely
of Hindu 'idol-worship' which he compared most unfavourably to the
enlightened faith of Christians. Bankim, who was not present at the
rite, was one of those who protested against Hastie's comments, and he
entered into a controversy about Hindu worship with Hastie through
the columns of *The Statesman*, first under a pseudonym and finally in his
own name. In the process, he gives an account of his own understanding
of what passed for 'idol worship' among his compatriots, and it is in this
context that his views are relevant for our own discussion. In a long
letter, published on 8 October, Bankim wrote as follows:

Modern science has shown what the Hindus always knew that the phenomena of
nature are simply the manifestations of *force*. They worship, therefore, Nature as
force. *Sakti*, literally and ordinarily means force or energy. As destructive energy,
force is *Kali*, hideous and terrible, because destruction is hideous and terrible. As
constructive energy, force is the bright and resplendent Durga. The universal soul
is also worshipped, but in three distinct aspects. ... I translate them as love, power,
and justice. Love creates, power preserves, justice dooms. This is the Hindu (idea)
of Brahma, Vishnu and Siva ...

I now pass on to the worship. Much of the Hindu ritual is mere mummery. ...
Idol worship is permitted, is even belauded in the Hindu scriptures, but it is not
enjoined as *compulsory*. ... The orthodox Brahmin is bound to worship Vishnu and
Siva every day, but he is not bound to worship their images. He may worship their
images if he choose, but if he does not so choose, the worship of the Invisible is
accepted as sufficient ...

And I must ask the student of Hinduism when he comes to study Hindu Idolatry, to forget the nonsense about dolls given to children. ... The true explanation consists in the ever true relations of the subjective Ideal to its objective Reality. ... The passionate yearnings of the heart for the Ideal in beauty, in power, and in purity, must find an expression in the world of the Real. Hence proceed all poetry and all art. Exactly in the same way the ideal of the Divine in man receives a form from him, and the form an image. The existence of Idols is as justifiable as that of the tragedy of Hamlet or of that of Prometheus. The *religious* worship of idols is as justifiable as the *intellectual* worship of Hamlet or Prometheus ...

Nor must the student fall into the error of thinking that the image is ever taken to be the God. The God is always believed, by every worshipper, to exist apart from the image. The image is simply the visible and accessible medium through which I choose to send my homage to the throne of the Invisible and the Inaccessible. ... The image is holy, not because the worshipper believes it to be his god—he believes in no such thing—but because he has made a contract with his own heart *for the sake of culture and discipline* to treat it as God's image.[22]

There is much to decipher here, but we are given an insight into what Bankim thought about the worship of images in the context of Hindu worship as a whole at the time of the publication of the hymn as part of the novel. It is clear that Bankim does not repudiate belief in a transcendent spiritual being (the 'universal soul ... the Invisible and Inaccessible') which is characterized as love, power and justice (= 'Brahma, Vishnu, and Siva'). He also affirms that Hindus worship Nature as power or force (*śakti*) represented, depending on the manifestations of this force, by Kālī as hideously destructive or Durgā as resplendently creative, and so on. But they do not worship Nature in its own right; they 'worship' Nature as permeated by the universal soul which is the Ideal of beauty, power and purity, and which finds artistic expression in the sacred image. This image is not the divine universal power. It is separate from it—a human way of representing the Invisible and Inaccessible Ideal by means of a 'contract with [the worshipper's] heart *for the sake of culture and discipline* to treat [the image] as God's image'.

Thus vande and mātaram, the latter a fusion of land and transcendent divine Ideal, are, from the standpoint of the author of the novel, not 'anti-Muslim' or 'idolatrous' in any obvious or traditional sense, for according to Bankim the 'image [whether of Durgā or the motherland] is holy, not because the worshipper believes it to be his god—he believes in no such thing', but because it is an expression of a contract his society and he have made to treat that image, '*for the sake of culture and discipline*' (emphasis in original) as God's image. We are speaking here of a *cultural and personal contract* initiated by the worshipper, and one either opts into this contract or one does not. Nevertheless, this does emphasize the peculiarly Hindu nature of the arrangement.

Further, there can be no talk here of actual polytheism, since there is only one Supreme Being which manifests through different (culturally determined) forms and images. One cannot over-simplify, then, the theology of the hymn in context. Still, it does seem that in Bankim's estimation the hymn has force because it evokes this contract, and that actual worship of the supreme, 'invisible', 'inaccessible' transcendent 'universal soul' is intended to take place in and through homage paid to the motherland and various other representations of the deity. Thus a strong if indirect sense of 'worship' does seem to be intended by both Vande and Mātaram by the author of the novel. And it is important to note that the symbolism of the song as a whole is unapologetically Hindu.

But of course this does not resolve the problem, chiefly for two reasons: first, because by an official act, endorsed on countless political occasions, only the first two stanzas, and not the whole hymn, became the national song, and second, because the force of worship lies not primarily in the words used to carry it out (or even in the intention of the composer of the words), *but in the intention of the actual user of the words in question.* Let us inquire into both these points.

So far we have looked at the first two stanzas in the context of the hymn as a whole. In this context vande and mātaram do seem to carry the connotations of worship as latria, that is, worship in the strong sense; neither the historical usage of language nor that of the author of the novel militates against this understanding. But if a special gloss is put on the first two stanzas *as divorced from the rest of the hymn,* does this alter the situation? Let us consider now how the first two stanzas became the national song.

To begin with, it must be pointed out that from its earliest association with the novel, the hymn seems to have had a life of its own; there is evidence to show that the song, at least in embryonic form, was composed even before the novel was written. It then seems to have been completed and inserted into the story.[23] Indeed, it was sung at a public function or two as a hymn in its own right (though apparently not with political intent) after it appeared in the serial version of the novel but before the novel had been completed.[24] So there is precedent for saying that the hymn can be detached or at least dislodged from its narrative context. This makes it easier to see how the first two stanzas could be further detached from the song as a whole.

Soon after the publication of the song it attracted the notice of several writers and critics. It inspired a picture of Mother India by Harishchandra Haldar which was printed in 1885 in a journal called *Balak*. In 1886 Hemchandra Banerji wrote a poem, 'Rakhi Bandan', wherein he included the first two stanzas of Vandemataram.[25]

Here we must add that in contradistinction to the song *Vande Mātaram*, the title-words 'Vande Mātaram' also took on an independent existence. In the novel itself this expression is used a number of times in this way—as a password, and as a rallying or battle cry. Thus, both the song and the slogan 'Vande Mātaram' ran separately on parallel tracks, associated with but resorted to independently from the novel. On the one hand the song, or rather its first two stanzas, began to assume a profile on the nationalist stage. Rabindranath Tagore, Bengal's rising star as a poet towards the end of the nineteenth century, 'set to music the first two stanzas of Vande Mataram and sang it in the Congress session in Calcutta in 1896'.[26] On the other hand, the slogan began to have a political ring of its own: 'The first enthusiastic plea for the extensive use of the slogan Vandemataram was made by Yogendranath Vidyabhushan in his biography of Garibaldi published in 1890.'[27]

But the pro-active and inexorable politicization of both song and slogan took place in connection with the first partition of Bengal in 1905, which was to come into effect in October of that year. Earlier, on 7 August, thousands of students, who included Muslims, marched on the Calcutta Town Hall, chanting *Bande Mātaram*,[28] in protest against the impending partition. This governmental act to split greater Bengal into two parts on what Bengalis perceived to be sectarian grounds (with Hindus preponderantly in the west and Muslims preponderantly in the east), acted as the catalyst for the mass politicization of song and slogan among Indians seeking to defy British rule. Rameshcandra Datta, in his article 'Chatterji, Bankim Chandra', in the well-known eleventh edition of the *Encyclopaedia Britannica*, writes,

During Bankim Chandra Chatterji's lifetime the *Bande Mataram*, though its dangerous tendency was recognized, was not used as a party war-cry; it was not raised, for instance, during the Ilbert Bill agitation, nor by the students who flocked round the court during the trial of Surendra Nath Banerji in 1883. It has, however, obtained an evil notoriety in the agitations that followed the [1905] partition of Bengal.[29]

'Dangerous tendency' and 'evil notoriety', that is, in the eyes of those who sympathized with the machinations of the British government.

Evidence indicates that in the very early days of these agitations in defiance of the British and their loyal Indian civil servants, Muslims did not offer serious objection publicly to either song or slogan. We have already mentioned the Calcutta protest against the 1905 partition where people of both communities took part. S. Bhattacharya, in the book mentioned earlier, gives another example of joint action, this time in Rajahmundry in the Madras Presidency:

The *Hindu* reported in February 1907 that a Bala Bharati Samiti was organized and in Rajahmundry, 'students, all wearing Vande Mataram badges, and carrying aloft beautiful banners glittering with bold letters of Vande Mataram and Allah-o-Akbar' marched around the town and here and there the procession halted to sing the immortal song of Bankim Chandra Chatterjee.[30]

It did not take long, however, for both slogan and song to acquire sectarian resonances and in consequence to incur strong Muslim objections. This process began to crystallize as early as the first half of 1907. The *swadeshi* movement, viz. the favouring of products manufactured in one's own land (swadeshi) and the boycotting of foreign-made goods, had begun in Bengal; because of the rhetoric and symbolism associated with it, it was soon perceived by Muslim leaders in eastern Bengal as a Hindu movement, which had the effect of alienating Muslims. It was alleged that 'the Hindu Zemindars [landholders], by closing their *hāts* or bazars to those using or purchasing foreign goods, were coercing the [Muslims to] join the Boycott movement and thus helping the yawning of the gulf (*sic*) between the Hindus and the Muslims'.[31] This was adduced as one of the reasons underpinning the creation of the All India Muslim League at the end of 1906 to represent Muslim interests before the British as a counter-measure to the Indian National Congress which was seen as a Hindu-orientated organization. In short, partition exacerbated Hindu–Muslim rivalries and divisive allegiances.

Serious riots broke out between the two communities in eastern Bengal in 1907. The English-language militant paper, entitled *Bande Mataram*, which had started in August 1906 under Bengali Hindu editorial control, played a significant role, inadvertently perhaps, both by its title and its editorials, in Hinduizing the post-partition nationalist movement and alienating Muslims. Its reportage of the riots in Jamalpur is illustrative of this bias.

Here [in Jamalpur] Muslim rowdies attacked Hindu volunteers who were destroying foreign-made goods at a fair. Then they went on a rampage, burning down shops where swadeshi products were sold. ... Mobs attacked landlords' houses, destroyed debt bonds, and smashed an image of Durga. This act of desecration outraged Hindus in every part of the country. *Bande Mataram* fanned the flames by publishing an etching of the broken image along with headlines like 'Hindu Women wait with Knives in Their Hands/ Rather Death than Dishonour'. ... The cry of religion in danger and womankind in danger had predictable results. *Bande Mataram*'s sub-editor Hemendra Prasad Ghose spoke for hundreds when he wrote: 'It makes one's blood boil to think of it. ...Revenge is the word that escapes one's lips'.[32]

At around this time, a controversial Muslim publication, called *Lal Istahar* ('The Red Pamphlet'), did the rounds encouraging Muslims to have nothing to do with *Vande Mātaram*.[33] The die was thus cast for a collision course between Hindus and Muslims over use of both slogan and song during the increasingly fraught times of political turmoil that lay ahead.

It was in the early 1920s that a fresh head of steam built up over the issue. In his book, S.K. Das notes that in the Calcutta riots of 1921, Hindu rioters used *Vande Mātaram* as a provocative watchword against Muslims, and 'from this time onwards Vandemataram began to be used as the war-cry of the Hindu fanatics'[34] The scene was thus set for a resolution to be passed during the twenty-fifth annual session of the All India Muslim League in October 1937 condemning

... the attitude of the [Indian National] Congress in foisting *Bande Mataram* as the national anthem [*sic*] upon the country as callous, positively anti-Islamic, idolatrous in its inspiration and ideas, and definitely subversive of the growth of genuine nationalism in India. This meeting further calls upon Muslim members of various legislatures and public bodies in the country not to associate themselves in any manner with this highly objectionable song.[35]

Henceforth, for many Muslims, *Vande Mātaram* would be eyed with implacable suspicion.

But while Muslim opposition was hardening, moves were afoot at the same time on another front to exalt the song, or at least its first two stanzas. The Congress party was in search of a national anthem, and various patriotic songs were up for consideration, including *Vande Mātaram*. In an article on the modern theme of Mother India, Geeti Sen writes,

In [October] 1937 Nehru wrote to Subhas Chandra Bose, 'Certainly as suggested by you I shall discuss the *Bande Mataram* song with Dr Tagore'. The poet laureate confirmed that the second stanza describing the goddess enshrined in temples was inimical to Islamic tenets against the worship of icons. And after considerable debate, in the wisdom of things as they had changed, *Bande Mataram* was not chosen as the national anthem.[36]

The reference to the 'second stanza' as describing the goddess enshrined in temples is puzzling. From my enumeration of the verses of the hymn given earlier, the reader will see that this would include the first six stanzas—well in excess of half the song! Perhaps the poet was nodding, or meant something like the first two major sections of the hymn! In any case, no one else of note, least of all the principal personalities involved in seeking to identify a national song at the time, was ambiguous on this matter. All (including Nehru and Bose) understood the first two stanzas to comprise the first two verses as enumerated in my translation of the hymn, viz. the eulogistic description of natural features of the land identified as Mother.

The relevant committee of the Congress party in the main followed Tagore's advice in making its recommendation. It seems that Tagore came to the conventional view of what the first two stanzas were; in a letter to Nehru dated 26 October 1937, he wrote:

To me the spirit of tenderness and devotion expressed in [the hymn's] first portion, the emphasis it gave to beautiful and beneficent aspects of our motherland made a special appeal, so much so that I found no difficulty in dissociating it from the rest of the poem and from those portions of the book of which it is a part. ... I freely concede that the whole of Bankim's 'Vande Mataram' poem, read together with its context, is liable to be interpreted in ways that might wound Moslem susceptibilities, but a national song, though derived from it, *which has spontaneously come to consist only of the first two stanzas of the original poem,* need not remind us every time of the whole of it, much less of the story with which it was *accidentally* associated. *It has acquired a separate individuality* and an inspiring significance of its own in which I see nothing to offend any sect or community (emphasis added).[37]

In the relevant matter of predilection for the nationalist history and evocative power of the first two verses of the song, this is perhaps a case of like writing to like. Both Tagore and Nehru had grown up acculturated to what we may generically call Hindu beliefs and practices, irrespective of the humanistic turns of thought their minds had subsequently acquired. They had an a priori disposition, as it were, to regard the land as 'Mother' and to sit lightly to detaching the first two stanzas from both the rest of the song and the novel. For Tagore, this was a 'spontaneous' act.[38] But this could not be said for those disciplined in a staunchly monotheistic faith with sharply divergent theological presuppositions, and who were convinced that the song was idolatrous and that both author and novel had a history that was implacably anti-Muslim![39]

Let us now ask: can Bankim be regarded as having a bias against Muslims (which allegedly emerged in his work), and is *Ānandamaṭh* anti-Muslim, so as to justify such adverse Muslim opinion where both author and song were concerned? I have considered this question at some length in *ASB* (see esp. pp.61–70, 102–04); it is a matter of considerable complexity and resists a simplistic answer. I have discussed how Bankim tends to distinguish in his writings between, as he saw it, the Muslim as *deśi* ('home-grown', viz. locals who converted to Islam, large numbers of whom spoke Bengali, practised age-old Bengali ways and lived preponderantly in the eastern part of Bengal) and the Muslim as *jaban* or 'outsider', whose ancestry was derived from foreign lands such as Afghanistan, Turkey, or Persia, and who came to India to loot or rule and refused to integrate with the ways of the established Hindu majority. There is evidence to show that a particular *angst* emerged especially in some of Bankim's later writings with regard to the Islamic presence of the second category of Muslim. As for *Ānandamaṭh*, anti-Muslim sentiments may well be detected in the narrative, but these are expressed largely against a degenerate elite and in the mouths of impassioned characters of the story. The fact is that as *Vande Mātaram* embarked on its sectarian career, Muslim antipathy against song and slogan incorporated bias, not without reason, against their author.[40]

After they had completed their deliberations on the status of *Vande Mātaram*, Nehru's Working Committee reported as follows:

Working Committee feel that past associations, with their long record of suffering for the cause, as well as popular usage, have made the first two stanzas of this song a living and inseparable part of our national movement and as such they must command our affection and respect. There is nothing in these stanzas to which anyone can take exception. The other stanzas of the song are little known and hardly ever sung. ... [T]he Committee wish to point out that the modern evolution of the use of the song as part of national life is of infinitely greater importance than its setting in a historical novel before the national movement had taken shape. Taking all things into consideration therefore the Committee recommend that wherever the Bande Mataram is sung at national gatherings only the first two stanzas should be sung, with perfect freedom to the organisers to sing any other song of an unobjectionable character, in addition to, or in the place of, the Bande Mataram song.[41]

So here we have the makings of the current official view that has remained consistent to the present day. The characteristics of this view are that: (i) the song, especially the first two stanzas, is steeped in the history of the sacrifices made in the nationalist cause leading to India's freedom from foreign rule—this justifies its preferred status; (ii) the first two stanzas have acquired a 'separate individuality'; (iii) as such, the first two stanzas are religiously unobjectionable; and (iv), all things considered (a concession to the possibility of legitimate objections being made from a wider perspective), the singing of the song on nationalist or official occasions need not be compulsory. And yet it is the *national* song of a democratic, 'secular' republic!

Jinnah and the Muslim League were not convinced, and continued to object strenuously and tendentiously to the song, but to no avail. Neither side was prepared to compromise or give ground, and we have seen earlier, how, on 24 January 1950, the Chairman of the Constituent Assembly, Rajendra Prasad, finally made the decision making *Vande Mātaram* the national song. As *VMBS* points out, this was on the last day of the Assembly's last session, and a motion that was 'not debated upon or put to the vote, unlike the numerous resolutions debated and voted upon in the process of making the Constitution of the Republic', was accepted.[42] As noted before, since then on countless occasions the first two stanzas of *Ānandamath*'s song have been sung or chanted under official sanction in a national context that has remained contentious, and throughout this saga, to the present day, the matter has been exacerbated by right-wing Hindu organizations opportunistically vaunting the song and striving to make its singing compulsory at official functions and occasions. The issue has given no evidence of going away or subsiding with the passage of time, and it would be irresponsible to close one's eyes to this. Indeed, the promulgation or implementation of directives such as that of the HRD ministry referred to at the beginning of this essay often leads to violence on the streets.[43]

Perhaps the time has come for a national debate to be undertaken by the leadership on all sides, sanctioned by a responsible government, so as to resolve the matter. The alternative is a prolongation of a religio–political issue that remains highly charged and potentially explosive. With regard to the subject of this essay, this debate could include, besides the specific matters raised here, such wider issues as the distinction between a national song and a national anthem, the purpose of a national song/anthem in a secular, multicultural democracy, the implications of history in the context of India's nationalist movement, and determining the appropriate occasions and appropriate language(s) for singing a national song/anthem in a nation-state such as India.

But to return to the immediate crisis, it has been suggested by a recent participant that an investigatory body of experts be set up to elicit the true meaning of vande in the context of the national song. This suggestion is really a cry for political leadership in the matter. I noted earlier that the force of worship lies really in the intention behind the use of the relevant terms, not primarily in the words themselves. One cannot legislate to determine intentions behind words. But there is sufficient ambiguity in the meaning of vande so as to leave room for manoeuvre. It may be used, as we have seen, in the sense of latria or the worship due to the Supreme Being alone, but it *can also* signify 'worship' or homage in the weak sense of dulia, in the sense, that is, of salutations or reverence offered to a non-divine object. As an immediate measure to defuse the situation (in preparation for the wider debate), it would be a constructive step if the Indian government exploited this ambiguity with respect to the national song, and issued a clarification to the effect that not only should its singing be non-obligatory, but also that it would be open to the utterer of vande to invest this word with the intention dictated by the utterer's conscience. This could then be adopted by individuals and communities as they saw fit. Such promulgation would go a long way towards immediately removing the sting of religious and political contentiousness that has lurked for so long in India's national song.

NOTES AND REFERENCES

1. I am grateful to Vinay Lal, the editor of this volume, for a number of helpful suggestions.

2. According to the Indian census of 2001, over 80 per cent of the 1.25 billion or so of the population were designated as Hindus, 13.4 per cent as Muslims, 2.5 per cent as Christians, and about 2 per cent as Sikhs among the various religious traditions. In this context, the term 'secular' carries a predominantly negative connotation, viz. *not* granting privileged status. This is in direct contrast to the situation in nation-states which define themselves in terms of one or more religious traditions.

3. The title-words of the national anthem are *Jana Gana Mana* (composed by Rabindranath Tagore), but the sense and context of this song are entirely different and, by comparison, largely uncontroversial; we shall return to the national anthem in due course.

4. Some of which is factually disputable!

5. This is how the adoption of *Vande Mātaram* as the national song by the Constituent Assembly on 24 January 1950 is reported to have taken place (the

President of the Assembly, Rajendra Prasad, is speaking in session): 'There is one matter which has been pending for discussion, namely the question of the national anthem. ... [It] has been felt that, instead of taking a formal decision by means of a resolution [by the House], it is better if I make a statement with regard to the national anthem. Accordingly, I make this statement. ... The composition consisting of the words and music known as "Jana Gana Mana" is the national anthem of India, subject to such alterations in the words as the Government may authorise as occasion arises, and the song "Vande Mataram", which has played a historic part in the struggle for Indian freedom, shall be honoured equally with "Jana Gana Mana" and shall have equal status with it. (Applause). I hope that will satisfy the Members,' See Julius Lipner, Ānandamaṭh, or The Sacred Brotherhood by Bankimcandra Chatterji (New York: Oxford University Press, 2005), p. 81 n128. So it appears that both the national anthem and national song were adopted not on the basis of a formal resolution, but on the basis of a statement it was 'felt' that the Chair should issue. As if to indicate the confusion underlying the choice of date for the centenary celebrations on 7 September 2006, The Times of India online, in an article entitled, 'Vande Mataram not compulsory in W[est] B[engal]', reported from Kolkata (6 September 2006) that 'Congress officials said the party has lined up a series of programmes, including ... hoisting the Vande Mataram flag, the first national flag hoisted at the Parsi Bagan here in 1906.'So was this incident, in the mind of the Kolkata Congress, the occasion for the centenary celebrations rather than that mentioned by Soni, the Culture Minister, in the extract quoted above?

6. Thus, 'No Muslim can sing "Vande Mataram" if he considers himself to be a true believer,' said Maulana Mahmood Madani, general secretary of Jamiat Ulama-i-Hind, New Delhi, during his visit to the city [of Surat] on Tuesday [5 September 2006].' Available at: http://www.timesofindia.indiatimes.com (posted 5 September 2006; accessed 12 March 2007). 'We are ready to say Jai Bharat Mata [Victory to Mother India], Jai Hind [Victory to India] and sing Jana Gana Mana but don't force us to sing Vande Mataram,' says noted Shia cleric and vice-president of the All-India Muslim Personal Law Board, Maulana Kalbe Sadiq.' The Indian Express online, available at http://www.indianexpress.com/story/12096.html (accessed 12 March 2007).

7. http://www.timesofindia.indiatimes.com (posted 5 September 2006; accessed 12 March 2007). Apparently the SGPC then relented and permitted the singing of the song; see article entitled 'India sings Vande Mataram in unison', available at http://www.timesofindia.indiatimes.com (posted 8 September 2006; accessed 12 March 2007). As we shall point out, the title of this article was somewhat optimistic. 'Communal/communalism' is India-speak for 'sectarian/sectarianism'.

8. Translated with an extensive 'Introduction' and 'Critical Apparatus' by Julius J. Lipner (New York: Oxford University Press, 2005).

9. It is this centenary edition that formed the basis of my English translation of the novel, and to which I shall refer in this essay.

10. The description has been taken from my translation in *ASB*; see Part I, ch.11 of the novel (p.150).

11. 'Alien' because for Bankim, the Muslim rulers of greater Bengal and their civil-servant co-religionists, were, like the British, outsiders. As discussed in *ASB*, Bankim tends to distinguish between *desi* Muslims—sons and daughters of the soil (most of whom came from convert stock)—and *jabans*, Muslims whose ancestry was foreign and who made no real effort to integrate with the people of the land. See *ASB*, pp.63–7.

12. Taken from *ASB*, pp.144–6. The hymn is annotated in the Critical Apparatus, pp. 242–5.

13. For a discussion of the derivative history of the hymn, both as to format and content, see *ASB*, pp.86–91.

14. This last gave rise to divisive tendencies since the early nationalist movement in Bengal, to which *Ānandamaṭh* contributed conspicuously, displayed a bias in favour of Hindu symbolism.

15. 'To be a stotra ... a composition must conform to some purely formal properties of style. Incomparability of the deity to whom the stotra is offered is conveyed by the mannerisms of descriptive excess. Stotras also exhibit a usually circular, repetitive movement, coming back, after each cycle of excessive praise, to the signature phrase describing the essential attributes of the object of worship.' Sudipta Kaviraj, 'Laughter and Subjectivity: The Self-Ironical Tradition in Bengali Literature', *Modern Asian Studies* 34, 2 (2000), p. 389. Early forms of stotras to the Goddess occur in the *Devī Māhātmya* section of the *Mārkaṇḍeya Purāṇa* and in some versions of parts of the Mahābhārata, that is, several centuries before the beginning of the second millennium CE. See Thomas B. Coburn, *Devī Māhātmya: The Crystallization of the Goddess Tradition* (Delhi: Motilal Banarasidas, 1984), especially Part III. The fact that the hymn is in the style of a stotra lends credence to the view that Bankim may well have derived part of it from the liturgy of a Kālī temple in Lalgola in Murshidabad district where he was staying for some time in 1873–4. See *ASB*, pp.37–8, 90–1.

16. It is no accident that in some, especially Hindu fundamentalist, circles today, as a direct consequence of the traditional veneration for Sanskrit, there is a reluctance either to sing only a part of the hymn or to sing it in translation. Tanika Sarkar has recorded the ideology underlying this reluctance. 'The song [*Vande Mātaram*] is chanted in full, at prescribed times, at all daily *shakhas* or training sessions of the RSS [a right-wing militant Hindu organization, often associated with the BJP]. To the combine [= the Sangh Parivar, a "family" (*parivār*) or "combine" of religiocultural bodies of the extreme right, including the RSS], this remains the real national anthem. Rabindranath's song, *Jana Gana Mana*—the official anthem of the Indian state—is widely condemned [by the Parivar] as a paltry substitute. ... The RSS thus restores [*Vande Mātaram*] to its old status as a sacred chant, not a word of which can be altered. Neither the Bengali nor the Sanskrit passages may be translated, since the original words are supposed to contain sacred energy. When I asked why the song is never abbreviated, members of the organization told me that it is symbolic of the integrity of the Motherland. It is always displayed against a map of undivided

India, expressing the organization's refusal to accept the partition [into India and Pakistan] of the subcontinent.' Tanika Sarkar, *Hindu Wife, Hindu Nation: Community, Religion and Cultural Nationalism* (New Delhi: Permanent Black, 2001), p. 273. This ideological appropriation of a national symbol is to some extent politically analogous to the appropriation of the national flag and/or national anthem by right-wing organizations in other contexts, for example, the British National Party in the UK. It remains to be seen whether this Parivar ideology, with its veneration for the original language(s) of the national song, especially Sanskrit, and the song's historical associations, could in due course be prepared to abandon or substitute the present national song for one in the official (national?) language of the Indian state, Hindi.

17. From the article, 'Jai Bharat Mata is fine, but don't force Vande Mataram', *The Indian Express* online, Lucknow, 5 September 2006, available at: http://www. indianexpress.com/story/12096.html (accessed 12 March 2007).

18. From 'Furore over AP's diktat on *Vande Mataram*', *The Times of India* online, available at: http://www.timesofindia.indiatimes.com (posted 5 September 2006: accessed 12 March 2007).

19. *Prahlāda uvāca: śravaṇaṃ kīrtanaṃ viṣṇoḥ smaraṇaṃ pādasevanam/ arcanaṃ vandanaṃ dāsyaṃ sakhyam ātmanivedanam// iti puṃsārpitā viṣṇau bhaktiś cennavalakṣaṇā....BhPu.* 7.5.23-4.

20. For example, there are a number of instances in the great Sanskrit epic, the *Mahābhārata*. Thus, in his address to Duryodhana, the Kaurava Karṇa says, 'You are greeted, O king, by the twice-born (Brahmins), and revered by kings (*vandyamāno dvijai rājan pūjyamānaś ca rājabhiḥ*)', 3.226.9 of the Bhandarkar Oriental Research Institute critical edition.

21. The bowdlerized translation of the hymn given in Basanta Koomar Roy's rendering of the novel, first published as *Dawn Over India* with an eye to India's freedom movement (and re-published much later as *Bankim Chandra Chatterji: Anandamath, Translated and Adapted from Original Bengali* (sic), by Vision Books, New Delhi, 1992), seeks to sidestep the problem by unabashedly omitting all specific Hindu references in the song, including those referring to the Goddess as Mother. Here, for example, is how verses 6 and 7 are translated by Roy (p. 39):

Thou as strength in arms of men,
Thou as faith in hearts dost reign. (verse 6)

Himalaya-crested one, rivalless,
Radiant in thy spotlessness,
Thou whose fruits and waters bless,
Mother, hail! (verse 7)

I append my own translation of these two verses with the original Bengali/ Sanskrit, for comparison:

Mother you're our strength of arm (*bāhute tumi mā śakti*)
And in our hearts the loving balm (*hṛdaye tumi mā bhakti*)

Yours the form we shape in every shrine! (*tomāri pratimā gaḍi mandire mandire*).

For you are Durga, bearer of the tenfold power (*tvaṃ hi durgā daśapraharaṇadhāriṇī*)

And wealth's Goddess, dallying on the lotus flower (*kamalā kamaladalavihāriṇī*)

You are Speech, to you I bow

To us wisdom you endow (*vāṇī vidyādāyinī namāmi tvām*).

I have annotated these two verses, justifying my translation, in *ASB*, p.245. The reader will note that Roy has omitted the last line of verse 6 which speaks of worship in shrines/temples (mandir), and has expurgated specifically Hindu connotations and names in verse 7. In fact, his translation of verse 7 has little, if any, bearing on the original text! This reductive attempt has failed signally to mollify either Hindus or Muslims.

22. *The Statesman*, 8 October 1882.

23. See *ASB*, pp. 86–91. Here I have also considered the possibility, raised by some commentators, as to whether part or all of the hymn was already in existence in some form which Bankim took over and adapted or completed for inclusion in the novel. This possibility has recently been discussed again in the pages of the Bengali paper, *Ānanda Bājār Patrikā*. See the article by Amitrasudan Bhattacarja in the 7 November 2006 issue, and subsequent letters to the Editor on 22 and 23 November 2006. However, whether the hymn was wholly or partially composed by Bankim is not strictly relevant for our purposes. We are mainly interested in that part of the hymn which became India's national song after it started its career in *Ānandamaṭh*.

24. See *ASB*, p.74.

25. S.K. Das, *The Artist in Chains: The Life of Bankimchandra Chatterji* (New Delhi: New Statesman Publishing, 1984), p. 215.

26. See S. Bhattacharya, *Vande Mataram: The Biography of a Song* (New Delhi: Penguin Books, 2003), p. 106 n1 (abbr.*VMBS*). But this date is contested by A. Chakrabarti who says that Tagore's performance was at the Congress session in Calcutta six years earlier. See A. Chakrabarti, *Gāner Bhelāy Belā Abelāy* (Kolkata: Primer Publications, 1996), p. 29.

27. S.K. Das, *The Artist in Chains*, p. 215.

28. The Bengali form of the title-words (since Bengali has no v sound).

29. Rameshcandra Datta, 'Chatterji, Bankim Chandra', *Encyclopaedia Britannica*, vol. 6, eleventh edn, 1910, pp. 9–10.

30. Bhattacharya, *Vande Mataram*.

31. H. Mukherjee and U. Mukherjee, *India's Fight for Freedom or The Swadeshi Movement (1905-1906)* (Calcutta: Firma K.L. Mukhopadhyay, 1958), p. 148.

32. Peter Heehs, *The Bomb in Bengal: The Rise of Revolutionary Terrorism in India, 1900-1910*, (Delhi: Oxford University Press, 1993), p. 106.

33. 'In the same year [1907], an anonymous Bengali pamphlet, printed on lurid red paper, began to circulate among Muslims exhorting them: 'Not a single

Muhammadan should join the perverted *Swadeshi* agitation of the Hindus. ...
Oh Muhammadans, sing not Bande Mataram!', *VMBS*, p. 25.

34. Das, *Artist in Chains*, p. 220. 'In the 1920s what is new is a critique of Bankim
    and his works in ideological terms from the Muslim point of view (p. 26).
    ... The opinion in the Muslim press was that Bankim "was a Muslim-hater to
    the innermost core" (1918); that "he forever alienated a large community" by
    displaying "intense communal hatred" (1920); and that his works "had unjustly
    stigmatized the Muslims" (1925). These typical examples of the evaluation of
    Bankim in Bengali Muslim literary journals naturally influenced the attitude to
    his most celebrated creation, Vande Mataram.' *VMBS*, p. 29.

35. Ram Gopal, *Indian Muslims: A Political History (1858-1947)* (London: Asia
    Publishing House, 1959), pp. 256–7.

36. Geeti Sen, 'Iconising the Nation: Political Agendas', *IIC Quarterly*, vol. 29, nos.
    3 and 4 (Winter 2002–Spring 2003), p. 160.

37. Quoted from *VMBS*, pp. 33–4.

38. In *ASB*, pp. 99–100, I show how the personification of the land (*bhūmi*) as
    female and as spouse of the king and thus mother of his subjects is rooted in
    Hindu tradition.

39. Similarly, even Gandhi, in his weekly paper *The Harijan* (1 July 1939), could
    write rather naively: 'As a lad when I knew nothing of *Ananda Math* or even
    Bankim, *Vande Mataram* gripped me. I associated the purest national spirit
    with it. It never occurred to me it was a Hindu song or meant only for Hindus.
    Unfortunately, now we have fallen on evil days. All that was pure gold before
    has become base metal today.' Quoted from *India Today*, international
    edition, 1 September 1997, p.55. But here is a representative Muslim view of
    the cultural blindness governing those Hindu Indians who could accept as
    unobjectionable the description of the land as 'Mother' of a song whose first
    two verses Tagore regarded as only 'accidentally associated' with the story
    in which it occurs: 'The context of the story entirely excludes the idea of the
    "Mother" being interpreted as the common motherland of all Indians, Hindus,
    Muslims and others. She symbolizes the motherland only as representing the
    culture, religion and political history of Hindus exclusively. ... It is a typical
    illustration of the psychology of a very large majority of Congress leaders in
    India that, when they address a public meeting about the necessity of separating
    religion from politics, they open the proceedings with this song.' Quoted
    from *The Civil and Military Gazette* (Lahore), 12 October 1937, in W. Gould,
    Hindu Nationalism and the Language of Politics in Late Colonial India (Cambridge:
    Cambridge University Press, 2004), p. 231. It may be of interest to note that,
    to the best of my knowledge, Indian Christians, currently numbering about
    2.5 per cent of the population (some thirty or so millions), and belonging to a
    variety of denominations, have never protested officially or en masse against
    the adoption or singing of the song. I suggest that an important reason for this
    may be grounded in Christian theology of Incarnation.

40. Certainly there is no call to say, on the basis of a reading of *Ānandamaṭh*, as
    Professor Tanika Sarkar unfortunately does in her contribution to the jointly-
    authored polemic, *The Vedas, Hinduism, Hindutva* (Ebong Alap, 2005), p.123,

that 'The goddess demands the blood of Muslims' (this is nowhere justified by text), or even that 'the mantra [viz. the song *Vande Mātaram*] is first heard in the aftermath of a battle between British-led troops of the nawab and the santans, who lead a mob of villagers', as if the song is introduced in a context that encourages and legitimates violence, which is extendable to Muslims; cf. her book *Hindu Wife, Hindu Nation*, p.178. From my translation of the hymn's introduction in the novel referred to earlier, the reader will note that the hymn is sung by the santān-leader Bhabananda in a non-martial context. Overcome by the beauty and tranquility of the moonlit landscape, he is 'no longer ... the skilled, valiant figure of the battlefield' as he sings the hymn. In a footnote in the original, Bankim points out that the hymn is to be sung in the musical mode Mallār, a non-martial mode (see my annotation of this mode in *ASB*, pp. 243–4).

41. Quoted in *VMBS*, pp. 35–6.
42. Ibid, pp. 43–4.
43. It is a common practice among analysts of Indian politics to avert their eyes from the religious dimensions of the issues they discuss and adopt a reductive approach, seeking to give a full account of their subject in non-religious terms. Such attempts at analysis misrepresent their subject and have little or no bearing on the realities they profess to clarify. From earliest times in the nationalist movement, Indian politics have been steeped in theological and religious issues. These must be fully acknowledged if proper discussion is to take place.

JOANNE PUNZO WAGHORNE

Global Gurus and the Third Stream of American Religiosity
Between Hindu Nationalism and Liberal Pluralism

When some of the true Samnyâsins, however, devote their thoughts and meditations to philosophical and religious problems, their utterances, which sway large multitudes that gather around them in their own country, cannot fail to engage our attention and sympathy, particularly if, as in the case of Râmakrishna, their doctrines are spread by zealous advocates not only in India, but in America also, nay even in England.

—F. Max Müller[1]

F. Max Müller, still famous for his edition of the Vedas, the holiest texts of orthodox Hindus and usually credited as the founder of the comparative study of religion, published only one book on contemporary religion in India[2], a small almost forgotten volume, *Râmakrishna, His Life and Sayings*. In his preface, Müller explains that this saint 'has been so often mentioned in Indian, American, and English newspapers that a fuller account of his life and doctrine seemed to me to be welcome'.[3] I now have a discarded copy from the Free Library of Menomonie, a small city in Wisconsin, which shows the wide appeal, even in 1899, of this particular strand of Hindu religiosity. The presence of such a volume in the Midwest is not surprising considering the impact of Sri Ramakrishna's most zealous disciple, Swami Vivekananda, at the World's Parliament of Religions held in Chicago just seven years earlier. The 1890s witnessed 'the dawn of religious pluralism'[4] in the World's Parliament, the founding moments of the academic study of religion in the United States, and the first serious export of not just Hindu thought but Hindu teachers. The often reviled and just as often-revered gurus, we cannot forget, came long before over a million 'Asian–Indians', as the official census terms them, built the temples and religious organizations that made 'Hinduism' obvious even to the most oblivious eye. The confluence of the founding of the academic study of religion, the dawn of pluralism, and the first popular wave of Americans—at that time mostly middle or upper middle-class white Protestants[5]—dappling with or outright joining Hindu-based, guru-centred organizations requires some serious reflection.

Today the conjoined matter of Euro–American adoption of Hindu religiosity and Euro–American production of knowledge about Hinduism are entangled in complex and controversial issues as *heritage Hindus*[6] lay claim to their heritage. Indeed, the study of Hindu religiosity and the option of adopting Hindu practice fall into two periods: 1890s to 1965, and then post-1965 with the opening of the United States to immigration from India. With the second wave of new immigrants from not only India but also Asia in general, a new consciousness of ethnic identity re-emerged in the 1980s, which had almost faded with the intense patriotism fostered during and after the Second World War. At the same time a renewed consciousness of Hinduism as a national identity gained power in India. In *Diaspora of the Gods: Modern Hindu Temples in a Middle-Class Urban World*, I charted the growth of new Hindu temples among urban Anglophone Indians of Washington DC, London, and Chennai (Madras). These temples rarely became a religious home to those outside the Indian ethnic fold and indeed that was not my interest. But now as I reflect on the broad topic of Hinduism in America, I see that the current 'ethnization' of Hinduism within the American context can no longer be ignored. Debates have raged within the academia over 'who speaks for Hinduism'[7] and within the energetic Dharma Association of North America whose meetings now conjoin with the annual meeting of the American Academy of Religion. The current use of the term 'pluralism' reflects these realities. But the current sense of pluralism assumes *difference* while gesturing toward understanding, tolerance, and even re-visioning personal faith in the light of this encounter. However pluralism eschews—I would argue—the possibilities for the kind of *third stream* of mixing, matching, adopting, and adapting that characterized the earliest period of American encounter with 'Hinduism' and further appears to be re-emerging within the American religious context—in both the academic attention to rising guru movements and in the now shared experience of both Euro and Indian American as devotees of common divine teachers. Confronting all of the problems of race, ethnicity, and nationalism involved in these encounters confounds me, but following the old route of a historian of religions, I propose that a return to origins is in order. The actions of Swami Vivekananda in America and later in India, the continued conversations between the Swami and the most influential advocate of the comparative enterprise, Max Müller, and the willingness of some affluent Americans to join Hindu-oriented movements at the turn of the last century hold, I will argue, the keys to understanding the multidimensional processes of the 'universalization' of Hinduism beyond the diaspora and beyond Hindu nationalism.

I fully admit that as a recovering historian of religions of the Chicago School, I lapse into the uncontrollable desire to *compare*, fully aware of the issues with universalism/s and generalization/s. However, I remind my readers that understanding processes of universalization of any religious system has long been central to religious studies—with 'Hinduism' often kept in limbo within our categories. In the 1870s and 1880s, the years just prior to the World's Parliament, 'often regarded as the beginning of *Religionswissenschaft*, or the modern science of religion',[8] academics in the United States and Europe debated classifications between 'natural religions' and 'high religion' or 'race religions' and 'founded religions', or between 'world religions'/'universal religion', and 'national religions'.[9] Apparently the major point of disagreement between the turn-of-the century's foremost scholars of the field 'had to do with the broad-stroke distinctions they were apt to draw among the so-called higher religions, namely the distinction between the ethnically or geographically specific "national religions", on the one hand, and religions that transcended such ethnic and national boundaries, or "world religions"'.[10] Keeping Masuzawa's warning about such arbitrary classifications in mind, Hinduism has nonetheless lived between these two categories for over a century with its status see-sawing between inclusion in a universalist framework via its classical Sanskrit texts, but then equally understood as mired the relentlessly bounded system of *caste*. At the very moment when scholars were at work constructing the differences between world religions and national religions, Swami Vivekananda rose in the Parliament of Religions not only to present Hinduism as universal but to leave his audience with suggestion that the catholicity of his Hinduism, its inherent inclusion of all from all walks of life, could serve as the very model for a rising new kind of universal religion,

The Hindu might have failed to carry out all of his plans, but if there ever is to be a universal religion, it must be one which would hold no location in place and time, which would be infinite like the God it would preach, whose sun shines upon the followers of Krishna or Christ; saints or sinners alike; which would not be the Brahman or Buddhist, or Christian or Mohammedan, but the sum total of all of these, and still have infinite space for development; which in its catholicity would embrace in its infinite arms and formulate a place for every human being ...[11]

With this grand leap over the widely accepted universality of Christianity, with some scholars including Islam and/or Buddhism as 'universal', Vivekananda redefined the terms of the debate but in subtle ways that moved between persons, bodies, nations, and races and spoke to certain members of the American public in a delightfully ambiguous and yet mutually intelligible language.

Any attempt to untangle the treads of nationalism, ethnic consciousness, emerging pluralism, and universalisms for Swami Vivekananda, and indeed what is often called Neo-Hinduism, would be impossible without three insightful new books: *Guru English* by Srinivas Aravamudan (2006), *A History of Modern Yoga* by Elizabeth De Michelis (2004), and *Religious Revivalism and National Discourse* by Shamita Basu (2002).[12] In addition, the last decades have seen a revival of intensive work, sometimes controversial, on Sri Ramakrishna by Sudhir Kakar (1991) and Kripal (1998) and the Ramakrishna movement and Swami Vivekananda by Gwilym Beckerlegge (2000 and 2006) and Carl T. Jackson (1994).[13] These are my valued conversation partners crisscrossing between India, the United States, and the United Kingdom. I offer this essay, then, not as a re-engagement with primary materials or with new ethnographic insights on the worldwide Ramakrishna Missions but as a *reading* of new readings of Vivekananda—a prolegomena to larger issues in the processes of the globalization of Hinduism.

SWAMI VIVEKANANDA'S CURIOUS DOUBLE ROLE

'Don Yellow Robes Chicagoans to Imitate the "Holy Men" of India', the *Chicago Daily Tribune* reported on 11 July 1897 (p. 25). The article featured a group of Chicago 'believers in occultism, meditation, concentration, and the general "practice of yoga"' who would gather in Michigan with their Swami 'Abayananda' [Abhayananda] a French émigré, 'the only woman monk in the world, and the latest follower of the yellow-robed order of East Indian religious mendicants'. This 'yellow-robed order' referred to those—including this Mme Marie Louise—initiated by Swami Vivekananda at Thousand Islands near the Canadian border of New York State.[14] Four years before, the young Swami from Calcutta had electrified the World's Parliament of Religions. At this moment, in 1897, Swami Vivekananda had just returned to India, after fruitful years of lecturing and writing in the United States and the United Kingdom. His newly founded Ramakrishna Mission was less than two months old and sadly he was within five years of his early death. Out of these brief years, the complex and often controversial life story of Swami Vivekananda came to signify seemingly opposite trends that continue to characterize the globalization of Hinduism: the coterminous re-linking of Hindu religion to 'a way of life' embedded within Indian cultural, ethnic, and some strongly argue *national* identity and the equally intriguing un-linking of Hindu religiosity from the very same ethnic-cultural and national ground. However, whether acting as spokesman for 'Hinduism' at the Parliament in Chicago, teaching yoga to a few Western disciples in a Victorian cottage in upstate New York,[15] or speaking at triumphal gatherings in Madras,[16] Vivekananda came to be envisioned by the Indian and American public as a turbaned and saffron-robed swami—the way he appeared in a popular poster widely distributed during the World's Parliament of Religions and as he chose to present himself at the Parliament.[17]

Today such peripatetic world teachers, now more commonly called gurus, and the organizations that surround them remain deeply venerated by some, yet suspected by others as they apparently were even in the 1890s. The *Chicago Daily Tribune* reported on Vivekananda at the World's Parliament in almost breathless terms describing him as he took the podium, 'Dr Nobel then presented Swami Vivekananda, the Hindoo monk, who was applauded loudly as he stepped to the center of the platform. He wore an orange robe, bound with a scarlet sash, and a pale yellow turban. The customary smile was on his handsome face and his eyes shown with animation.'[18] Six years later the same newspaper would report on 'Chicago Followers of Strange Religions', which included those Western followers associated with Vivekananda's teachings. Writing with undisguised cynicism in the same style as the earlier report on the woman swami, the reporter concluded, 'all of the followers after strange gods and even stranger religions labor, talk, and practice their rites. ... the "sacred word" of the Hindoos, the Buddhists, the Confucians, the Brahmans ... the Persians, and the Mohammedans, alike is recited over and through Chicago daily'.[19] At this point, many in the press seemed to make no distinction between the occult and what most textbooks now classify as the major religions of Asia.

This shift from awed veneration to sarcastic quips seems to parallel the two very public faces of global gurus: their function as spokespersons, apologists, and unifiers of the Hindu religion for Hindus in India and heritage Hindus in the United States as well as the broad-minded international public (for which they are respected), and their other role as synthesizers and creators of newer and more universalized religious forms that break the bounds of territory, race, and ethnicity (for which they and their followers are often treated with suspicion). Again, the great Swami Vivekananda took on both functions—indeed he is credited with pioneering the current popular fusion of generalized Hindu spirituality, yogic techniques, with pre-existing Euro–American esotericism.[20] The monks of the worldwide organization that he initiated continue to serve, like their founder, both constituencies and to perform both functions, although not without tension.[21] Today this conflicting picture of Swami Vivekananda reappears as seemingly divergent organizations claim him as an icon of modern Hindu nationalism, or as an early apostle of a new world theology, religious pluralism, and even New Age movements.

After years of obscurity, re-enactments of the World's Parliament of Religions once again made headlines and, once again Swami Vivek-ananda's spirited defence and articulation of 'Hindu religion', as he phrased it, re-emerges along with the memory of his universal message. In 1993, the Vishwa Hindu Parishad (VHP) of America organized 'Global Vision 2000' in Washington DC to mark the centenary of the Parliament in Chicago. At the same time, the newly formed Council for a World's Parliament of Religions, in which the monks of the Ramakrishna–Vedanta Society of Chicago 'played a leading role',[22] held the second Parliament in Chicago exactly one hundred years later with 8,000 people attending. The second Parliament produced, as its organizers put it, 'a groundbreaking document, *Towards a Global Ethic: An Initial Declaration*. The declaration is a powerful statement of the ethical common ground shared by the world's religious and spiritual traditions'.[23] This second Parliament intended to carry on—albeit in a distinctly modified form[24]—what Joseph Kitagawa described as the focus of the first Parliament, 'not the critical, scholarly inquiry concerning religions, but rather the religious or philosophical basics for the unity of all religions'.[25] Speeches at Global Vision 2000 also invoked Swami Vivekananda's 'Universal Religion'[26] and spoke of 'lifting the thoughts of people to higher ideals of peace, harmony and unity',[27] but the emphasis as recorded in the speeches and the descriptions of the conference centred on 'our culture' and the 'great son of our motherland'.[28] Although the event in Washington DC was very well attended, many other Indian–American organizations waged strong protest before and during the conference, in part, over their seeming co-opting of Swami Vivekananda. The *Washington Post* quoted one protester, 'Swami Vivekananda's ... message is very universal, but the World Hindu Organization takes a very narrow view, to exclude everybody else except those who accept their political agenda'.[29]

Organizers of Global Vision 2000 retorted by saying 'that the Washington conference was purely a cultural and religious gathering intended to help reconnect Indian expatriates to their Hindu roots',[30] and indeed, many first and second generation Indian Hindus settled in the United States viewed the event as celebration of their Hindu heritage. Speeches at Global Vision invoked Swami Vivekananda's message 'to unify the religious vision of humanity' but created though Hindu religious sensibilities.[31] A speech by Sri Tarlabalu Jagadguru of Sringere on 'Hindu Visions of Global Peace' affirmed: 'To those who are enlightened and noble, the whole world is one family. Here is the Hindu vision of the whole world as one Global Family based on pure human love.'[32] Others later reflected that the conference had succeeded in 'deepening the understanding our culture and what it stands for, and broadening our vision of the world we live in'.[33]

For others, Swami Vivekananda's universalizing message to a divided world elided into his brilliant articulation of a generalized Hindu religion to unify a divided nation. In a speech arguing that the 'RSS fulfills the mission of Swami Vivekananda', a leader of the social service projects of this nationalist Hindu organization built the case, through a careful selection of quotes from Swami Vivekananda, that '[h]is life mission was to rejuvenate and reestablish this Hindu nation'.[34] He quotes the foremost apostle of Sri Ramakrishna as saying: 'It is specially for the preservation of the Hindu race and religion that Bhagawan Sri Ramakrishna, the embodiment of mercy, has incarnated himself.'[35] He provided no reference for the quote but may be relying on the ongoing work in India of the Vivekananda Kendra, 'a spiritually oriented service mission which reflects Swami Vivekananda's vision of a glorious India in action', founded by former General Secretary of the RSS, Eknath Ranade. In a memoir, Ranade recalls defending his joint involvement with the RSS and Vivekananda's philosophy, '... it is Vivekananda's philosophy that made me an R.S.S worker. ... R.S.S. is nothing but the extension of Swamiji's work'.[36] Ranade spearheaded the construction of the now famous Vivekananda Rock Memorial at Kanyakumari.

While many who protested Global Vision 2000 and others who extolled the new World's Parliament of Religions, saw clear contrasts between the universalism of *their* Swami Vivekananda and the icon of Hindutva that the RSS and VHP had constructed, their differences are not so easy to theorize. The second World's Parliament of Religions and Global Vision 2000 shared a common understanding that there are bounded religions in this world and that these boundaries should be accepted even celebrated, but that an overall *commonality* exists on some generalized level under certain conditions. They also share common sensibilities that modernization acts on older systems and demands new configurations, reformation, and re-formation. Importantly, they *both* contrast with another realm of the modern religious world—now even more apparent as contemporary globalization exceeds the worldwide penetration of the Pax Britannia at the time of the first Parliament of Religions—a *third stream* of highly syncretic newly wrought or 'discovered' religious systems. My major concern will be this 'third component', which the Dutch scholar of New Age religions, Wouter J. Hanegraaff, identifies in Western culture[37] and which I also see as an important component of global Hinduism, especially in connection to the contemporary rise of guru-centred movements worldwide. Thus, I am identifying three modes of the globalization of Hinduism within the American context (there may indeed be more and many individuals mix these models):

(1) The 'liberal' mode of Hindu heritage citizens identifying with the generalized system of *pluralism* as 'Hindus' in a multi-religious domain.

(2) The 'conservative' mode of heritage Hindus identifying their Hinduness (Hindutva) with an ethnic identity derived from India as the Motherland.

(3) The 'spiritual' mode of Hindu consciousness and yogic practices as open to worldwide participation usually via a guru and guru-centred communities.

THE LIBERALS AT THE PARLIAMENT AND SHARED SENSIBILITIES BEYOND LIBERALISM

On the opening day of the first World's Parliament of Religions, the Revd John Henry Barrows, the prime organizer of this unprecedented congress, addressed the assembled invited representatives of the world's 'major' religions,

We are met as religious men, believing here in this capital of material wonders, in the presence of an Exposition which displays the unparalleled marvels of stream and electricity, that there is a spiritual root to all human progress ... We are met, I believe, in the temper of love, determined to bury, at least for the time, our sharp hostilities, anxious to find out wherein we agree, eager to learn what constitutes the strength of other faiths and the weakness of our own. And we are met as conscientious and truth-seeking men, in council where no one is asked to surrender or abate his individual convictions, and where, I will add, no one would be worthy of a place if he did. [38]

Barrows brief address simply assumes distinct and even codified religious traditions with clear 'representatives'—all in common consort with the engineering miracles of the century and the lauded *progress* of modernity tempered by religious values. The very notion of 'representatives' and even the term 'Parliament' assumes a democratic polity. Interestingly the organizing committee invited only the 'leading representatives from the great Historic Religions of the world',[39] and apparently assumed that the common language would be English. Representatives delivered their addresses in this de facto lingua franca. 'Delegates' included African American Christians and several prominent women. Notably absent were any of the popularly known Native American chiefs and holy men,[40] like Sitting Bull who died violently as part of the hysteria to end a Native American messianic movement in 1890.[41] The religions of Africa, still the 'Dark Continent', were apparently too shadowy to notice and delegates from Latin America were similarly excluded, 'a particularly conspicuous absence given that the celebration of Christopher Columbus's achievements was the occasion for the event'.[42]

Note the marks of almost classic American religious liberalism: the acceptance of diversity (within carefully defined limits), the assumption of a representative democracy, English as the obvious cosmopolitan language, and the affirmation of material progress defined within a capitalist world tempered by religious values. However, Richard Seager observes a paradox in the Parliament in Chicago heralded as a sign of the growing 'religious pluralism in our nation': while the conveners of the Parliament assumed a growing liberal Protestant agenda, 'the assembly embraced an extraordinary variety of positions simultaneously'.[43] These included a delegation of Theosophists from the new world headquarters in Madras (now Chennai), India, as well as scientists with a religious bent:

One suspects that such eclectic religious sensibilities, although rarely studied sympathetically, are quite prevalent in many quarters today. But they were also there on the Parliament floor, a harbinger of a later day when religious humanism would not be synonymous with liberal Christianity.[44]

These understudied and underestimated *shared eclectic religious sensibilities* were indeed alive in 1893.

Diane Eck, the most articulate and passionate spokesperson for *pluralism* provides clear distinctions between several modes of religious encounter in *Encountering God: A Spiritual Journey from Bozeman to Banaras*, also published in 1993 during the centenary of the World's Parliament,

First there is the exclusivist response: Our community, our tradition, our understanding of reality, our encounter with God, is the one and only truth, excluding all others. Second there is the inclusivist response: There are, indeed, many communities, traditions, and truths, but our way of seeing things is the culmination of the others, superior to the others, or at least wide enough to include the others under our universal canopy and in our terms. A third response is that of the pluralist: Truth is not the exclusive or inclusive possession of any one tradition or community. Therefore the diversity of communities, traditions, understandings of truth, and visions of God is not an obstacle, but an opportunity for our energetic engagement and dialogue with one another.[45]

After further delineating the important distinction between pluralist and inclusivist perspectives, she explains that in the inclusivist sense 'the other is not so much dangerous as immature and in need of further enlightenment' and this was 'the kind of thinking that lay behind Swami Vivekananda's mission to bring spiritual growth to the immature materialist West'.[46] A few pages later, Eck discusses relativism:

Relativism for me and for many others becomes a problem when it means the lack of commitment to any particular community or faith. If everything is more or less true, I do not give my heart to anything in particular. There is no beloved community, no home in which the context of values are tested, no dream of the ongoing transformation of that community. Thus the relativist can remain uncommitted, a perpetual shopper, set apart from a community of faith, suffering from spiritual ennui.[47]

While deeply committed to his nation and its common community of fellow Hindus—a wide community sense that he helped to articulate and construct—Vivekananda remains, it seems, an inclusivist and yet in many ways 'set apart' from his community and alive in the worldwide set of religious shoppers as the founder of the first Hindu mission to the West. Something is simply missing from this charting of exclusivism, inclusivism, and pluralism. And as an inveterate 'uncommitted' shopper with an ambiguous sense of *my* community, I think these elusive yet powerful *shared eclectic religious sensibilities* remain unacknowledged and misunderstood within the pluralist framework. Hence I choose not to discuss 'Hinduism' here as community property, but the *other* Hinduism of that first global guru as the carrier of that kind of *eclectic universalism*.

These shared eclectic religious sensibilities, evidence suggests, were perhaps more global in range than American liberal Protestantism but equally a part of the growing worldwide middle-class—including many in the United States and the United Kingdom—who shared a modern outlook also derived from the Enlightenment, but not *liberal* and certainly not *pluralistic*. They challenged borders between nature and culture, between nature and science, and between human and divine. It was these *unspoken religious values* that the many speeches would now make public in this first global arena. Swami Vivekananda's presentation of Hinduism as the model for a new universalism is perhaps the most famous, the most contentious, and the most problematic for the liberal world of pluralism, then as now. Rather than framing this as inclusivist, I shall rather call it *eclectic*—the difference is important if global gurus can be understood as doing more than 'selling spirituality'.[48]

CHANGING BODIES, CHANGING MINDS

Returning to the paradox of Vivekananda's message, Swami Vivekananda as he emerges in contemporary scholarship also assumes a Janus face with one side looking toward the West, and the other to India: 'Ecumenical and almost Unitarian during his sojourn in the United States, Vivekananda demonstrated his chauvinistic colors on his return to South Asia',[49] and, 'In India, the swami hotly defended Hinduism against attacks while simultaneously urging renewal and programs of humanitarian reforms that frightened orthodox Hindu leaders. In the West, meanwhile, he undertook a separate work, launching the first Vedanta societies in the United States and Europe to disseminate Hinduism to Western people'.[50] Just how separate were these two faces of the Swami?

In De Michelis's *A History of Modern Yoga: Patañjali and Western Esotericism*, Vivekananda emerges not only as a disseminator of

Hinduism but more importantly as a conduit for a rising interest in esotericism, not only in American cities but also in the capital of British India, Vivekananda's hometown of Calcutta. She provides an important clue in her description of Vivekananda's ease in settling into the many parlours of his American admirers during his two sojourns in the United States:

It was, *mutatis mutandis*, the social group corresponding to the Bengali cultic milieu from which he himself came. Except that these American circles were far more widespread, affluent, secularized, individualistic and far more intent on engaging in 'occult' endeavours.... It was therefore not surprising that, with relatively minor adaptation on both sides, he was readily accepted and accepting. This pattern of social interaction continued throughout his stay in the West: embraced by the more fluid, unchurched, affluent strands of the cultic milieu, he in turn adapted to them. Flattered by their admiration and support, he also admired them, and the reciprocation of positive feelings led to mutual admiration.[51]

Her description of this relationship conflicts with earlier biographers who see the Swami distressed by the 'tutelage of his rich protector';[52] nonetheless, the point remains: many upper middle-class young Hindus in Calcutta and the other colonial port cities of the Empire already shared *religious sensibilities* with their American, and indeed British, counterparts. De Michelis points to common international organizations like the Freemasons. Another, the Theosophists, had around that time moved their headquarters to Adyar in Madras city and would begin a century of close interactions between Europeans, Americans, and a rising Indian middle class. A small but powerful segment of urban Indians and urban Americans shared a common milieu at the turn of the nineteenth century. And that milieu was far more radical than our clichés of the Victorian period usually allow: 'Vivekananda gave shape to Modern Yoga by blending Neo-Vedantic esotericism and avant-garde American occultism. Thus Neo-Vedantic ideology became an integral part of Western occultism and, conversely, Western occultist ideas were integrated into Neo-Vedanta.'[53] The important point here being that much of this happened *within* an American context amid the highly receptive, increasingly wealthy American middle classes of the late nineteenth century.

In the American context, Vivekananda's teachings began with the *person* as the site of religious experience and not with the community as a whole. Without a doubt these persons joined Vedanta Centres in the United States with a few joining the Ramakrishna Missions and Cultural Centres in India—but these remained voluntary organizations and not the kinship groups associated with belonging 'naturally' to a Hindu family and to a *jati / varna* ('caste'). Their goal, after all, was some form of 'personal salvation'—to borrow an evangelical term. These early years of the turn of the century saw both the rise of a worldwide middle class, unmoored from older community configurations and an increasing operating as 'individuals' and a new scholarship focusing on the *person*—the middleclass person. Dr Freud analyzed the ills of society through the neurotic gestures and dreams of his affluent patients. Max Weber built a theory of the rise of capitalist modernity out of 'this-worldly' but *personal* asceticism of Protestant merchants—interestingly in the midst of a visit to the United States. He also created his long-standing theory of *charisma*—a personal quality of the leader—as the key to new community formation. So too in Calcutta, the group of mostly university educated middle-class young men and older householders gathered around Ramakrishna, each looking to him as *their* teacher while he fashioned them into an inner and outer *circle* of disciples—the *antaranga* and the *bahiranga*.[54] Interestingly, the Sanskrit term *ranga* can be translated 'circle' in the sense of an 'assembly', but has its root connotations in arena, theatre, and stage.[55] The term perfectly captures the ambiguity in this kind of teaching via the revered guru: Were minds or bodies transformed? I ask this in full cognizance of Sigmund Freud the physician moving the ailing body into the mind and apparently incorporating insights on Ramakrishna's 'oceanic feeling' into his later *Civilizations and Its Discontents*,[56] or Weber's strange circle from asceticism—which was corporal—to his arguments over the processes of 'rationalization' through which discourse appears to devalue bodily practice—issues Foucault would surely raise. Recall that the issue of bodily change / mental change has implications for the globalization of Hinduism and the possibility for that *third stream* of 'de-ethnicized' universalism. In other words, is there some middle ground between a Hindu identity based on 'birth'—that is, having the right kind of body and belonging *naturally* to a community—and the other model based on the 'universal' religion of Christianity (or Islam or Buddhism) that requires—supposedly—only a confession of 'belief'?

THE SWAMI, THE SAINT, AND THE SCHOLAR
In the last year of his life, The Right Hon. Friedrich Max Müller published his little book on Ramakrishna and a second volume of his reminisces titled, *Auld lang syne: My Indian Friends*. In *Râmakrishna, His Life and Sayings*, Müller initially presents the Bengali saint, as a contemporary

example of an old process that 'will give us insight into the way a new religion, or rather a new sect, springs up and grows'.[57] His concerns were the many fabulous tales of Ramakrishna that circulated within a mere decade of his death: 'they are so strangely exaggerated, nay so contradictory, that it seemed almost hopeless to form a correct and true idea of his earthly career and his character'.[58] (In)famous for his earlier theories on myth as the 'disease of language', the old professor in the face of such a contemporary scene appears to have softened his terminology calling this the *Dialogic Process* ... distinguished from the *Mythological Process*, which forms indeed a part of it, but acts under special rules'.[59] Müller then tells his reader that his 'as much a possible unaltered' account of Ramakrishna comes directly from Swami Vivekananda at his personal request:

I had made it clear as possible to Vivekânanda that the accounts hitherto published of his Master, however edifying they might be to his followers, would sound perfectly absurd to European students, that stories of miraculous events of his childhood, of apparitions of goddesses (dêvi) communicating to the Samnyâsin a knowledge of languages and literatures which, as we know, he never possessed in real life would be thrown away on his poor unbelievers... Vivekânanda himself is a man who knows England and America well, and perfectly understood what I meant. Yet even his unvarnished description of his Master discloses here and there the clear traces of what I call the Dialogic Process, and the irrepressible miraculising tendencies of devoted disciples. And I am really glad that it does so, if only to teach us that no historian can ever pretend to do more than show us what a man or a fact seemed to be to him.[60]

In the remarkable account that follows, the aging Müller reveals—amid his fluid and often-florid Victorian prose—his near glorification of the practically illiterate saint, and his own oddly troubled mind about the practices of asceticism, about conversion, and about Christians turning East in a way that his lifetime of scholarship, which ironically opened the *Sacred Books of the East* to the West, perhaps never quite expected.

Max Müller ironically provides the Bengali saint with a clear lineage within the then accepted scholarly construct of the ancient Hindu world—a world that he had carefully constructed over many decades. The later Ramakrishna movement recognized what Gwilym Beckerlegge calls his 'rescuing' of Ramakrishna.[61] After delineating the meaning of *mahâtmans*, the place of renunciations in the four stages of life, the ideal of the *samnyâsins* and the saints, and the development of the Yoga, Müller concludes:

And if they have been brought up in a philosophical atmosphere, or are filled by deep religious feelings, they would naturally become what the Mahâtmans are described to be—men who can pour out their souls in perfect eloquence and high-flown poetry, or who are able to enter even on subtle discussions of the great problems of philosophy and answer questions addressed to them ... Such a man was Râmakrishna.[62]

Later Müller expends several dense pages to explaining Vedanta philosophy 'in order to show the background from which Râmakrishna emerges, and the light and shades of the atmosphere in which he moved',[63] but after having earlier said that, 'I am not concerned with Indian philosophy, *pure and simple*, but with the effects on the popular mind of India as shown by one of its recent representatives, Râmakrishna'.[64] Such an interest in contemporary practice seems a late concern for the scholar who is most frequently associated with the construction of 'the aristocracy of book religions'.[65] Beckerlegge confirms, 'The judgments that Müller passed on Vedanta during the last decade of his life bear witness to the way his early ambivalence toward Hindu religious traditions had given way to a positive acceptance of Vedanta'.[66] And the poor and seemingly mad Bengali saint became, in Müller's little book, 'an authentic expression of the sublimest form of India's spiritual heritage—Vedanta'.[67] Further, I would add that Ramakrishna, the man, becomes the summation of the spiritual community of India through Müller's own—to borrow an uneasy term—re-enchantment of Vedanta. Moreover, Ramakrishna becomes something more than an interesting subject to Professor Max Müller, something more subjectively vital.

After expressing his doubts, but no longer his outright denial, of miraculous aspects of the 'ascetic exercises or yoga', such as feeling no pain or sitting for weeks without food, Müller adds, 'I confess I find it equally difficult to believe or not to believe them.' But 'that what is called a state of Samâdhi, or trance, ... is ... admitted by medical and psychiatric authorities; and though imposters certainly exists among Indian Yogins, we should be careful not to treat all these Indian Saints as mere impostors'.[68] This seems a remarkable turnabout for the scholar whose published edition of the Vedas turned these once orally transmitted texts literally into *scriptures*. The issues, as Max Müller was fully aware of, involved re-situating Vedanta philosophy in the context of Ramakrishna whose ardent ascetic practices, whose ability to enter *Samadhi*, transformed his body in some remarkable way; and at the same time, whose ardent devotion to Kali and other deities rendered him a *bhakta*, a theistic devotee, as well. At this point in his narrative Müller has related Vivekananda's version of the saint's life and is about to append Ramakrishna's 'sayings'—now that he must reconcile the embodied saint with the Vedantic philosopher. Throughout this intriguing section—clearly both dense and yet aimed at the educated public—the Kantian Müller argues for taking the human bodily senses seriously as a means of knowledge and of discovery of that Self of 'true being', at the same time that the deeply theistic Müller argues for the reality of the 'Godhead'. Yet both the bodily senses and the notion of God, then and now, pose problems within the very Vedanta philosophy that Müller, using a significant metaphor, declares 'is the very marrow running throughout all of the bones of Rāmakrishna's doctrine'.[69]

Moving between the major Vedanta philosophers Samkara (Shankara) and Rāmânugan (Ramanujan), the 'Western'—as he calls himself—Müller struggles to affirm the 'manifold phenomenal world' and its 'individual subjects', and an omniscient God in the context of a monistic—read unified—world. His focus becomes the Self. Müller argues, 'our instruments of knowledge, whether senses or mind, nay our whole body ... are they not, like everything we call created, the result also of that universal beginningless Avidyâ [Unknowing or the great Unknown], without which Brahman [the Absolute–the Totality] could never have become phenomenally created?'[70] His description of the Self in relationship to the body borrows unambiguously from Kant although the full implication of Müller's reading of Rāmakrishna via Kantian epistemology awaits a philosopher of religion moving where unfortunately too few tread:

But if we see that all we know comes to us through the five senses of seeing, hearing, touching, tasting, and smelling, that we cannot go beyond the senses, that we never have nor can have more than sensuous images of the world and of ourselves, and that what we call our knowledge consists in the first instances of these images, not of any realities, which we may postulate, indeed, as underlying these images, but which we can never reach except by hypothesis, might we not say our senses as a whole are our *autos* or Self?[71]

In Müller's interpretation of the texts, the mind lies in the body, as with 'the ten senses ... what is sometime called an eleventh sense, the Manas, all treated as material, and as products of the earthly elements'.[72] This 'inner organ' is 'sometimes reason, sometimes understanding, or mind or thought'.[73] With this newly embodied sense of Vedanta, Müller is ready to reintroduce the Bengali saint.

Enfolding the saint's yogic and ascetic practices—making special mention of the importance of controlling 'the vital breaths', 'the Prânas'—into what he sees as the ultimate goal of Vedanta, liberation or Samadhi, Müller concludes with a section called 'tat tvamasi' [*tat tvam asi*] usually translated with a Biblical flourish, 'thou art that' and understood as the equation of the individual self with the Absolute. Returning directly to Ramakrishna, Müller acknowledges that though the 'powerful control of his breath' and 'long continued ascetic exercises', the saint achieved the kind of 'Samâdhi' that allows a real master to remain in his body and to return to teach others, '... his Self, no longer his, had recovered its Brahmahood, had become what it had always been and would always be, the Atman, the Highest Self, in all its glory freed from all the clouds of appearances, and independent of individuality, personality, and of the whole phenomenological world'.[74] Ramakrishna now is 'freed' and 'independent' but still very much here working in the world in a state of—what might be temptingly called another kind of—'this-worldly asceticism'.

I believe that Müller positions Ramakrishna as a living solution to his own dilemma—and many other 'Orientalists' of the period—as a Godly, goodly, yet scientific (affirming some kind of materiality) European, how could such a public man justify long years working with a seemingly 'otherworldly' and 'mystical' system. Müller hesitates at the point of 'conversion' but he re-envisions a Ramakrishna whose bodily transformation signalled a universal process based on the *human* body and the *human* mind akin to the work of the Immanuel Kant, Müller's philosophic hero. Is this another kind of *humanism*? The Vedantic milieu that he created for Ramakrishna seems to echo or perhaps foretell Vivekananda's own 'practical Vedanta' with its deep involvement with the world—with the political and social life of India, and at the same time with the personal/spiritual lives of his American followers.

FROM THOUSAND ISLANDS, NEW YORK, TO CALCUTTA, INDIA—A PLACE IN THE WORLD

In his preface to *Râmakrishna*, Müller carefully declares, 'We need not fear that the Samnyâsins of India will ever find followers or imitators in Europe, nor would it be at all desirable that they should ...'.[75] But just a few years before Müller wrote these lines, a small band of Americans were meeting in Thousand Islands Park, New York in the summer of 1895 seemingly to do exactly this. A published record of this event is now widely available through the devoted eyes of Vedantist Marie Louise Burke, 'the movement's most indefatigable scholar',[76] as part of her six volume series on Swami Vivekananda's two visits to America, in 1893–6, in connection with the Parliament of Religions, and again in 1899–1900. The Thousand Islands meeting attracted a very small company but Vivekananda wrote, 'I have arranged to go to Thousand Islands, wherever that might be. There is a cottage belonging to Miss Dutcher, one of my students, and a few of us will be there in rest and peace and seclusion. I want to manufacture a few "Yogis" of the material of these classes'.[77] And according to Burke, he indeed initiated several of them. She reverently describes the fruit of his work:

His desire, as he often intimated, was to see many hundreds of men and women of the West formally renounce the world. 'The yellow robe of the sannyasin is the sign of the free,' he said in one of his last classes at Thousand Islands Park. 'Give up your beggar's dress of the world; wear the flag of freedom, the ochre robe.'[78]

And, she comments:

Was not his stay at Miss Dutcher's cottage only the occasion, then, for releasing a flood of spiritual energy into the very heart of the nation? Was he not teaching generations of Americans in those few weeks? One cannot but think that the immense power generated by Swamiji's teaching day and night at the height of spiritual consciousness must have transcended and out distanced its effects in the lives of the twelve students who gathered around him and asked, 'What have we done to ever deserve this?'[79]

Marie Louise Burke, thoroughly enmeshed the swami into the American landscape—not only in this passage but also throughout her text—and he in turn liberally borrowed potent American tropes: Swami Vivekananda will give real freedom to those in the land of the free. He will revitalize America from its own heartland.[80]

However, the most curious feature of these potent weeks in upstate New York remains Swami Vivekananda's reconstruction of what Elizabeth De Michelis terms 'Modern Yoga'. De Michelis positions Vivekananda's stay at this 'camp' as the key moment of his refashioning of yoga. She sees him emerging from this retreat with his 'basic tenets' for a practical and universalized type of yoga and ready to dictate his soon-to-be very popular *Karma Yoga*, followed by his most famous work, *Raja Yoga*.[81] Her intriguing study carefully unravels the ingredients of multiple Western occult ideas that Vivekananda blended with classical yoga to produce a new 'secularized' practical and pragmatic formula for worldwide consumption. But her interest is in this East–West process of mutual interpenetration, mine is to return to the issue of the possibilities of a de-ethnicized Hinduism. We are both concerned with bodies because Vivekananda chose to present his 'teachings' as yoga, always a bodily practice even in its most meditative forms. Ethnicity also is identity perceived, assumedly, in bodily practice and bodily form—such identity requires birth into the fold—or to put it another way, the right kind of 'body'. She shows us how Vivekananda constructed yoga within an American milieu and on American soil. Here, like De Michelis, I have 'to piece together ... the hidden or untold parts',[82] but at this point in an even more speculative manner than her exhaustive work. I ask, why did Vivekananda turn to yoga at all and why did he develop his Raja Yoga here in the United States but on returning to India, redefine a unifying Neo-Hinduism for an emerging Indian nationalism.[83] In other words, what is this Janus face about and how does it relate to a 'universalized' Hinduism?

De Michelis presents Vivekananda's Raja Yoga thus: 'Its message was what many in cultic milieus worldwide had been waiting for: a flexible set of teachings that would meet their craving for exotic yet accessible and ideologically familiar forms of practical spirituality'.[84] The key here is *practical*, *accessible*, and accommodating a worldwide following. To this end, Vivekananda, De Michelis argues, presents two models of yoga, the *Prana* model and the Samadhi model. The Prana model begins with processes of gaining control, via control of the vital breath, over 'gross' and 'subtle', 'internal' and 'external' aspects of the cosmos.[85] In the Samadhi model, 'the more prominent' one, Vivekananda,

... construes yoga in terms of the mind undertaking a proprioceptive journey back to the 'source of intelligence' through various level of meditative practice. Each individual mind is part of 'universal mind', he postulates, and by accessing higher or 'superconscious' states (*samadhi*) each of us can tap into the omniscience of the universal mind and obtain gnosis. *This profound transformative effect on the adept*, eventually brings to the fore his or her forgotten almighty, omniscient, and divine nature [my emphasis].[86]

At the risk of summarizing too much of this careful history of borrowings and reinterpretations, I understand De Michelis as making several major suggestions. Swami Vivekananda tries to salvage the 'natural laws' of the Enlightenment with their materialist and empiricist principles by reworking this model of the humans as part of nature and under its laws into another model of humans *homologized* to nature. Hence by 'occultist' sensibilities, comes the formula that what a person does with their body, they do with the world:

An equation between 'knowledge', 'power' and 'control' underlies Vivekananda's recommendations for practice: if one becomes aware, feels, perceives gross and subtle energy movements within oneself ... then one will come to know and control fully. ... Further still, if one controls one instant (usually one's *prana*, one's own body), then one will control all (all *pranas*, all bodies).[87]

Vivekananda harnessed, at that time, a whole series of conceptions which saw no distinction between the material and spiritual in the multiple theories of universal energies or fluids that moved between divine and material principles. These are 'magic correspondences of microcosm and macrocosm' that Vivekananda 'activates'.[88] In this sense, the 'religious' becomes 'secular' via occultist sensibilities that understand the material world as infused with what others would call 'otherworldly' or 'transcendent' powers, now available to the human transformed through yogic practices.

I continue to question why Vivekananda would release such potent power initially to his American followers. Certainly persons in India may have some knowledge of these practices but his fellow Bengali middle class university-educated cohort would be as unlikely as Americans to take up practices, which until then would have remained within an ascetic milieu, within the world of renouncers, not householders. Jeffrey Kripal argues that Ramakrishna, a temple priest and although unconsummated nonetheless married, had already broken this 'householder/renouncer division' and began to teach his more 'secret' practices to selected members of both.[89] De Michelis describes a series of teachers from the Calcutta intelligentsia that became renouncers of sorts, but all of this was a break from tradition and affected very few in Calcutta. Vivekananda on the other hand looks first to producing a 'few yogis' in America and then hopes for 'many hundreds of men and women from the West' to undergo this profound transformation. The key here is the transformative power of yoga, the power to heal, to purify, and to rebuild a subtle body from the gross body. I would suggest, in what I recognize as a controversial leap of interpretation, that Vivekananda never let go of his sense of the spiritual superiority of the Indian person and of Indian religious sensibilities to grasp these powers. But Indians remained too bounded by tradition and by the multifold communities at that moment, and would require another kind of transforming release. The American person, on the other hand required a personal (bodily) transformation, to move onto and into his new universal religion that he introduced on the floor of the World's Parliament of Religions just three years back.

Upon returning to Calcutta and prior to his departure, Shamita Basu argues in an equally fine grained and sensitive study *Religious Revivalism as National Discourse*, Vivekananda constructed a 'universal Hinduism' for a new nationalist India. Her argument moves through some of the same Hindu philosophical concepts and the same nineteenth century

Indian reformers that De Michelis mentions, but she sets these within their Bengali and finally an all-Indian context. She summarizes his project thus:

This is the national context in which the Advaita principles of Universalism was to be employed: to organize the sociologically decentralized people by invoking a single absolute core of Hindu philosophy of non-dualism that is supposed to represent and incorporate all sectarian beliefs, practices, and institutions of various communities. The universalization of Hinduism was the task that Vivekananda had set himself to achieve in his nationalist endeavor.[90]

Both she and De Michelis focus on Vivekananda's creative use of *Advaita* (non-dualist) philosophy but rather than frame her reading in the context of common occult sensibilities, Basu uses Gramsci's theories of language, politics, and public intellectuals to frame her analysis. In her introduction, she presents her selected material and methods for *Religious Revivalism as National Discourse*: '[Vivekananda's] commentaries on Hinduism, which I have sought to study as part of a history of thought, are treated as a document, and his appearance in America as a form of performative utterance: an event in the history of the genesis of nationalism in nineteenth-century Bengal'.[91] Basu presents Vivekananda's 'discursive practices' as generating powerful, performative words but nonetheless concludes that Vivekananda maintained what is frequently termed the Enlightenment compromise, 'The Swami wanted to advocate a form of Hinduism that was a far cry from the parochial version of religion which the orthodox Hindu leaders wanted to popularize. Vivekananda followed the Reformation model in *depoliticizing* Hinduism, confining in a Lutheran manner the *spiritual to the private sphere of life*' [my emphasis].[92] At one point she describes his words as 'a classical example of the language of ideology'.[93]

However her own choice of language throughout her text make me suspicious that something more than performative language was at work in Vivekananda's teachings even in Bengal. For example: 'To Vivekananda, the personality of Ramakrishna was the embodiment of the idea of national unity: a practical illustration of how Hinduism could be conceived in the context of heterogeneity and could be successfully used as the organizing factor in creating *a collective self* [my emphasis].[94] She titles a section, 'The Self and Subject in National Discourse' and argues that: 'This was the source of the insight into the concept of the nation as *the greater self* and the secret that the self-determination of the people of a nation could only be achieved through the path of self-mastery *as was the case with individuals*' [my emphasis].[95] And,

Within the neo-Hindu philosophy, the nation which is now generally represented as Nationalism, to Vivekananda, was an act of self-revelation, *a going back to the origin of this Hindu self, and a Hinduism rising to self-consciousness*. In the subsequent period of nationalistic struggle those who adopted the religious idiom and rose in defense of Hinduism often borrowed from Vivekananda this gigantic conception of Hinduism as the *custodian of universal enlightenment* [my emphasis].[96]

Later Basu argues that, 'Vivekananda made religious discourse open to rational analysis, and spiritual realization *as exclusively a subjective affair'* [my emphasis].[97] But then she adds,

Neo-Vedantism was created as a spiritual discourse of power which called upon the nation to reinterpret its ancient texts, to search within it the spiritual source of the combative spirit, the inner strength, and the sublime knowledge of the *eternal freedom of the soul* which could never be held in subordination, be it political bondage, social discrimination or material deprivation. It was *the pure unconquered self* which was the seat of God [my emphasis].[98]

What is this national 'self'? Within these passages in Shamita Basu and within Vivekananda's own speeches and teachings, the problem of the political and the religious re-emerges with full force but in some very tricky ways. At stake here is Basu's unspoken but clear intention to bracket Vivekananda and his religious nationalism from the current Hindu Nationalism of the RSS and the then ruling BJP. And, recall that the Ramakrishna Mission in the United States helped to initiate the second World's Parliament of Religions staying clear of the VHP-sponsored Global Vision 2000. She reads Vivekananda as initiating a transformation of a multitude of individual subjects into a realization of their commonality. But how corporate and how intense was this 'collective self' to be? Is this incorporation a matter of brilliant performative discourse that would transform minds, or was this a subtler in-corporation, a 'magical' means of creating a national body? Here, reading De Michelis's discussion of the occultism in Vivekananda into the Indian context, I would argue that not only the microcosm and the macrocosm of the some inner and outer universe are homologized—as in his eclectic American-made Yoga, but here Vivekananda may be homologizing the public sphere and the private sphere as well. The Indian people may well be invited into a massive yogic exercise, to *realize* their unity to willingly become a part of this glorious Whole.

THE THIRD STREAM IN A CONFLUENT WORLD

This is the tricky part of the Swami's two faces—one does point almost uncomfortably close to the trope of the 'Nation as Person' used by the

Hindu nationalists—images of Mother India, the divine holy land, Our Nation, 'Our Culture', or 'Our Heritage'. But here Swami Vivekananda's 'occultism' and his 'yoga' cannot be ignored. As both Basu and De Michelis make clear, Vivekananda in his role as guru/swami begins and ends his discourse within the person, within the self, and not the community. His is more than 'performative language'. Yoga does more: there is physicality here with talk of *forces* that are understood as instrumental in a 'scientific sense' or, as De Michelis suggests, in the sense of a new 'magic'. His scientism and his occult naturalism forces his language into a notion of the human body and the earth as composed of universal substances, energies, and forces working under common, albeit occult, 'laws'. I do not claim that Vivekananda abjured all of the many racial theories of his day, rife among his fellow occultists, especially the Theosophists,[99] but that his ontology was so thoroughly universalistic—and yes, literally *inclusive*—that his nationalism never merged into an exclusive ethnicity, but assumed the very Hindu sense that mind and matter entangle within the human self. So, while his yogic spell meant to re-form Indians into a single body—a powerful religio-political entity fit to be free—his American yogis needed to re-form their bodies, to build a self fit to learn and to teach. In classical terms, they needed to gain *adhikara*—the right to learn and the right to teach. Vivekananda then, and as global gurus do now, released what had been an exclusive birthright of certain caste communities into anyone willing to undergo that transformation of the self–body–senses that the guru's touch and teaching can effect.

Without accepting all of the implications of Jeffrey Kripal's controversial book, *Kali's Child*, his insight into the physicality of the guru–disciple relationship cannot be easily put aside. Whether the disciple touches or even washes the guru's feet, or receives a chaste touch on the forehead, or a massive hug, or—as in the case of Vivekananda—beholds his shining countenance, more than a verbal message is shared. A transformation of the *self* involves a transformation of the body—in the context of acquiring a new discourse. Here, I think Srinivas Aravamudan is right and yet wrong that the modern gurus constructed a new cosmopolitan language, 'Guru English' and that this new language fits, perhaps dangerously, well into our postmodern consumer world. Aravamudan views the ambiguity of Guru English and its almost empty message as part of the world of style participating 'in an era when value has resolutely shifted from mechanical to mental labor, and where consumer culture is meeting the challenge by rising to target levels of immaterial lifestyle, experience, and ethos that can bypass the cruder measures of material product'.[100] However, I would counter that that new worldwide guru-engendered 'theo-linguistics'—to use Aravamudan's term— rides on a body of more than words. These are not simple dialogues or even encounters—but baptism by fire. They are felt within the person. The question as to whether they spell the end of metaphysics or onto-theology, or whether they herald a strange return of magic, a 're-enchantment' as Lawrence Babb suggested a decade ago, remains, but I no longer think that either the liberal language of pluralism, nor of ethnic 'identity politics' can contain them.

NOTES AND REFERENCES

1. Friedrich Max Müller, *Râmakrishna: His Life and Sayings* (New York: Charles Scribner's Sons, 1899), p.vi.

2. The same year, he also published *Auld lang syne. Second series: My Indian Friends* (New York: C. Scribner's Sons, 1899).

3. Müller, *Râmakrishna*, p. v.

4. Richard Hughes Seager, *The Dawn of Religious Pluralism: Voices from the World's Parliament of Religions, 1893* (La Salle, Illinois: Open Court, 1993).

5. Carl T. Jackson, *Vedanta for the West: The Ramakrishna Movement in the United States* (Bloomington: Indiana University Press, 1994), pp. 97–9.

6. I have adopted this term for those who are born into Hindu-Indian families in India or in the diaspora in lieu of another term 'birthright' used by Christian denominations to indicate someone born into the church.

7. This was the title of a panel at the annual meeting of the Journal of the American Academy of Religion later published as a symposium in the *Journal of the American Academy of Religion* 68 (2000), pp. 703–835.

8. Tomoko Masuzawa, *The Invention of World Religions: Or, How European Universalism Was Preserved in the Language of Pluralism* (Chicago: University of Chicago Press, 2005), p. 107.

9. Jonathan Z. Smith, *Relating Religion: Essays in the Study of Religion* (Chicago: University of Chicago Press, 2004), pp. 188–91.

10. Masuzawa, *Invention of World Relgions*, pp. 108–9.

11. John Henry Barrows (ed.), *The World's Parliament of Religions* (Chicago: The Parliament Publishing Company, 1893), p. 977.

12. Srinivas Aravamudan, *Guru English: South Asian Religion in a Cosmopolitan Language* (Princeton: Princeton University Press, 2006); Elizabeth De Michelis, *A History of Modern Yoga: Patañjali and Western Esotericism* (London: Continuum, 2004); Shamita Basu, *Religious Revivalism as National Discourse: Swami Vivekananda and New Hinduism in Nineteenth-Century Bengal* (New Delhi: Oxford University Press, 2002).

13. Sudhir Kakar, *The Analyst and the Mystic: Psychoanalytic Reflections on Religion and Mysticism* (Chicago: University of Chicago Press, 1991); Jeffrey J. Kripal, *Kali's Child: The Mystical and the Erotic in the Life and Teachings of Ramakrishna,*

second edn. (Chicago: University of Chicago Press, 1998); Gwilym Beckerlegge, *The Ramakrishna Mission: The Making of a Modern Hindu Movement* (New Delhi: Oxford University Press, 2000) and *Swami Vivekananda's Legacy of Service: A Study of the Ramakrishna Math and Mission* (New Delhi: Oxford University Press, 2006); Carl T. Jackson, *Vedanta for the West: The Ramakrishna Movement in the United States* (Bloomington: Indiana University Press, 1994).

14. Marie Louise Burke, *Swami Vivekananda in the West: New Discoveries*, vol. 3 (Calcutta: Advaita Ashrama Publications, 1985), pp. 125–7. In her discussion of the Thousand Islands retreat headed by Vivekananda, Marie Louise Burke presents a picture of this French woman who 'exasperated some of Swamiji's other disciples' but apparently was highly regarded by Vivekananda. The new Swami Abhayananda had been a labour organizer but after her turn towards the new order apparently 'softened wonderfully' (p. 127).

15. His talks to those disciples at Thousand Islands, New York were published as *Inspired Talks: My Master and Other Writings* (New York: Ramakrishna-Vivekananda Center of New York, 1987). The Ramakrishna Center celebrated the centenary of this event in 1995. See http://ramakrishna.org/activities/events/MEvents2.htm (accessed on 29 December 2006).

16. Vivekananda left for Chicago via Madras and returned the same way stopping there in 1887 as he made his way back to Calcutta. The website of the Sri Ramakrishna Math in Chennai carries the story as part of its campaign to restore the house where he stayed during this period, now called the Vivekananda Illam. See http://www.sriramakrishnamath.org/activity/illam.shtml (accessed on 28 December 2006).

17. The poster is now available online at the website of the Vivekananda Center, Boston. See Photo 22 in their archive, http://www.vivekananda.org/archivephotogallery.asp (accessed on 29 December 2006).

18. *The Chicago Daily Tribune*, 20 September 1893, p. 10.

19. Ibid., 16 April 1899, p. 46.

20. De Michelis, *History of Modern Yoga*, pp. 110–12.

21. Beckerlegge, *The Ramakrishna Mission*, pp. 61–81.

22. Jackson, *Vedanta for the West*, p. xii.

23. Available at: http://www.cpwr.org/who/history.htm (accessed on 29 December 2006). The statement was initially drafted by Dr. Hans Kung, the controversial Catholic theologian currently President of the Global Ethic Foundation: For Inter-cultural and Inter-religious Research, Education, and Encounter see http://www.weltethos.org/dat_eng/index_e.htm.

24. See Diane L. Eck, *A New Religious America: How a 'Christian Country' Has Become the World's Most Religiously Diverse Nation* (New York: HarperSanFrancisco, 2001), pp. 366–70.

25. Joseph M. Kitagawa, 'Humanistic and Theological History of Religions with Special Reference to the North American Scene', *Numen*, vol. 27, no. 2 (1980), p. 199.

26. Mahesh Mehta, 'Swami Vivekananda's Message—Modern Perspective'. Posted on the website of Global Hindu Electronic Network: Swami Vivekananda Study Center, which is sponsored by the Hindu Student Council, available

at: http://www.hindunet.org/vivekananda/mm_gv.txt (accessed on 29 December 2006). See 'Report on the Global Vision 2000', available at the same website.

27. Nagulapalli Srinivas, 'World Vision 2000 Success/Failure?' available at: http://www.hindunet.org/vivekananda/ns_success_failure (accessed on 29 December 2006).

28. 'Vision 2000—Vivekananda Celebrations Report', available at: http://www.hindunet.org/vivekananda/jm_report.

29. *The Washington Post*, 9 August 1993.

30. Ibid.

31. Mehta, 'Swami Vivekananda's Message'.

32. See http://www.hindunet.org/vivekananda/gv_2000_talks/t_vision_global_peace (accessed on 29 December 2006).

33. Srinivas, 'World Vision 2000 Success/ Failure', http://www.hindunet.org/vivekananda/ns_success_failure (accessed on 2 January 2007).

34. See http://www.hindunet.org/vivekananda/gv_2000_talks/sr_rss_fulfills_viveka.

35. As termed in the official website of the Ramakrishna Mission Institute of Culture. See http://www.sriramakrishna.org/.

36. Eknath Ranade, *The Story of the Vivekananda Rock Memorial*, second edn. (Chennai: Vivekananda Kendra Prakashan, 2000[1995]), p. 93.

37. Roelof van der Broek and Wouter J. Hanegraaff (eds), *Gnosticism and Hermeticism from Antiquity to Modern Times* (Albany: State University of New York Press, 1998), p. x. The source of the term 'third stream' is unclear, but Wouter Hanegraaff has popularized the concept of an important strain of early and continuing 'Western esotericism' which has been used by Elizabeth De Michelis in *A History of Modern Yoga*, her excellent study of yoga and Swami Vivekananda. The term is also used in music for a new confluence of jazz and contemporary new music.

38. Barrows, *The World's Parliament*, p. 75.

39. Ibid, p. 18.

40. Alice C. Fletcher, who Seager identifies as 'an anthropologist and student of Franz Boas', presented a very short paper titled, 'The Religion of the North American Indians'. See Richard Hughes Seager, 'Pluralism and the American Mainstream: The View from the World's Parliament of Religions', *Harvard Theological Review*, vol. 82, no. 3 (1989), p. 316.

41. The slaughter of almost 400 Sioux participants in the Ghost Dance movement at Wounded Knee, South Dakota by the US military was headline news in late 1890. The conveners of the conference could not have failed to know the names of many of these Native American religious leaders.

42. Seager, *The Dawn of Religious Pluralism*, p. 7.

43. Seager, *Pluralism and the American Mainstream*, p. 312.

44. Ibid., p. 315.

45. Diana L. Eck, *Encountering God: A Spiritual Journey from Bozeman to Banaras* (Boston: Beacon Press, 1993), p. 168.

46. Ibid, p. 185.

47. Ibid, p. 195.

48. Jeremy Carrette and Richard King, *Selling Spirituality: The Silent Takeover of Religion* (London and New York: Routledge, 2005).

49. Aravamudan, *Guru English*, p. 56.

50. Jackson, *Vedanta for the West*, p. 5.

51. De Michelis, *History of Modern Yoga*, p. 114.

52. Romain Rolland, *The Life of Vivekananda and the Universal Gospel*, trans. E.F. Malcolm-Smith (Kolkata: Advaita Ashrama, 2006 [1933]), pp. 33–4.

53. De Michelis, *History of Modern Yoga*, p. 110.

54. Kripal, *Kali's Child*, p. 11.

55. See Monier Monier-Williams, *A Sanskrit-English Dictionary* (New Delhi: Motilal Banarasidas, 1956 [1898]), p. 862, columns b and c.

56. Aravamudan, *Guru English*, p. 57.

57. Müller, *Râmakrishna*, p. 23. Beckerlegge includes an analysis of Müller's earlier work on Ramakrishna called 'A Real Mahatma', published in *The Nineteenth Century* (August 1896). For a careful analysis of the difference between the early version and the later book, see Beckerlegge, *The Ramakrishna Mission*, pp. 8–15.

58. Ibid, p. 24.

59. Ibid, p. 25.

60. Ibid, p. 30.

61. Beckerlegge, *The Ramakrishna Mission*, p. 8. Shri Ramakrishna's disciples could never unequivocally confirm that their master, whose only official position was as priest in a very new temple to Kali, was initiated into a clear guru-*parampara*, an unbroken succession of religious teachers, although the life stories told of the saint include his initiation into Advaita by a 'teacher' known as Totapura. See Swami Nikhilananda and Dhan Gopal Mukerji, *Sri Ramakrishna: The Face of Silence* Swami Adiswarananda (ed.) (New York: Ramakrishna Center of New York, 2005), pp. 41–9. This text may well rely on Max Müller.

62. Müller, *Râmakrishna*, p. 10.

63. Ibid., p. 94.

64. Ibid., p. 93.

65. Masuzawa, *Invention of World Religions*, p. 210.

66. Beckerlegge, *The Ramakrishna Mission*, p. 17.

67. Ibid., p. 15.

68. Müller, *Râmakrishna*, p. 9.

69. Ibid., p. 70.

70. Ibid., p. 73.

71. Ibid., p. 81.

72. Ibid., p. 84.

73. Ibid., p. 86.

74. Ibid., p. 95.

75. Ibid., p. vi.

76. Jackson, *Vedanta for the West*, p. 32.

77. Quoted in Burke, *Swami Vivekananda*, p. 109.

78. Burke, *Swami Vivekananda*, p. 129.

79. Ibid., p. 119.
80. And, emphatically following this trajectory, a Bengali long settled in Chicago proposes, 'Chicago, along with other such places around the world touched by Swamiji, a God-man, can be called a *punyatirtha*, a holy place of pilgrimage.' Asim Chaudhuri, *Swami Vivekananda in Chicago: New Findings*, second edn. (Kolkata: Advaita Ashrama Publications Department, 2005 [2000]), p. 21.
81. De Michelis, *History of Modern Yoga*, pp. 124-5.
82. Ibid., p. 5.
83. See Basu, *Religious Revivalism*, for a detailed analysis.
84. De Michelis, *History of Modern Yoga*, p. 150.
85. Ibid., p. 151.
86. Ibid., p. 153.
87. Ibid., p. 167.
88. Ibid., p. 167.
89. Kripal, *Kali's Child*, pp. 11–14.
90. Basu, *Relgious Revivalism*, p. 71.
91. Ibid., p. 10.
92. Ibid., p. 127.
93. Ibid., p. 128.
94. Ibid., p. 82.
95. Ibid., p. 33.
96. Ibid., p. 39.
97. Ibid., p. 190.
98. Ibid., p. 191.
99. Gauri Viswanathan, *Outside the Fold: Conversion, Modernity, and Belief* (New Delhi: Oxford University Press, 1998), pp. 177–207.
100. Aravamudan, *Guru English*, p. 268.

JYOTIRMAYA SHARMA

Digesting the 'Other'
Hindu Nationalism and the Muslims in India

In a lecture delivered in Nagpur on 19 October 1949, M.S. Golwalkar warms to the theme of the imagination and realization of a Hindu Rashtra. The idea of a nation, he argues, does not change with circumstances. Articulation of Hindu nationalism during British rule in India was difficult and was often seen as reactionary. In a veiled reference to the Muslims, he asserts that some communities took advantage of this and became insolent under foreign patronage. The Sangh (RSS), he continued, had articulated the idea of Hindu nationalism despite foreign rule. The British now had left India, and he felt no reason why the task of Hindu unity, consolidation, and empowerment could not be carried out with greater vigour.[1]

He briefly returns to the theme of the Muslims. Golwalkar is unusually circumspect in talking about the Muslims here. The RSS had been banned after Gandhi's assassination and Golwalkar had been imprisoned. This was his first major public lecture after his release from prison and the lifting of the ban on the Sangh. The manner in which he approaches the subject of the Muslims is, therefore, circumscribed by several momentous events. He says, 'The Muslim community was there during foreign rule. It is now demoralized and defeated. Therefore, we must make them part of ourselves. But do we still have the capacity to digest such a process of assimilation or not?'[2] This partial restraint was only temporary. In lectures delivered in Uttar Pradesh the same year in December, Golwalkar would return to spewing venom on the efforts to bring about Hindu-Muslim unity which he likened to converting the nation into a *dharmashala*, calling the Muslims *parakiya* or outsiders, and dismissing Pakistan as the *toota-phoota ghar* or ramshackle house of the Muslims.[3]

In the passage quoted above from Golwalkar, it is easy to miss the weight of the word 'digest'. It does not indicate assimilation. The idea of assimilation is used independently of the word 'digest'. Eating and digesting are terms that Golwalkar uses frequently in referring to the Partition and to Muslims. The Muslims had 'gobbled' a part of 'our body', he says in a speech at Sindi in 1954.[4] Speaking of the Partition, Golwalkar, elsewhere, speaks about the insatiable hunger of the Muslims during and in the immediate aftermath of Partition for grabbing parts of the land that was not too long ago undivided India.[5] However, the situation, he felt, had radically changed after Partition. A thousand years ago there were only Hindus in this country. The Shakas, Huns, and Greeks came but they had to become Hindus. They could not corrupt the original inhabitants of this land—Golwalkar was prone to likening the Hindus as the 'founders' of the 'original' Hindu nation in this fashion like many other Hindu nationalist leaders. But what is the situation today, he asks, and offers an answer:

Are there only Hindus in India today, and if there are others, will they be digested? No, the situation is not the same as before. Whereas there were Hindus all over earlier, today there are millions of a-Hindus trying to preach and spread themselves among our own people. ... The son of Lord Krishna's guru had been taken away by a daitya. He went and churned the ocean, terrorized the inhabitants of the ocean and brought him back. Till such time that we had the belief of not allowing anyone to go out of our fold, only till such time were we able to digest outsiders. Today we are a laughing stock [after Partition] and our society has been insulted.[6]

In short, he urges Hindus to consolidate and wash away the stain and insult of Partition. Golwalkar's resentment towards Partition or the creation of Pakistan is neither surprising nor unusual; it partakes of the rhetoric common to Hindu nationalist thought. What is unique about his rhetoric, however, is the use of the word 'digestion' while speaking of the Muslims who remained within India after Partition. Is the employing of words like *paachan* and *hazam* merely accidental or is the use of these words part of a larger pattern?

The idea of 'digesting' the non-Hindus in India is not merely a careless metaphor thrown in to indicate the possibility and extent of assimilating those communities Golwalkar considered outsiders. From the middle of the nineteenth century onwards, debates about the appropriateness of the food consumed and its larger social and psychological ramifications were subjects hotly debated, and these fraught and highly contested discussions produced alarmingly contradictory arguments. There was, in the first instance, a widely shared recognition among almost all nationalist thinkers spanning the nineteenth and the twentieth centuries about the primacy of the three *gunas* or qualities of nature, namely, *satva* (purity or goodness), *rajas* (activity or passion), and *tamas* (darkness, ignorance, gloom, or inertness). A discussion of these qualities is also central to traditional Indian treatises on nutrition, medicine, and well-being like the *Carakasamhita* and the *Sushrutasamhita*. Drawing upon the threefold characterization of the gunas as also their salience for the choice of food for an individual and a society, nationalist leaders came to a dazzling constellation of ideas.

A central strand that separated Hindu nationalists like Swami Dayananda Saraswati, Bankimchandra Chatterji, Swami Vivekananda, Sri Aurobindo, V.D. Savarkar, and M.S. Golwalkar from Gandhi, was the allied question of the place of violence and its legitimacy. While all Hindu nationalist leaders agreed that the use of violence, be it direct or indirect, in obtaining food and consuming it rendered such individuals violent, they also affirmed the virtues of food like milk and fruits, considered *satvic*; a satvic diet was desirable towards obtaining the ultimate goal of merging one's self with the divine self. But this affirmation was only in theory. An important idea within the Hindu nationalist discourse was the need to make Hindus more masculine, violent, and aggressive in order to fight their enemies and end their enslavement.[7] In practice, therefore, rajas had already replaced satva in the hierarchy of qualities in the eyes of the Hindu nationalists in their project to end their subjugation and raise a proud Hindu nation. An early nationalist like Swami Vivekananda, therefore, prescribed three Bs for the salvation of India: beef, biceps, and the Bhagavadgita. Hindu nationalists saw vegetarianism, non-violence, and non-harm as part of the unfortunate legacy bequeathed by Jainism, Buddhism, and shades of the Bhakti movement in making Hindus weak and effeminate. Cosmetic adherence to the theory of the three gunas had to be balanced with legitimizing violence. Addressing the World Vegetarian conference on 23 November 1967, this is how Golwalkar synthesizes the two seemingly contradictory strands:

All our sacred texts first extol us to follow non-violence. Truth only comes second to non-violence ... But if we follow non-violence literally, the human race will perish ... Even then, there are people in our country who eat meat, but the ideal situation would be one if they did not ... Human beings are affected by the food they eat. Those who rely on violence in their food would certainly be violent in his behaviour. Satvic food will make a man pure and good. After many experiments, the learned men in ancient times came to the conclusion that cow's milk, fruit and vegetarian food makes an individual pure and self-restrained, something which helps in one's spiritual progress in order to become one with the universal soul.[8]

Since Golwalkar specifically mentions cow's milk as part of the satvic diet, a word here needs to be said about the centrality of the cow in Hindu nationalist discourse. The stigma attached to beef eating and its association with Muslims became increasingly fraught and occupied a pre-eminent place in the entire Indian nationalist context.[9] Once again contradictions abound. Vivekananda's exhortation to Hindus to eat beef in order to become more 'manly' has already been cited above. An early Hindu nationalist like Swami Dayanada Saraswati argued in favour of protecting the cow in terms that were purely pragmatic and economic. Savarkar too argued that though there were compelling reasons to rear cows, there was no justification in the deification of the animal. In an essay titled, 'Rear Cows, Do not Worship Them',[10] Savarkar argues that to consider an animal like the cow as divinity is an insult to humankind. He also ridicules the idea that cow dung and urine could purify the impure. He argues that in order to save a few temples, a handful of Brahmins and a few cows, orthodox Hindus allowed the Hindu nation's subjugation for centuries. When the Muslims were invading India, Savarkar continues, they quickly understood the Hindu tendency to deify the cow and used it to their advantage. They used to use cows as a shield against the Hindu armies, knowing that the Hindus would not shoot a single arrow to kill the cows. The consequence of this blind worship of cows led to opening the gates for the Muslim invaders and facilitated the future butchering of millions of cows for centuries. In order to escape from the sin of killing a few cows, the blind followers of the Hindu scriptures handed over the entire nation to the *Mlecchas*. He adds that the arguments in favour of the cow's usefulness are also overstated. In terms of usefulness, a buffalo, a horse, a dog, and even a donkey are animals that are equally useful. Therefore, to consider the cow as holy is not only madness, but also a sign of utter foolishness, concludes Savarkar.

Savarkar's rationalist argument was an exception in the corpus of Hindu nationalist thought as it unfolded in the twentieth century. Over the years, the question of cow protection became a contentious political issue, and resurfaced prominently during Gandhi's support of the Khilafat movement.[11] But the politics of Hindu nationalism saw the question of the cow differently from the way both Savarkar and Gandhi perceived it. The theory of the threefold gunas or qualities had already been reversed. It was broadly acknowledged among almost all votaries of Hindu nationalism that Hindus had become soft and effeminate and had to be made 'manly'. Along with the inversion of the characterization of the gunas, the questions of the fourfold *varna* system (classification of castes) too had to be reconsidered. This was imperative for bringing about a viable Hindu consolidation that would, in turn, be the foundation for the argument for a Hindu nation.[12] Vegetarianism could no longer be held as an ideal. It could not be imposed as a normative value representing the satvic tendencies—the Hindu nationalists had already drawn a connection between non-violence, passivity, and vegetarianism and the capitulation of the Hindus at the hands of meat-eating foreigners. Nor did it help the cause of Hindu unity by imposing a largely Brahminic ideal on other castes that were traditionally meat eaters.

In order to stitch together these contradictions, beef came to be recognized as the food of the 'other'. The Muslims, therefore, came to be identified as beef eaters and the killers of the holy cow. It allowed a large section of the Hindu population to remain non-vegetarian, eat meat in order to become strong and manly, while forgoing just one category of meat, namely, beef. Golwalkar and the RSS made the question of cow protection and the ban on killing cows for meat a central plank of their organizational agenda ever since Independence in 1947. Writing on the issue in 1952,[13] Golwalkar asks why did the Muslims who came to India choose to selectively destroy symbols of Hindu national piety and faith? Why did they destroy temples and erect mosques in their place? Why did they burn scriptures and destroy idols? Hidden behind all these acts, concludes Golwalkar, was an *asuric* or demonic tendency, exhibited often in people who are underdeveloped and uncultured. The same impulse, he elaborates, was also behind the Muslim predilection to cow slaughter. It was this asuric tendency that made the Muslims fashion cow slaughter into an act of religious merit. The argument is clear enough: Muslims were outsiders, barbarians, and uncivilized and betrayed asuric tendencies, and those with asuric tendencies, among other things, were prone to slaughtering cows and eating beef.

At this point, there is yet another evocative element within Golwalkar's quote about digesting the non-Hindus that deserves careful delineation. The 'outsider' is introduced in the quote, not merely as someone who needs to be digested, but also as someone who, in a moment of weakness, can take Hindus away from their community and religious affiliations. The parallel is drawn carefully and the suggestiveness of the parallel is hard to miss. The *daitya* or demon who carried away the son of Lord Krishna's guru had to be overpowered, vanquished, and brought back. Similarly, Muslims were the contemporary versions of daityas who had led Hindus astray from their parent faith, a situation whose remedy had already been suggested by Lord Krishna's example.

Golwalkar uses the word 'a-hindu' or non-Hindu to indicate the 'otherness' of Muslims and all other foreign faiths that happen to live and flourish in India and need to be digested in Independent India. Elsewhere, he uses the word *parakiya* to indicate the Muslims as alien outsiders, a word that also carries within itself the etymological connotations of the prefix *'para'*, which, among a complex of meanings, signifies attributes such as 'strange', 'foreign', 'alien', 'adverse', and 'hostile'.[14] It is a word that gained currency in the Hindu nationalist literature popularized by the likes of Savarkar and Golwalkar, and does not have the rich and suggestive history of words like Mlecchas and *Yavana*. Despite the contextual use of words such as 'a-hindu' and parakiya, all Hindu nationalists without exception continued to use terms like Mleccha and Yavana to portray the Muslims in a generic sense. Much original work has been done on the history of these terms;[15] their use for centuries continues to cast a shadow on the ways in which Hindu nationalists evolved their ideological apparatus in relation to the Muslims.

From the eighth century onwards, written sources in Sanskrit and other Indian languages exhibit a familiarity with Islam in general, and terms and concepts in Islam in particular, but existence of such evidence is sparse. What is significant, however, is that these written sources do not refer to Muslims in generic terms, as is the case today. There were terms that were used before the coming of the Muslims to indicate outsiders and aliens and in many instances these terms were effortlessly interpolated on to the Muslims without even cosmetic modifications.[16] Of all the terms used to connote the Muslims—*Tajika, Turushka, Gauri, Mudgala, Turuti, Turbati, Pathana, Parasika, Garjana, Hammira,* and *Suratrana*[17]—Mleccha and Yavana became generic terms to indicate outsiders, but continued to be used to identify Muslims. Sanskrit texts often used the terms Mlecchas, Yavanas, and Turushkas interchangeably, but there is no evidence that the use of these names, even as a literary motif, in any way signalled the emergence of a single foe or an antagonistic 'other'. Rather, till almost the fifteenth century, the uses of the terms Mleccha and Yavana have to be understood as acts of multiple representations within the political, cultural, and ideological parameters in early India. A few examples would suffice.

The early representation of the Mlecchas was complex and consisted of intricate layers of meanings arising out of a variety of contexts. The Mlecchas were seen as agents of political upheaval as well as desecrators of all that was pure and revered. They were perceived as people who were violent and vile, and as those who caused distress to the gods and the Brahmins. In certain situations, they triggered off calamity, but were not necessarily the originators of the ultimate grief. In other situations, they were seen as the very cause of social and political devastation and ruin. In some epigraphic and textual sources, the Mlecchas are represented as shouldering the burden of the earth to an extent where they relieve Vishnu of his burden and responsibilities as the preserver of order. In yet another example, they assume the role of the burden of the earth and the cause of its woes. The Ajaigarh Fort Rock inscription of 1261 is an example of this kind of description. The Kotihar Inscription of 1369 traces the lineage of a sultan from the epic family tree of the Pandavas, while the Delhi Sultan who brought distress to Andhradesha is seen as continuing the tradition of Parashurama, the mythical destroyer of the Kshatriyas. These contradictions are to be explained, as suggested above, by attention to the political and cultural context in which they arose.

The Mlecchas and Yavanas were seen, firstly, as one of many raiders and contestants to political power. Even within this spiral of intense competition, there is no single representation that is privileged over the other. Brajdulal Chattopadhyaya suggests that 'there could be various empirical realities in political relations between Yavana and non-Yavana powers, and there could be various representations too. Historical reconstruction has to contend with these various representations'.[18] Moreover, the Sanskrit texts also betray a representational slant that works in favour of exclusion and inclusion, legitimation, and distancing. Therefore, the Mleccha/Yavana as a theoretical category had a timeless quality to it that made it both an instrument of exclusion by designating the 'outsider' but also as a strategy of accommodation of diverse ethnic groups from outside the geographical boundaries of India within its rubric. The Mleccha, literally, the 'dirt of mankind', then, for the Brahminical discourse also could be a hunter from the Vindhya forest or a Turushka of the early medieval or medieval period. The designation of an individual as Mleccha depended also on his conformity with the *varnashramadharma*.[19]

It is crucial to note that at no juncture and in no instance in the epigraphic and literary sources from the eighth century to the fourteenth century were ethnicity or religion,[20] factors that determined the representation of the Mleccha.[21] Neither do these sources project the image of the Muslims as Mlecchas in a seamless and undifferentiated way as the 'other', nor is there an all-encompassing xenophobia evident. Further, Muslims were not projected as a community of believers whose faith was antithetical to orthodox religious practices of the Brahminical order.[22] Given the highly inflamed sense of religious exclusivity and national identity evident in the nineteenth and twentieth centuries, this gloss becomes an extremely useful point of reference.

In the early decades of the nineteenth century, Hindu nationalist leaders and ideologues continued with the tradition of calling Muslims Mlecchas, perceiving them as aliens who had invaded India. In addition to this, the picture was one of the sensuous and decadent Muslim, who could also at once be fanatical, aggressive, and a fiery defender of the faith. The context, political and cultural, had, of course changed. The Muslims were no longer the rulers. Any deference to their sentiments would hardly have invited repercussions. Moreover, the fledgling nationalism of the nineteenth century variety was negotiating several elements at one and the same time, where preoccupation with constructing a viable 'national' history went hand in hand with theories of racial and ethnic purity, Hindu India's 'unbroken' civilizational history, and rampant theories of victimhood. A common element that ran through this preoccupation to define and delineate the 'nation' was the positing of a 'Golden Age' from which contemporary India was perceived to have degenerated. The responsibility for this fall from an imagined ideal in the distant past was put variously at the doorstep of feuding kings, theories of non-violence, but most importantly, the Muslim invasions. The way Muslims and their rule in India was perceived and analysed increasingly assumed shades of demonology, some subtle, but a large number of such narratives were vicious and plainly incorrect.

By the time Bankim published *Ānandamath* in the 1880s, the portrayal of Muslims was already undergoing a subtle change. In *Ānandamath*, the nawab, Mir Jafar, a lazy opium eater, was 'evil', and was 'a vile, treacherous blot on the human race'.[23] In the novel, Muslims are 'bearded degenerates', who had destroyed the Hindu way of life, caste status, self-respect, and identity.[24] Somewhere in the middle of the narrative, in Chapter 18 of Part I, there is an outburst that alters the very course of the way Hindu nationalists would speak about the Muslims in a generic way. This is what Jnanananda says:

For a long time we've been wanting to smash the nest of these weaver-birds, to raze the city of these Muslim foreigners and throw it into the river – to burn the enclosure of these swine and purify Mother Earth again! Brothers, that day has come! The teacher of our teachers, our supreme preceptor – who is full of boundless wisdom, whose ways are always pure, the well-wisher of all, the benefactor of our land, who has pledged to give his life to proclaim the Eternal Code anew, whom we regard as the very essence of Vishnu's earthly form, who is our way to salvation – today lies captive in a Muslim jail! Is there no edge to our swords? ... Is there no courage in his heart? Brothers, cry out 'O Hari, enemy of Mura, of Madhu and Kaitabha!' We worship Vishnu – who destroyed Madhu and Kaitabha, who wrecked the downfall of such powerful demons as Hiranyakashipu, Kamsa, Dantavakra, and Shishupala, by the loud whirling of whose discus even the immortal Shambhu became afraid, who's invincible, the giver of victory in battle ... Come, let's raze the city of foreigners to the dust! Let's purify that pigsty by fire and throw it into the river! Let's smash that nest of tailor-birds to bits and fling it to the winds! Cry, 'O Hari, enemy of Mura, of Madhu and Kaitabha!'[25]

Who are Mura, Madhu, Hiranyakashipu, Kaitabha, and Dantavakra? Bankim returns to explain this in Chapter 4 of Part II of the novel. The context is a discussion between Mahendra and Satyananda regarding the true nature of *Vaishnava* practice. Mahendra till this moment believes that followers of the Vaishnava code ought to be non-violent. Satyananda tells him that he has a mistaken view of what being a Vaishnava entails. He says:

Non-violence is the mark of the false Vaishnavism that arose in imitation of the atheist Buddhist code of practice. The mark of authentic Vaishnava practice is subduing the evildoer and rescuing the world. For is not Vishnu himself the protector of the world! It is He who destroyed the demons Keshi, Hiranyakashipu, Madhu, Kaitabha, Mura, Naraka and others in battle, as well as the ogres Ravana and so on, and the kings Kamsa, Shishupala and the rest. That Vishnu wins the victory, and bestows it.[26]

The word Bankim uses in Jnanananda's speech to identify demons and their contemporary likeness to Muslims is *asura*. In Satyananda's speech, the same demons—Mura, Keshi, Hiranyakashipu, Madhu, Kaitabha and Naraka—are called daityas, whereas Ravana is called a *rakshasa*. Asura in popular Hindu mythology is an evil spirit, demon, ghost, and opponent of the gods. They live under the earth, in *paatala*, as contrasted with the *devas*, who live in Amravati, a heavenly city above the skies. A modern text on Hindu mythology describes them in this way:

Both the Asuras and the Devas invoke God in their quest to be triumphant. Typically, the story begins with an Asura invoking God and seeking immortality. God refuses to give such a boon, for all jivas are mortal. So the Asura asks for a boon that makes him almost invincible, hence almost immortal. Using this boon, the Asura launches an attack against the Devas and drives them out of Amravati. The Devas then invoke God, who defeats the Asuras either through force or through trickery. God is thus responsible for the alternating victories and defeats of the Devas and the Asuras.[27]

Daitya, in contrast, is the son of Diti, an asura, by the sage Kashyapa, and also implies the status of a demon. A rakshasa is also a demonical being, corresponding to 'nocturnal demons, imps, fiends, goblins, going about at night, haunting cemeteries, disturbing sacrifices and even devouring human beings'.[28] A contemporary reading suggests that a 'more appropriate word for them would be barbarians, *jivas* who follow the law of the jungle, known in Hindu scriptures as *matsya nyaya* or the code of fishes. According to this code, "might is right, big fish eat small fish".'[29]

A few very important strands emerge from the quotes above. Bankim seeks to abrogate to his characters the power and the mandate to kill demons that once belonged only to Vishnu. The suggestion is that the sacred brotherhood of the *santans* had the legitimacy to kill demons in its time and that they were not merely on the side of righteousness but also god-like in their earthly, human form. But more significantly, the parallel between Vishnu slaying the demons and the call to purify the pigsty of the Muslim foreigners by fire by characterizing them as demons is an important step in the increasingly fraught and invective-filled rhetoric of the Hindu nationalists. To a great extent this is due to the passing over of political power from the hand of the Muslims to the British. Writers like Bankim did not have to look over their shoulder while portraying Muslims as asuras and daityas and were safe from any manner of retribution. For instance, Viashnava texts in Bengal in the sixteenth century were much more circumspect and confined themselves to the generic terms already in use like Mleccha and Yavana.[30] Moreover, there are almost no Hindu daityas, asuras, and rakshasas from the nineteenth century onwards, though there are instances of their existence in the early period. Therefore, the Vadavali plates of Silaahaara Aparaaditya (AD 1127) talk of Chittukka, a demon born to destroy the world. Having been vanquished by Aparaaditya, Chittukka took refuge among the Mlecchas.[31] Further, while Vishnu as the slayer of demons is still invoked and his status as God is still acknowledged, he now had to share space with another potent and mighty God, namely, nationalism. In Bankim, as in the rest of the Hindu nationalists, the 'nation as God' becomes a very significant category.

In the nineteenth and the twentieth centuries, there is a regular reappearance of the deva–asura binary, used invariably to portray the Muslims, and at other instances, the West, as repositories of asuric tendencies. Hindus, in this discourse, depending on the subtlety or crudity of exposition, are perceived as devas out to deal with the asuras without the mediation of God, or as sons of the devas. Swami Vivekananda suggests that without going into the question of whether the devas were better than the asuras, it would be safe to assume that asuras were more like human beings and far more manly than the devas.[32] Indeed, in many respects, the devas were far inferior to the asuras. Vivekananda puts it thus: 'Now, to understand the East and the West, we cannot do better than interpret the Hindus as the sons of the Devas and the Westerners as the sons of Asuras.'[33] Not only were the Westerners the sons of asuras, he continues, Central Asia and the deserts of Arabia too were the home of the asuras, who, united in hordes, chased the civilized devas and scattered them all over the world. He goes on to argue that those who conquered the Hindus were Turks and Tartars who had converted to Islam. And what are these Muslims of Turkish and Tartar origins, who conquered the Hindus like? Vivekananda asserts that, 'These Asuras never care for learning and cultivation of the intellect; the only thing they understand is fighting.'[34] It is another matter that only a few pages earlier, the Swami had spoken about the Vedantic ocean, in which the Hindu, Mohammedan, Christian, or Parsi were all one, all children of the Almighty God.[35]

Another important figure who straddled both the nineteenth and the twentieth centuries, Aurobindo Ghosh, in his justification of violence, which he called repayment of man's debt to Rudra, returns to the deva–asura distinction. Without violence, he argues, the law of Vishnu—peace and well-being—would be devoid of meaning and substance. The spirit of violence, however, could be purified. For this, one had to return to the old Hindu system where the fighting spirit of the Kshatriya was spiritualized: the Kshatriya oppressed no one and did not allow oppression. He was always governed by dharma, a code of right conduct. For him, violence was always a moral and ethical option.

It was part of being masculine. Its legitimacy derived from the need to hold together society by righteous means rather than pursue selfish ends. Increasingly, Aurobindo's justification of kshatriyahood and violence began to take a religious colour:

[B]ut even the greatest Rishis of old could not, when the Rakshasas were fierce and determined, keep up the sacrifice without calling in the bow of the Kshatriya. We should have the bow of the Kshatriya ready for use, though in the background.[36]

War and violence were justified by the nobility of the objective, namely, slaying asuric forces. The act of killing itself was seen as favouring the immortality of the soul. To kill asuric individuals was to prepare oneself for immortality. Moreover, since all actions were for the sake of the Divine, they were to be seen purely as acts of sacrifice undertaken without attachment or desire. Further, drawing upon the Gita, Aurobindo argued that it was the Divine who 'has already slain the Dhritarashtrians, he of whom Arjuna is only the human instrument'.[37]

This power of kshatriyahood was not beyond limits. Though Aurobindo held the ideal of kshatriyahood (exemplified by Arjuna) was a virtue worthy of emulation in colonial India by weak and unmanly Hindus, he also paid due attention to the delineation of asuric qualities among human beings. While there is scant detail in the *Essays on the Gita* or other works about how this mission to impart kshatriyahood in Hindus was to be actualized, Aurobindo's explanation of asuric qualities is interesting.

Asuric qualities comprised of harshness, hardness, fierceness, and satisfaction in slaying enemies, amassing wealth, and unjust enjoyments.[38] An asura was one whose dominant rajasic nature was 'turned towards egoistic greatness, satisfaction of desire, the indulgence of their own strong will and personality which they seek to impose on the world, not for the service of man or God, but for their own pride, glory and pleasure.'[39] Asuric nature was imbued with wrath, greed, cunning, treachery, doing wilful injury to others, pride, arrogance, and excessive self-esteem. In contrast, the deva nature was characterized by self-control, sacrifice, the religious habit, cleanness and purity, candour and straightforwardness, truth, calm and self-denial, compassion to all beings, modesty, gentleness, forgiveness, patience, and steadfastness, along with a freedom from restlessness, levity, and inconstancy.[40]

In other words, the deva qualities were part of the satvic ideal. As for the asuric qualities, Aurobindo described their nature as fierce, Titanic, destructive, and arrogant. Adding a very important gloss on the question of asuric qualities he says that, 'The Asuric Prakriti is the rajasic at its height ... [F]or the unbridled force of the rajasic nature, when exhausted, falls back into the weakness, collapse, darkness, incapacity of the worst tamasic soul-status.'[41]

Rajas, it is worth recalling, was the attribute of the Kshatriya. An asura was, therefore, a Kshatriya who did not recognize any limits and was not subject to any moral law. Arjuna was of the deva nature and not the asura *prakriti* because God was his charioteer. He was asked by the Divine to establish the kingdom of dharma, or righteousness.

In the absence, therefore, of a commonly accepted moral universe and ethical framework, kshatriyahood was bound to lapse into *asuratva*, demonic forces. It is interesting to note that despite a clear understanding of the asura qualities, Aurobindo did not make the connection between unbridled rajas and asura qualities. There is a clear exposition of the asuric and the rajasic qualities as independent entities. These are presented as independent, mutually exclusive, theoretical ideals by Aurobindo without a sense of the thin line that divides the two ideals in practical life. Shorn of its status as an ideal, kshatriyahood in practice could easily lapse into asura prakriti. Put differently, asuratva is 'Ksatriyahood which has run amuck'.[42]

There is ambiguity in Aurobindo's thought regarding the question of making Hindus more 'manly'. There are instances where he proposes the Kshatriya ideal for curing the weaknesses and cowardice of the Hindus. This was part of his nationalist mission and part of his early revolutionary activities. Elsewhere, he speaks of kshatriyahood as the governing principle of politics alone. In this instance, the kshatriyahood principle is spoken of as a normative concept rather than as a practical one. What is absolutely clear, however, is that Aurobindo equated kshatriyahood with manliness.

This is yet another inversion in his thought which inaugurates a separate set of problems. In the Indian cosmology, it was the cerebral, self-denying, and ascetic Brahmin who represented the masculine principle. The violent, virile, and active Kshatriya, on the other hand, stood for the feminine principle. Ananda K. Coomaraswamy in his *Spiritual Authority and Temporal Power in the Indian Theory of Government* clearly says that, '[T]he King, who is unquestionably the "feminine" party in the "marriage" of the Sacerdotium (brahma) and the Regnun (ksatra)'.[43] Coomaraswamy clarifies that the King, traditionally a Kshatriya, was feminine to the Brahmin but male to his own realm. Just as a woman was assimilated to a man, so was the Kshatriya to the Brahmin. In the

Atharvaveda Samhita, III. 4.1, the priest tells the king: 'Bear thou rule' (*tvam vi raja*). *Atharvaveda Samhita*, II. 36.3 cites the instance of the same words spoken to a wife: 'Let her bear rule' (*vi rajatu*). The *Aitareya Brahmana*, III. 11 says: 'Forward the Spiritual-authority, forward the Temporal-power! Unto their Union.' Aurobindo conflated the ideals exemplified in the scriptures; the Kshatriya was a feminine principle in the marriage of the sacred realm (*brahma*) and the kingly realm (*ksatra*). This balance of the sacred and the temporal ensured clear demarcation of authority and put limits on their respective functions. It is only when the sacred and the spiritual act together that they possess the right to counsel and command the populace. In other words, the Kshatriya was meant to implement the purpose, delineated by dharma, set out by the spiritual authority representing the will of God on earth.

Bankim's characters in *Ānandamaṭh* had already appropriated the right to kill asuras and daityas, a right that once belonged to Vishnu. In Vivekananda, there is a subtle inversion of the popular conception of the desirability of devas, seen by him as ineffective, lacking in strength and purpose, and, unlike the asuras, not oriented towards war and aggression alone. Aurobindo's project of making Indians more manly was by means imparting them the qualities of kshatriyahood without necessarily being conscious of the perils of unbridled kshatriyahood lapsing into asuric qualities.

In Savarkar, the idea of a god-like Chhatrapati Shivaji killing the Muslim demons is without frills and without few of the metaphysical niceties that one encounters in Vivekananda and Aurobindo. Shivaji is for him 'Hindu-Nrsimha'. A poem written in 1926 has the refrain 'Hindu-Nrsimha, Prabho Shivajiraj'.[44] He was the vehicle for crushing of the Muslim pride, the *mada-mardan* of the Muslims.[45] In another poem, Savarkar castigates the Hindus for abandoning Nrsimha, the half-lion, half-man incarnation of Vishnu, and resorting to worshipping cows.[46] How did Shivaji, the Hindu-Nrsimha accomplish this? By ripping open the stomach of Afzal Khan and ritually sacrificing him, '*Afzal Khan ka udar-vidaaran kiya, bali chadhhayi*'.[47]

The retelling of the Nrsimha–Hiranyakashipu encounter and the fate Hiranyakashipu meets at the hands of Nrsimha is elaborated further:

Lifeless piece of roti. The stomach of the enemy. Tear it apart.
Appease your hunger with the entrails.
Appease your hunger with blood.
Appease your hunger with flesh.
Bejaan roti ka kor. Shatru ka udar. Abhi chir kar.
Aanthon sey bhookh mitao.

Khoon sey bhookh mitao.
Maans sey bhookh mitao[48]

Savarkar's invoking of the Nrsimha imagery in poems written between 1902 and 1937, betrays the poet deriving a sadistic and almost cannibalistic pleasure in describing the state of the enemy. The Maratha hero, therefore, provides to Savarkar a paradigm for avenging the encroachment of the motherland by the Mlecchas (*mlecchatikramana*).[49] It consists, for Savarkar, of a simple formula: A hundred thousand skulls of the enemy must be broken, powdered, and applied as a balm.[50] Only then can Independence be celebrated in the true sense, 'This is a festival of independence. A festival of the enemy's blood. It is a bloodbath that gives great happiness.'[*yeh parva swatantrata ka. Shatru key lahu ka. Snan bahu such ka.*][51]

Shivaji, the poet suggests, piles up a heap of carcasses of the enemy, which results in a slush of flesh being trampled upon and a deluge of blood. Shivaji was not merely Hindu-Nrsimha, but also Rama who killed the rakshasa Ravana, also Krishna who killed Kamsa,[52] and also one whose chest was adorned with a garland of skulls.[53] The latter association with Kali is woven into Savarkar's extolment of Shivaji. The poems are also replete with references to slitting the throats of the enemy and bathing the motherland with their blood.[54]

Is Savarkar's detailed description of the ripping of Afzal Khan's guts unusual, or does it partake of a tradition of narrative already extant?[55] Texts from the seventeenth century such as the ballad by Ajnandas titled *Afzal Khan Vadh* (1659), *Shivabharat* (1674) composed by Shivaji's court poet Kavindra Paramananda, *Srisivaprabhuce* (1697), a historical account by Krishnaji Anant Sabhasad, and the Jedhe chronology maintained by the Jedhe family, all attest to the details of the Shivaji–Afzal Khan encounter much in the way Savarkar describes it. Though the ripping apart of Afzal Khan's guts is described in detail, the seventeenth century accounts swiftly move to comparing Shivaji's god-like status, likening him to incarnations of Vishnu, Rama, and Krishna, as also the valorous lineage of the Pandavas. The cannibalistic relish with which Savarkar describes the eating of entrails, flesh, and blood is significantly missing in these accounts. Epic poetry has always been less squeamish about blood and gore in its pages. Roberto Calasso's sweeping restatement of the idea of sacrifice in *The Ruin of Kasch* is another instance of how the 'stench and dizzying perfumes' of human flesh continues to fascinate poets and philosophers alike into metaphysical flight.[56]

A reading of the 'Streevilaapaparva' in the Mahabharata brings home the vividness with which not only bones, blood, decapitated heads, and flesh of dead bodies is described, but also description of these human remains being consumed by foxes, cranes, crows, dogs, vultures, and cannibalistic rakshasas.[57] Even if one were to move away from the realm of the epics and consider epigraphic material such as the Navasari plates of Pulakeshiraja (dated 21 October AD 739),[58] these are replete with violent descriptions of killing and blood being spilt:

[T]he bodies (of warriors) in which appeared dreadful as their armours, were reddened by very large streams of blood (gushing) from the intestines which came out of the cavities of their big bellies, as they impetuously rushed forth and were completely pierced by spear-heads ... who though they were great warriors and had their sharp swords reddened by the mass of blood that flowed when the sides of their loins and the trunks of hostile elephants were rent on several extensive battlefields, could not attain success.

Nothing prepares the reader of Savarkar's poem in comprehending his celebration of victory over the Mleccha foes in the form of a cannibalistic appeasing of hunger even if the hunger so illustrated is for revenge and retribution. To understand this element, it is crucial to turn to Savarkar's theory of digestion. Recounting his days in the Andaman prison,[59] Savarkar speaks about the trend among Hindus to boycott another Hindu who happened to eat something offered by a Muslim. He blames the Brahmins for this custom among Hindus, which he feels had pushed scores of Hindus towards Islam. He says:

If a Muslim who eats something offered by a Hindu and does not become a Hindu in the process, and digesting food offered by the Hindus remains a Muslim, and so does a Christian, then why do Hindus begin to suffer from loose motions of dharma the moment something is offered by a Muslim? Why has the strength of your Hindutva gone so feeble? Your powers of digestion must be such that after eating from the hands of a Muslim and after being offered food and water by a Christian, a Hindu ought to remain a Hindu.[60]

In a speech in 1927, Savarkar further elaborates the point.[61] He suggests that Muslims eat from the food of the Hindus not merely by accident, but also snatch food from the Hindus and yet remain Muslims. In fact, they live and survive on the food of the Hindus and yet make it their community's trait to call Hindus kafir. He asks the Hindus to regain the ability to digest everything and offers an example:

Why does the food offered by the Muslims result in loss of religion? Why has the digestive power of the Hindu become so feeble? Now we must develop the power of digestion comparable to Agastya Rishi, so powerful and inflamed an appetite that is capable of digesting the whole world.[62]

While these attempts on the part of Savarkar to encourage Hindus to give up traditional notions of purity and impurity were part of his mission to unite Hindus as well as bring back converted Hindus to the parent faith, two points need highlighting here. Savarkar's invocation of Agastya is significant, and it is a theme this narrative will return to shortly. It would suffice to say that the mythical sage Agastya had eaten an asura named Vatapi and digested him. Vatapi masqueraded as a goat that was killed and fed to Agastya with the intention of killing him. Savarkar not only uses the word Mleccha to signify the Muslims, but his writings and speeches are replete with references to Muslims as asuras, daityas, and rakshasas. But he goes a step further. He often refers to Muslims as a goat with thirty-two teeth.[63] This imagery is not original. The first instance of its use is in the earliest chronicle of Shivaji's killing of Afzal Khan written in 1659. The poet, Ajnandas has the goddess Bhavani say to Shivaji: 'A goat with thirty-two teeth has come for the slaughter.'[64] Savarkar holds Agastya as an exemplar, not merely because he digested well, but, more importantly, he digested an asura in the form of goat meat.

Savarkar takes one final leap in the process of demonizing the Muslims. Not content with calling them asuras, daityas, rakshasas, Mlecchas, and goat with thirty-two teeth, he goes a step further. In an essay titled, 'The Unclean Vows of the Muslims', he argues that despite converting thousands of Hindus to Islam by force and terror, Muslims do not consider these acts as sin but as virtue.[65] He adds provocatively that the Muslim definition of God is Khuda, who considers even rape to be a just instrument for the conversion of Hindus and perceives such an act as deserving merit. Pushing the boundaries of invective even further, he says that: 'A true Muslim ought to kill Hindus in this way – someone who gives such a tough order ... Where God himself is a rakshasa of this sort, where can one find discrimination, a semblance of thought?'[66]

Therefore, for Savarkar, all those who fought foreign invaders in the country had actually penetrated the battle-formation of daityas. Those who converted to Islam were that tainted, sinner segment who had been raped by the asuras [asura balatkaarit, patitvarg].[67] Alexander, the Yavanas, the Shakas, the Barbars, and the Huns, were all asuras and were vanquished in the way that Rama defeated and killed Ravana. The Muslim invaders who came after them were rakshasas and the Hindus defeated them as well.[68] In fact, the Muslims, English, and Portuguese were all asuric powers and all those who opposed them were 'living Nrisimha' [moort Nrsimha].[69] Similarly, the Maplas were rakshasa-like [*rakshasa-sama*], because they were once Hindus, and now having converted to Islam, were ready to slit the throats of the Hindus.[70]

Before and after Independence, equating Muslims with asuras, daityas, and rakshasas became an important element in Hindu nationalist discourse. There is hardly any strand of this discourse that remains impervious to this demonology. An important extension of this theme was the exhortation, sometimes explicit, and at other times implicit, that these demons had to be vanquished, destroyed, or eliminated in ways that Vishnu had done in his various incarnations, or the manner in which Rama had killed Ravana, or the fierce way in which Durga and Kali take on these demons and herald their inevitable end.

Golwalkar [with whom we had begun] was no exception to portraying Muslims as rakshasas. For instance, in his foreword to Pandit Satyanarayan Pande's book on Shivaji, he begins by saying that every nation went through periods of glory and degeneration.[71] India too had its share of these ups and downs. One such period was when Ravana, the rakshasa king sought to disrupt all that was good, noble, and desirable in this land. Therefore, Rama and Sita had to revive all that was lost by winning the battle against the rakshasas in order to revive hope, self-esteem, and cultural pride. Having offered this background, he embarks on a discussion of the advent of Islam in India. Islam, after its birth in Arabia, sought to bring all humanity under its flag on the strength of the sword. They destroyed kingdoms, old religions, and ancient places of religious veneration in order to do so. They murdered, raped, and kidnapped women and looted. India at the time of the Muslim invasions was a fragmented country; there was a loss here of a sense of nationalism and cultural memory, and the local rulers capitulated by pleasing their new masters by supplying girls and surrendering their wives and wealth to them. Just as Rama was the answer to Ravana in the ancient times, Golwalkar concludes, Shivaji was the answer to the same problem in contemporary times. 'People,' he says, 'saw Shivaji as an incarnation of God.'[72]

Independence, however, created a number of challenges to this formulation of Hindu nationalists like Golwalkar. Independence had been won largely through peaceful means rather than ripping apart the entrails of the projected asuric enemy. The bloodbath at the time of Partition could be used by the Hindu nationalists to argue that their theories of the asuric nature of the Muslims had, after all, stood the test of verification; while the Muslims who fled to Pakistan could also claim that self-righteous claims regarding Hindu tolerance were a veritable sham. But more than anything else, the Hindu nationalists had to contend with the large number of Muslims that had stayed behind in India, which was far from becoming a Hindu Rashtra.

When Golwalkar speaks of the problems faced in 'digesting the Muslim', its context is singularly the status of Muslims in Hindu nationalist thought in post-Independence India. At this juncture, ideologues such as Golwalkar broker a synthesis of several elements in order to come to terms with Muslims in India. The idea that Muslims were asuras, daityas, and rakshasas is not abandoned, neither is the view that they had to be killed when they dared provoke the self-styled Hindu devas. In the absence of a Hindu Rashtra, however, the possibility of pursuing this goal was limited, if not impossible. Another ingenious way had to found in order to kill the Muslim asuras, daityas, and rakshasas, even if, in this instance, the killing was merely symbolic.[73] Hindu epics and Hindu mythology proved to be handy once again.

In the Mahabharata, there is a daitya by the name of Ilvala, who amassed great riches by killing and stealing from people, especially the Brahmins. He had the powers to transform his younger brother, Vatapi, into a goat. Once so transformed, Ilvala would slaughter him and cook his meat. He would, then, invite a Brahmin as guest and feed him with the meat of Vatapi transformed into a goat. After the guest had eaten, Ilvala would call his brother back to life. Vatapi would pierce the belly of the guest and come out of the stomach of the dead guest. The sage Agastya kills Vatapi by digesting Vatapi masquerading as goat meat.

The Agastya story had a wider resonance for Golwalkar. Earlier Muslims were aliens, who had to be fought and vanquished. But after Independence, they had formally become part of India. He saw the creation of Pakistan as an incomplete attempt on part of the Muslims to re-establish Muslim rule over India.[74] For him, the creation of Pakistan was yet another attempt at shaking the core of Hindu values.[75] Independence for him was meaningless till such time that 'in our own home, enemies of our dharma, our culture, our tradition and social life, even if they are Hindu originally, continue to behave arrogantly and insolently towards us and we cannot stop them ...'[76] Golwalkar's bitterness towards Muslims increased over the years. In 1952, he called the Muslims undeveloped, uncultured, and demonic [asuri prakriti].[77] The only way to digest the Muslims, therefore, was to either warn them by telling them that their days of rule were over and that they must learn to love India, or to bring them back to the Hindu fold.[78] But as Muslims with a distinct identity, they would always remain enemies.[79] Speaking to RSS workers in 1954, Golwalkar clearly states his position by clarifying that Muslims [and Christians] were neither *rashtradohi* or traitors, nor *shatrusevi* or servant of the enemy. They were just enemies, pure and simple and ought always to be treated as enemies.[80] For Golwalkar, digesting the 'Other' was far less easy than it was for Agastya. After digesting Vatapi, Agastya won the affections of Lopamudra. Golwalkar and the Hindu nationalists have no claims to such a sublime legacy.

NOTES AND REFERENCES

1. M.S. Golwalkar, *Sri Guruji Samagra*, vol. 2 (Nagpur: Dr. Hedgewar Smarak Samiti, 2005), p. 13.
2. Ibid., vol. 2, pp. 13–14.
3. Ibid., vol. 2, p. 51 and pp. 63–5.
4. Ibid., vol. 2, pp. 130–1.
5. Ibid., vol. 10, p.171.
6. Ibid., vol. 2, p. 131.
7. There is a detailed discussion of this strand within Hindu nationalist thought in Jyotirmaya Sharma, *Hindutva: Exploring the Idea of Hindu Nationalism* (New Delhi: Penguin–Viking, 2003).
8. M.S. Gowalkar, *Sri Guruji Samagra*, vol. 5, pp. 70–1.
9. See Therese O'Toole's excellent essay, 'Secularizing the Sacred Cow: The Relationship between Religious Reform and Hindu Nationalism', in Anthony Copley (ed.), *Hinduism in Public and Private: Reform, Hindutva, Gender, and Sampraday* (New Delhi: Oxford University Press, 2003), pp. 84–109.
10. V.D. Savarkar, *Savarkar Samagra*, vol. 7 (Delhi: Prabhat Prakashan, 2003), pp. 433–45.
11. Therese O' Toole, 'Secularizing the Sacred Cow', pp. 94-101.
12. See Jyotirmaya Sharma, *Hindutva*, chapters 4 and 5.
13. M.S. Gowalkar, *Sri Guruji Samagra*, 'Let there be ban on cow slaughter', vol. 6, pp. 11–14.
14. M. Monier-Williams, *A Sanskrit English Dictionary* (Delhi: Motilal Banarasidass Publishers, 1999), p. 586.
15. Two of the most significant works are Aloka Parasher, *Mlecchas in Early India* (New Delhi: Munshiram Manoharlal, 1991) and Brajdulal Chattopadhyaya, *Representing the Other? Sanskrit Sources and the Muslims* (Eighth to Fourteenth Century) (New Delhi: Manohar, 1998). For a short summary of Brajdulal Chattopadhyaya's book, see Aloka Parasher-Sen (ed.), *Subordinate and Marginal Groups in Early India* (New Delhi: Oxford University Press, 2004), pp. 374–404; see also Aloka Parasher, 'The Foreigner as the "Other" in Early India', *The Indian Historical Review*, vol. XVI, nos. 1–2 (1995–6), pp. 109–29.
16. Brajdulal Chattopadhyaya, 'Representing the Other? Sanskrit Sources and the Muslims', in Aloka Parasher-Sen (ed.), *Subordinate and Marginal Groups in Early India* (New Delhi: Oxford University Press, 2004), p. 375.

17. Several of these were ethnic names, others were indicative of names of countries of origin, and some were derived from titles.

18. Brajdulal Chattopadhyaya, 'Representing the Other?', p. 391.

19. Ibid., p. 394.

20. It is crucial to note that the medieval Muslim view of Hindus and their religious practices followed more or less the same trajectory. See Yohanan Friedmann, 'Medieval Muslim Views of Indian Religions', *Journal of the American Oriental Society*, vol. 95, no.2, pp. 214–21.

21. Aloka Parasher, *Mlecchas in Early India*, p. 20.

22. Brijdulal Chattopadhyaya, 'Representing the Other?', p. 396.

23. Bankimcandra Chatterji, *Ānandamath, or The Sacred Brotherhood*, trans. Julius J. Lipner (New Delhi: Oxford University Press, 2005), p. 140.

24. Ibid., p. 147.

25. Ibid., p. 169.

26. Ibid., p. 179.

27. Devdutt Pattanaik, *Myth=Mithya: A Handbook of Hindu Mythology* (New Delhi: Penguin, 2006), pp. 85–6.

28. M. Monier-Williams, *A Sanskrit English Dictionary*, (Delhi: Motilal Banarsidass Publishers, 1999), p. 871.

29. Devdutt Pattanaik, *Myth=Mithya*, pp. 97-8.

30. J.T. O'Connell, 'Vaisnava Perceptions of Muslims in Sixteenth-Century Bengal', in Aloka Parasher-Sen (ed.), *Subordinate and Marginal Groups in Early India* (New Delhi: Oxford University Press, 2004), pp. 405–28.

31. Brijdulal Chattopadhyaya, 'Representing the Other?', p. 380.

32. *The Complete Works of Swami Vivekananda*, part V (Almora: Advaita Ashrama, 1936), p. 373.

33. Ibid., part V, p. 373.

34. Ibid., part V, p. 430.

35. Ibid., part V, p. 214.

36. Sri Aurobindo, *Bande Mataram* (Pondicherry: Sri Aurobindo Ashram, 1973), p. 122.

37. Ibid., pp. 273–4.

38. Ibid., p. 83.

39. Sri Aurobindo, *Essays on the Gita*, Second Series (Calcutta: Arya Publishing House, 1942), p. 275.

40. Ibid., pp. 277–8.

41. Ibid., p. 281.

42. Ashis Nandy, *The Intimate Enemy* (New Delhi: Oxford University Press, 1983), p. 78.

43. Ananda K. Coomaraswamy, *Spiritual Authority and Temporal Power in the Indian Theory of Government* (New Delhi: IGNCA and Oxford University Press, 1993), pp. 1–2.

44. V.D. Savarkar, *Savarkar Samagra*, vol. 10 (Delhi: Prabhat Prakashan, 2003), p. 172.

45. Ibid., vol. 10, p. 178.

46. Ibid., vol. 10, p. 191.
47. Ibid., vol. 10, p. 70.
48. Ibid., vol. 10, p. 71.
49. Ibid., vol. 10, p. 49.
50. Ibid., vol. 10, p. 73.
51. Ibid., vol. 10, p. 72.
52. Ibid., vol. 10, p. 82.
53. Ibid., vol. 10, p. 84.
54. Ibid., vol. 10, p. 93.
55. All reference to the legend of Shivaji have been taken from two highly unlikely sources. The first is the nationalistic rendering of Shivaji's life by Jadunath Sarkar titled *Shivaji and His Times* (Mumbai: Orient Longman, 1997). The second is James Laine's controversial book, *Shivaji: Hindu King in Islamic India* (New Delhi: Oxford University Press, 2003).
56. Roberto Calasso, 'Sacrificial Crumbs' in *The Ruin Of Kasch* (London: Vintage, 1995), pp. 206–18.
57. *Mahabharata*, 'Streevilaapaparva', vol. 5, verses 5–38 (Gorakhpur: Gita Press, 1996), pp. 4399–401.
58. Cited in Brajdulal Chattopadhyaya, 'Representing the Other?', pp. 377–8.
59. V.D. Savarkar, *Savarkar Samagra*, vol. 2, pp. 288–9.
60. Ibid., vol. 2, pp. 288–9.
61. Ibid., vol. 7, p. 309.
62. Ibid., vol.7, p.309.
63. Ibid., vol. 10, p. 354.
64. Y.N. Kelkar, *Aitihasik Povade*, vol. 10 (Pune: Bharat Itihas Samsodhak Mandal, 1928), p. 12.
65. V.D. Savarkar, *Savarkar Samagra*, vol. 8, pp. 351–5. The original title of the essay is 'Musalmanon Ka Aghor Vrat'. The connotations of the word 'aghor' and 'aghori' is all too well known.
66. Ibid., vol. 8, p. 352.
67. Ibid., vol.10, p. 343.
68. Ibid., vol.10, p. 352.
69. Ibid., vol.10, p. 327.
70. Ibid., vol.10, p. 342.
71. M.S. Golwalkar, *Sri Guruji Samagra*, vol. 10, pp. 163–4.
72. Ibid, vol. 10, pp. 167–8.
73. In recent years, killing Muslims is no longer merely symbolic. It is often done effortlessly by Hindu ideologues with the active collusion of the State's machinery and these instances are often legitimized in the name of nationalism. See Siddharth Varadarajan (ed.) *Gujarat: The Making of a Tragedy* (New Delhi: Penguin Books, 2002); Ornit Shani, *Communalism, Caste and Hindu Nationalism: The Violence in Gujarat* (New Delhi: Cambridge University Press, 2007).
74. M.S. Gowalkar, *Sri Guruji Samagra*, vol. 2, pp. 205–6; vol. 4, p. 68.
75. Ibid., vol. 6, p. 60.
76. Ibid., vol. 2, p. 204.

77. Ibid., vol. 6, p. 13.
78. Ibid, vol. 6, pp. 82–3.
79   Ibid., vol. 4, p. 260–1. This was said in 1968.
80   Ibid, vol. 4, p. 89. For a detailed account, see Jyotirmaya Sharma, *Terrifying Vision: M.S. Golwalkar, The RSS And India* (New Delhi: Penguin–Viking, 2007).

AJAY SKARIA

'No Politics without Religion'
Of Secularism and Gandhi[1]

The essence of superstition is that it isn't amenable to reason.
—COMMANDER DALGLIESH[2]

In both cases (re-legare and re-ligare), what is at issue is indeed a persistent bond that bonds itself first and foremost to itself. A resistance or a reaction to dis-junction. To absolute alterity.
—JACQUES DERRIDA[3]

Enlightenment is mythic fear turned radical.
—THEODOR ADORNO and MAX HORKHEIMER[4]

If totalization no longer has any meaning, it is not because the infiniteness of a field cannot be covered by a finite glance or a finite discourse, but because the nature of the field—that is, language and a finite language—excludes totalization. This field is in effect that of play, that is to say, a field of infinite substitutions only because it is finite, that is to say, because instead of being an inexhaustible field, as in the classical hypothesis, instead of being too large, there is something missing from it: a center which arrests and grounds the play of substitutions.
—JACQUES DERRIDA[5]

PARADOX
A striking paradox marks Gandhi's arguments: he insists both that there can be 'no politics without religion', and that the post-Independence Indian state should be 'secular'. In November 1924, for example, Gandhi wrote a piece in *Young India* announcing that he had '[a]fter much prayer, after much heart-searching, and not without fear and trembling' decided to accept the invitation to preside at the next session of the Indian National Congress. But, he added:

I must not deceive the country. For me there is no politics without religion [*dharmathi bhinn raajniti*]—not the religion of the superstitious [*vahem*] and the blind [*andhshraddha*], religion that hates and fights, but the universal [*vishwavyaapi*] Religion of Toleration [*sahisnuta*]. Politics without morality [*niti*] is a thing to be avoided.[6]

After reviewing the considerable challenges he would face as President, he ended his piece by remarking: 'May God help us all'. But by the 1940s, Gandhi himself explicitly affirmed a secular vision of the state over and again. In a conversation with a Christian missionary in 1946, Gandhi insisted:

If I were a dictator, religion and State would be separate. I swear by my religion. I will die for it. But it is my personal affair. The State has nothing to do with it. The State would look after your secular welfare, health, communications, foreign relations, currency and so on, but not your or my religion. That is everybody's personal concern![7]

And in a similar vein he argued after Independence:

After all, we have formed the Government for all. It is a 'secular' government, that is, it is not a theocratic government, rather, it does not belong to any particular religion. Hence it cannot spend money on the basis of communities. For it, the only thing that matters is that all are Indians. Individuals can follow their own religions. I have my religion and you have yours to follow.[8]

And in February 1947 he argued in a letter published in the *Harijan*:

I do not believe that the State can concern itself or cope with religious education. I believe that religious education must be the sole concern of religious associations. Do not mix up religion and ethics. I believe that fundamental ethics is common to all religions. Teaching of fundamental ethics is undoubtedly a function of the State. By religion I have not in mind fundamental ethics but what goes by the name of denominationalism. We have suffered enough from State-aided religion and State Church. A society or a group, which depends partly or wholly on State aid for the existence of its religion, does not deserve or, better still, does not have any religion worth the name.[9]

It is tempting to think that his formulations about secularism and about religion belong to different periods in his life, and that while he insisted till the 1930s or early 1940s that there could be 'no politics without religion', he came to affirm secularism as Hindu–Muslim violence spiralled upwards in the 1940s. There is certainly something to this argument, for it is only by the late 1940s that he insists on separating religion and state. Yet, it is not as though there is a significant change in his arguments on this subject. In his earlier writings too, he does on occasion warn against theocratic rule, and he never seems to have suggested that religion and state be melded. In the 1940s, he kept up his insistence on practising a religious politics: one only has to recall the epic fasts that he undertook as a Hindu. So, while by the late 1940s there might have been a sharper emphasis on separating religion and the state, this is not so much a change of perspective as a more explicit elaboration of what had earlier been an implicit argument.

If we resist the temptation of quick chronological explanations, then we can discern three divergent conceptual registers on which Gandhi affirmed a religious politics and secularism. Each of these takes in a different direction his consistent emphasis on 'the religion which stays in all religions'. In my book under preparation, *Gandhi's Faithful Rendering: Secularism, Religion and Immeasurable Equality*, I explore each of these registers. The first register on which Gandhi could affirm both a religious politics and secularism was, curiously enough, classical Western secularism itself. Gandhi's efforts to do so are especially marked in his attempt to translate a book by William Salter titled, *Ethical Religion*. Salter tries simultaneously to affirm a theistic understanding of religion, and to make secularism itself into a religion. In the process, Salter affirms the civilizational hierarchies and historicism that are everywhere the mark of secular and humanist thought. Gandhi too, especially in the early years, was hardly innocent of these hierarchies. Nevertheless, he translated Salter at a time when he was increasingly beginning to challenge these hierarchies. Perhaps because of this, his translation of Salter quite displaces Salter's arguments, even though they do not develop an alternative perspective.

In this failure, there also emerges Gandhi's distinctive concept-ualization of religion. Gandhi's book *Hind Swaraj*, for instance, is organized as a 'dialogue' between two figures—the Editor and the Reader. Both share a commitment to *swaraj*—independence or 'home rule'. But they differ quite radically on what swaraj means, or how it might be achieved. The Reader is a figure who makes the conventional nationalist arguments about why and how the British need to be driven out of India. For the Reader, swaraj involves India securing, as he puts it in Gandhi's English translation of Chapter 4 (titled 'What is swaraj?'), the same powers as England or Japan: 'We must own our navy, our army, and we must have our own splendour, and then will India's voice ring through the world.' And to achieve this goal, the Reader is willing to use any means possible. As he puts it in Gandhi's English translation of Chapter 15: 'Why should we not obtain our goal, which is good, by any means whatsoever, even by using violence?'

But the Editor, ventriloquizing Gandhi's explicit positions, argues that such violence would not bring about swaraj or 'home rule', Independence. For the Editor, the swaraj that the Reader seeks is only 'English rule without the Englishman'. He insists not only that swaraj in this sense is not only inappropriate for India, but that it has reduced England to a 'pitiable' condition. For this pitiable condition, the Editor blames not the English themselves but 'modern civilization'. This religion is central to his politics, and here religion is opposed to 'modern civilization' itself. That phrase is used for the first time towards the close of Chapter 5 ('The condition of England'), and is Gandhi's translation of the Gujarati phrase *aajkaalna sudhaara*. Leaving for another occasion the appropriateness of this translation, what I wish to stress for now is that while the Editor attacks 'modern civilization' on several registers, its irreligiosity is an overwhelming concern. The stress on this irreligiosity emerges in Chapter 6:

In it there is no thought for niti [ethics; 'morality'] or dharma ['religion']. The votaries of sudhaara ['modern civilization'] say quite clearly that it is not their job to teach people dharma. So many believe that religion is only a false pretense [*dhong*, 'superstitious growth']. Also, so many wear the mantle of *dharma*; they even talk of *niti*; nevertheless I tell you after twenty years of experience that *aniti* is taught in the name of *niti*. ... This sudhaaro is *adharma* ['irreligion'], and it has spread to such an extent in Europe that the people there ['the people who are in it'] appear half-mad.

The Editor again devotes much of Chapter 8 (the first of five Chapters named 'The condition of India') to dharma:

Dharma is dear to me, and so my first reason for grief is this that Hindustan is becoming ever more corrupt in *dharma* [*dharmabhrasht*; 'irreligious.']. By *dharma* I do not here mean Hindu or Mussalman or Zorastrian religion. But the religion which stays in all these religions has gone. [Here I am not thinking of the Hindu or the Mahomedan or the Zoroastrian religion but of that religion which underlies all religions.] We are turning our faces away from Ishwar [God].

In Gandhi's argument, then, 'modern civilization' was making India 'irreligious', much as it had made England 'irreligious'. This opposition that Gandhi sets up between 'modern civilization' and 'religion' perhaps explains his insistence that there could be 'no politics without religion': for him, only a religious politics could oppose 'modern civilization' in any constitutive sense.

Here, religion is no longer thought within the terms of the Enlightenment, but is thought instead as *dayadharma*, a phrase that can only be quite wrongly if literally translated as the religion of compassion. Dayadharma, I suggest, thinks religion (sticking for the purpose of this essay to Gandhi's translation of dharma as religion) as the proper practice of finitude. In this essay, I would like to tease out some aspects of Gandhi's affirmation of dayadharma. Most of all, I would like to argue that his emphasis on dayadharma provided a way of questioning the secular conception of equality, and elaborating on another equality. This other conception of equality is organized around finitude, and is opposed to 'modern civilization', which Gandhi elsewhere associates with infinitude. While conservative nationalists also tried to conceptualize a distinctively Indian equality, they did so through an emphasis on constative finitude—a finitude that various groups were inescapably marked by, and of which caste was exemplary. In contrast, Gandhi's finitude, I shall argue, involved the giving of a very distinctive equality to both self and other. This equality to the other made possible a distinctive secularism that was internal to the concept of religion rather than imposed on it from the outside, or practised by it for contingent reasons.

DAYADHARMA

To attend to what is at stake in Gandhi's concept of dharma or 'religion,' and how it might have produced a 'secularism', perhaps we can take our cues from Gandhi's discussions in his never-completed book (which he wrote sometime during his internment in Yeravda jail between 1922 and 1924) on his early interlocutor, the Jain thinker Shrimad Rajchandra, who Gandhi also called Raychandbhai (from his everyday name, Raychandbhai Mehta) or simply Kavi, 'the Poet'. That book was eventually published in 1926 as Gandhi's foreword to the book, *Shrimad Rajchandra*. In the additional remarks he made for the foreword, Gandhi gently intimated some of his differences from Raychandbhai. He refused to accept Raychandbhai as his guru. He also disputed the claim made by Raychandbhai's disciples that the latter had attained *moksha* or salvation. Nevertheless, Gandhi identified Raychandbhai, along with Tolstoy and Ruskin, as three individuals who 'have influenced me deeply'. In the book itself, Gandhi mentions that he met Raychandbhai in 1891 in Bombay 'on the very day on which' Gandhi returned from England. Gandhi was deeply impressed by him at their first encounter, and the two were soon in regular conversation.

Even after Gandhi left for South Africa, Gandhi appears to have continued to have conversations with Raychandbhai which were central to Gandhi's developing understanding of Hinduism:

When I began to feel doubts about Hinduism as a religion [*Hindu-dharma*], it was Raychandbhai who helped me to resolve them. In the year 1893, I developed close relations with some Christian men in South Africa. Their lives were pure, and they were devoted to their religion [*dharma-chust*]. Their main work in life was to persuade followers of other faiths to embrace Christianity. Though I had come into contact with them in connection with practical affairs, they began to feel solicitude for my spiritual welfare. I could understand one duty I had. Until I had studied the teachings [*rahasya*] of Hinduism and found that they did not satisfy my soul, I should not renounce the faith in which I was born. I, therefore, started reading Hindu and other scriptures. I started reading, and I read Christian and Musalman books ['read books on Christianity and Islam']. I carried on correspondence with some English friends I had made in London. I placed my doubts before them. I entered into correspondence with every person in India in whom I had some trust [*aasta*], Raychandbhai being the chief among them. I had already been introduced to him and a close bond had grown between us. I had respect for him, and so I decided to get from him everything he could give. The result was that I gained peace [*shaanti pamyo*; 'gained peace of mind'] I felt reassured that Hinduism could give me what I needed.[10]

That a Jain like Raychandbhai should be the figure who reassured Gandhi about Hinduism is all the more striking since Raychandbhai was often quite critical of the Vedas, insisting that the Jain tradition had thought more systematically and better about dharma. If, nevertheless, Gandhi could be reassured about Hinduism by his conversations with Raychandbhai, this probably had to do with the latter's understanding of dharma. Elaborating on 'the nature of dharma as explained by him [Raychandbhai]', Gandhi remarks:

Dharma does not mean various sectarian beliefs [*amukh matmatantar*; 'any particular creed or dogma']. Nor does it mean reading or learning by rote books known as Shastras or even believing all that they say.

Dharma is a quality [*gun*] of the soul [*atmaan*] and it resides in humanity [*manavjaati*; 'every human being'] in visible or invisible form. Through it we know the duty of human life [*manushyajivannu kartavya*; 'our duty in human life']. Through it we can recognize [*olakhiye*] our true relation with and other living things [*beeja jivo*; 'other souls']. It is evident that all this is not possible till we have known the self in us [*potaney na olakhiye*]. Hence dharma is the means [*sadhan*] by which we can know ourselves.

We may accept this means from wherever we get it, whether from India [*Bharatvarsha*] or Europe or Arabia [*Arabistaan*]. Anyone who has studied the scriptures of different faiths will say that the general nature of this means as expounded in them is the same.

Thus, while Raychandbhai 'believed that the *Jinagamas* [Jain holy books] contained the perfection of spiritual knowledge', Gandhi further remarks that he

... did not, however, lack respect for other faiths. ... In all his discussions with me, he never told me that if I wished to attain *moksha* I should follow a particular dharma and no other. He advised me only to think about my actions [*aachaar*]. When the question arose of what books I should read, he thought of my personal inclinations [*valann*] and the world of my youth [*bachpan-na sanskaar*] and advised me to continue the *Gita* which I was then reading.[11]

This multiplicity of dharma was worked out through a central motif which is asserted in Raychandbhai's *Mokshamala*, the only book by him which we know he recommended Gandhi to read. There, Raychandbhai insisted that 'any one religion is on this srishti completely true. Now in calling one religion [*darshan*] true, other religions may have to be called wholly [*keval*] untrue, but I cannot say so.'[12] An intriguing argument is involved here—that each dharma, darshan, or religion is a totality and perfectly true as a totality. And yet, it can and must tolerate other totalities. He defended this position briefly by drawing on the Jain distinction between *nischaya dharma*, or the dharma that sought to know things in their intrinsic form, and *vyavahara dharma*, or the dharma that was concerned with everyday transactions. He suggested that while it might be possible to call some religions untrue in terms of nischaya dharma, all religions were true by the terms of vyavahara dharma.

Mokshamala does not systematically follow up on the implications of such a statement, and reverts elsewhere to hierarchy of dharma, with the way of the Jains clearly privileged. For Raychandbhai, while the equality of all religions was something he presumed, he never systematically elaborated on it. For his purposes, an exploration of the *Jinagamas* was adequate. Nevertheless, Raychandbhai's argument there about vyavahara dharma is extremely suggestive: 'The principal thing [*mukhya*] in *vyavahara dharma* is *daya* [compassion].' Having made this claim, *Mokshamala* proceeds to explicate vyavahara dharma in terms of the four vows involved in daya, and the eight forms of daya. In the process it subtly, perhaps even inadvertently, casts nischaya dharma as secondary to and even a form of vyavahara dharma. Thus its extended account of the various practices of daya involved in vyavahara dharma concludes with nischaya daya—the daya towards the self involved in 'single mindedness in search of one's pure self'. And nischaya dharma itself is discussed only very briefly, in terms that subsume it within the practice of daya involved in vyavahara dharma.[13]

I do not have either the desire or the competence to situate these arguments in relation to the internal debates within Jainism, where it is possible to situate this argument. I am more concerned here with the way Gandhi takes up these concerns. Gandhi does not seem to use the phrase vyavahara dharma in his writings, but his understanding of dharma is in some ways very close to what he ascribes to Shrimad Rajchandra. This is so on many registers, but we could begin with the observation that the term daya is picked up by him to make an assertion very similar to Raychandbhai's. In Chapter 17 of *Hind Swaraj*, for instance, he cites Tulsidas on daya:

The poet Tulsidas has said: 'Of religion, pity, or love [*daya*], is the root, as egotism of the body. Therefore, we should not abandon pity so long as we are alive.' This appears to me to be a scientific truth. I believe in it as much as I believe in two and two being four. The force of love is the same as the force of the soul or truth. We have evidence of its working at every step. The universe would disappear without the existence of that force.

Daya, thus, is constitutive of the universe and of religion. A phrase that recurs in his writings is dayadharma—the religion of love. And the force of *satyagraha* itself was described in *Hind Swaraj* as *dayabal* and *atmabal*—terms that are translated as love force and soul-force.

TOLERANCE

Daya—Gandhi's difficulties with this word are indicated by the hesitation in the English *Hind Swaraj*, which resorts to two words to translate daya—pity and love. Elsewhere, he also translates it as compassion. Through the word daya, I would like to suggest, Gandhi eschewed the problematic of agency and power, whether that agency takes the form of domination, subordination, or equality. There can be no agency in daya, for in the experience of daya, one gives oneself to the other in ways that one is no longer is control of, where one is neither powerful nor powerless.

And the concept-word dayadharma names an especially audacious move. Through that word, Gandhi does not only attempt to conceptualize a dharma organized around daya. Even more audaciously, he suggests that dharma itself needs to be conceptualized as always the working of daya.

Now, the suggestion that there is anything audacious in this invocation of dayadharma might seem a little puzzling. If we stick with the standard translation of daya as compassion, what Gandhi argues for here seems neither particularly original nor particularly compelling: compassion in closely related forms, after all, has been a staple of world religions, secular religion, and spiritualized secularism. One might also well say of this kind of spiritualized secularism, that it is a good and even laudable sentiment, but what political and philosophical purchase can it give?

All this makes for a compelling question: what is involved in dayadharma?

Perhaps what is most salient for our arguments here is that dayadharma involves a very distinctive equality and pluralism. Secular thought insists that religion cannot allow for equality to other religions (or more broadly to others), that religious rule will result in a theocracy rather than pluralism. As Ashis Nandy has repeatedly pointed out, secularism claims a monopoly on religious and ethnic tolerance and on political rationality. It insists that only it can practice a pluralism that defends the right to diverse religious practices. But to rehearse in a brutally abbreviated form two key elements of the secular concept of tolerance, it rests, first, on a double disengagement, of which the distinction between public and private spheres is symptomatic. In the public sphere, secular tolerance involves not an engagement with the singularity of what is included within it, but rather a subjection of what is included to the criteria of a public and communicative reason. And though the right to a private sphere is absolutely central to secularism and is what makes for much of its tolerance, the irrationality of the private sphere (the realm to which religion is usually relegated) can be tolerated both because it is being constantly remade in the image of public reason, and because the public sphere dominates the private.

Second, and consequently, this double disengagement (which is also a double domination) inscribes a statist inequality and violence within the very core of secularism. Secularism rests on the premise that the other is inferior to the extent that the other does not conform to public and communicative reason. What is tolerated is thus rarely equal (tolerance is thus a very appropriate word here). Even where secular tolerance extends an abstract equality to the other, this abstract equality is always undercut by the insistence that full equality requires the exercise of reason. Thus it is that secularism can, without contradicting itself in the slightest, always justify colonialism or the expropriation of land from Native Americans, or the treatment of some religions as inferior. There is thus a constitutive violence to secularism and its statist projects.[14]

There is absolutely no tolerance in this disengaged sense involved in dayadharma. Indeed, Gandhi is disturbed by the secular concept of tolerance precisely because of these hierarchical implications. He dwells on them explicitly in one amongst his series of letters (later published as the book *Mangalprabhat*, in Gujarati, and *From Yeravda Mandir*, in

English) that discussed ashram vows. The letter was devoted to the vow *sarva dharma sambhavna*, a phrase which he translated into English as 'equality of all religions':

This [*sarva dharma sambhaav*] is the new name we have given to the Ashram observance which we know as *sahisnuta* ['tolerance']. 'Sahishnuta' is a translation of the English word 'tolerance'. I did not like that word. But I could not think of another ['a better'] one. Kakasaheb [Kalelkar], too, did not like that word. He suggested 'Respect for all religions' [*sarva dharma aadar*]. I didn't like that either. In tolerating other religions, they are considered deficient [*unap*]. In respect there always enters a sense [*bhav*] of patronage [*maherbaani*; Tolerance may imply a gratuitous assumption of the inferiority of other faiths to one's own and respect suggests a sense of patronizing ...]. Ahimsa teaches us *sambhaav* for other religions [to entertain the same respect for the religious faiths of others as we accord to our own]. Tolerance and respect is not enough from the perspective of *ahimsa*. In the fundamental principle [*moolma*] of keep *sambhaav* towards other religions, there is also an acceptance [*svikaar*] of the incompleteness [*apoornata*] of one's own religion.[15]

These and other remarks suggest an understanding of *sarva dharma sambhavna* that is somewhat at odds with the implications usually associated with the phrase. Like many other words in Gandhi's vocabulary, the term has been appropriated in fascinating ways for statist purposes, most notably for a Nehruvian secularism. From a broadly Nehruvian point of view, it might even be said that what sets the secularism of the Indian state apart from its Western counterpart is that while the latter insists on a separation of religion and the state, the Indian state's *sarva dharma sambhavna* stresses the equality of religions, or an equal participation by the state in all religions. There is a very important difference between these two formulations. The separation of the state from religion does not mean that the state has nothing to do with religion. That would anyway be impossible (even though many liberal theorists have difficulty recognizing this impossibility). What secularism conceptualizes as the separation of the state from religion is rather an abstract equality of religions, where the state is formally equidistant from all religions. From the point of view of Nehruvian secularism, such an abstract equality of religions smuggles in the presumptions of the dominant religion, and does not recognize the social inequality that prevails amongst various religious formations. The separation of the state from religion in this abstract sense produces a majoritarian secularism. It is this majoritarian secularism, for example, that the BJP seeks to impose in India (and BJP ideologues are in this sense not incorrect in saying that they seek to practice true secularism, for it is their version of secularism that is more consistent with classical European secularism and its genocidal impulses); similarly, it is this majoritarian secularism which enables decisions such as the recent French one to deny citizenship to a woman who wore a veil.

If Nehruvian secularism in contrast affirms *sarva dharma sambhavna*, this is because its postcolonial inheritance allows it to see all too acutely (in ways that European liberalism is perhaps only beginning to encounter and conceptualize) the limitations of a secularism based on formal equality. For Nehruvian secularism, true plurality requires substantive equality. Such substantive equality requires certain protections for minority religious formations, rather than simply a formal equality between religious formations. What the statist version of *sarva dharma sambhavna* thus practices, is a secularism that seeks a substantive equality between various religious formations. (It is at least in part, though by no means entirely, this Nehruvian attempt at a substantive equality that leads to charges against it of 'minorityism'.) This substantive equality still remains within a humanist or liberal problematic, since it claims an external relation to religion, and seeks primarily to realize more effectively the humanist vision of equality.

SPIRIT
But I do not wish to be sidelined here into an exploration of the fascinating implications of the Nehruvian reworking of the European humanist or liberal problematic. My point is quite different: it is that while Gandhi would in all likelihood have been quite sympathetic to the statist appropriation of *sarva dharma sambhav*, his arguments are organized around another notion of equality—an equality that is neither formal nor substantive, one that is constituted by dharma rather than in a break with it. His *sarva dharma sambhav* is not just about the equality of all religions (the way Gandhi himself translated the phrase) but—if we follow Gandhi in allowing the word religion to translate dharma— an attempt to conceptualize religion itself differently, where religion always gives equality between the self and the other.

In order to make this point, it may be appropriate to very briefly trace the genealogy of Gandhi's almost obsessive concern with equality. The post-facto evidence of his autobiography suggests that Gandhi was from quite early in his youth deeply upset at the subordination involved in colonialism, and sought to redress it through meat-eating and other practices that sought to make him more like the Englishmen with whom he sought equality. At least by the time he was a student in

Britain, he seems to have been convinced that European intellectual and political traditions themselves affirmed equality. In one of his earliest available writings, he remarks on how Indian converts to Christianity had embraced the idea of equality from the Europeans. This conviction that the value of equality was affirmed in European traditions remained central to his thinking. During a tour to the French influenced areas of south India in 1934, for instance, he remarked that it was 'France that first gave the world the three significant words "Liberty, Equality, Fraternity" ["*swatantrata, samaanta, aney bandhuta*"].'[16] Speaking just a day later in Pondicherry, he again remarked: 'Equality [*samaanta*] and brotherhood were brought into France several hundred years before people began to realize that there was anything like brotherhood of man. The bravest of them fought and bled for that realization.'[17]

Similarly, when he claimed to be a loyal subject of the British Empire, as he notoriously did on several occasions, he did so through the profoundly subversive claim (made much to chagrin of his imperial protagonists) that the Empire provided for equality to its citizens. In 1895, in one of his earliest petitions to the British, he protested against the injustice of the treatment meted out to Indians in South Africa by pointing out that the Proclamation of 1858 provided for the equality of all 'Her Majesty's subjects' and specifically mentioned that Indians should be treated as equal.[18] In later years too, this insistence on equality remained central and he argued, much to the chagrin of the representatives of the very Empire to which he professed loyalty, that 'equality [*samaanta*] is the cornerstone of the Imperial edifice'.[19] Especially suggestive is a Gujarati essay he wrote on the occasion of King George's coronation. The essay became for him an occasion to explore the nature of his loyalty to the British Empire as a colonial subject. Arguing for loyalty to King George, he suggested:

Moreover, the British Constitution aims at securing equality of rights [*sarkha hak*] and equality before the law [*sarkho nyaya*] for every subject. Those who are not accorded this ["those who do not enjoy such equality"], they are free to fight for justice [*nyaya*], the only restriction being that the mode of agitation shall not harm others. Not only is every British subject free to fight in this way, but it is his duty [*faraj*] to do so.

Indeed, he insisted that he could even express loyalty only by claiming equality: 'The loyalty of a slave is no loyalty. He only serves. If a slave can be loyal, that must be due to coercion. The loyalty of a free man [*swatantra manas*] is willed [*marajiyat*].' He went on to argue: 'If the British Constitution were to change and lay down that there would be no equality [*eksarkhapan*], not even in theory, as between whites and blacks [*kala*, "Coloureds"], we could no longer owe allegiance to such a constitution and would have to oppose it.'[20]

But he identified the French Revolution and the British Constitution with 'legal equality', or what he also often called 'theoretical equality' or 'fictitious equality'. Many of his campaigns in both South Africa and India were concerned with securing this kind of equality. He argued that such fictitious equality was worth fighting for, and was preferable to the inscription of inequality in law. In an early interview, a British interlocutor, Lord Crewe, suggested to him that the inscription of inequality in law in South Africa still granted more than, and was therefore preferable to, a fictitious equality of the Australian kind which was accompanied by the 'Australian policy of excluding by imposing ridiculous tests'. Gandhi responded that while fictitious equality [*krutrim samaanta*; artificial equality] was 'unsatisfactory', it was still 'the lesser of the two evils'.

And after all, is not the British Constitution itself founded on many fictions [*krutrimtao*]? I have myself been nurtured in those traditions. As a student I learnt the value of this kind of fiction. Indeed, after mature consideration, I have come to the conclusion that there is a very reasonable basis for these so-called fictions.[21]

Thus, over and again, he claimed and affirmed the equality of the British Empire and the French Revolution (and these two equalities are not as far apart as they might seem).

But he was also ambivalent about fictitious equality, perhaps because it is impossible to think of such equality without reference to the 'modern civilization' that Gandhi attacked. This ambivalence is evident in his attacks on democratic institutions over and again, most notoriously in *Hind Swaraj*, where he describes the English Parliament as a 'prostitute'. He also insisted that democratic institutions were unsuitable for India. Over and again, he made remarks similar to the ones that he made in his response to the conservative Hindu Central Committee in 1933: '[S]o far as I am concerned there is no desire indiscriminately to import Western ideals of society, civilization [*sabhyata*] and equality'.[22]

Yet these attacks on democratic institutions were accompanied by a constant affirmation of the 'spirit of democracy'. In 1920, for example, as he campaigned against the British, he insisted:

If we wish to evolve the spirit of democracy [*lokshahina bhaavna*] out of slavery, we must be scrupulously exact in our dealings with opponents. We may not replace the slavery of the Government by that of the non-co-operationists. We must concede to our opponents the freedom we claim for ourselves and for which we are fighting.[23]

There was thus a *spirit* of democracy that he sought to separate from the parliamentary institutions of democracy. Indeed, it was in the spirit of democracy that he attacked parliamentary institutions.

This spirit of democracy that he separated out from the institutions of parliamentary democracy was equality. Gandhi was insistent that it was not only in these European institutions of democracy, with their stress on fictitious equality, that equality was to be found. He discerned the practice of equality also in various dharma, or 'religions'. As early as 1905, in a lecture on Hinduism, he argued that the 'key-note of Islam' was

... its levelling spirit. It offered equality to all that came within its pale, in the manner that no other religion in the world did. When, therefore, about 900 years after Christ, his followers descended upon India, Hinduism stood dazed. It seemed to carry everything before it. The doctrine of equality could not but appeal to the masses, who were caste-ridden.[24]

Later too, Gandhi was to insist on Islam's spirit of equality and fraternity. In 1926, he wrote:

Someone has said (I do not know where, but only recently) that Europeans in South Africa dread the advent of Islam,—Islam that civilized Spain, Islam that took the torchlight to Morocco and preached to the world the Gospel of Brotherhood [brathrubhaavna]. The Europeans of South Africa dread the advent of Islam, for they are afraid of the fact that if the Native races embrace Islam they may claim equality with the white races. They may well dread it. If brotherhood is a sin, if it is equality [samaanta] of Coloured races that they dread, then that dread is well founded. For I have seen that any Zulu embracing Christianity does not ipso facto come on a level with all Christians, whilst immediately he embraces Islam, he drinks from the same cup and eats from the same dish as a Mussalman.[25]

Elsewhere, Gandhi's arguments about Islam, for example, suggest that what it brought to Hinduism was precisely an awareness of Hinduism's obscuring of equality. Through its encounter with Islam, Hinduism could for Gandhi be infused with equality.

But Gandhi's claim was not only that some social practices associated with some religions instituted equality. If such were the case, it could equally be claimed (and Gandhi himself made the claim on occasion) that other religious practices instituted inequality. Gandhi was acutely aware of the inequality that characterized Hinduism. His remarks about the French Revolution cited above, for instance, went on in the following vein:

It can be said that it was France that first gave the world the three significant words, 'Liberty, Equality and Fraternity'. But it is not given to all to enforce the three things in practice and I am ashamed that Hindus have been the worst criminals in this respect. It was reserved for them to invoke the name of God for untouchability.[26]

Religious practices were thus as capable of promoting equality as inequality. It was thus not at all his argument that religion or dharma involved a greater or more consistent practice of equality than parliamentary democracy. Instead, more interestingly and productively, in the arguments that he makes especially from 1909 onwards, it is possible to discern the claim that religion itself is constituted by a distinctive finitude and equality, and that this finitude and equality sustained a secularism internal to the concept of religion.

CONSTATIVE

The sense that there was alternative Indian or Indic concept of equality was pervasive amongst early twentieth-century nationalists. Indeed, many Indian nationalists perhaps sensed such an equality in the concept-word, dharma. While I have neither the desire nor the competence to provide a history of dharma (that task is one with which scholars of South Asia have long been concerned, and the difficulties of that task are well illustrated by P.V. Kane's monumental classic *History of the Dharmasastras*), nationalists discerned a certain kind of finitude and plurality in that word, a certain difference from the word religion. For them, across many of its various formulations, the word dharma usually involves not so much a concern with the ontology or theology as the obligation to carry out, to be given to a task. Dharma in this sense is not an object as much as an activity. This activity makes dharma always very concrete and plural, even when the formulation appears to be abstract (as when dharma is declared to be the pursuit of *sat*—for now, being or truth). Put differently, while on the one hand dharma is universal, there is no abstract.

Many upper-caste nationalists in the early twentieth century picked up on this to argue for the distinctive plurality of Indian civilization. Around the time of *Hind Swaraj*, the young Aurobindo had defended the boycott of British goods against the criticisms made by 'a poet of sweetness and love' (Tagore, it seems safe to presume). The poet, he remarked, demanded a 'saintliness of spirit' that was impossible. In contrast, he remarked,

Hinduism recognizes human nature and makes no such impossible demand. It sets one ideal for the saint, another for the man of action, a third for the trader, a fourth for the serf. To prescribe the same ideal for all is to bring about *varnasankara* the confusion of duties, and destroy society and the race. If we are content to be serfs, then indeed boycott is a sin for us, not because it is a violation of love, but because it is a violation of the Sudra's duty of obedience and contentment. Politics is the field of the Kshatriya and the morality of the Kshatriya ought to govern our political actions. To impose on politics the Brahminical duty of saintly sufferance, is to preach *varnasankara* [the destruction of *varna*].[27]

Such formulations are framed, whether consciously or not, by the liberal understanding of the task of politics as that of balancing the claims of equality against those of difference. What such formulations suggest is that the caste order of *varnadharma* achieves that task in a way that is both just and uniquely Indian. For here, each varna is constituted on the one hand by a constative finitude that makes difference possible (every varna has a different role to play, and the roles cannot be mixed up), and on the other hand a functionalist understanding of Indian civilization where various castes complement each other and come together to produce a modern Indian nation-state that would not be significantly different from European nation-states. The word *swadharma*—one's own dharma, the duty assigned to one by caste—was often invoked in the late nineteenth and early twentieth centuries to describe this functionalist organization of constative finitude. For upper-caste nationalists, such a functionalist understanding entailed a distinctive equality, one they thought to be different from Western concepts. For them, swadharma prescribed not the abstract equality of all humans, but rather the equality of different varnas to their dharma—their equality in other words to their difference and finitude, and in this equality their equality to each other.

Thus, nationalists explained caste hierarchies through a distinctive functionalism, which claimed that the oppression of caste was merely a later accretion, and that varnadharma in principle and as concept only instituted a functional hierarchy. Effectively, this functionalist thinking of equality through a constative finitude justified an order where various castes were separate but equal. (An argument on these lines about caste as making for a distinctively Indian modernity occurs even in the writings of such a self-proclaimed modernist as Nehru. But Nehru himself limits this constative finitude to Indian prehistory, treating it simultaneously as a sign of potential and of inadequacy.)[28] It was the monstrous inequality of this formulation that was instituted in the very name of equality that thinkers like Ambedkar were to so brilliantly question.

LIMITS

There can be little doubt that Gandhi participated on many occasions in invocations of swadharma and varnadharma. Like other nationalists, he often discerned this swadharma at work in the Gita. There, Arjuna expresses doubts about the war with the Kauravas, and says that he does not want to go to war. Krishna points out to Arjuna that his dharma as a Kshatriya requires him to fight the Kauravas, and urges Arjuna to perform his swadharma as a Kshatriya. Gandhi returned on many occasions to this section of the Gita, noting for instance in a lecture that occurs as the culmination of a series of discourses given at the Sabarmati Ashram on the Gita:

With this, the Lord concluded the argument: 'Better one's own duty, bereft of merit' [*Shreyan swadharma viguna ityadi*]. That means that, whatever one's swadharma, even if it be without merit ['seemingly without merit'], and even if the other's seems full of merit [*gun-vaalo*], even then one's swadharma is better than the other's dharma.[29]

But even where he did so, he also questioned, wittingly or unwittingly, the constative and functionalist reading of finitude propounded by early twentieth century upper-caste nationalists. In order to discern how this happened, we might begin with his obsessive insistence on the observance of limits. For him, such an observance of limits was not a given trait of Indian civilization to be harnessed to create a distinctive Indian modernity. Rather, it was itself a politics, and one with very distinctive entailments. (Indeed, this was the sense in which he was never quite part of the nationalist problematic despite being the most prominent leader of the Indian nationalist movement.) The centrality of limits emerges in his remarks about swadeshi, which for him was necessary if swaraj or self-rule was not to produce an English rule without the Englishman:

After much thinking, I have arrived at a definition [*lakshan*] of swadeshi that perhaps best illustrates my meaning. Swadeshi is that spirit [*bhavana*] in us which restricts us to the use and service of our immediate surroundings [*paaseyni paristhithi*] to the exclusion [*tyaag*, sacrifice or surrender] of the more remote. Thus, as for religion, in order to satisfy the requirements of the definition, I must restrict myself to [*vadgi rahevu*, adhere to] my ancestral religion. That is the use of my immediate religious surroundings. If I find it defective, I should serve it by purging it of its defects. In the domain of politics, I should make use of the indigenous institutions and serve them by curing them of their proved defects. In that of economics, I should use only things that are produced by my immediate neighbours [*maari paasey vasnaraoey*] and serve those industries by making them efficient and complete where they might be found wanting.[30]

Indeed, limits marked dharma itself. Consider Gandhi's contrast in Chapter 8 of *Hind Swaraj* between dharma or religion and 'modern civilization':

Hinduism, Islam, Zoroastrianism, Christianity and all other religions teach that we should remain passive [*mand*] about worldly things [*dunyavi vastu*] and active about religious things [*dharmik vastu*], that we should set a limit [*hadh*] to our worldly ambition and that our religious ambition should be open [*mokda*; 'illimitable']. Our activity should be kept only to that ['latter channel'].

It is all too easy to read 'limit' or *hadh* privatively, to presume that the call is to limit 'worldly ambition' in order to transcend the worldly and reach an illimitable religious ambition. Such a privative understanding presumes that the limit involves ascesis, where ascesis is understood as the practice of austerities in order to transcend the physical for something spiritual, infinite, and larger. Here, the limit is not itself the concept of religion; it is merely the requirement for an absorption into the transcendent infinitude that is God. Such an understanding of Gandhi's argument seems all the more persuasive since Gandhi himself seems over and again to explicitly resort to it.

But such an understanding of Gandhi's argument in terms of limits misses out on its more far-reaching implications, implications which convert it into a conceptual argument about finitude, and about how an acknowledgement of finitude involves questioning secular certitudes, beginning with the commonsensical secular certitude about how the distinction between secularism and religion is to be thought. A recent magisterial reiteration of the certitude by Charles Taylor put it this way:

[W]e have moved from a world in which the place of fullness was understood as unproblematically outside of or 'beyond' human life, to a conflicted age in which this construal is challenged by others which place it (in a wide range of different ways) 'within' human life. .... The great invention of the West was that of an immanent order in Nature, whose working could be systematically understood and explained on its own terms, leaving open the question whether this whole order had a deeper significance, and whether, if it did, we should infer a transcendent Creator beyond it. This notion of the 'immanent' involved denying—or at least isolating and problematizing—any form of interpenetration between the things of nature on one hand, and 'the supernatural' on the other, be this understood in terms of the one transcendent God, or of Gods or spirits, or magic forces, or whatever.[31]

And what marks this ethics is a focus on what Taylor calls 'human flourishing': 'a secular age is one in which the eclipse of all goals beyond human flourishing becomes conceivable; or better, it falls within the range of an imaginable life for masses of people'.[32]

Now, this secular contrast between the immanent and transcendent worlds is never (not even in the case of Taylor, who tries exceptionally hard to avoid this) simply a description. It always valorizes the immanent, which is regarded as ethically, politically, and intellectually more compelling. Even where it is not stated in these terms, it is presumed that the values of liberty, equality, and fraternity, or freedom broadly, are best served where a distinction between the immanent and the transcendent is maintained, and where the immanent is privileged and dominant.

Gandhi's religion however refuses the secular narrative which sees secularism on the side of immanent, and religion on the side of the transcendent. The point I am making is simply that it is not the case that for figures like Gandhi other things are more important than human flourishing—that he suggests abandoning the immanent for the transcendent (though it often seems that way because we operate with the modern secular concept of the human). Rather, Gandhi's category religion offers a different thinking of the human altogether, which is very ill-served by the secular distinction between the immanent and the transcendent.

The terms that organize Gandhi's thinking are intimated in a passage in Chapter 8 of *Hind Swaraj* that follows soon after the one above. It adds of the adherents of 'modern civilization', those who infinitize themselves: 'They remain neither of faith nor of the world. They completely forget the real things.' [*Teo nathi raheta din-na ke nathi raheta duniya-na. Teo khari vastu-ne taddan bhooli jaaye chhe.*]

This phrase, with its conjoining of *din* and *duniya*, is widespread not only in Gujarati but in other related languages too. The conjoining is suggestive of a thinking that does not fit with the secular narrative. The originally Arabic word din, central to Islam, is not quite religion or faith but much more—it is a way of living. Din, in this sense, always already involves an attitude to the world—it is a way of being worldly. Furthermore, here there is no choice between din and duniya. Rather than an oppositional choice between the two, the two terms are paired and work together: To give up on din is thus also to give up on the duniya, and vice-versa. In other words, when Gandhi says that they remain neither of faith nor of the world, he struggles to contest the familiar secular opposition of the worldly and the religious—the very opposition that he himself succumbs to in his contrast just a little earlier between 'religious things' and 'worldly things'. And the duniya proper to din is not unworldly or otherworldly, as secular thought would have it, but rather a distinctive worlding, a worlding for whom dharma or din involves the real or true [khari] things. Dharma and din are thus never about an asocial relation to an otherworldly or transcendent God: both these terms name a way of being social.

The stakes of this sociality are indicated perhaps also by the difficulty that Gandhi has translating the two sentences above into English. He renders it as: 'They become utterly irreligious and, in reality, derive little advantage from the world.' A very suggestive bit of floundering goes on here. Trying to translate his description of the consequences of the infinitizing of modern civilization, he fails, and resorts instead to remarking that 'they become utterly irreligious'. To stay neither with din nor with duniya—this is to be utterly irreligious. To become irreligious, furthermore, would be to derive little 'advantage' from the world. Again, then, what is reiterated is that being religious is about a distinctive sociality. Conjoined with the Gujarati text, the argument is also that it is in this sociality that 'advantage' occurs, that 'real things' abide.

It is this other sociality that I have tried to point to with the concept-word finitude. Religion, to axiomatically indicate the argument I am making, always involves the practice of finitude. And when Gandhi suggests that dayadharma is the root of dharma, what he argues is that dayadharma is the practice of finitude. And if finitude matters in this way, this is because finitude sustains a sociality that is unrecognizable from a sociological or historical perspective, just as this sociology is incomprehensible from the perspective of dayadharma. Dayadharma must always proceed by setting aside the sociological or historical understanding of things, for the latter understanding must, as I have argued elsewhere, necessarily involve the creation of a world organized around infinitude.[33]

GUESS

But what are the stakes of this emphasis on finitude, of this refusal of the transcendent-immanent distinction? From a secular perspective, Gandhi's refusal of the distinction seems to lead to the enchanted world that is the stock of secular descriptions of the religious, the world that fails to make the proper distinctions between the transcendent and the immanent. Gandhi's God is not dead, and indeed intervenes all the time in the world. Notoriously, for instance, he described the 1934 earthquake in Bihar as a 'divine chastisement [*saja*] sent by God for our sins', specifically the sin of untouchability.[34]

From a secular perspective, such a remark reveals the dangers of a perspective that fails to maintain the distinction between the immanent and the transcendent: not only does such anthropocentrism rest on a complete misunderstanding that mixes up even orders of causality, but it implies an ethics which shifts responsibility away from humans to the divine. One might for example ask in the outraged secular vein (which I for one most certainly cannot not share) that marked many of the letters that Gandhi received: if earthquakes are divine chastisement for sins, why does God punish the innocent? Does this mean that it is presumptuous to save oneself from an earthquake or from other natural processes by learning more about natural causality? Secularism can only consign such remarks to its prehistory, to a time when people had not learnt to think rationally enough.

But this very term enchantment perhaps needs to be deployed cautiously, given how inextricable it is from secular conceptions of the religious. Even where we celebrate and affirm enchanted worlds, we perhaps limit ourselves to opposing secularism in secularism's own vocabulary; we perhaps remain within a secular problematic. It is worth attending to the way that Gandhi interrogates the secular conceit that allows the distinction between the secular and the superstitious or enchanted:

I share the belief with the whole world—civilized and uncivilized—that calamities such as the Bihar one come to mankind as chastisement for their sins. When that conviction comes from the heart, people pray, repent [*pashtaap*] and purify themselves. I regard untouchability [*asprishyata*] as such a grave sin as to warrant divine chastisement. I am not affected by posers such as 'why punishment for an age-old sin' or 'why punishment to Bihar and not to the South' or 'why an earthquake and not some other form of punishment'. My answer is: I am not God. Therefore I have but a limited knowledge of His purpose. Such calamities are not a mere caprice of the Deity or Nature. They obey fixed laws as surely as the planets move in obedience to laws governing their movement. Only we do not know the laws governing these events and, therefore, call them calamities or disturbances. Whatever, therefore, may be said about them must be regarded as guess work. But guessing [*anumaan*] has its definite place in man's life. It is an ennobling thing for me to guess that the Bihar disturbance is due to the sin of untouchability. It makes me humble [*namra*], it spurs me to greater effort towards its removal, it encourages me to purify myself, it brings me nearer to my Maker. That my guess may be wrong does not affect the results named by me. For what is guess to the critic or the sceptic is a living belief [*jeevtijaagti shraddha*] with me, and I base my future actions on that belief. Such guesses become superstitions [*vahem*] when they lead to no purification and may even lead to feuds. But such misuse of divine events cannot deter men of faith from interpreting them as a call to them for repentance for their sins. I do not interpret this chastisement as an exclusive punishment for the sin of untouchability. It is open to others to read in it divine wrath against many other sins.'³⁵

Several disconcerting and even uncomfortable moves occur here. Perhaps we can grope our way through the passage with the word 'superstition'. As in the passage above, Gandhi often attacks superstition, vahem, in the name of religion. He opposes religion and 'old traditions' to the superstitions of both modern civilization and those of religion. But what he calls superstition simply cannot be governed by the usual Enlightenment triad of superstition/myth, reason, and religion. In that triad, superstition names those beliefs which fail to maintain the division between the orders of the divine and the secular, which presume that the divine intervenes in everyday life through miracles and other wondrous events; conversely, religion names those beliefs which are concerned with the transcendent in a way that sustains the distinction between the immanent and the transcendent. This triad clearly cannot work for Gandhi, for whom miracles and divine intervention are clearly important and constitutive of his religion. To a secularist, Gandhi's religion is not truly religion: it is merely superstition. And even to the critics who might question Enlightenment's perception of itself, who might insist that the Enlightenment is mythic fear turned radical, Gandhi's fear would smack of precisely that mythic fear which they charge the Enlightment with radicalizing.

So we come to the question: what is Gandhi's concept of religion, and correspondingly of superstition? How does he organize this triad of reason, religion, and superstition, if not in the usual Enlightenment way?

Perhaps we can begin addressing that question by attentiveness to the guess that has its definite place in man's life, but that can become either religious and 'ennobling' or superstitious. Gandhi elaborates on the distinction between the two in terms that are deceptively tautological and simplistic: the guess is religious where it leads to purification and superstitious where it leads to feuding. The guess properly observed 'makes me humble', and leads to faith, belief. There can be (as will be indicated later) disagreement and conflict where there is humility, but there cannot be a feud.

But what is the nature of this *anumaan* or guess? Gandhi's guess does not belong to the reasonable realm of that which is probable but unprovable; there is nothing reasonable about it. It is just that—a guess. As a guess, it does not have to and does not claim to answer several questions—why here, why now, and how? With the guess, one is in the realm of faith. The guess is centrally thus about a conviction and a belief that cannot be justified by the criteria of causal reason, that will not submit to reason, and will yet intervene in the domains of science and ethics and everyday life that Enlightenment traditions would consider reason's own.

This suggests why humility or *namrata* should be proper to the guess. Gandhi presents the matter sometimes in somewhat conventional terms, as in the passage above where he says that he cannot know the workings of God. In such a formulation, the humility and finitude of the guess of faith is only understood in a metaphysical manner—privatively, as an acknowledgement of the way that human agency is limited and can always be overcome by 'acts of God' (and it is surely not accidental that the agential understanding of the divine enshrined in this phrase is central to insurance law today); that the finitude of the human glance cannot take account of the infinitude of God. And the infinitude of God is also thought metaphysically here—as that which is too large and too huge for comprehension by the finite human being.

But the guess of faith is also humble in another way here: even where it is absolute (as it must be where it becomes a 'living belief' or faith) such a guess must acknowledge its singular limit—that it is constituted by and constitutes only its own singular relation to God, that it must be both absolute and yet not make any ontological or epistemological claims. As such, there is a finitude and a limit that is constitutive of the guess of faith. In order to be faithful, it must practice this singularity, or observe limits. In this very observing of the limit, the 'living belief' is always already open to the other. For even though Gandhi's faith can never be proven wrong, it remains only his living belief.[36] As such, the rightness or wrongness of either Gandhi's or the other's guesses becomes completely unimportant ('that my guess may be wrong does not affect the results named by me').

This openness to the other is the original equality that 'living belief' must always give to the other. In this openness, we receive an intimation of an equality that is not organized by the abstract epistemological criteria of knowledge.[37] This equality that is always involved in living belief—is this what Gandhi names in the previous passage as making him humble? If it is an ennobling thing for Gandhi to guess that the earthquake was because of untouchability, is this because the practice of untouchability denies the equality that the faithful guess gives to both itself and the other?[38]

FAITH

The nature of this equality to the other can be elicited by attentiveness to the word dayadharma. Neither that word nor the word daya occurs in the passage above. But it is intimated in the word 'purification'. Here, purification involves a hewing to the nature of the guess as faith. And the practice of 'purification' involved the observance of various vows or *vrat*. Gandhi usually stressed on eleven vows. The vows were modelled on the Jain and Hindu traditions of the major vows (*mahavrat*). Five of these were the conventional mahavrat of truth (*satya*), non-violence (*ahimsa*), celibacy (*brahmacharya*), non-stealing, and non-possession. He supplemented these, moreover, with six more: fearlessness, removal of untouchability, bread labour, equality of religions, humility, and swadeshi. To rehearse, though only in abbreviated form in this essay, his reading of the vows, he always started out with the primary vow of satya or truth. As he put in the first of a series of letters devoted to ashram vows that inmates of Sabarmati Ashram should observe (these letters were later published as a book, *Mangalprabhat*), and meant to be read out as discourses at Sabarmati Ashram: 'the word Satya is derived from Sat, which means Being. That is why Sat or Truth is perhaps the most important name of God.'[39]

But what was Gandhi's concept of satya? Whether translated as truth or being (and the two cannot of course be separated in any rigorous accounting), it is after all a notoriously underdetermined term, one of the stakes of the conventional debate between science and religion. What is striking, perhaps, is that Gandhi's notion of satya does not accord with either (expectedly) the scientific conception of truth and being or (less expectedly) with what is usually regarded in the metaphysical tradition as the religious conception of truth and being. This discordance emerges only gradually. The discussion in *Mangalprabhat* of the vow of satya strikes a preliminary note. The letter suggests that the 'devotion [aradhana] to satya is the sole justification for our existence [hasti]'; that it is not merely a matter of speaking the truth but rather that 'all knowledge is necessarily included in it'. This satya, moreover, does not require consensus:

what may appear as truth to one person will often appear as untruth to another person. ... there is nothing wrong in every man following *satya* according to his lights. Indeed it is his duty to do so. Then if there is a mistake on the part of anyone so following Truth, it will be automatically set right.

How this will happen is not indicated. Instead, just a few sentences later, the letter says: 'But now we have come to the border-line beyond which lies *ahimsa*. We will discuss it next week.'[40]

This pattern is repeated. In order to understand the vow of satya, it becomes necessary to turn to its supplementation by ahimsa. In order to understand the vow of ahimsa, it becomes necessary to turn to the vow of brahmacharya, and so on. The various vows that followed satya are thus extraordinarily important because of the way that in them the vow of satya unfolds. This unfolding is most marked in the second vow, ahimsa. For Gandhi, truth was inseparable from ahimsa, which he described as 'the foundation of the world':

Indeed, without ahimsa it is not possible to seek and find Truth. Ahimsa and Truth are as inseparable [*othproth*] as two sides of a coin, or rather of a smooth unstamped metallic disc. Who can say which is the obverse and which is the reverse? Nevertheless, ahimsa may be considered [*ganiye*; 'is'] the means and Truth may be considered ['is'] the end. The means is what is within our reach ['Means to be means must always be within our reach'], and this is why ahimsa is the supreme dharma [*paramdharma*; 'supreme duty']. Satya becomes God. If we keep attending to the means, we will someday behold [*darshan*; 'reach'] satya.[41]

But ahimsa could not for him be thought only its privative form, as simply abstention from violence towards others. It was a form of compassion, daya. This emphasis on daya or—to resort to another word that he often deployed—prem or love, was pervasive and constitutive of all his arguments. In a leaflet published in 1919, for instance, he argued: 'There cannot be hatred [*tiraskaar*] of any individual in my writings, because it is my belief that this world is founded [*nabhi*] on love [*prem*]. Only where there is love is there life. A life without love is like death [*mrityu samaan*; "is death"]. Love is the reverse of the coin of which the obverse is *satya*.'[42] This love and truth, moreover, were constitutive of religion: 'Only truth is religion [*satya eyj dharm*] is one axiom. Only love is religion is another axiom. Since there cannot be two religions ["as there can be only one religion"], it follows that truth is love and love is truth.'[43]

In words such as prem or daya, the distinctiveness of the finitude and equality that Gandhi associates with religion emerges. Here, the words daya and *prem* point to the practice of ahimsa as the infinite giving of oneself, and such infinite giving can be conceptualized, paradoxically, only as the very practice of finitude. For one cannot give to oneself— that would only be taking. One can only give to that which is constitutively apart from oneself. In order to sustain the other's constitutive separation from that to which one gives, thus, it is necessary to practice finitude.

To think of daya in this way is to venture a very distinctive conceptualization of both God and the human. God is the prime practitioner of daya, which is to say that God constantly gives of God's own self. God, as Gandhi insists on several occasions, is infinite. But Gandhi understood the infinitude of God in a distinctive way. For him, the infinitude of God could not be thought as infinitude in the metaphysical sense—so familiar to us from dominant traditions within Christianity, Islam, or Hinduism—of mastery as power without limits. Rather, God's infinitude involves a radical finitude. Thus Gandhi argued: 'God is no dispenser of rewards and punishments [*fal*], nor is He an active agent [*karta*]. ... At no time and in no circumstances do we need a kinglike God [*raja jeva*]. By thinking that we do, we put a limit to the power of the *atman*, which is infinite.'[44] In such an argument, perhaps human freedom is exemplary of the way that God's infinitude works by making itself finite: such freedom must include freedom from God, and equality with God.

This insistence that God cannot be an agent, that the very concept of God gives an equality with God, leads Gandhi to contemplate an erasure of the word God itself. Thus, the 1930 *Mangalprabhat* letter about Satya went on: 'In fact it is more correct to say that Truth is God than to say that God is Truth. But as we cannot do without a ruler or general, the name God is and will remain more current. On deeper thinking, however, it will be realized that *sat* or *satya* is the only correct and fully significant name.' Less than a year before, in December 1929, Gandhi had described this formulation—that Truth is God—as a new and better formulation of his earlier claim that God is Truth.[45] On several occasions in the years after *Mangalprabhat*, he referred to this transition: 'I used to say that "God is Truth". But that did not satisfy me. So I said, "Truth is God".'[46] He did not regard the new formulation as a shift in his perspective, but rather as a better articulation of a perspective that he had articulated inadequately before (and he is not incorrect in this, since he does on several occasions in earlier years state that 'Truth is God', though he seems to treat this as interchangeable with the statement 'God is Truth'.)

What are the stakes of the new formulation? Perhaps we can approach it by turning to an event in 1925 that may have played a role in problematizing for him his formulation 'God is Truth'. This was the response of a Congressman to Gandhi's use of the word God. The Congressman objected 'because "God" has now a place on pledges and vows such as that administered to Congress volunteers, which begins "with God as witness, I ...".' The Congressman suggested that atheists or many Buddhists could not, in good faith, take such a pledge and asked: 'is it proper to exclude from Congress service any such merely because of their religious faith?' In his reply, Gandhi acceded that it was not, and said that the 'mention of God may be removed if required from the Congress pledge of which I am proud to think I was the author. Had such an objection been raised at the time, I would have yielded at once. I was unprepared for the objection in a place like India.' He went on to argue, in the usual vein, that God was Truth, and was as such even 'the atheism of the atheist'.[47]

It was his experience—using that word in its strong sense—of this question that seems to have led to the reformulation, 'Truth is God'. Indeed, in a speech at Lausanne about a year after *Mangalprabhat* letter where he ventured the distinction, he remarked that 'it was because of their [atheists'] reasoning that I saw that I was not going to say "God is Truth", but "Truth is God."'[48] By conceptualizing God as satya, he was not simply discarding theological baggage to affirm a secular truth that would remain after the death of God, that secularists too could affirm, that could provide a new truth that secularists too were amenable too. Rather, he was conceptualizing satya itself in a distinctive way, where satya was marked by a giving of itself to the other, and the radical finitude that emerged in such giving. It is this radical finitude which also makes him suspect that the sat or being of satya and satyagraha is not a being that 'is' in the metaphysical sense of a constative or eternal being or truth, but rather itself marked by non-being.

Symptomatic of this is his resort on several occasions to the phrase 'neti, neti' ['not this, not that']: 'Even God vanishes and we have only neti neti.'[49] Here, it would be mistaken to read the emphasis on neti neti as the working of an Indian apophaticism. Rather, neti neti has to be understood in conjunction with the emphasis on daya and prem. Conjoined thus, what the emphasis on neti neti foregrounds is the insistence that it is the giving involved in daya or prem, rather than even the object of that act, which is the stake. In this giving, there remains no trace of an agential God, or even of some transcendent presence—there is only the transitivity of the giving.

(It might seem as though there is a glaring contradiction here: how can the God who causes earthquakes—a kingly act, if there ever was one!—be reconciled with this other God who is not an actor at all. But we perceive this contradiction primarily because we operate with a metaphysical understanding—and I will not here develop the argument, which nevertheless needs someday to be made, that secularism is the apogee of the metaphysical understanding, and as such equally its moment of greatest danger and greatest opportunity—of miracles, where a miracle is the act of God as agent. But for Gandhi, a miracle is not a constative event. For the faithful, indeed, a miracle can never be a constative event. To understand a miracle as a constative event—this is the conceptual error that he describes as superstition; it is the failure of faith, the pre-eminent mark of inadequate faith. For the Gandhi who makes the distinction between the guess of superstition and the guess of faith, the miracle is an event only for the faithful witness. Even in the belief that God had caused the earthquake, thus, God does not act as a divine sovereign. The proper response of the faithful to the event of the miracle, Gandhi's earlier argument suggests, can only be purificatory; it can only involve the practice of radical finitude.)

In this rending of God into a satya that is thought through daya and prem (and the neti neti that is always constitutive of them), a distinctive argument about the human also becomes possible. Since the human is the *pratibimb* (silhouette or reflection) of God, humans too are marked by this paradox: the infinitude that is proper to them can be sustained only by the practice of finitude. In other words, finitude in Gandhi's argument is organized and made possible by an infinite giving, the giving that gives always freedom and equality to both self and other. The finitude that Gandhi conceptualizes is in this sense perhaps better described as an in/finitude. In this infinite giving, faith provincializes both itself and the other. It provincializes itself by limiting itself, not simply in the negative sense of an ahimsa that abjures the force of arms, but in the more active sense of ahimsa as daya, or the productive giving of onself to the other. This giving in daya also provincializes the other, for it refuses to accept the other's claims to domination, and in its combination of finitude and infinitude insists on the other's singularity.

This worlding in in/finitude is neither transcendent nor immanent if we are to use these words in their conventional secualr senses. It is not transcendent because it does not find meaning in a divinity beyond the world; from its perspective, indeed, secular thought's humanism—its privileging of the human—is transcendent. And it is not immanent because it refuses to accept the world in the sociological or historical sense. Thus, when in Chapter 17 of *Hind Swaraj*, the Reader asks for examples of the working of atmabal (which he also elsewhere describes as dayabal, or the force of daya), the Editor responds:

The universe would disappear without the existence of that force. But you ask for historical evidence. It is, therefore, necessary to know what history means. The Gujarati equivalent means: 'It so happened'. If that is the meaning of history, it is possible to give copious evidence. But, if it means the doings of kings and emperors, there can be no evidence of soul-force or passive resistance in such history.

I have elsewhere discussed this passage in detail. Here, I wish to only stress that daya or prem (which in this argument always the proper of faith) is resistant to the disciplines of immanent knowledge, of which sociology and history are exemplars. The disciplines are necessarily constituted by measure: they must analyse social relations in terms of determinate and regular relations of power, culture, class, and so on. But the finitude of religious or faithful actors is sustained by an immeasurable and infinite giving. Of this giving, and correspondingly of the finitude of these actors, there can be no disciplinary knowledge.

SUPERSTITION

Now it is possible to turn to the question of what makes a guess into superstition. Perhaps we can take our cue from another word that appears in the passage above—'feud'. A feud is premised on a conviction in the rightness of one's guess, or in other words, the conversion of a guess into a matter of ontological and epistemological knowledge. Once a truth is ontological and epistemological, that which does not accord with it is false. The only way such a truth can be tolerant is by being weak. But it obviously cannot be too weak, for it will then no longer be a truth. It must continue to be defined and centred, however surreptitiously and unconsciously, by its truth (this surreptitious persistence of the centre is what many radical critiques of multiculturalism have pointed to). In other words, an ontological and epistemological truth can only feud with other claims to truth. The only equality it can grant to its other is what Gandhi describes on occasion as the equality established by the sword, when it is opposed by a truth of equal ontological and epistemological power. Hierarchy, in other words, is central to ontological and epistemological truth. Such a truth does not 'purify' itself by establishing its own limits, as faith does; rather, for such a truth to purify itself is precisely to make its ontological and epistemological claims stronger.

It turns out, thus, that what separates faith from superstition is that the former is constituted by the practice of equality with the other, that contrary to secular thought the giving of equality to the other is possible only where there is faith, belief, or religion. Indeed, since secular thought must always draw, however weakly, on an ontological and epistemological truth, the spectre of superstition is internal to the concept of secularism rather than to the concept of faith. And it is precisely where faith models itself after reason, or where reason claims sovereignty, that superstition occurs.

Gandhi pointed in this vein on some occasions to the privileging of reason. Responding on one occasion to a correspondent who had written him a letter suggesting that religious faith was at the root of Hindu–Muslim tensions, and that 'secular education is the remedy for Hindu-Muslim riots', he responded thus:

But the correspondent has yet another word that holds him in its chains. It is the mighty word 'rationalism' [buddhivad]. Well, I had a full dose of it [mein dharai dharaine eno swaad chaakhyo; I have over and again assumed its mantle and tasted its flavors]. Experience has humbled me enough to let me realize the specific limitations [chokkas maryaada] of reason. Just as matter misplaced becomes dirt, reason misused becomes lunacy . . .

Rationalists are admirable beings, rationalism is a hideous monster [rakshas] when it claims for itself omnipotence . . .

Works without faith [shraddha] and prayer are like an artificial flower that has no fragrance. I plead [daleel] not for the suppression of reason [buddhi], but for a due recognition [yogya swikar, appropriate acceptance] of that in us which sanctifies [paavan] reason itself.[50]

Involved here is a provincializing of reason, a stress on its 'distinct limitations'. But to provincialize is never to reject. The move of provincializing operates here on two registers. First, reason is affirmed. Both here and even more emphatically in the years around and after the Mangalprabhat letters, there is the insistence that 'on matters which can be reasoned out, that which conflicts with Reason must also be rejected'.[51] Also, that which is 'amenable to rational enquiry' must be submitted to it.[52] Gandhi stressed the centrality of reason even in conversations between faiths. Thus, when asked in a discussion with a missionary, Dr Crane, what he would do with 'a man who says he is commanded by God to do violence', Gandhi insisted: 'There you would not put another God before him. You need not disturb his religion, but you will disturb his reason. ... You will not pit one word of God against another word of God. But you will have to bear down his reason.'[53]

Second, the relation between faith and reason is refigured. That faith is not opposed to reason is for Gandhi already given in the Gujarati words he uses for faith and superstition—*shraddha* and *andhshraddha*. Shraddha, in other words, is by its very nature not blind or unreasonable; when it becomes andhshraddha or 'blind faith', it is no longer faith but superstition. For Gandhi, 'faith begins where reason fails. That is to say, faith is beyond reason'.[54] But it is not beyond reason in the sense that it transcends reason (though he says precisely that it does in the English interview with Dr Crane). Rather, faith is 'that in us which sanctifies reason', and it does so by supplementing reason. For the word 'sanctify' is suggestive, as is its translation by the powerful word *paavan*. To sanctify is to make holy. In other words, reason itself is marked by sanctity, but that sanctity comes from faith, and from the work of faith as daya and prem. To sustain reason in accordance with this sanctity is one of the tasks that a religious politics sets itself.

But what is the line between reason and faith, and how is it to be governed? This is the secularist question that Gandhi's affirmation of faith and religion cannot escape. And the explicit answer he gives is quite anodyne: that the line that determined where reason failed and faith become inescapable was itself rational and clear, that all could agree on where reason had its provenance. But the anodyne answer is misleading, as even a slight consideration suggests. If the answer were indeed so anodyne, there would not have been the tension between faith and reason that he seeks to address. An alternative understanding is also suggested by his various positions. Thus, while his faith led him to believe that the Bihar earthquake was divinely ordained, for him the belief that Jesus was 'the only begotten son of God' was one of those that 'conflicts with reason'.

We would be reading too quickly if we simply pounced here on an inconsistency in his different responses to two very similarly structured claims. Rather, this is another of those occasions where his argument has to be produced by rending it from his own rendering. The inconsistency, I would suggest, is quite consistent with the nature of the faith that

Gandhi affirms. Faith is marked by its singularity. As one essay on the relation between reason and faith remarks, 'the faith of one man is of no use to another man'.[55] It is of the very nature of faith in its singularity that it will on occasion find that it will regard other faiths as unreasonable, that to 'bear down on his reason' does not lead to consensus. This does not mean that they are wrong. Rather, this is the moment at which a faith can encounter another faith as faith, and no longer through the abstract third term of secularism. Faithfully encountering the other faith as faith, this is the moment at which an according of equality to the other faith becomes both possible and necessary. This is the moment at which the equality accorded to the other faith will result simultaneously in another concept of secularism and tolerance and, where faiths clash, in the practice of satyagraha.

SAMBHAV

It is this other concept of secularism and tolerance that he names with the phrase *sarva dharma sambhav*. Its potentialities can be elicited by considering the way he conceptualized relations with Muslims. He refused to participate in the celebration (which one finds for instance in Nehru's *The Discovery of India*) of India as a syncretic culture where Hindu and Muslim identities were deeply and on occasion almost indistinguishably intertwined. As I have suggested elsewhere, syncretism is a profoundly secular category. It represents the secular attempt to envision a figure other to itself that can be celebrated. As such, syncretism is the answer to the secular question: how can different religions tolerate each other in the absence of or before secularism, before the third term or neutral meeting ground represented by secularism, civil society, and reason exists. And the answer is syncretism, where different religions or cultures mix together without conflicting.[56] While Gandhi was not hostile to cultural miscibility of Hindus and Muslims, since religion was for him a faith rather than a sociological object, miscibility could not provide a conceptual answer to the problem of the relation between religions in the absence of conventional secularism:

I hope that nobody will bring up here the history of the attempts by Guru Nanak and Kabir to unite Hindus and Muslims; for the effort today is not for uniting the religions, but for uniting hearts while maintaining the separateness of religions. The efforts of Guru Nanak and others were towards fusing the two by showing the basic unity of all religions. The effort today is at tolerance [*titiksha*]. The effort is to see how the orthodox Hindu, while remaining staunchly Hindu, can respect and sincerely wish prosperity to an orthodox Muslim. True, this attempt is altogether new, but its spirit is there at the roots of Hindu dharma.[57]

It was from such a perspective that Gandhi could simultaneously affirm religion and secularism. Faith, conceptualized through the emphasis on the limit and on finitude, already had internal to it the daya which allowed it to 'tolerate' other religions. It is this *religious* capacity to tolerate other religions that Gandhi was to describe as *sarva dharma sambhavna*—'equality of all religions' as Gandhi translated it, or more precisely, the treating of other religions as one's own. In other words, 'equality of all religions' no longer described a secularism that emerged through a transcendence of religion, or through the creation of secular religion that would confine itself the private sphere; rather, it described the secularism that was internal to religion thought properly—which is to say, as dayadharma, as an abiding by the in/finitude that is proper to both God and the human who's is God's pratibimb, and practices religion as a way of being this pratibimb.

It was in this spirit that Gandhi appropriated Gopal Krishnayya's definition of what was involved in the struggle for swaraj:

It is not the common political suffering that is to weld together the Hindu and the Muslim like the Greeks of old during the Persian invasions, but the mutual respect, regard and love for each other's dharma. ... and the necessity for its individuated preservation that can and shall achieve it. Swaraj, therefore, means the preservation of Hindu dharma, Muslim dharma, Christian dharma, Parsi dharma, Sikh dharma, in short *swadharma* of all and a co-ordinated federation of all.[58]

'Equality of all religions' was in this sense a secularism internal to religion; it was the following of swadharma or one's own dharma which involved each religion preserving both itself and the other religion. Perhaps Gandhi's participation in the Khilafat movement (much before he coined the phrase 'equality of all religions', but in complex ways anticipating that formulation) prefigures what would be involved in such a pursuit of swadharma. For him, the Khilafat movement's call for the restoration of the *Khalifa* was a religious demand made by Muslims. A religious demand—this is to say that it arose from a faith that sanctified reason. Such a demand had to be pursued by reason to the extent that it could, but when reason failed to obtain to it, then it had to be still pursued. And that pursuit had to be supported even by those faithful to other religions unless it was antithetical to one's own religion, in which case it had to be opposed, but opposed religiously.

Furthermore, both religious demand and religious opposition could only proceed through ahimsa, the word that is casually translated as non-violence. To resort to violence was to fail to recognize the in/finitude that was constitutive both of the other who was one's antagonist, and of one's own demand as a religious demand. It was to become irreligious. And 'irreligion cannot be cured by irreligion, but only by religion. There is no room in religion for anything other than *daya* [compassion]'.[39] But even where a religious demand was pursued irreligiously, even where it became irreligious, Gandhi as a figure who abided by religion had to respond to it religiously, whether that response took the form of opposition or support. It is as such a religious demand that Gandhi supported the Khilafat movement.

I will not go here into how both opposition and support, when conducted in a religious vein in Gandhi's sense, took the form of satyagraha. I only wish to stress that *sarva dharma sambhav* envisioned an equality of religions quite unlike that envisioned by what we usually know as the secular tradition. It entailed fighting religiously for the other's religion; it entailed the giving of oneself or daya to the other who remained absolutely other.

Perhaps this also suggests why Gandhi often resorted almost interchangeably to the terms dharmarajya, which he associated with Yudhisthira, and *ramrajya*, which he associated with Rama. Both were gestures in the direction of a state that practised the equality internal to religion. Unlike, say, Bruno Bauer, who as the young Marx notes in his 'On the Jewish question' regards the Christian state as incapable of emancipating the Jew (and Marx does not disagree with this formulation), what Gandhi seeks to envisage here is a religious state that will as part of its very practice of religion emancipate the Hindu as Hindu and the Muslim as Muslim. What Gandhi seeks to put in place here, in other words, are the protocols for conceptualizing those state forms which are not secular, but which nevertheless recognize the equality of other religions not only as a matter of interest, but conceptually. By describing such a state form as secular, Gandhi pushed in entirely another direction the stress on equality that marked conventional secularism—towards a consideration of what would be involved in religious equality, and what kind of 'secularism' came forth in the practice of religious equality.

But what could be the relation between the abstract and measurable equality that conventional secularism involved, and the immeasurable equality involved in religion? This was a question to which Gandhi gave two quite conflicting answers, both of which belong together as conceptual possibilities, and each of which can nevertheless be pursued only by the destruction the other (though Gandhi himself almost never acknowledges this relation between the two). Symptomatic of this is the conflict between the profoundly conservative politics that Gandhi practised on some occasions, and the profoundly radical politics that emerges on other occasions. But an exploration of these two impulses of Gandhi's affirmation of religion and its immeasurable equality, and of the relation between them, will have to await another occasion.

NOTES AND REFERENCES

1. This paper is the result of ongoing conversations with many of my colleagues and friends at the University of Minnesota, but especially to those with Vinay Gidwani, Qadri Ismail, and Simona Sawhney. I was also very fortunate to be able to discuss the arguments of the paper with Saurabh Dube, Ishita Bannerjee-Dube, David Hardiman, Vinay Lal, and Mrinalini Sinha. Writing this essay has been an especially thought-provoking task for somebody like me, who has been brought up as an atheist, and who is not aware of experiencing a desire to give up on his atheism.

2. P.D. James, *Original Sin* (New York: Warner Books, 1994), p. 38.

3. Jacques Derrida, *Acts of Religion* (London: Routledge, 2002), p. 74.

4. Theodor Adorno and Max Horkheimer, *Dialectic of Enlightenment* (London: Verso, 1997), p. 16.

5. Jacques Derrida, 'Structure sign and play in the discourse of the human sciences', *Writing and Difference* (London: Routledge, 1978), p. 289.

6. 'May God help', *Young India*, 24 November 1924; in *The Collected Works of Mahatma Gandhi* (CWMG), second edn., Ministry of Information and Broadcasting, Government of India (Ahmedabad: Navjivan Press, 1958), vol. 29, p. 373f; *Akshardeha*, vol. 25, p. 340.

7. *Harijan*, 22 September 1946, in *CWMG*, vol. 92, p. 190. In these notes, I first refer to the language in which Gandhi originally wrote, and where it has proved possible provide a reference to the translation. Whereas Gandhi originally wrote/spoke in Gujarati, I have wherever possible tried to adhere to the official translation. However, I have sometimes modified the official translation. In such cases I have also provided the official translation, wherever necessary. I have provided the official translation in parentheses. Where Gandhi originally wrote/spoke in Hindi, I have depended on the English translation. When citing from *Hind Swaraj*, I have given the number of editions available, tried to make things easier for the reader by indicating the chapter from which the citation is taken. Since these chapters are fairly short, it will presumably not be a problem to find the citation within the chapter.

8. Speech at a prayer meeting, 28 November 1947, *CWMG*, vol. 97, p. 414.

9. Letter to R.W. Aranyakum, *Harijan*, 23 March 1947; in *CWMG*, vol. 94, p. 19.

10. 'Some Reminiscences of Raychandbhai', *Akshardeha*, vol. 32, p. 3; *CWMG*, vol. 36, p. 468.

11. 'Some Reminiscences', *Akshardeha*, vol. 32, p. 8; *CWMG*, vol. 36, p. 476f.

12. 'Mokshamala', *Shrimad Rajchandra*, tenth edn. (Agaas: Shrimad Rajchandra Ashram, 2006), p. 100.

13. Ibid, p. 64ff.

14. In identifying these two aspects of secularism, I reprise from my book under

preparation, *Gandhi's Faithful Rendering: Secularism, Religion, and Immeasurable Equality*. These two aspects emerge when we attend to Gandhi's faithful rendering of William Salter's secularism.

15. Letter to Narandas Gandhi, 21–23 September 1930, *Akshardeha*, vol. 44, p. 165; *CWMG*, vol. 50, p. 78.

16. Speech at Public Meeting, Karaikal, 16 February 1934, *CWMG*, vol. 63, p. 167; *Akshardeha*, vol. 57, p. 171.

17. Speech at Public Meeting, Pondicherry, 17 February 1934, *CWMG*, vol. 63, p. 172f; *Akshardeha*, vol. 57, p. 177.

18. Petition submitted to Lord Ripon, Principal Secretary of State for the Colonies by Indians Resident in the South African Republic, [Before] 5 May 1895, *CWMG*, vol. 1, p. 229. During this period, his commitment was to a very restricted notion that sought to claim 'the Indian's fitness for an equality with the civilized races'. See *CWMG*, vol. 1, p. 285.

19. 'Indians under the Union', *Indian Opinion*, 25 June 1910; in *CWMG*, vol. 11, p. 73; *Akshardeha*, vol. 10, p. 329.

20. 'Rajyabhishek', *Indian Opinion*, 24 June 1911; *Akshardeha*, vol. 11, p. 129f; 'The Coronation', *CWMG*, vol. 11, p. 452ff.

21. Interview with Lord Crewe, 16 September 1909, *CWMG*, vol. 10, p. 88; *Akshardeha*, vol. 9, p. 466.

22. Letter to Hindu Central Committee, 13 February 1933, *CWMG*, vol. 59, p. 262; *Akshardeha*, vol. 53, p. 331.

23. 'Social Boycott', *Young India*, 8 December 1920, in *CWMG*, vol. 22, p. 66; *Akshardeha*, vol. 19, p. 73.

24. 'Hinduism', *The Star*, 11 March 1905; in *CWMG*, vol. 4, p. 208. We do not have the text of Gandhi's talk, only a newspaper report of it.

25. Speech on resolution on South African Indians, Kanpur Congress, 26 December 1925, *CWMG*, vol. 33, p. 356; *Akshhardeha*, vol. 29, p. 287ff.

26. Speech at Public Meeting, Karaikal, *CWMG*, vol. 63, p. 167; *Akshardeha*, vol. 57, p. 171.

27. Aurobindo, *Bande Mataram: Political Speeches and Writings, 1890–1905*, vols 6 and 7 of *Complete Works of Sri Aurobindo* (Pondicherry: Sri Aurobindo Ashram Press, 2002), p. 1118.

28. See, for instance, Jawaharlal Nehru, *The Discovery of India* (Delhi: Oxford University Press, 1994), 245ff.

29. 'Gandhijinu Gitashikshan', *Akshardeha*, vol. 32, p. 290; 'Discourses on the Gita', *CWMG*, vol. 37, p. 343

30. Speech on Swadeshi at Missionary Conference, Madras, 14 February 1916, *CWMG*, vol. 15, p. 159; *Akshardeha*, vol. 13, p. 202ff.

31. Charles Taylor, *A Secular Age* (Boston: Harvard University Press, Boston, 2007), p. 15f.

32. Ibid., p. 19f.

33. I explore Gandhi's criticisms of the secular tradition in *Gandhi's Faithful Rendering*.

34. Speech at Tinevelly, *Harijan*, 24 January 1934, in *CWMG*, vol. 63, p.38; *Akshardeha*, vol. 57, p. 45.

35. 'Bihar and Untouchability', *Harijan*, 2 February 1934, in *CWMG*, vol. 63, p. 82; *Akshardeha*, vol. 57, p. 90.

36. On another occasion, I will explore a related theme which would take us too far afield from the concerns of this essay—that of how this living belief also conceptualizes one's equality with oneself.

37. Here equality with the other is conceptually prior to the fact that the other too has his or her own guess, and that the possibility that they are as faithful as Gandhi's own living belief is constitutive of these other guesses too. When equality is granted only to those who can guess, the human would merely be redefined as the figure who can guess. Gandhi's insistence on the finitude proper to the guess would strictly speaking not allow for a hierarchical distinction between the animal and the human.

38. Despite evident differences, my discussion here clearly owes a great deal to Akeel Bilgrami's article. See Akeel Bilgrami, 'Gandhi's Integrity: The Philosophy behind the Politics', *Postcolonial Studies*, vol. 5, No. 1 (2002), pp. 79–93.

39. Letter to Narandas Gandhi, 18–22 July 1930, *Akshardeha*, vol. 44, p. 42; *CWMG*, vol. 49, p. 384. These letters were written while he was jailed at Yeravda. The Gandhian press Navjivan, collected and published the letters same year under the title *Mangalprabhat*. Valji Govindji Desai translated the letters into English; Gandhi went over this translation, which was published by 1932 under the title *From Yeravda Mandir*.

40. Letter to Narandas Gandhi, 28–31 July 1930, *Akshardeha*, vol. 44, p. 42; *CWMG*, vol. 49, p. 383.

41. Letter to Narandas Gandhi, 28–31 July 1930, *Akshardeha*, vol. 44, p. 60; *CWMG*, vol. 49, p. 409.

42. *Satyagraha Patrika* no. 5, 17 April 1919; *Akshardeha*, vol. 15, p. 228; *CWMG*, vol. 17, p. 437.

43. 'What is Satyagraha', *Satyagraha Patrika* no. 6, 25 April 1919; *Akshardeha*, vol. 15, p. 240; *CWMG*, vol. 17, p. 448.

44. Letter to Jamnadas Gandhi, 30 May 1913, *Akshardeha*, vol. 12, p. 76f; *CWMG*, vol. 13, p. 153.

45. See, for instance, his letter to Prabhudas Gandhi, 2 December 1929, *CWMG*, vol. 48, p. 48.

46. Discussion with D. Ramaswami, *CWMG*, vol. 84, p. 266.

47. 'God and Congress', *Young India*, 5 March 1925, in *CWMG*, vol. 30, p. 332ff.

48. Speech at a meeting in Lausanne, 8 December 1931, vol. 54, p. 268.

49. 'Gandhijinu Gitashikshan', *Akshardeha*, vol. 32, p. 170; 'Discourses on the Gita', *CWMG* vol. 37, p. 199

50. 14 October 1926, in *CWMG*, vol. 36, p. 401f; *Akshardeha*, vol. 31, p. 463ff.

51. Interview with Dr Crane, 25 February 1937, *CWMG*, vol. 71, p. 2; *Akshardeha*, vol. 64, p. 426.

52. Reason vs. Faith, *Hindi Navajivan*, 19 September 1929, in *CWMG*, vol. 47, p. 108; *Akshardeha*, vol. 41, p. 427.

53. Interview with Dr Crane, *CWMG*, vol. 71, p. 2; *Akshardeha*, vol. 64, p. 426.

54. Reason vs. Faith, *Hindi Navajivan*, 19 September 1929, *CWMG*, vol. 47, p. 108; *Akshardeha*, vol. 41, p. 427.

55. Reason vs. Faith, *CWMG*, vol. 47, p. 108; *Akshardeha*, vol. 41, p. 427.
56. I restate here an argument that I had made in a more preliminary terms in 'Gandhi's Politics: Liberalism and the Question Of the Ashram' *South Atlantic Quarterly*, vol. 101, no. 4 (Fall 2002), pp. 955–86.
57. 13 January 1921, in *Akshardeha*, vol. 19, p. 270; *CWMG*, vol. 22, p 289; translation modified.
58. 'Notes', *Young India*, 12 January 1921, *CWMG*, vol. 25, p. 173.
59. 'The late, great Tolstoy', *Indian Opinion*, 26 November 1910, in *Akshardeha*, vol. 10, p. 461; *CWMG*, vol. 11, p. 176.

PAULA RICHMAN

The Politics and Print Career of Rajagopalachari's Tellings of Ramkatha

It may come as a surprise to learn that C. Rajagopalachari (1878–1972), a statesman so prominent in the freedom struggle of Madras Presidency that he earned the moniker 'Gandhi of the South', and so central to the nationalist movement that many assumed he would be appointed India's first President, would deem his retellings of Ramayana and Mahabharata 'the best service I have rendered to my people'.[1] Indeed, he found it 'a source of great joy' that these works, written toward the end of his life, had helped readers 'realise their higher selves'.[2] From 1954 to 1972, there was no time when he was not involved in reading, interpreting, writing, translating, broadcasting, glossing, or writing prefaces to Ramkatha (Rama's story)—in Tamil or English.[3]

Scholarly studies of Rajagopalachari's oeuvre have neither taken into account how recursive was his attention to certain episodes in Ramkatha nor examined the complex and ambivalent relations between his three ways of telling the narrative. His biographers have focused mainly on the fortunes of his career in political offices, with only passing attention to his Ramkatha writings.[4] In contrast, Rajagopalachari's writings on Ramkatha take centre stage in this essay, and are contextualized less in the light of the ebbs and flows of his career as a political leader than in relation to his deepest moral and political concerns during the final decades of his life.

Many people today assume that his widely-distributed English paperback, titled Ramayana, conveys Rajagopalachari's sole interpretation of

Ramkatha but in fact he retold parts of Rama's story in different ways in three genres: short story, prose epic, and translation:[5]

1. A set of Tamil short stories published in Tamil magazines or anthologies; later translated into English.
2. *Cakkaravartti-t-Tirumahan* [Venerated Son of an Emperor], a serialized Tamil prose epic; later a Tamil book, best known in English translation as Ramayana.
3. *Bharat Milap* [Reunion with Bharata], a transcript of radio talks based on an excerpt from a twelfth-century Tamil devotional text he translated into English verse.

Each of the three performs distinctive kinds of cultural work. The short stories delve into psychological motivations of characters. The prose epic presents a heroic tale to inspire the newly-free citizens of the Indian nation, while the translation glorifies Lord Rama.

In order to avoid mistaking Rajagopalachari's Ramayana as his authoritative interpretation of Rama's story, one must examine it in light of the other two tellings. His three tellings were shaped not only by the genre in which they were written but also by particular aspects of print culture at the time of publication. Only by examining the circumstances under which all three of Rajagopalachari's tellings were composed and circulated can one apprehend Rajagopalachari's diverse, and sometimes contradictory, responses to Ramkatha, which range from deep unease to admiration to intense piety.

This essay explores the range of interpretations present in Rajagopalachari's tellings of Rama's story. In relation to print culture, I argue that he wrote his prose epic and his translation to link readers to what he saw as 'classical' wisdom and that those books were promoted by literary institutions that propagated Indian national integration, and distributed them over time to an ever-widening circle of readers. In contrast, his short stories probed the psychological motivations of Ramkatha characters more deeply but earned only a limited readership. In relation to literary genres, I argue that the short story allowed him to grapple imaginatively with knotty moral dilemmas downplayed in his prose epic and absent in his translation. By viewing Rajagopalachari's Ramayana in light of his efforts to rationalize problematic actions in his short stories and by taking into account the devotion that drives his translation, we obtain a more comprehensive and balanced view of his interpretations of Ramkatha than if we take his Ramayana as his sole—and authoritative—telling.

LITERARY CLASSICS AND PRINT CULTURE

Moral Discourse, Enduring Texts, and Hindu Epics

Rajagopalachari's manner of recounting Ramkatha draws upon the multiple roles he played over the course of his long life. Born in 1878 in Salem district, Madras Presidency, into an orthodox, Brahmin, Sri Vaishnava family, C[akkaravartti] Rajagopalachari trained in, and entered, the legal profession. At the age of forty-seven, he renounced a successful law career to join a Gandhian ashram (religious community) which promoted self-reliance (swaraj) among rural villagers. Later, he played a crucial role in the Indian National Congress, and served as Chief Minister of Madras twice (1937–9 and 1952–4), Governor of West Bengal (1947–8), India's head of state (1948–50), and Home Minister in Nehru's cabinet (1950–1). In 1959, he co-founded a rightist political party to contest Nehru's socialist policies. His legal training schooled him in accurate and concise wording, his Gandhian work shaped his development of a pedagogical narrative voice, and his political speeches gave him practice in addressing a wide variety of audiences.

Rajagopalachari's impetus to publish emerged from specific experiences. At the ashram in the mid-1920s, he published his first short stories in support of Gandhi's liquor boycott. While serving a jail sentence under the British in the early 1940s, he and his fellow-prisoners daily studied Valmiki's ancient poem, Ramayana, a literary endeavour that provided the foundation for his subsequent retelling of the epic in prose.[6] He began it in 1954 when he was coping with a radical diminution of his political stature after another man was chosen as President of India (a position he coveted). Retelling Rama's story turned his attention away from the disappointments of political office and allowed him to enter, as he put it, 'a different world, with the characters of the Ramayana'.[7]

Rajagopalachari's writings on Ramkatha form one part of his broader effort to provide instruction about matters that he considered crucial to the cultural and practical education of Indian citizens. In addition to his retellings of Mahabharata and Ramayana, his publications encompass an impressive range of subjects: an analysis of Krishna's teachings in Bhagavadgita, a guide to the classical poems of Auvai, short stories about rural life, a chemistry primer, a biography of Socrates, an essay on the inevitability of Partition, attacks on nuclear proliferation, a summary of Shankara's philosophy, and topical columns for Tamil and English magazines. Yet, he returned again and again to ponder the nature of proper action, refracted through the lens of Ramkatha.

When writing for a general audience, Rajagopalachari's goal was to inform rather than create works of literary originality. He sought to facilitate understanding among non-specialists with little other access to substantive information on the subject. He gave lucid explanations of complex topics, and earned a reputation for cutting to the heart of the matter. A prominent scientist marvelled that, in a two-page article in a magazine for general readers, Rajagopalachari explained a complicated scientific discovery in the field of physics more clearly than any physicist had managed to do.[8] His *Cakkaravartti-t-Tirumahan* and English Ramayana were among the most widely read non-Hindi tellings of Rama's story in Independent India, at least partially due to his concise exposition and his ability to relate the story to the times in which his readers lived.

Rajagopalachari often used narrative to present moral advice, a tendency that some critics condemned as a literary flaw.[9] Although his writings were frequently denigrated by critics as 'preachy', he took pride in seeing them instead as purposive.[10] He admits in a preface to an anthology of short stories, for example, that many of the selections were composed 'not by an author aspiring to be an author but for furthering the public causes in which he was involved'. He hoped to aid readers on the path to wisdom by inculcating truths about how to live, writing that he 'held fast to the skirts of Mother Truth'.[11] In using stories for ethical instruction, in choosing genres that captured audiences' attention, and in picking rhetoric suited to his targeted readers, he joined a long lineage of respected Indian storytellers.[12]

Like many other nationalist intellectuals of his era, he took for granted that 'high civilizations' produced 'epics' which reflected their national character and, for him, India's epics were Ramayana and Mahabharata. In addition, he often conflated ancient and modern India, exclaiming, for example, that his retelling of Ramayana presented 'the people of Bharat just as they *are*, with all their virtues and their faults' [my emphasis]. Similarly, he saw Mahabharata as a text that 'has moulded the character and civilisation of one of the most numerous of the world's people' through 'its gospel of dharma, which like a golden thread runs through all the complex movements in the epic'.[13] He viewed the Hindu epics as 'classics' that encapsulated the values central to 'civilization', and proclaimed that they 'really embody our national character in all its aspects'.[14] And yet, of course, the concept of 'nation' as conceived by twentieth-century Indian nationalists did not exist when the ancient Hindu epics were originally composed.[15]

To illustrate the value of the epics, he described a visit to the site of an ancient temple with a friend, where the high quality of its architectural remains led him to praise the work of the masons of those days. His friend countered that not all ancient masons produced such outstanding work; because the poor quality of inferior masonry led to their disintegration, they have not survived to the present. Rajagopalachari saw the situation as parallel to preservation of great literary works: noting that they continue 'to speak to our lives and concerns' long after they were written, he declared that the Hindu epics survived due to their ability to put Indians in conversations with 'learned, divinely-inspired sages of India's ancient civilization'.[16] Because these texts continued to address the concerns of Indians of his day, Rajagopalachari dedicated himself to making concise renderings of them available. Thus, instead of seeking to create original literary works, he retold classics to transmit to modern readers the moral lessons contained in the epics.

Print Venues and Cultural Institutions

By the mid-1940s, relatively inexpensive technology for printing in English and in Tamil was available in India, shaping the trajectory of Rajagopalachari's publications. Both private and public institutions took advantage of the new technology, which influenced the forms Rajagopalachari's writings took and their circulation among specific audiences. Consequently, the history and goals of four private or public literary institutions shaped how Rajagopalachari's Ramkatha texts were ushered into print: *Kalki*, the Sahitya Akademi, All-India Radio (AIR), and the Bharatiya Vidya Bhavan.

Rajagopalachari's retellings of the Hindu epics appeared first in *Kalki*, a weekly Tamil magazine founded in 1941 by its eponymous editor, R. Krishnamurthy, known by his nom de plume, 'Kalki'. The two men had a history of joint ventures dating back to the 1920s when they both worked on the same ashram in Tiruchengode, an impoverished area in Salem district. There they started cottage industries in spinning, hand-weaving, bee-keeping, and manufacture of soap and non-edible oils to supplement the local villagers' limited income earned through agricultural labour.[17] Their bond as writers deepened when they co-edited *Vimochanam*, a magazine that printed Rajagopalachari's first extant Tamil short stories, on the dangers of alcohol.[18]

Journalist Kalki, statesman Rajagopalachari, and T. Sadasivam (*Kalki*'s business director)—all Brahmins and staunch Gandhian nationalists—wielded significant influence among the Brahmin elite active in the Madras cultural arena in the mid-1940s. They helped promote the growth and appreciation of forms of south Indian music and dance which were being 'revived' (as well as reconstituted) and dominated the performing art scene in Madras at that time.[19] When Sadasivam married M.S. Subbalakshmi, a talented, exquisitely beautiful, beloved vocalist from a *devadasi* background, *Kalki* actively publicized her concerts. Her association with the magazine, in turn, linked it with the piety of the devotional songs she favoured in concert. As a nationalist magazine that foregrounded 'classic' south Indian culture, *Kalki* proved a particularly appropriate venue for Rajagopalachari's first retellings of Mahabharata and Ramayana in Tamil.

Many new Tamil periodicals in the 1940s appeared irregularly or went bankrupt during their first year, but *Kalki* survived the many challenges of start-up and went on to provide a steady stream of issues filled with articles geared to readers of various ages and interests, thereby building a solid base of subscribers. Precise circulation figures for *Kalki*'s earliest years are not available, but we know that in its very first year of operation, it became the largest Indian language magazine in the country.[20] *Kalki* published many serials, among them Rajagopalachari's retellings of epics, which were thus showcased in one of the most prominent and widely read Tamil magazines of his day.

Rajagopalachari's first Tamil retelling of an epic for *Kalki* was his Mahabharata, titled *Viyasar Viruntu* ('The Feast of Vyasa'). In this 107-instalment work (1 January 1944–9 May 1946), he presents the story as a rich cultural repast for readers. Right after *Kalki*'s last episode, Pari Nilayam Press published the entire Tamil serial as a 691-page book. Until then most Tamil books had print runs of 1,000–3,000 copies, but printer Sakthi Govindan opted for unprecedented scale, using a press that belonged to a newspaper magnate to produce 1,00,000 copies on newsprint.[21] Cheap paper and huge volume allowed him to price the book at just one rupee. It sold out within a few days, breaking all previous records in Tamil publishing.[22]

The success of the Mahabharata serial soon led Kalki to request a Ramayana serial and, in response, Rajagopalachari composed *Cakkaravartti-t-Tirumahan*. Thinking back over the seventeen months he spent writing the serial, he admitted to being 'greatly encouraged by the warm reception' to his Ramkatha 'in the homes of the Tamil people all over the country'.[23] By July 1954, shortly after the serial began, *Kalki*'s circulation increased to 68,500, rising to 78,000 by the end of the year, and to 86,000 by October of 1955.[24] Rajagopalachari's publication in *Kalki* influenced the format and linguistic register of his Ramkatha retelling. For the small-format weekly, each instalment had to be short yet maintain its coherence as an episode. To scale down a huge, highly ornate, epic narrative into everyday prose for a family magazine, Rajagopalachari combined lucidity with accessibility and suspense. In addition, he wove in messages about the centrality of patriotism, richness of Indian civilization, and value of self-sacrifice, themes well-suited to the first decade after Independence from British colonial rule.

While he was retelling Ramkatha for *Kalki* in 1954, he also wrote five talks for All India Radio (AIR). Begun under British rule in 1927, AIR inherited the colonial protocol of vetting a written transcript, submitted in advance, of each radio talk to insure it did not contain seditious material, and oversight continued after Independence.[25] In 1953, AIR's central office in Delhi instituted a National Programme of Talks in English and during 1954–5 they were broadcast weekly throughout India.[26] The protocols of advance scrutiny of radio talks made it possible to monitor contents. Programmes were meant to enhance cultural unity without offending particular religious, linguistic, or social groups.

Rajagopalachari's 1954 radio talks focused upon Kamban's twelfth century *Iramavataram* ('Rama the Avatara') with the goal of educating listeners about Tamil literature.[27] By representing Tamil literature on radio, AIR advanced the national agenda by including literature from various regions of India in programming for the nation's airwaves. His radio talks contained short translations from, and exegesis of, *Iramavataram*, a sophisticated work of poetry that connoisseurs deem the 'classic' retelling of Rama's story in Tamil.

The Ministry of Information and Broadcasting chose certain AIR talk shows for publication, including Rajagopalachari's set on Kamban. In 1955, his AIR talks appeared in a slim forty-page book with a plain aqua cover, titled *Bharat Milap* ('Reunion with Bharata'). Subsidized by the government, it was priced at 8 annas, or half a rupee.[28] The work sought to educate listeners with 'high brow' poetry vetted by government officials. *Bharat Milap* had a small print run; since it rendered Kamban into English poetry, its readers were few, limited primarily to those familiar with English poetry. In contrast, the show's symbolic role was great since it presented the state as a patron of Tamil literature.

Bharat Milap contains a one-page foreword by Rajendra Prasad, India's first President (1950–62), which highlights similarities between Kamban's text and the sixteenth century *Ramcaritmanas* by Tulsidas, the classic Hindi telling of Ramkatha. Prasad, who grew up in a Hindi-speaking state, presents Kamban and Tulsidas as kindred poets from different areas in India, thereby advancing the national project to encompass regional literatures within the rubric of the nation and furnishing 'palpable proof of India's unity in diversity, hidden but persistent and everlasting'.[29] Prasad thereby links two of the most influential regional tellings of Ramkatha, a narrative that teaches citizens respect for their rulers, buttressing the authority of the state that funds AIR to promote 'national' culture.

President Prasad's foreword also carries a significant political charge in light of a contentious cultural debate in the south India of his day. As early as the 1930s, Non-Brahmin Tamil-speaking groups had attacked Indian National Congress (INC) policies which they denigrated as the efforts of high-caste elites to subordinate speakers of Dravidian languages to the hegemony of north Indian, especially Hindi, culture.[30] A Gandhian and national leader, Rajagopalachari had spearheaded a campaign for south Indians to learn Hindi so they could be 'integrated' into the nation, earning a reputation among some Tamil aficionados for selling out his 'mother tongue' [Tamil] to promote Hindi. Rajagopalachari condemned such critics, who had threatened to secede from India to form their own state, an aspiration that threatened the fragile unity of the new nation. Hence, that Rajagopalachari, rather than a 'Tamil nationalist', represented Tamil literature on AIR was not accidental.

In conformity with AIR's aims, Rajagopalachari shaped his language and choice of material to conform to the format of a radio talk. *Kalki* gave him more than a year to tell Ramkatha, but AIR allotted only five shows. Rather than try to convey the entire narrative, he chose a single section of Kamban's text as his focus, a section that depicts how Rama willingly went into exile to maintain the honour of his father. Since most Hindus admired Rama's sacrifice on behalf of his father, Rajagopalachari's choice enabled him to present a Tamil text in an inspiring and largely non-controversial way.

Rajagopalachari's next publication house was founded by lawyer, friend, and fellow freedom-fighter, K[anaiyalal]M[aneklal]Munshi (1887–1971). Munshi founded the Bharatiya Vidya Bhavan [Indian Knowledge Centre] in 1931 to promote Hinduism as the answer to dilemmas of modernity in India. He feared that, without guidance in reading, the Indian masses might fall prey to Western-style 'sensationalist' novels that would rob them of 'moral fibre'. To prevent that eventuality, Munshi sought to 'cater wholesome intellectual food to them and endeavour to arrest the corroding influence of mass-produced unwholesome literature'.[31] His 'Book University' would provide affordable, widely-distributed paperbacks to dispense 'Indian knowledge'. Munshi sought books that would teach 'permanent values', instil 'character', and build 'faith in India among the masses'. He chose Rajagopalachari's retelling of Mahabharata and Ramayana, translated from Tamil into English, to inaugurate his Book University. Soon, bookstores, bazaars, pavement book dealers, train stations, and lending libraries all stocked the Bhavan's inexpensive and relatively short paperback copies of Rajagopalachari's Ramayana. Between 1957 and 1962, the Bhavan sold 82,000 copies, an astonishing figure compared to other English books, except school textbooks, printed in India.

The Bhavan aimed to enhance knowledge in three areas of Hindu culture: Sanskrit and Sanskrit-derived literatures; religious teachers and exemplars such as Rama and the Buddha; and Hindu 'reformers' such as Ramakrishna, Aurobindo, and Gandhi. Since Rama's story took its earliest extant form in Sanskrit, described Rama as an exemplar of dharma, and was beloved by modern reformers such as Gandhi, it fit well with all three of the Bhavan's foci. Reciprocally, the Bhavan played a major role in the print history of Rajagopalachari's retellings of Ramkatha, extending his telling beyond its earlier Tamil readership to a pan-Indian group of English readers across the nation.

Some of Rajagopalachari's following among readers came from the widower's own sage-like reputation for an ascetic, 'wholesome' life.[32] Rajagopalachari, emulating Gandhi, set rigorous standards for himself and other political leaders, urging them to live frugal, righteous lives, free of self-aggrandizement. Even today, these qualities are spotlighted in Bhavan marketing flyers, which note Rajagopalachari's refusal to accept royalties from the 18 books he wrote for the Bhavan as evidence of his non-attachment to monetary rewards. It continues to use his 1957 assessment, 'That the Bhavan's books and periodicals devoid of sex, smut, sensationalism, crime and gossip, are selling so well is proof positive that the soul of India is still sound', to endorse Bhavan publications.[33]

Even though the Bhavan was re-publishing a book whose format and linguistic register had been customized to the needs of *Kalki*, Munshi still shaped the way that readers first encountered Rajagopalachari's book by writing a preface that situated the book within the general goals of the Bhavan and its Book University (3 October 1951), that subsequently appeared in every book in the series. Munshi also added a second preface specifically for the Bhavan's Ramayana (12 May 1957). Munshi's general preface explains the urgent need for books to teach 'Indian values'. He embraces modern print technology to revive and disseminate the 'Indian values' that constitute the 'soul of India', warning that uncontrolled technology has the potential to destroy those values. To combat that threat, he had undertaken this publishing endeavour to further 'the integration of the Indian culture in the light of modern knowledge' and urges readers to resuscitate Indian culture's 'fundamental values in their pristine vigour'. They can combat the chaos of modern life by delving into the Hindu epics, which teach about the 'Moral Order' that inheres in 'true culture'. These epics, says Munshi, are 'the Collective Unconscious of India' which contains 'her message to man'. He commends Rajagopalachari's Ramayana for eloquently conveying that message.

While the Bhavan was championing Rajagopalachari's Ramayana in English, the Sahitya Akademi in New Delhi awarded its prize for best Tamil book published between 1955 and 1957 to *Cakkaravartti-t-Tirumahan*. The Sahitya Akademi, a government-funded institution founded seven years after Independence was charged 'to set high literary standards, and to foster and promote literary activities in all the Indian languages' by awarding prizes to writers who had published outstanding works which unified the country and enriched its cultural life.[34] The Akademi celebrated literary works whose poetic traditions were rooted in both pan-Indian and regional languages that pre-date the modern period, yet did so under the auspices, and with the fiscal support, of the modern state. By honouring ancient Sanskrit and the regional languages of India, the Sahitya Akademi signifies not only the classic *and* the modern, but also the nation *encompassing* regional culture. Rajagopalachari presents *Cakkaravartti-t-Tirumahan* as a retelling of a classic text that prompts reflection about modern life; he publishes it in Tamil, a regional language, but it wins recognition from a national literary institution.

Many prominent literary figures approved of awarding the Tamil prize to Rajagopalachari, but based their approval on strikingly divergent criteria. S. Sivapatha Sundaram, who wrote the prize's citation, characterized Rajagopalachari as a writer of 'great subtlety and charm'. By praising the presence of 'Kamban's original touches', Sundaram indicates that Rajagopalachari's incorporation of classic literary elements added to the quality of his writing.[35] 'Masti' Venkatesa Iyengar, fellow Brahmin and prominent Kannada writer, also defended the choice upon the basis of didactic criteria, noting: 'Very competent [Tamil] people consider Rajaji's book an expression of his own view of life and when a book is this, and reaches such a high level in writing, it deserves an award that is meant as recognition of the production of good literature.' Prime Minister Jawaharlal Nehru, then also President of the Akademi, saw the book's popularity as justifying the choice. Pointing to the magnitude of the book's sales, he asked, 'How can anyone object to the award?'[36]

Lack of unanimity about criteria for judging literary works is clear not only in such support for awarding the prize to Rajagopalachari but also in reasons given for criticizing the choice. V. Swaminathan, whose views were representative of widespread dissatisfaction with the choice among Tamil literary connoisseurs, called *Cakkaravartti-t-Tirumahan* 'an Enid Blyton's version of the Ramayana', rather than 'serious literature of the creative variety', and labelled Rajagopalachari 'more concerned with dishing out moral fables than with literary pursuits in a serious sense'.[37] Swaminathan judges literary works upon their mastery of literary techniques and originality. His assessment also implies that serious literary endeavours preclude moralistic storytelling.

More broadly, Swaminathan also raises substantive questions about the integrity of the award process. Members of the Sahitya Akademi, who included prominent Indian writers, academicians, and government officials, bore multiple responsibilities.[38] On the one hand, they initiated major scholarly projects, such as writing histories of regional literary traditions. On the other hand, they bestowed awards on creative writers. A person might not be the most qualified for each kind of endeavour. Swaminathan criticized the selection committee as lacking 'top rank' Tamil writers qualified to judge ground-breaking literary talent. For example, pioneering modernist Pudumaippittan, one of Tamil's most respected and talented writers, was long ignored by the Akademi while Rajagopalachari's book was designated the finest Tamil literary work of his day. In addition, Swaminathan pointed out that fair evaluation of literary works by the committee is not possible without proper protocols that guard against conflict of interest.

It is not irrelevant that award-winning Rajagopalachari had served as a member of the Akademi's Advisory Board for Tamil in 1954–5 and 1955–6.[39]

In addition, links to the Akademi meant that literary opportunities came to people more easily than those without such links. For example, Rajagopalachari's link to the Akademi identified him to outsiders as an appropriate representative of Tamil literature. When UNESCO (United Nations Educational, Scientific, and Cultural Organization) decided to identify texts and translators suitable for a series called 'Collection of Representative Works' to promote mutual appreciation of the cultural values of East and West, they worked closely with national literary institutions. Prime Minister Jawaharlal Nehru, leader among non-aligned nations, cultivated close ties with UNESCO to enhance coalitions among nations, especially formerly colonized ones.[40] Upon the Akademi's advice, Rajagopalachari was requested to expand his AIR translation of Kamban's *Iramavataram* for the UNESCO Representative Works series.[41]

The analysis of cultural institutions that promoted Rajagopalachari's two volumes of Ramkatha in Tamil and English demonstrates the extent to which his own ideological commitments paralleled those of his patrons. With Kalki and Munshi, he shared a view of the Hindu epics as central to Indian nationalism. For AIR, he represented Tamil literature as one of many regional literatures that created the diversity of Indian unity, ignoring the hostility that many Tamil speakers felt towards the central government and Hindi propagation. Rajagopalachari's shared ideological commitments shaped reception of his prose epic, which won him a Sahitya Akademi award and *Bharat Milap*, which earned him global marketing with the UNESCO imprimatur. Yet his most original Ramkatha works were his short stories, which were largely beyond the purview of the major cultural institutions just examined.[42]

QUESTIONING RAMKATHA IN SHORT STORIES

Sita's Accusations of Lakshmana Absolved

Ramkatha episodes that troubled Rajagopalachari were minimized or absent from his two volumes linked to the four cultural institutions discussed above. In contrast, all three Ramkatha short stories focus on episodes that seem to disturb him because the supposedly exemplary prince, wife, and brother appear to deviate from proper behaviour.[43] The first short story, 'Pachattapam', which focuses on Sita and Lakshmana, appeared in print before Rajagopalachari retold Ramkatha for *Kalki*. He wrote 'Sitadeviyin Avataram', which deals with Rama's banishment of Sita, before he began his *Kalki* serial but after he agreed to write it. The last, 'Vali Vatam', which considers Rama's shooting of Vali, appeared in print after the serial ended. Thus, his questioning of Ramkatha began before he started his prose epic for *Kalki* and continued after he completed it.

'Pachattapam' [Remorse], does not appear in the earliest collection of Rajagopalachari's stories, a 1926 anthology about the ruinous effects of alcohol.[44] Nor is it found in the next collection, published in 1937.[45] The third anthology, printed in 1944 does include the story, so it was probably composed after 1937 but before 1944.[46] 'Pachattapam' assumes familiarity with an episode present in virtually all tellings of Ramkatha: Lakshmana's refusal to accede to Sita's demand that he leave her alone so that he can help Rama chase the golden deer. When Sita interprets Lakshmana's refusal as signifying that he has sexual designs on her and threatens suicide, he is so shocked that he leaves immediately to aid Rama.

'Pachattapam', the most radical Ramkatha story that Rajagopalachari ever wrote, is unique among his oeuvre in attributing intensely unsettling emotions—anger, anxiety, and resentment—to those usually promoted as ideals of devotion and modesty. In order to keep such passions from sullying the reputation of his characters, Rajagopalachari employs the narrative conceit that his story reveals the content of one of Sita's dreams. Neither the narrator nor Sita can be held responsible for events in her dream; in it she expresses feelings that are almost never voiced elsewhere. The (somewhat confusing) sequence of Sita's dream is: Lakshmana forgives Sita her for her accusation against him; she reprimands him for abandoning her; Narada tries to stir up trouble between them; and Lakshmana admits that when he left to aid Rama he almost returned to protect Sita from danger but desisted, fearing that his honour would be lost.

The story begins with the narrator announcing that, after many sleepless nights, a sad and exhausted Sita had fallen asleep 'without realizing it' (p. 97)—a phrase that distances her from what transpires next.[47] Next comes a break, indicated in the story's format by a blank line and asterisks, that sets this portion apart from what follows. Rajagopalachari then recounts from his imagination how he thinks Sita's guilt and regret might influence her unconscious thoughts. In her dream, she attempts to focus her thoughts on Rama but, instead, Lakshmana's accusing face keeps looming before her. She imagines him asking her how she could have spoken to him in such a way. Intensely ashamed, she withers under his denunciatory gaze.

Sita's remorse weighs so heavily on her that she deems her allegations toward Lakshmana more of a sin (*pavam*) than Ravana's abduction of her. This seems a harsh self-judgment from one who believed she was sending her brother-in-law to save her husband's life and was subsequently captured by a terrifying demon. Then, Lakshmana suddenly appears in Sita's dream, admits that he should not have left her alone, and asks forgiveness for his misdeed (pavam). Abruptly shifting tone, he laughs when he recalls how fiercely obstinate she had been at that moment, thereby endangering their lives. In spite of the criticism present in his words, he smiles and the narrator then asks, with a rhetorical flourish, 'How can one express in words the beauty of that mixture of sorrow, tears, laughter, and happiness?' (p. 97). By achieving reconciliation with her brother-in-law, to whom she owes respect, Sita finds relief from her previously overwhelming guilt.

In another rapid shift in emotions, Sita now reprimands Lakshmana for abandoning her. She admits that she wrongly accused him, but castigates him nonetheless for departing from his vow made to his elder brother. Sita knows she transgressed the bounds of decency when she denounced Lakshmana; the phrase she uses to refer to her allegations against Lakshmana is 'words that should not be spoken' (*solli-k-kudata pechu*) (p. 97). Nonetheless, she still condemns Lakshmana for leaving her vulnerable to abduction, shifting the burden of blame from herself to him.

Suddenly, the meddlesome Sage Narada involves himself in the already contentious discussion.[48] Acknowledging the oddity of the sage's abrupt arrival, Rajagopalachari pauses in his narration to note that the reader might wonder when Narada arrived, since he was not mentioned previously in the story. Rajagopalachari suggests that one need not worry about such questions since Narada 'somehow or other' (*eppatiyo*) came upon the scene, 'as was his custom, as all those who study the puranas know' (p. 98). Narada then declares that, technically, Lakshmana was not bound to guard Sita. When Rama asked Lakshmana to protect her, he left before hearing whether Lakshmana assented. A promise is only binding when open assent has been elicited, argues Narada. Although *rishis* might consider such arguments hair-splitting, Lakshmana responds that to a Kshatriya it is irrelevant since warriors must obey the commands of their superiors.

Sita observes that Rama endured exile to uphold his father's vow, reiterating that one must keep a promise, no matter what the cost. Lakshmana implores her to refrain from pursuing her point any further because it reminds him of her unbearable (*porukka mudiyata*) accusations against him (p. 98). Again Sita's allegations surface, but only in this euphemistic way. Sita then declares that even if the whole world had slandered him (not just she), he should have remained to guard her and fulfil his vow.

Cowed, Lakshmana confesses that, after leaving their forest cottage to aid Rama, he regretted his decision and started to walk back toward Sita. The narrator then reveals that at that very moment, Ravana, who was waiting nearby in the disguise of an ascetic, shook with fear and prepared to flee. Just then, Narada appeared and assured Ravana that Lakshmana would not return so Ravana need not flee.[49] That Narada encouraged Ravana in this way strikes even Rajagopalachari as odd, as indicated by another of his interruptions in the narrative, this time to comment that the story seems 'mixed up' (*tinusaha*). He even suggests that the intense suffering that Sita had undergone accounts for the strange events in her dream (p. 98).

The narrator then details how Lakshmana considered what Sita would probably do if he returned. He imagined that she would be so furious with him that, like an avatara of Goddess Kali, she would attack him. Envisioning her terrible anger, he thought of nothing but Sita's allegations and his own pride (*ahamkaram*). Losing his intellectual discernment, his mind became focused only on retaining his honour (*manam*) and thus his vow to Rama slipped his mind (p. 99). Lakshmana's choice of words here indicate that he found Sita's allegations deeply unsettling to his notions of propriety and self-respect.

One wonders whether Lakshmana imagined Sita turning into an avenging goddess out of concern for the danger threatening her husband or because of her anger with him. Also unanswered is whether Lakshmana viewed his honour as at risk because he had made a vow and broken it or because if he remained by Sita's side, others might assume that he had sexual designs on his sister-in-law. Such issues are never resolved, nor even made explicit. Instead when, in her dream, she imagines Lakshmana shaking her violently, she awakes to find instead her female wardens at Ravana's approach.

In his concluding comments on the story, Rajagopalachari observes that dreams in ancient India were seen as prophecies, so this one might foretell the arrival of Rama's messenger, Hanuman.[50] Rajagopalachari also notes, in a comment related to Sita's accusations against Lakshmana, that when Hanuman arrives, the first question that Sita—famed for single-minded devotion to Rama—asks, 'Is Lakshmana well?' That she would first inquire about a man other than her husband would seem deeply peculiar without some explanation. Rajagopalachari provides one: Sita asked this question because she had just awakened from her dream of Lakshmana.

Ending on a pious note, Rajagopalachari reminds readers that if they bear their suffering with fortitude and pray to God, Hanuman will come to their aid, as he did to Sita. The short story attests to Rajagopalachari's dismay that noble Sita articulated such ignoble allegations against Lakshmana, but also assures the reader of Sita's remorse, which bears fruit when Hanuman arrives bearing Rama's signet ring. The story's ending also insures that the volatile resentments and dangerous emotions expressed in the story have been safely contained and explained away. The story culminates with a standard devotional suggestion: Rajagopalachari exhorts readers to accept their suffering and pray to God for succour. Thus, he safely relegates improper desires to the world of dreams.

Justifying Sita's Fire Ordeal

Rajagopalachari's second Ramkatha short story, 'Sitadeviyin Avataram' [Sita Devi's Descent], published in 1953, possessed the basic tripartite structure of an Indian moral tale.[51] Framed by an imagined prologue and epilogue, the story focuses on Sita's abduction and fire ordeal, two of Rama's most questionable actions. The story's structure emerges if we compare the relative lengths of its parts:

Prologue and narration of earthly birth, 4 pages
Referral to other renditions of Ramkatha, 1/2 page
Sita's abduction and captivity, 1 page
Sita's fire ordeal and banishment, 1 ½ pages
Epilogue, 1 page

The space devoted to each component shows that the prologue, sorrow-filled incidents, and epilogue form the story's core. The prologue shows how the goddess takes human birth as an experiment, the sorrow-filled events provide the experience she seeks, and the epilogue indicates the lesson learned on earth.

As the story opens, in the celestial world Goddess Sridevi asks why, if worldly existence is the result of Lord Vishnu's *lila* (play), do human beings experience suffering as real? To understand their situation, Lord Vishnu invites her to accompany him during his avatara-ship, so she can experience life as human beings do. Hence, the rest of the story focuses almost entirely on incidents that foreground Sita's tribulations. When Sita is living contentedly in Panchavati, 'delusion' (*moham*) overcomes her, causing her to send Rama after the golden deer and insist that Lakshmana join him: 'Sita unfairly doubted Lakshmana, who took avatara only out of devotion [to Vishnu], and then abused him, spoke insultingly, caused him trouble. After sending him away, she got caught in terrible danger since she was all alone' (p. 68). When Ravana abducts Sita, she grieves when he kills Jatayu and grows so disheartened in Lanka that she contemplates suicide. Yet Rama's later demand that she provide evidence of her purity surpasses all the suffering that she has already endured, prompting her to say: 'At this moment, I understand the true meaning of sorrow' (p. 69).[52]

When she learns of her pregnancy, again delusion overtakes her, this time with a desire to visit the forest, providing Rama with the pretext to banish her. The narrator states, 'During Rama's avataram, there wasn't a sorrow in the world that Sita did not experience' (p. 68). In an epilogue, set again in the celestial world, Sridevi assures Vishnu that her time spent on earth has revealed to her how human beings experience suffering and she promises to help relieve their suffering (p. 70). In 'Sitadeviyin Avataram', Rajagopalachari has created an etiological narrative to explain why devotees pray to Sridevi rather than Lord Vishnu when they suffer. Ending the story with a devotional exhortation, he urges readers to call upon the compassionate goddess for aid.[53]

Like 'Pachattapam', 'Sitadeviyin Avataram' focuses upon an episode where Ramkatha characters seem to deviate from dharma. Yet by depicting Sita's suffering as lasting only for a limited time and as the result of a choice she has made to take birth on earth, Rajagopalachari exonerates Rama from possible blame for his harsh treatment of her. The story also protects Sita against criticism that she endangered herself and husband out of desire for a deer. Instead of her desire, it was delusion that overcame her and compelled her to send Rama after the deer. The story neatly ends with Sridevi testifying that she learned about human torment on earth, just as Vishnu had predicted. Rajagopalachari does not change Ramkatha's incidents in the story. Instead, he reframes them so that seemingly *adharmic* actions are part of the play of divine lila so that Rama can continue to be regarded as heroic and just.

Rationalizing Vali's Death

Rajagopalachari's third Ramkatha story, 'Vali Vatam' [Slaying of Vali] published in *Kalki* in 1958, concerns one of Rama's most controversial deeds. Rama has vowed to help his friend Sugriva win back his kingdom from his brother Vali. Vali has the power of drawing to himself half the strength of any foe who faces him in combat, so he cannot be killed in a conventional battle. Rama knows he will incur *papam* (sin, impurity) if he deviates from his dharma to his friend Sugriva by not fulfilling his promise to slay Vali yet Rama also realizes that if he does so in a face-to-face battle, he cannot defeat him, so he will fail in his dharma as a warrior.[54] In 'Vali Vatam', the knowledge that it is impossible to comply with both dharmas initially paralyses Rama. 'Vali Vatam' does not rationalize or glorify Vali's death, as do some other Ramkatha texts.[55] Instead, Rajagopalachari presents Rama's dilemma as the consequence of the practical alliances into which every political leader must enter.

Rajagopalachari sets up 'Vali Vatam' so that Rama's situation parallels that of Arjuna in Mahabharata. In 'Vali Vatam', Rama cannot will his hand to release his arrow because shooting Vali transgresses the warrior's code for conduct. Similarly, Arjuna's bow slips from his hand as he prepares to enter into battle against his kinsmen. Arjuna's dilemma is resolved only when Lord Krishna, discoursing on the necessity of action, persuades Arjuna to perform his dharma as a Kshatriya. Similarly, Rama's dilemma in 'Vali Vatam' is resolved when Lakshmana warns that he will reap only shame if he breaks his vow to his friend Sugriva. In response, Rama acknowledges that he must slay Vali, announcing: 'Dharma itself (*taruman cumappatee*) makes us commit this sin (papam)' (p. 112). Rajagopalachari stresses the similarities between the two paralysed young warriors: both must adhere to the divine command to take action, despite the deviation from dharma that each will perpetrate as a result of being caught between two dharmas.

Rama's experience of a dharmic dilemma can be seen as having some parallels with Rajagopalachari's time in political office. He believed that he acted honourably, and hoped to serve as President of his newly free nation, the Independence of which he had fought for in long and hard battles where he exercised leadership and self-restraint. He viewed his departure from office as a form of exile. His depiction of Vali's slaying suggests that political alliances, such as that between Rama and Sugriva, entail great costs. Rama's honest admission that even he (the epitome of dharma) cannot escape acquiring papam acknowledges that politics can never be entirely pure, even for the greatest heroes.

The realism that infuses Rama's fight with Vali gives way to a sanitized ending that flattens a morally ambiguous situation. Vali, who now lies dying, angrily castigates Rama for deceit. Rajagopalachari abruptly introduces a dramatized audience from the celestial world into the story: tearful Goddess Parvati in heaven has watched the battle and worries that Vali will die filled with anger at Rama, thereby losing his chance for a fortunate rebirth in his next life. One of her tears falls on Vali's face, and its divine power calms his mind (p. 117). As a result his mind turns serene; he accepts the blame for deeds that led to his death, and dies. Saddened by the passing of this mighty warrior, Rama sadly tells Lakshmana that earlier they suffered [exile] due to the papam of others, but now they will suffer due to the papam produced by his own lethal deed (p. 119).

'Vali Vatam's' ending smoothes over morally difficult issues. For example, why should Tara suffer a future as a widow because Rama killed her husband in the back from behind a tree? Rajagopalachari provides an etiological explanation for the great respect traditionally accorded to Tara, who is classed among the great epic women loyal to their husbands. In 'Vali Vatam', Goddess Parvati finds Tara's grief so devastating that Shiva promises that, by living an ascetic life after Vali's death, Tara's fame as a devoted wife will endure forever.[56] Shiva also assures Parvati that whenever grieving people pray to her, she will destroy their delusion and bestow peace upon them. Once again, without changing Ramkatha's plot in significant ways, Rajagopalachari uses celestial intervention and devotional practice to justify Rama's deeds and create an unproblematic ending.

All three of Rajagopalachari's Ramkatha stories seem well-described by 'Vali Vatam's' subtitle, putu-c-caayal [New Perspectives]. Each one examines, but does not alter, unsettling actions in Ramkatha that have been questioned and debated across the centuries. Yet only 'Pachattapam' is truly original in its use of a dream to imagine Sita's anger, anxiety, and remorse toward Lakshmana. The last two stories debate ethical complications of a deed that turns out to conflict with dharma, yet neither delves into morally troubling deeds in the same frank, courageous way as 'Pachattapam'. Instead, the last two stories incorporate divine intervention to airbrush away moral complexities and portray Rama's deeds as parts of a grander divine plan.

PROSE EPIC AND TRANSLATION FOR THE NATION

Exemplary Heroic Actions in Prose

Despite the reservations he expressed in his short stories about some actions performed by Rama and Sita, Rajagopalachari shows little ambivalence in his triumphal prose epic for *Kalki*, where Rama's victory over Ravana signifies the end of cruel tyranny. Also notable in his *Kalki* serial is Rajagopalachari's choice to write in clear and accessible Tamil prose (rather than verse, as he did in his Kamban translation). Rama's heroism enabled him to defeat evil and inaugurate an era of righteous rule, just as Indian nationalists defeated British imperialism and established an independent nation ruled according to a new Indian Constitution.[57] The dependence upon prose in *Kalki* expresses a confidence in an ever-increasing literacy among Tamil speakers, a literacy which will provide a faithful readership for the magazine.

Until the twentieth century, most serious creative writers of Tamil had composed in poetry when writing about significant subject matter, with prose denigrated as useful only for journalism, government reports, and other mundane tasks.[58] Both Rajagopalachari and his editor, Kalki, realized the growing power of prose, its potential to cut across class and caste boundaries, and the boost it received from the increasing number of educational institutions in the Tamil-speaking region of the country which provided opportunities for children to become literate. Readers of *Cakkaravartti-t-Tirumahan*, neither needed grounding in ornate Sanskrit nor familiarity with Kamban's elevated style of verse to read Rajagopalachari's telling of Ramkatha, written in straightforward, easily intelligible prose.

That Rajagopalachari chose to tell his serial in prose relates to his historical moment and intended audience. It had now become possible to launch a successful popular magazine in Tamil and reach a wide set of readers including children, newly literate mothers, and college students. Rajagopalachari remarks that he deliberately used 'simple words and short sentences' so that children could understand his Tamil. Prose makes his writing more accessible to the citizenry of the democratic republic of India than poetry. His prose enabled Tamils to enter Rama's story with ease, week after week, savouring its episodes one by one. While children might be reading the story for the first time, adults could reacquaint themselves with it afresh.

Furthermore, even in *Cakkaravartti-t-Tirumahan*, Rajagopalachari does not limit himself solely to Valmiki's telling. Instead, he builds upon Kamban's text as well. In addition, he continually contextualizes the story by inserting comments that explain otherwise puzzling passages. By drawing upon more than one telling of Ramkatha and by supplementing his narrative with advice on how to draw comparisons between ancient events and the modern social equivalents in the society of his day, Rajagopalachari shows that he is not wedded to a single, static telling of Ramkatha.

By bringing together elements from both Valmiki and Kamban, Rajagopalachari mediates between two older texts and his present-day readers, judiciously highlighting treatments of character or episodes that are distinctive to either Kamban or Valmiki.[59] For example, he recounts Shurpanakha's mutilation twice, once according to Valmiki's version (26 December 1954) in which Shurpanakha presents herself as a female demon throughout the incident, and one week later, according to Kamban's version (2 January 1955) in which Shurpanakha first appears as a lovely woman and only later takes on her full demonic form. Since the two poets differed in how they presented the key elements of this episode, Rajagopalachari insures that *Kalki*'s readers get the gist of both, again playing the role of mediator between multiple texts. While those learned in Valmiki's ancient Sanskrit or Kamban's classical Tamil had no need for a prose rendition, readers unschooled in poetry of either or both languages could read Rajagopalachari's version and gain some insight into the works of both Valmiki and Kamban.[60]

Rajagopalachari frequently draws morals from the selfless acts of Rama, Bharata, Hanuman, and Sita, to whom he points as models of ideal political leaders, good citizens, loyal family members, conscientious messengers, and devoted wives.[61] Indeed, this purposive intent stands as one of the most striking characteristic of *Cakkaravartti-t-Tirumahan*. He often interrupts his narrative to explain how readers should interpret the ancient story in the midst of the twentieth century. Rajagopalachari portrays Rama's time in forest exile as parallel to the trials faced by Indians who struggled to throw off British rule; Sita's tribulations in captivity show how determined one must be to fulfil one's commitments. The havoc that Ravana wrecks by transgressing the boundaries for appropriate action illustrates what occurs when people do not respect the norms for proper behaviour.

Unlike many other devotees of Rama, Rajagopalachari was familiar with philological scholarship about Valmiki's text and drew upon it when it suited his purposes. For example, since there had been public debates recently about Rama's seeming departures from dharma when he killed Vali in the back and doubted Sita's fidelity, he includes in *Cakkaravartti-t-Tirumahan* (and its translation, Ramayana) a summary of the scholarly view that the story had been passed on for generations orally before Valmiki wrote it down, which accounts for what he labels 'the difficult features in the story' (p. 15).[62] Similarly, he cites scholarly views that the *Uttara-kanda* (Valmiki's final book), with its account of Sita's banishment, is a later interpolation added by 'the people'. Hence, he relegates it to an epilogue and comments that 'my heart rebels against it' (p. 311). Such explanations allow him to distance himself from actions that might cast the characters he sees as ideal in ways that discredit them.

Gearing his telling to modern times, he acknowledges that readers will encounter aspects of the story that extend beyond credibility, even acknowledging that sometimes a passage in the text directly contradicts common sense. For example, 'According to the *Raamaayana*, Sagara lived for 30,000 years. Figures like 30,000 and 60,000 need not confuse us; "thirty-thousand" may mean either a very large number or just thirty' (p. 37). He also takes the liberty of dismissing what he regards as 'popular traditions'. For example, some local tellings recount that during the forest exile Lakshmana stayed awake 24 hours per day in order to protect Rama and Sita while they slept. To disapprove this unlikely idea, Rajagopalachari calls the reader's attention to a passage in Valmiki where Rama has Lakshmana awakened in the morning (p. 90).[63]

Where readers might not understand a description, he provides useful analogies. For example, he likens ancient *yagnas* to 'our present-day State-sponsored big scale conferences and exhibitions' (p. 17), an analogy that fits in with Rajagopalachari's tendency to connect kingly events in the epic with the present-day Indian state. Such comments guide his audience in how to read an ancient text as relevant to the present without dismissing its teachings, just because some details are obscure or not credible in the light of knowledge acquired in recent decades.

Rajagopalachari also takes pains to re-contextualize the story in places. For example, he sanitizes the story of Ahalya, an understandable strategy when writing for a Tamil family magazine in the 1950s. In his account of the story, he euphemistically remarks that Indra 'approached the lady [Ahalya] with urgent solicitation', and is cursed to have his 'manhood fall away' (p. 40). Here Rajagopalachari avoids explicit reference to sex even at the cost of possible obfuscation. On the other hand, he does not accept pious desires to deny what Valmiki unambiguously states. For example, he declares that even if today's strict vegetarians find it hard to bear, Valmiki 'makes it quite plain' that Rama and Lakshmana hunt in the forest, subsisting 'mostly on meat' (p. 90).

In addition to such specific comments, Rajagopalachari incorporates into *Cakkaravartti-t-Tirumahan* a thoughtful protocol for reading which addresses the issue of Rama's seeming deviations from dharma. Rajagopalachari specifies two categories of incidents. Lapses of the virtuous should function to illustrate 'the dangers of adharma' (p. 42), rather than lead readers to criticize characters or mock the story. In contrast, the great deeds of the virtuous are worthy of emulation. As he notes of Bharata's refusal to accept the throne: 'There have been through the ages great and noble souls whose virtue shines eternally in the midst of the sordid and self-seeking of a sinful world, as a beacon of light to seekers of the right path' (p. 106). In *Cakkaravartti-t-Tirumahan* and Ramayana, the most noble and self-sacrificing character is not Rama, but Bharata, the regent who rules by day but practices asceticism by night in sleeping on the hard forest earth. He provides a model of conscientious and selfless stewardship that political leaders should emulate.

Besides presenting Ramkatha as a means for instilling moral guidelines, Rajagopalachari also encourages the reader to approach the text with devotion rather than suspicion. He declares, 'in every episode of the Raamaayana, some lesson is taught for daily life,' and urges, 'If one reads with reverence and thinks deeply, it is found' (p. 180). In some places, he sounds exactly like a religious preceptor as, for example, when he piously exclaims about Bharata and others who forsake their own desires for the welfare of others, 'May these heroic figures and that culture live for ever in the land of Bharata!' (p. 107). For Rajagopalachari, the text abounds with national, ethical, and devotional messages to inspire and guide readers in daily life.[64]

Two Strands of Hindu Nationalism

Although Rajagopalachari and his publisher Munshi shared many fundamental assumptions about post-Independence India, each conceptualized nationalism in his own distinct way. The two men shared bonding experiences as lawyers, freedom-fighters, members of Nehru's cabinet, and—most relevant to Ramkatha—as co-founders in 1959 of the anti-statist Swatantra party, whose members sought to conserve the 'traditional' order that they now perceived as under threat.[65] Nonetheless, I argue that they differed in the type of nationalism they embraced. Munshi actively promoted a Hindu nationalism that explicitly denigrated Muslims and excluded them from 'Indian culture'. In contrast Rajagopalachari, who read widely in areas such as religion, philology, political theory, literature, and general knowledge, expressed the wisdom he found in the Hindu epics in ways that did not necessarily exclude readers from differing religious backgrounds. This point can best be seen if we compare some of the major tenets held by the two men.

The prefaces that Rajagopalachari wrote for Bhavan editions of Ramayana showed his ever-increasing anxiety about the nation's stability. (In the late 1940s, he likened the Mahabharata's war between cousins, for example, to the impending Partition of India.) His anxiety about encroaching disorder mounted while he served as Chief Minister of Madras in the early 1950s; he faced violence and threats of secession from some Tamil groups who rejected government efforts to elevate Hindi to a pan-Indian link language. His preface to *Ramayana*'s first edition (10 May 1957) cautioned that the new nation must be firmly linked to the past, promoting 'a re-communion between us and the sages of our land, so that the future may be built on rock and not sand'. The second edition's preface (14 October 1957) questioned whether Indian civilization would decline as did that of ancient Greece, leaving only its epics. His preface to the third edition (19 October 1958) expressed fear of the fate not only about Indians but of all humankind: 'Thorough familiarity with our ancient heritage is necessary if we desire to preserve our individuality as a nation and serve the world through dharma which alone can save mankind from error and extinction.' A prescient critic of nuclear proliferation, he looked to Indian morality and non-violence to help prevent an atomic holocaust.[66]

To battle such threats, Rajagopalachari turned to India's 'national character,' as he saw it expressed in Ramkatha. Although hindsight today reveals that the concept of 'national character' is a cultural construct that developed in modern Europe for particular historical reasons, the nationalist movement focused upon a concept of decolonialization that raised the notion of 'nation' to a nearly sacred status. Noting that Valmiki and Vyasa created their epics from 'the inherited bricks of national memory prior to their own time,' he read nationalism back to the ancient days when bardic stories first crystallized. To him, Ramkatha was 'national' because if citizens emulated its self-sacrificing heroes, they would eschew egoism and work together for the common good.

He, therefore, lauded the epic for its ability to 'bind our vast numbers together as one people, despite caste, space and language that seemingly divide them.' Thus, he trusted that if Indians steeped themselves in the Hindu epics, 'our ancient heritage,' the nation would prosper.[67]

Like other intellectuals of his day, Rajagopalachari believed that India's 'ancient heritage' originated during a golden age. He saw Ramkatha as a tale of valiant kings and wise sages from the 'epic age' and he praised the actions of people who lived during a glorious era quite different from his own degenerate time. He was one of many Indian writers in this period who set their narratives in the ancient past, performing significant cultural work by creating vivid visions of a pre-colonial Indian past with which to combat imperial claims about the superiority of British culture. He wrote during the period when Indologists were rediscovering ancient Indian texts that existed long before those of ancient Greece. In setting his narratives in the pre-modern period, Rajagopalachari joined many nationalist writers who looked to India's past for inspiration.[68] Such writings facilitated a process by which readers came to see themselves as rooted in a glorious and sophisticated Indian civilization.

For Rajagopalachari, regional and national identities were linked through the notion of one's 'mother tongue'. He lauded the fact that Hindu epics had been passed down in regional languages from mother to child for centuries. In fact, it was only because 'modernity' had disrupted such transmission that he felt it necessary to retell epics in Tamil for *Kalki*. And he too chose to pass on his interpretation of Ramkatha in his mother tongue of Tamil. In that framework, regional languages provided the local medium for inculcating loyalty to the nation. Conceptually, therefore, he viewed *Iramavataram* by Kamban first as an Indian literary work and second as a Tamil ('mother tongue') one.[69]

For Rajagopalachari, Ramkatha provided a precedent for linking good governance with morality. The moral basis of action plays such a large role in his framework that he declares it the basis of the nation's right to rule. Without it, he argues that credibility would be lost. Consequently, Rajagopalachari considers teaching morality integral to transforming India from a colonized state into an independent one:

It is true of everything that what is bad morality, according to the scriptures revered by nations, is also bad in the sense of worldly policy. This is so, because man's physical, social and moral evolution has been an organic process and necessarily, therefore, a single integrated development. The Culture, the civilization, the morality, the religious spirit and the accepted axioms of life are the results of one intertwined process of evolution.[70]

This quote demonstrates Rajagopalachari's belief in an evolutionary scheme in which civilization advances only if political rule rests on sound morality. He takes the Hindu epics as storehouses of moral teaching upon which good government should draw.

Hindsight, however, reveals that Rajagopalachari's prose epic includes a dangerous conceptual flaw, one that becomes even more dangerous in the writings of other Hindu nationalists: slippage from Hindu epics to 'Indian epics'. Several factors encouraged his identification of the Hindu epics with 'Indian culture'. His upbringing as a Brahmin Sri Vaishnava Hindu in Tamil Nadu deeply shaped his devotional proclivities towards Vaishnava avataras, especially Rama, known for his noble self-sacrifices for the sake of his family and kingdom. In addition, Rajagopalachari's many years as disciple of Gandhi, who used epic characters to illustrate his points, contributed to his belief in the power of these religious narratives.[71] The population of Muslims in south India was much smaller than in north India and limited primarily to areas such as northern Malabar and eastern coastal Tamil Nadu. His formative years in the south, as well as his immersion in Valmiki, Kamban, and Vyasa, may have fixed Hindu epics at the centre of his intellectual universe.

Munshi shared with Rajagopalachari many of the views just listed, especially his fear that the nation might fragment into pieces and an evaluation of the Hindu epics as foundational texts for the Indian nation. In fact, Munshi's Book University plan coalesced in the tumultuous early 1950s while, as a member of Nehru's cabinet, he experienced the fissiparous tendencies of the fledgling nation. Like Rajagopalachari, Munshi responded to threats of disorder by idealizing values set out in Hindu epics as guides for the new nation.

Yet Rajagopalachari and Munshi differed in the extent to which they viewed Hindu epics in relation to the new Indian nation. On the one hand, Rajagopalachari idealized a Sanskritic Tamil golden age, and Munshi lauded a Sanskritic Gujarati golden age. As did other prominent Gujarati intellectuals in the first half of the twentieth century, Munshi envisioned and believed in 'a primeval Gujarati identity' when religion and social order flourished. On the other hand, Munshi villainized Muslims, claiming that the arrival of Muslims in India destroyed the golden age of Gujarat, a view of history that he gave life to in his historical novels.[72] Yashaschandra, a Gujarati literary critic, sees 'little historical evidence' for Munshi's claim that in the Chalukya period, a single people speaking a distinctive language established the boundaries of Gurjaradesa.[73] Further, as Isaha has shown, Munshi entirely erased from his literary history the role of Persian and Arabic literary works in western India, disseminating a distorted picture of the region to glorify Hindu sovereignty and blame Muslims for the 'decline of society and culture'.[74]

Furthermore, while Rajagopalachari emphasized the inclusive ethical norms of Hindu epics, Munshi sought to defend and propagate a particular strand of Hindu tradition, the one tied to brahmanical texts and an ideology of ranked social hierarchy. Munshi hewed quite closely to specific brahmanical narratives and motifs, in distinction to Rajagopalachari's emphasis on broader ethical and moral principles. Evidence of this elite hierarchical strand of Hinduism can be seen in the vocabulary Munshi developed for the Bharatiya Vidya Bhavan. He designated himself the Bhavan's *kulapati* (*pati*, lord; *kula*, lineage), a term for the spiritual head of a forest school (*gurukula*) or hermitage where one retreated to join a kula of disciples under the authority of a spiritual preceptor (pati).[75] Here, Munshi presents the Bhavan as analogous to a hermitage, students to ascetics, and Munshi to a guide whose wisdom should be unquestionably accepted.

Although Rajagopalachari and Munshi tended to conflate 'Hindu' with India, Rajagopalachari did not claim that his favourite texts or historical figures represented Indian culture as a whole, as did the Bhavan's Book University. For example, only one biography, out of the one hundred biographies of great Indians published by the Bhavan, concerns a Muslim, Emperor Akbar.[76] Similarly, with the exception of Zakir Husain (then President of India), no Muslims appear among the board or well-wishers of the Bhavan, whose photos appear in Munshi's retrospective about it.[77] Although spokesmen regularly describe the Bhavan as purely a cultural organization, the claim belies its deeply political definition of India as essentially Hindu.

Again, although both Rajagopalachari and Munshi both promoted Hindu texts, Munshi disparaged Muslim texts and culture in a way that Rajagopalachari did not. Instead, Rajagopalachari kept himself abreast of developments in India's Muslim communities, realizing sooner than many others that the creation of Pakistan was imminent and urging his fellow Hindus to take into consideration the alienation that some Muslims who remained in India would feel after Partition. Rajagopalachari's work during the first decade after Independence, especially in Bengal, kept him in close touch with the concerns of Indian Muslims. For example, in a speech to the Bengal Muslim Association on 6 December 1947, he said, 'I feel that one of the reasons why we have been fighting with one another is that we have not been eating together ... my view is that since we quarrel over trifling things, we can make up also by attending to trifling things.'[78] One doubts that Munshi would propose such a culinary project for the Bhavan.

In Munshi's 'emphasis on the making of a Hindu Bharat',[79] his campaign to reconstruct the Somanatha temple in western India reveals how integral a role anti-Muslim sentiment played. The Muslim ruler of the princely state of Junagadh had decided his state would join Pakistan but 82 per cent of the state's population that was Hindu revolted against the decision. After the ruler and his family fled to Pakistan, the Congress party took control of the state, providing an opportunity for Munshi (with Sardar Vallabhbhai Patel's support), to reverse what he took to be a great wrong. He had viewed the ruins of Somanatha temple as symbolic of Hindu shame because it had been looted and desecrated by a Muslim. Over the objections of Jawaharlal Nehru, other leaders committed to a secular state, and members of the archaeological survey, Munshi spearheaded the renovation of the temple. The main image was reinstalled in November 1951. Munshi's rationale for the project rested on his belief that the living past of the temple was part of the 'sentiment of the whole nation and its reconstruction was a national pledge'.[80] Here, he clearly conflates the whole nation with Hindus, even though many influential political leaders, both Hindu and non-Hindu, disagreed with him.

It would be inaccurate to tar Rajagopalachari with the same brush simply because he also viewed Ramkatha as a 'national' epic and published with Bharatiya Vidya Bhavan's press. Rajagopalachari's endorsement of Ramkatha for the nation is not exclusive in its spirit or manifestations. Rajagopalachari classes Valmiki's Ramayana with other illustrious epics that came to symbolize the culture of certain countries, such as the *Iliad*, *Odyssey*, or Shakespeare. Indeed, as Rajagopalachari's knowledge of foreign affairs expanded during the last decades of his life, his concern with non-proliferation of nuclear arms broadened his view of the international relations and he developed a global perspective on many issues, his concerns for human welfare expanded to encompass the planet as a whole, while Munshi's remained focused narrowly on

Hindu India as he envisioned it in his historical novels and tried to enshrine it in the Somanatha temple.

Devotional Sentiment and Selective Translation

Rajagopalachari's radio talks on Kamban differ radically from his short stories and his prose epic; unlike his short stories, the Kamban talks exhibit no ambivalence toward Rama and Sita and, unlike his prose epic, heroic Rama is eclipsed by divine Rama. For *Kalki*, Rajagopalachari had presented Rama's life from birth to coronation, so he had to include Rama's morally flawed, as well as his great, actions. In contrast, the selections Rajagopalachari chose to translate from Kamban's text for AIR uniformly portray Rama in a positive light.[81] Following Valmiki, Rajagopalachari presented Rama for his *Kalki* serial primarily as 'a great and unique man, not an incarnation of God', but in translating Kamban's *Iramavataram* he needed to portray Rama as fully God and convey the devotional power of Kamban's poetry in praise of Rama.[82]

Each of Rajagopalachari's five selections of Kamban verses provided the basis for one of his five radio talks for AIR, broadcast in Madras during July and August, 1954. Each show begins with an explication of a theme or technique in the poetry, followed by Kamban's poetry translated into English verse by Rajagopalachari in a manner that highlighted *Iramavataram*'s literary craft and devotional spirit. The verses focus upon several ideals to which Rajagopalachari was committed: renunciation of political power, overcoming anger, and forging connections between people of different castes.

Each *Iramavataram* selection attests to the self-sacrifice and love shown by Rama or his brother, Bharata. The first radio show features Rama winning Sita as his wife by breaking the celestial bow, a favourite incident that depicts Rama's superhuman martial prowess and unites him with his loving wife. The second and third portray Bharata rejecting his mother's plan that he ascend the throne. The fourth explores friendship between the low-caste forest chieftain, Guha, and Rama. The last centers on Bharata's reunion with Rama in the forest, which heals the rift in the family. These emotionally evocative episodes showcase Rama's awesome martial power, emphasize his love for family, depict him transcending caste divisions, and laud his self-denial in accepting forest exile for the sake of the honour of his lineage.

Each radio talk culminates with devotional praise. When Rama breaks the bow, the king, courtiers, Sita's friends, and gods laud Rama. After Bharata tells Rama's mother how deeply he loves his brother, the show ends with verses about her joy at Bharata's devotion to Rama. When Bharata vows to bring Rama home, the programme ends with the residents of Ayodhya praising him. When Guha shows Bharata the earth where Rama slept while guarded by Lakshmana, the poem eulogizes the love all three bear for Rama. The reunion of Bharata and Rama culminates with a joyous reunion of brothers.

While *Bharat Milap*'s title assumes a reader knows the basic story of Rama even if unfamiliar with Kamban's rendition, the lengthy UNESCO title, *The Ayodhya Canto of the Ramayana as Told by Kamban* [henceforth *Ayodhya Canto*], is targeted to an audience unfamiliar with Ramkatha. The word 'canto' to translate *kanda*, for example, brings to mind the cantos of European texts such as those of Dante. *Ayodhya Canto* translates one full kanda, set in the capital city, which depicts Rama and Sita's years in the palace of Ayodhya before exile. More than twice *Bharat Milap*'s length at 117 pages, it contains twenty-two chapters.

Unlike *Bharat Milap*, *Ayodhya Canto* contains the usual three-part format for translations into English and European languages: 1) introduction, 2) full translation, corresponding verse by verse to the original, and 3) back matter. Virtually all the prose in *Ayodhya Canto*'s introduction, except a short Ramkatha synopsis, is taken from the remarks at the beginning of each *Bharat Milap* chapter, but it is assembled into a single introduction whose footnotes are keyed to a glossary in the back matter. Published by George Allen and Unwin of London in 1961, the volume was marketed abroad.

While UNESCO's imprimatur branded Kamban as worthy of international literary attention, one must keep in mind that Rajagopalachari's choice of selection resulted in a volume in which the only Rama whom readers see is the one who calmly agrees to renounce the throne and live for fourteen years in the forest. Since the translation does not include any of the problematic incidents in which Rama could be interpreted as deviating from proper behaviour, the world has been given a translation of Kamban's text that is not representative of the entire corpus of Rama's deeds. *Ayodhya Kanda* lack any incidents that had bothered Rajagopalachari enough for him to probe their psychological motivations in short stories. Instead, the devotion that occasionally surfaced in some stories and the prose epic turns into the predominant tone in his translation of Kamban. Depicting Rama as flawless and worthy of utter devotion, the translation presents yet a third facet of Rajagopalachari's interpretation of Ramkatha, together with psychological analysis in the short stories and heroic deeds in the prose epic.

CONCLUSION

So connected did Rajagopalachari's name become with epic literature after the Bhavan's publication of his English retellings that, when Munshi served as Governor of Uttar Pradesh, he heard a member of the Public Service Commission inquire of a job candidate, 'Who is the author of the Mahabharata?' Without hesitation, the young man replied, 'C. Rajagopalachari.'[83] As the anecdote suggests, by the late 1950s, many saw Rajagopalachari's Mahabharata as *the* Mahabharata, rather than a Tamil retelling of a Sanskrit epic later translated into English, and viewed his Tamil retelling of Ramkatha in the same way. Four months before Rajagopalachari passed away in 1972, Vanati Press received his permission to change the Tamil title of *Viyasar Viruntu* to *Mahabharatam* and the title of *Cakkaravartti-t-Tirumahan* to *Ramayanam*. Perception of his retellings as transparently *the* epics had become so widespread that even the original publisher now sought to identify the books as *the* epics. One reason for this outcome was that Rajagopalachari's desire to link national culture to Ramkatha coincided with developments in print technology, in the decade immediately following Indian Independence, which increased the size of print runs while lowering the cost of products.

Rajagopalachari's *Cakkaravartti-t-Tirumahan* carried out a particular kind of cultural work at a moment in Indian history when newly-freed Indians were seeking, conceptualizing, or contesting what they took to be 'shared' cultural features of their 'nation'. Rajagopalachari's prose epic functioned as a guide to moral action, presenting deeds of exemplary figures as models for proper behaviour in the modern state. At the same time, Rajagopalachari's commentary, dispersed throughout his epic, established a protocol for reading that disregarded anachronisms, obscurities, and supernatural elements, thereby facilitating a link between a 'classic' repository of wisdom and 'modern' citizens whom he deemed in need of a moral guide.

Bharat Milap performed a different kind of cultural work: it represented a regional literary tradition to those unfamiliar with it. On the one hand, it presented a 'classic' Tamil work to readers within India unfamiliar with Tamil. On the other hand, its expanded version for UNESCO presented an excerpt from a Tamil 'classic' to represent Indian literature to the non-Indian world. Its cultural work included lauding the glory of Lord Rama and the beauty of Tamil poetry to those otherwise unfamiliar with both. It also advanced the work of Indian nationalism by subsuming regional literature within a nation framework.

In contrast, Rajagopalachari's little-known short stories, especially 'Pachattapam', focus almost entirely on the ways in which Rama, Sita, and Lakshmana have deviated from dharma and, thus, show that Rajagopalachari harboured more complex responses to Ramkatha than displayed in his two books. Rather than concern with India's dilemmas as a new nation, each story grapples with Rajagopalachari's own ambivalence, doubts, and unease with incidents where characters do not live up to his expectations of proper action. Ironically, these short stories are a crucial resource for Indians. Rajagopalachari believed that the central government could not represent 'the nation' unless its citizens perceived themselves as bound by shared culture. Yet, creating a shared culture in a post-colonial society that includes multiple regions and religious groups runs the risk of generating representations of the past that submerge or erase differences and contradictions. Interpreting Rama's story as a source of wisdom and inspiration for post-colonial India can only be a service if one acknowledges the narrative's complexity and the manner in which Ramkatha has always fostered multiple interpretations.

While Rajagopalachari himself generated three different tellings, including short stories that raised questions about issues taken for granted in his prose epic and translation, Munshi homogenized the Ramayana tradition and sought to exclude Muslims from his conceptualization of the Indian nation. In the past two decades, Hindutva appropriations of major Hindu texts have worried social critics that India's protection of religious freedom is under attack. At such a time, one must scrutinize how a religious text is portrayed by groups with agendas linked to gaining electoral power. Hindutva groups have insisted on a single way to tell Rama's story correctly, draining it of its complexities and multivocality. In contrast, Rajagopalachari's relationship with the story was more multi-faceted and ambivalent, and therefore less exclusive, than that of Munshi. For much of his later life, Rajagopalachari wrestled with moral dilemmas in Ramkatha, viewing the epic from multiple perspectives rather than reifying or oversimplifying it. That he continued to rethink Ramkatha in three genres for thirty years may indeed have been a great service to the nation, because his Ramkatha writings, set side by side, bear witness to the multiple ways in which the story can be told and interpreted.

NOTES AND REFERENCES

1. Author's Preface (3 March 1956) in C. Rajagopalachari, *Cakkaravartti-t-Tirumahan* (Madras: Pari Nilayam, 1956), p. iv. English translation in C. Rajagopalachari, Ramayana (Bombay: Bharatiya Vidya Bhavan [henceforth BVB], 1957), p. 7.

2. Author's Preface (18 October 1955) in C. Rajagopalachari, Mahabharata, fourth edn. (B: BVB, 1955), p. 11.

3. Because this paper deals with a period of history when anglicized forms of English words are common in Indian public discourse, I eschew the distracting diacritical marks used by Tamil scholars for transliteration of literary works and inscriptions. Instead, the Tamil names are spelled out in roman transliteration that most closely matches their pronunciation. So, for example, Sita is spelled with an 's' rather than a 'c' and Tiruchengodu with a 'ch' rather than a 'cc'. Whenever I refer to Ramayana by Valmiki, I identify its author by name to avoid it being confused with Rajagopalachari's Ramayana. Ramkatha is used in this essay not to refer to a specific telling (such as, for example, Kamban's *Iramavataram*) but to the basic set of episodes generally included in, or taken for granted by, the vast majority of tellings of Rama's story, such as the wedding of Rama and Sita, the forest exile, and the battle with Ravana.

4. Books that focus primarily on Rajagopalachari's political career include Anthony R.H. Copley, *The Political Career of C. Rajagopalachari: 1937-1954* (Delhi: Macmillan, 1978); R.K. Murthi, *Rajaji: Life and Work* (New Delhi: Allora Publications, 1979); C.R. Narasimhan, *Rajagopalachari: A Biography* (New Delhi: Radiant Publishers, 1993); Rajmohan Gandhi, *Rajaji* (New Delhi: Penguin, 1997). An exception to this pattern is Joanne Punzo Waghorne, *Images of Dharma: The Epic World of C. Rajagopalachari* (Delhi: Chanakya Publications, 1985), which traces how his writings assess events of his day in light of dharmic ideals, with particular focus on his Ramayana and Mahabharata.

5. For full citations for the short stories, see notes 46, 51, and 54. For the prose epic, see note 1. For the translation, see note 29.

6. In 'Janaka of our Times', M. Ananthasayanam Ayyangar, also imprisoned during 1940–1, recalls Rajagopalachari guiding fifteen to twenty prisoners, himself included, through an analysis of a section of Valmiki each day. See *Rajaji '93 Souvenir* (Madras, 1971), p. 155.

7. Comment reported in *The Hindu*, 2 April 1952, as quoted in R. Gandhi, *Rajaji*, p. 340.

8. Rajagopalachari wrote about 'the Raman Effect' in *Bhavan's Journal* (27 December 1970). R.K. Murthi, *Rajaji*, p. 157, provides the quote from the scientist, a researcher at the Bhabha Atomic Research Centre.

9. See S. Narayanaswamy, 'The Humanist with a Difference', *Bhavan's Journal* 25, no. 10 (December 17–30, 1978), pp. 59–63. 'Many unimaginative critics twitted

Rajaji on his parables and illustrations; which enabled him speedily to reach both the untutored millions of India and the young' (p. 62).

10. See Author's Preface (10 May 1957), Ramayana, p. 8.

11. Preface to new edn. (16 June 1967), C. Rajagopalachari, *Stories for the Innocent* (Bombay: BVB, 1964; rpt. 1982), p. iii. A disciple of Mohandas Karamchand Gandhi for decades, Rajagopalachari shared Gandhi's view of Truth as one of the highest goals of humankind.

12. For moral teaching in the Indian storytelling tradition, see Stuart H. Blackburn, *Moral Fictions: Tamil Folktales from Oral Tradition* (Helsinki: Suomalainen Tiedeakatemia, Academia Scientiarum Fennica, 2001); Kirin Narayan, *Storytellers, Saints, and Scoundrels: Folk Narrative in Hindu Religious Teaching* (Philadelphia: University of Pennsylvania Press, 1989); and Paula Richman, *Women, Branch Stories, and Religious Rhetoric in a Tamil Buddhist Text* (Syracuse: Syracuse University Press, 1988).

13. Preface to second edn. (10 January 1952), Rajagopalachari, Mahabharata, p. 10.

14. Preface to first edn. (10 May 1957), Rajagopalachari, Ramayana, p. 8.

15. The phrase 'Hindu epics' is used here to refer to the Ramayana and Mahabharata, because Rajagopalachari and many of his Hindu colleagues saw these texts as epics of the Indian nation. The word 'Hindu' emphasizes that many Indian nationalists were invoking not secular texts but ones rooted in a Hindu religious context rather than a pluralistic context that includes Hindu, Islamic, Buddhist, and Jain texts. The term 'epic' is used here to refer to a narrative identified with a country's identity. For other ways to define Indian epics, see James Fitzgerald, 'No Contest Between Memory and Invention', in Kurt A. Raaflaub (ed.), *Epic and History* (Malden, MA and Oxford: Blackwell, 2010).

16. 'Why I Believe in the Classics' in C. Rajagopalachari, *Satyam Eva Jayate: A Collection of Articles Contributed to Swarajya and Other Journals from 1956 to 1961,* 2 vols. (Madras: Bharathan Publications, 1961). Rajagopalachari credits classics with providing 'perpetual intellectual pleasure by re-uniting us with the great souls of the past' (vol. 2, pp. 932–3).

17. For Kalki, see Cunta [R. Cundaram], *Ponniyin Putalvar: Amarar 'Kalki'yin Valkkai Varalaru* (Madras: Vanati Press, 1976).

18. Temperance was central to Gandhi's plan for rural constructive work. First, money not spent on drink could be used to purchase spinning wheels, thereby supplementing family income through cottage industry. Second, the heavy liquor tax underwrote the cost of British rule so purchasing liquor could be viewed as collusion with colonialism. Finally, since high castes considered alcohol a source of pollution, renouncing liquor would help free 'untouchables' from 'social disability'. When the Indian National Congress (INC) asked Rajagopalachari to help with the boycott of alcohol, he took over editing the English language periodical, *Prohibition*, and launched the Tamil one, *Vimochanam*. See R. Gandhi, *Rajaji*, p. 111 and Narasimhan, *Rajagopalachari*, pp. 45–6.

19. See Indira Viswanathan Peterson and Devesh Soneji (eds), *Performing Pasts: Reinventing the Arts in Modern South India* (New Delhi: Oxford University Press,

2008) for the revival of classical music and dance in the south during this period.

20. This statistic for 1941 was provided by the Audit Bureau of Circulation. The high number of *Kalki*'s readers is striking, given that other regional languages in India boasted more native speakers than did Tamil.

21. Govindan used the press of Ramnath Goenka, who owned the Tamil newspaper, *Dinamani*, and the English newspaper, the *Indian Express*. See B.G. Verghese, *Warrior of the Fourth Estate: Ramnath Goenka of the Express* (New Delhi: Viking Penguin, 2005).

22. P. Seshadri, S. Krishnamurti, and Navaratna Rama Rao helped translate the Tamil into English and it was serialized in *Sunday Standard*, according to the Preface (1 July 1950) in Mahabharata, first edn. (B: BVB, 1950), p. 7. Rajagopalachari's son-in-law, Devadas Gandhi, had it printed, simply titled Mahabharata (rather than '*Vyasa's Feast*') by Devi Prasad Sharma, legal printer and publisher of *Hindustan Times*.

23. Preface (10 May 1957) to Ramayana, first edn. (Bombay: BVB, 1957).

24. Personal communication of circulation figures provided by Shankar Ramachandran, CEO of Bharathan Publications, from his analysis of *Kalki*'s long-term financial profile.

25. H.R. Luthra, *Indian Broadcasting* (New Delhi: Ministry of Information and Broadcasting, 1981), p. 291, notes that during the war years, 1939–1945, all stations were required to submit to the government copies of scheduled radio talks.

26. Ibid., p. 294.

27. David Lelyveld, 'Upon the Subdominant: Administering Music on All-India Radio', in Carol A. Breckenridge (ed.), *Consuming Modernity: Public Culture in a South Asian World* (Minneapolis: University of Minnesota Press, 1995), p. 57, sees parallels between the central government's early role in controlling basic industries and AIR's function of playing 'a leading role in integrating Indian culture and raising standards'.

28. *Bharat Milap* (New Delhi: Publications Division, Ministry of Information, Government of India, 1955). Note, however, that the title is transliterated into English according to Hindi (*Bharat Milap*) rather than Sanskrit or Tamil (*Bharata Milapa*).

29. Prasad even suggests, 'It will be doing a great service if someone were able to render Kamban into Hindi verse and Tulsidas into Tamil verse.' Given the anti-Hindi sentiment in Tamil country at this time, such a project would be unlikely.

30. The most vociferous protests against promoting Hindi emerged from Tamil-speaking areas of the south. See Sumathi Ramaswamy, *Passions of the Tongue: Language Devotion in Tamil India, 1891–1970* (Berkeley: University of California Press, 1997), especially the cartoon following page 78, 'Rajagopalachari's Bravado: The Dishonoring of Tamilttay', which shows the Tamils as Draupadi, being disrobed by Rajagopalachari's support of Hindi. In north India, in contrast, many found it offensive that Tamil speakers preferred English, the colonizers' language, to Hindi.

31. K.M. Munshi, 'Bhavan's Book University: Prospect and Retrospect', *Bhavan's Journal* 6 (November 1977), pp. 40–1.

32. *Bhavan's Journal* (15 December 2002), pp. 25–6, calls him 'a shining example of austere living and high thinking untainted by pride and egoism', and 'a relentless champion of clear and efficient administration'.

33. The multi-coloured, double-sided, oversize, cardboard advertising flyer available at the Bhavan in December 2002 says, 'The Bhavan has the proud privilege of publishing 18 books authored by Rajaji, the copyright of which he gifted very quietly, unobtrusively to the Bhavan.' The 'no smut' quote appears on the reverse side of the flyer.

34. Front matter, *Award Winning Books of Indian Languages* (New Delhi: National Book Trust, 1992). In its early years, Akademi prizes were virtually the only regular pan-Indian literary recognition available to India's writers. Prizes also informed Indians literate in one region's language about outstanding literary works in other regional languages. Duggirala Subba Rao notes, 'In 1954, writers and readers in one language knew next to nothing of what was being written in a neighbouring language within the same country.' Duggirala Subba Rao, *Five Decades, The National Academy of Letters, India: Short History of Sahitya Akademi* (New Delhi: Sahitya Akademi, 2007), p. 94,

35. *Sahitya Akademi Awards: Books and Writers (1955-1978)* (New Delhi: Sahitya Akademi, 1990), pp. 446–7.

36. Masti Venkatesa Iyengar, *Rajaji: A Study of his Personality*, 2 vols. (Bangalore: Jeevana Karyalaya, 1975), II, p. 102, provides his evaluation, as well as Nehru's comment.

37. V. Swaminathan, 'Literary Masquerades: Part Two', *Thought*, 5 April 1969, p. 15. The next five issues include letters to the editor debating the quality of the book.

38. Although the Akademi's funding came from the government, it managed to maintain autonomous status despite attempts by the central government to gain control over it.

39. Part One of Swaminathan's essay for *Thought* (29 March 1969) notes that eight of the ten prizes for Tamil literature were awarded to members on the Sahitya Akademi Board. Because of controversies about the selection process, the Executive Board recommended a change in the way that books were considered. See Rao, *Five Decades*, p. 30.

40. Raja Ram Merhotra, *Indian English: Texts and Interpretation* (Philadelphia: John Benjamins Pub., 1998), pp. 38–9, presents Nehru's inaugural address at a UNESCO conference as a model of Indian English. For UNESCO's translation efforts, see Humayun Kabir's 'Role of UNESCO in Promotion and Preservation of World Cultures' in *Twenty Years of UNESCO* (New Delhi: India International Center, 1967), p. 68. For a 1948 mission statement for the representative literary works series, (accessed 12 May 2003), see www.unesco. org/culture/creativity/literature/html_ eng/collection.shtml.

41. See *Sahitya Akademi Annual Report 1954-55*, p. 22.

42. Only after Rajagopalachari's retellings of the epics became bestsellers did the Bhavan in 1964 decide to print a collection of his short stories in English. Several

of them, including 'Pachattapam,' had been published in an early anthology of his stories, translated into English. See C. Rajagopalachari, *The Fatal Cart and Other Stories* (New Delhi: Hindustan Press, 1945).

43. Some ambivalence toward Rama comes out in his letter to Navaratna Rama Rao, an old and dear friend (20 October 1955). There Rajagopalachari expresses his disgust that Rama treated Sita so harshly in Lanka: 'Yesterday I finished the last chapter of the Tamil series of Valmiki [for *Kalki*] and sent Rama back to Ayodhya after his disgraceful performance on the battlefield with Sita.' Quoted in R. Gandhi, *Rajaji*, p. 357.

44. Rajagopalachari's best-known story on alcoholism, about a wife ruined by her husband's drinking, 'Tikkarra Parvati' [Destitute Parvati] appeared first in *Kudi ketukkum kal* [Liquor that Ruins the Household] (Tiruchengode: Gandhi Ashram, 1926), his earliest extant collection of stories.

45. *Rajaji Katti-k-Kataikal* [Rajaji's Collected Stories] (Mylapore: Alliance Co., 1937).

46. *Siru Kataikal* [Short Stories] (Karaikkuti: New Publishers, 1944). 'Pachattapam' was reprinted eight years later in *Rajaji Kataikal* [Rajaji's Stories] (Madras: Bharati Press, 1952), and later translated into English as 'Repentance' in *The Fatal Cart*.

47. 'Pachattapam' was reprinted in *Kalki's* 17 January 1960 issue under a new name, 'Sitaiyin Kanavu' [Sita's Dream], pp. 97–9. My translations are based on this version. I cite page numbers from it parenthetically in the body of my essay, right after a quote.

48. Narada, a celestial sage, wanders in and out of various Puranic and epic stories. A busybody and a meddler, he frequently intrudes in the conversation of others to add some comment that is usually accurate but unwelcome.

49. The story hints that Narada was involved somehow in Sita's abduction, since he encouraged Ravana to stay. This detail does not appear in familiar tellings of Ramkatha. On the other hand, in a number of later tellings, the gods desire that the plot moves smoothly towards Sita's abduction and the battle in which Rama slays Ravana so Vishnu's divine plan will be fulfilled. Thus, Narada's presence may be interpreted here as insuring that Ravana plays his scripted role in the celestial plan.

50. Rajagopalachari speculates that, since Sita had never met Hanuman, *his* arrival could not be foretold in her dream so perhaps the dream puts Lakshmana in his place.

51. 'Sitadeviyin Avataram' first appears in Tamil in Rajaji, *Niranta-c-Celvam* (Madras: Vanati Publications, 1953; rpt. 1971), pp. 63–71. This is the version upon which I have based my translation and cite from it in my essay with page numbers in parentheses. *Stories for the Innocent* does not contain this story in English translation. It does, however, contain 'Uttara Kanda-Revised', a story that is much shorter than 'Sitadeviyin Avataram' and lacks the scenes set in heaven at the beginning and end. K.M. Munshi notes, in his Foreword to the anthology, that Rajagopalachari originally composed 'Uttara Kanda-Revised' in English. This rather underdeveloped story justifies Rama's banishment of Sita by having her tell Rama after the fire ordeal that she came to earth

from heaven to fulfil her duties and now only wants to retire to the forest. A translation from English into Tamil appears later in Rajaji, *Palkatal: putiya katai-t-tokuti* [Milk Ocean: A New Story Anthology] (Madras: Parati Publishers, 1960), pp. 96–102.

52. Rajagopalachari refers pointedly here to her as 'avatara of Sridevi' to emphasize that she is playing a temporary role, rather than actually being humiliated by Rama.

53. Rajagopalachari lists some of the many names of the goddess, such as Parvati and Gauri (p. 70), assuring readers that they are all manifestations of Sridevi.

54. 'Putu-c-caayal: Vali Vatam' [New Perspective: Slaying of Vali], *Kalki* 19 October 1958, pp. 10–11. It appears in English translation in *Stories for the Innocent*, pp. 219–26, subtitled 'not the version of Valmiki but a bold variation'.

55. David Shulman, 'Divine Order and Divine Evil in the Tamil Tale of Rama', *Journal of Asian Studies* 38 (1979), pp. 651–69, compares the Vali episode in Valmiki and Kamban.

56. For an analysis of what Tara shares with the other ideal epic women, see Pradip Bhattacharya, *Pancha-kanya: The Five Virgins of Indian Epics: A Quest in Search of Meaning* (Calcutta: Writers Workshop, 2005).

57. In relating Rama's story to present day India, Rajagopalachari followed the lead of his mentor, Mohandas Karamchand Gandhi, who used the concept of Rama's just rule as a way to envision post-colonial India. For a survey of modern political leaders who drew on language about Ramrajya, see Philip Lutgendorf, *The Life of a Text: Performing the Ramcaritmanas of Tulsidas* (Berkeley: University of California Press, 1991), pp. 378–82. Swami Karpartri of Rashtriya Swayamsevak Sangh referred to Ramraj often in speeches, but interpreted Rama's perfect rule as a time when caste hierarchy would be unquestioned. Political leaders on the opposite side of the spectrum saw Ramraj as a utopian society in which no one would suffer from lack of food or sickness.

58. As Pudumaippittan, one of Tamil's most masterful and celebrated prose writers, noted in 1934, 'Until the present time, prose had no standing.' See A.R. Venkatachalapathy (ed.), *Putumaippittan Kataikal: Mulu Tokuppai* [The Complete Stories of Pudumaippithan] (Nagercoil: Kalaccuvatu Patippakam, 2000), p. 101.

59. He engaged in long discussions with fellow-lawyer, friend, and Kamban expert, T.K. Chidambaranatha Mudaliyar (1882–1954), who founded the first chapter of Kambar Kalakam [Kamban Association] in Tirunelveli in 1938. An unflagging advocate of *Iramavataram*, he provided exegesis of complex verses, spearheaded publication of inexpensive editions, and wrote columns on it for *Kalki* (See, for example, 2 November 1943).

60. Rajagopalachari proceeds like a conscientious student who weaves into the story frequent comments on how aspects of it have been treated by two previous masters.

61. See Paula Richman, 'Epic and State: Contesting Interpretations of the Ramayana', *Public Culture* 7 (1995), pp. 631–54, for a detailed analysis of

Rajagopalachari's characterization of the main figures in Ramkatha, which will not be repeated here.

62. The most famous (and vitriolic) critic of Rama's actions in Tamil was E.V. Ramasami. See Paula Richman, 'E.V. Ramasami's Reading of the Ramayana', in P. Richman (ed.), *Many Ramayanas* (Berkeley: University of California Press, 1991), pp. 175-201.

63. For a folksong in which Lakshmana remains awake each night in exile, see Velcheru Narayana Rao, 'A Ramayana of Their Own: Women's Oral Tradition in Telugu', in *Many Ramayanas*, pp. 124–5.

64. The phrase 'national culture' appears, among other places, in the Author's Preface to the third edn. (19 October 1958), Ramayana, p. 9.

65. In *The Swatantra Party and Indian Conservatism* (Cambridge: Cambridge University Press, 1967), Howard Erdman notes that Swatantra party members reached consensus on twenty-one principles and deemed other issues irrelevant, a policy that 'reflects the conviction that the principal task is that of opposing Congress "statism," and that those who can agree on this should not be divided by other issues deemed to be less significant' (p. 189).

66. An accessible account of Rajagopalachari's views on nuclear proliferation appears in Monica Felton, *I Meet Rajaji* (London: Macmillan, 1962).

67. Preface (19 October 1958), Ramayana, third edn., pp. 9–10.

68. Kalki, too, wrote historical novels, setting them in ancient Tamil kingdoms.

69. Many Tamils vilified Rajagopalachari as a Brahmin whom they believed sought to force Hindi upon Tamils. Regarding such criticism as absurd, he asked in the Madras Legislative Assembly, 'Are we [Tamil speakers] not in India? Or has an earthquake converted Tamil India to an island, separated from the rest of India?' *Debates*, vol. XI, 24 February 1939, p. 359 cited in Copley, *Political Career*, p. 108 n88).

70. C. Rajagopalachari, *Swarajya*, 26 January 1974, as quoted in T.S. Devadoss, 'Sri C. Rajagopalachari—A Tribute', *Bulletin of the Institute of Traditional Cultures, Madras* (January–June 1977), p. 139.

71. For Mohandas Karamchand Gandhi on Sita, see Pushpa Joshi (comp.), *Gandhi on Women* (Ahmedabad: Navajivan Publishing House, 1988), pp. 175, 197.

72. Richard H. Davis, *Lives of Indian Images* (Princeton: Princeton University Press, 1997), p. 211, notes that Munshi 'made the reconstruction of a Gujarati golden age an important part of his literary agenda'.

73. Sitamshu Yashaschandra, 'From Hemanchandra to *Hind Svaraj*: Region and Power in Gujarati Literary Culture', *Literary Cultures in History: Reconstructions from South Asia* (Berkeley: University of California Press, 2003), comments, no matter 'however useful they might have seemed to the author in the service of the sociopolitical needs of his day', his writings were based on erroneous premises about historical events (p. 569). Yashaschandra notes the vulnerability 'to uncritical assumptions' in Munshi's writing, despite being a 'distinguished novelist' and 'keen student of Indian cultural history'.

74. Riko Isaha, 'The Perception of the Literary Tradition of Gujarat in the Late Nineteenth Century', *Journal of the Japanese Association for South Asian Studies* 14 (2002), pp. 1–19, shows how leading Gujarati scholars of the late nineteenth

century focused on Jain literature and Vaishnava bhakti poetry, while ignoring Persian and Arabic literature patronized by Muslim rulers in Gujarat and Ismaili religious songs (pp. 4–6). Isaha's 'Gujarati Intellectuals and History Writing in the Colonial Period', *Economic and Political Weekly* (30 November 2002), pp. 4867–72, shows how Munshi read Hindu animosity towards Muslims of his day back into earlier history in the region, ignoring evidence that Indian culture flourished during Muslim rule.

75. Munshi wrote a regular column, 'Kulapati's letter', for *Bhavan's Journal*. His fondness for themes drawn from ancient Sanskrit texts is also reflected in his novels and plays about ascetics such as Lopamudra, Vishvamitra, and Parashurama. The Bhavan published his novel *Bhagawan Parashurama* (earlier serialized in Gujarati) in abridged English translation. For analysis of his historical novels see Davis, *Lives*, pp. 210–12.

76. The list includes nationalist leaders such as Annie Besant, Gandhi, Rajagopalachari, Subas Chandra Bose, and Sardar Patel; leaders of Hindu 'reform' movements such as the Buddha, Aurobindo, Ramalingar, Vivekananda, and Swaminarayan; devotional saints such as Mirabai; and miscellaneous figures such as Joseph Stalin. Only a two-volume set on Akbar, by J.M. Shelet, deals with an Indian Muslim.

77. 'Kulapati's Letter', *Bhavan's Journal*, 4 July 1965, p.7.

78. *Speeches Delivered by His Excellency Sri Chakravarti Rajagopalacharya, Governor of West Bengal, 15 August 1947 to 19 June 1948*, p. 59. That a Brahmin Sri Vaishnava would suggest dining with Muslims shows how far he had moved from the views of purity and pollution with which he had been raised.

79. Ajay Skaria, 'Homeless in Gujarat and India', *The Indian Economic and Social History Review*, vol. 38, no. 3 (2001), p. 277.

80. See Davis, *Lives*, pp. 218–19.

81. Selections come from Bala and Ayodhya Kanda, the first two of the six-kanda poem.

82. Rajagopalachari, in *Bharat Milap*, concedes that Valmiki contains some references to Rama as God, 'but in the body of the narrative the Raama pictured by Sage Vaalmeeki is not God himself but a great prince endowed with divine qualities'(p. 15), showing his familiarity with philological research on the text's history. He notes that omitting Rama's divinity in Kamban 'would be like omitting the divinity of Jesus', which would have its lessons, he says, 'but it would not be the foundation of Christianity such as it now is' (p. 6).

83. This story appears in K.M. Munshi's essay, 'Our Bheeshmapitamaha', *Bhavan's Journal* (3 December 1967), p. 78.

Ronald Inden

Popular Patriotism in Indian Film

NATIONAL THEOLOGY

Popular patriotism has suddenly come to scholars' attention in the Western world mainly due to the rise of what they refer to as 'fundamentalism' or 'religious nationalism' in places as far apart as the US with its Nascar dads and the Middle East with its suicide bombers. Scholars of South Asia have assumed that the rise to power of the Bharatiya Janata Party (BJP) inaugurated a new era of what we are calling here 'Political Hinduism'. They have also assumed that this political Hinduism is somehow connected with these other fundamentalist movements. They have also tried to connect it with a phenomenon they refer to as globalization. The surprising defeat of the BJP and its National Democratic Alliance (NDA) in the last elections raises serious questions about the strategies of the BJP and its grip on the popular imagination, as I have argued in an interview.[1] Amazingly, scholars have made almost no effort to study what I refer to as popular patriotism in South Asia. They have assumed that it is either a reflex of official, national, or party ideas of the nation, synonymous with religious nationalism, or virtually nonexistent because India's masses are uneducated—and perhaps not even masses. They hold 'traditional' views instead, that is, they are loyal to family, caste, locality, and the religions of their forefathers.

I came across popular patriotism when I began to study popular Hindi films. It appears mostly in 'action' films, what people in the industry have classified as 'social' or 'historical' or 'war' films rather than 'mythological' (or 'devotional') films. Mythological films have all but disappeared from the cinema halls.[2] They have not, however, disappeared; they have been reborn as serials on television and have been the focus of scholarly attention on the links between Hindutva and the media.[3] To be sure, these serials may be controversial, especially for secularists, but they do not themselves problematize patriotism as many of the action films do.

It became quite clear to me while watching action films and listening to the songs in them, that there is not only a distinct popular patriotism in India, but that this patriotism itself comprises what I would call a *national theology* and what some US sociologists would call a 'civil religion'.[4]

The national theology of India, its civil religion, draws on and, in certain respects, recuperates certain features of Indian theisms (Hindu, Islamic, and Sikh).[5] Popular films and the patriotic songs both in the films and apart from them are, along with posters, the main evidence for this popular patriotism because they themselves have been integral to and expressive of the practices by which people have fashioned and sustained popular patriotism in India. The most important practices involving the songs have been protest marches and rallies as well as those occasions which memorialize these activities—including visits to the cinema hall—or prepare people to participate in them.[6]

The association of patriotic songs with films actually antedates the advent of sound films. Kohinoor Film's *Bhakt Vidur* [Loyal Vidur] (Kanjibhai Rathod, 1921) starred one of the owners, Dwarkadas Sampat, as the minister of the Pāṇḍavas in the Mahābhārata and drew a homology between himself and Gandhi. The film was accompanied by live music and the singing of a nationalist song in praise of a spinning wheel.

'Patriotism' and its sister, 'nationalism', are contested terms. People in the US and Europe commonly use the term patriotism (etymologically related to father and the notion of a fatherland) in everyday parlance to denote minimally loyalty to one's country. They may use the term nationalism as a synonym for patriotism or, more usually, to designate a heightened and perhaps fanatical patriotism (also called chauvinism or jingoism) attributed by Anglo-American liberals in the twentieth century to Nazis, Communists, and in many cases the 'new nations'. I use the term patriotism to refer to the ideas and beliefs involved in the practices covered by the Hindi and equivalent Urdu expressions for 'devotion to the country' (*deśbhakti* and *vatanparastī*, respectively). Indians have used the term nationalism in English (and its neologisms, *rāṣṭrtyatā* or *rāṣṭravād/itā,* Hindi; and *qaumparastī*, Urdu) to refer in general to a 'freedom struggle' (*āzādī kī laḍāī*) by which they formed themselves into an independent and modern nation. Because patriotism was a pre-requisite for nationalism the scholars of Indian nationalism have done little to distinguish the two. The British, of course, considered the nationalist movement unpatriotic if not traitorous.[7] Generally I shall use the term patriotism here in order to unpick it from nationalism, a term I use here in the positive Indian sense.

When I say *popular* patriotism I mean to distinguish it from *elite* patriotism. Elites in many countries, including India, often look down on patriotism altogether. They prefer to see themselves as 'international' or, nowadays, as 'transnational' in position and as 'cosmopolitan' in outlook. Nonetheless, elites do promote or condone certain forms of patriotism (especially if they are looking for popular support). Within India, officially sanctioned patriotism has come generally to be encapsulated in the term 'secularism'. I will spare us all a discussion of the endless debates over Indian secularism. Let me just say in summary that most have taken secularism to entail a *marginalization of the conventional religions*—Hinduism, Islam, Sikhism, Jainism, and Christianity. Proponents of a stronger secularism generally also saw it as involving the gradual diminution in importance of the conventional religions not just in the life of the nation, but in personal lives as well.

Nehru and his adherents, capturing the centre of the political stage, saw national development as the key to a secular India in which Western consumerism and personal spirituality would displace traditional religiosity. Gandhi saw an absolute morality that reworks and transcends the conventional religions as supplanting those religions. Advocates of liberalization see India's version of a free market economy as leading to the goals that national development failed to reach. On the right, Veer Savarkar called for the Hinduization of India through purification. His India would displace the non-Hindu religions and the divergent orders of Hinduism itself, with a generic, universal Hindu nationalism. To the left of Nehru, Naxalites and others called for the violent overthrow of a class-divided society (whether colonial or national). The social justice that emerged would leave no room for the false consciousness of the conventional religions or of bourgeois patriotism.

The representations of popular patriotism show us a situation in which the people of the nation have neither marginalized the conventional religions nor have they Hinduized the nation. Rather they have *nationalized* elements from the conventional religions. The terms they use for 'country' (*deś*, Hindi; *vatan*, Urdu) are often also used where we might use the term 'nation' (*rāṣṭra*, Hindi; *qaum*, Urdu).[8] Films have created a *god of the nation* generally referred to as *Ūparvālā*, 'the one above' (rather than the Hindu *Bhagvān* or *Īśvar* or the Muslim *Allāh* or *Khudā*). Often they also refer to it by one of the many terms from Islamic or Hindu theology as 'destiny' or 'fate' (*qismat, muqaddar, taqdīr*, Urdū; *karma, bhāgya*, Hindi). The nation and the god of the nation are, according to the representations of the films, to take precedence over the conventional religions upon which they draw. Yet the conventional religions are themselves not to be marginalized. Echoing Gandhi, they continue to be important for people and their families. Indeed there is and should be room for all of India's religions to be practised.

They see the *nation as a mother*—Mother India/Bhārat Mātā and her citizens as her sons and daughters. The aim of the nation is to support the family life of its citizens. They should enjoy prosperity with social justice. Marriage is the complex activity which should both bring prosperity and justice and display it (though often it does not). Filmmakers frequently, but by no means always, connect the main family of a Bombay film to the nation and see the two as homologous.

Numerous scholars have noticed the representation of India as a mother figure, but few have noticed another representation that is equally important—that of the nation as *paradise on earth* (*firdaus, jannat*, Urdu; *svarg*, Hindi/Sanskrit), one that takes the form of a quadripartite *garden of delights* (*cārbāg, gulistān, gulśan*) and its associated palaces and pavilions, themselves set in a beautiful landscape. Though the connection is not often made explicitly in words, this idea of a paradise on earth as a garden of delights has been constitutive of the Hindi film since its inception. Indeed films and songs have been responsible for the *massification* of this idea of a paradise on earth. They have taken a place which was walled off from the rest of the world and accessible only to a few available to the many at least in the cinema hall (and now on the television screen). They have also transformed the aristocratic aestheticism associated with the garden of delights into the consumerism of the middle classes.

The poet Allama Iqbal (1873-1938), a Kashmiri, wrote a famous poem called 'Song of India' (*Tarānā-e Hind*) characterizing India as a garden of delights while he was reading law in England. The first verse is the most popular, but the first four verses are also widely recited. Ravi Shankar Sharma (b. 1920) set the poem to music for a film:

The best in all the world is our Hindustan
We are nightingales in this our flower-garden.
Though I be in exile, (my) heart remains in (my) country.

Understand, it is for us alone there where our heart is.
Its mountains are the highest, neighbors to the sky;
They are our guardian, our sentinel.
In whose lap play a thousand streams;
Whose flower-beds are the envy of heaven.[9]

Kashmiris and Panjabis, and many other Indians and Pakistanis, too, have long considered one part of India special in this regard—Kashmir. It was not only filled with gardens of delights during Mughal times, people thought the entire country was itself a garden of delights. Consistent with this idea, a recent patriotic film, *Mission Kashmir* (Vidhu Vinod Chopra, 2000), represents Kashmir that way in three of its songs.[10]

It is, of course, ironic that films and songs should be the vehicle for creating India's civil religion. Like their British rulers, the leaders of the nationalist movement, Nehru and especially Gandhi, tended to view commercial film-makers and film stars, both foreign and domestic, with suspicion. The British were afraid that foreign movies showing Americans behaving in a vulgar fashion would undermine the authority of the British and worried that films made by Indians might try to support one or the other strands of the nationalist movement. Nationalist leaders considered the commercial films as at best trivial and vulgar and at their worst as degrading and immoral in their consequences for the masses of Indian viewers.[11]

Film-makers working with music composers and poets or lyricists and the stars and fans of films have responded to these different criticisms by fashioning a popular patriotism in the films they have made and viewed. They have, in effect, created a national theology. A national god or destiny, India as a mother, and as a paradise on earth are, however, not the only elements of this national theology. The other element is the *national hero*, usually a man, sometimes a woman, who acts to save the nation.

Three ideas, each drawn from a conventional religion, are at work in representing the patriotic hero. They are the Hindu, Muslim, and Sikh ideas of the *incarnation*, the *angel* or messenger, and the *martyr*.

INCARNATION OF THE NATION
Often the hero can be seen (in Hindu terms) rather loosely as an avatar, a descent to earth of a manifestation of the nation or the god of the nation. He is the outsider who intervenes to save the good people and, implicitly, the country. Incarnation (*avatāra*, *prādurbhāva*, Sanskrit) is crucial to one of the two main divisions of Hindus, the *Vaiṣṇava*. Viṣṇu is

a transcendent, but active god who maintains moral order in the world and removes wickedness. The incarnation is the means by which Viṣṇu acts in the world while remaining outside it. He causes these and other interventions in the world through his luminous, divine will (*tejas*). Theologians differ on the number and types of incarnations, but agree that full incarnations are to be distinguished from partial ones. Among the latter are kings and some religious gurus and images liturgically installed in temples. (Śiva, the God of the other division, is an ascetic, withdrawn from the world. His spouse and her variants are left with the task of managing the world.)[12]

Jeet (Raj Kanwar, 1996) is a film that features a hero as incarnation. As in many action films, punchy—and here, alliterative—dialogues (by Avtar Gill) do a great deal of the patriotic work.[13] An opening scene in the film has the villain respond to the charge that he is not a patriot (*deśbhakt*) but a traitor (*deśdrohī*). Gajraj (Amrish Puri), a godfather-like criminal boss cuts roses in the garden of a luxury mansion. Two businessmen enter. Govardhan (Deepak Shirke) reports success in arranging 'fixes' for licenses with government ministers. He has arranged for enough firearms deals to celebrate the Festival of Lights (Diwali, beginning of the merchants' year, accompanied by fireworks) every night. Gajraj replies that this is a small lamp in his glittering Sultanate of crime, over which he presides as a successor of Alexander. Govardhan speaks indirectly about their money-laundering. His partner, Pitambar (Mohan Joshi), says it is all a matter of 'common sense'. He reports that a journalist, Baljit Parmar (Sashi Kiran) has accused Gajraj of being a merchant of death (*maut kā saudāgar*) and 'traitorous' (*deśdrohī*). Gajraj replies sarcastically that he is a patriot (*deśbhakt*), a farmer (*kisān*) who grows rice and wheat, hash and cannabis, earning foreign currency for the country. He provides Mother India with golden wings. The associates say that when the pen starts writing it is mightier than the sword. Gajraj looks to his go-between and says: 'Gajjan. Karan (Sunny Deol)'.

After Karan, an orphan who looks like both Rāvaṇ and Rambo, saves Raju (Salman Khan) several times, Kajal (Karishma Kapoor), Raju's wife and Karan's former lover, explicitly calls him a saviour (*masīhā*). A bit later there is this interchange between the two heroes of the film:

Raju: 'Destiny', fortune (*taqdīr*), fate (*qismat*). Nothing. It's a chessboard and we're all just pawns. The player above (*khilāḍī uparvālā*) makes wondrous moves. From his mere indication, relationships are made and broken. And we are all scattered around. There's just one thing. The one thing that keeps us united is love (*muhabbat*), only love. Friend, if there were no love in this world, nothing at all would happen.

I came to know today why you continue to save me.
(*Then, looking at his wife:*) Kajal, from the day I placed the necklace of well-being around your neck, you have observed the rules and realized yourself as a wife, as only an Indian wife (*hindustānī aurat*) could do. Kajal, I honor what is past between you two.
(*Turning to Karan:*) In this small world, you have the largest of hearts. Only some god could act in such a way.
Karan: In this world of stones it is easy to become a deity. Becoming a man is very difficult. You are a truly civilized man, Raju.
Raju: Kajal, If we have a boy, we shall name him Karan.

Especially noteworthy is the post-Hindu comparison of a 'stone' *image of a deity* (*devtā* rather than a deity itself, *dev*) to a 'civilized human' (*nek insān*), that is, a citizen of the nation. Karan dies fighting off Gajraj while the pregnant Kajal goes into labour.

The connection between avatar and hero is explicit in *Narasimha* (N. Chandra, 1991) where Sunny Deol plays a character named after Narasimha, the Man-Lion, one of Viṣṇu's full avatars. Many films also invoke the characters of the Rāmāyaṇa. The film *Khal-Nayak* (Subhash Ghai, 1993), explicitly drawing parallels to the Rāmāyaṇa, calls its

Narasimha emerges from the pillar (*Narasimha*, US: Bollywood Entertainment Inc.)

villains rākṣas. The hero's name is Ram, another full incarnation, and the heroine's Ganga, a permutation of Sītā.

MESSENGER OF THE NATION

The hero of a Hindi film is seldom a Muslim, but Muslim characters do appear frequently in lesser roles. Many films feature an elderly, wise Muslim gentleman. He may be viewed (in Islamic terms) as resembling an 'angel' or 'messenger' (fariśtā) sent by God. Strictly monotheist Muslims disallow incarnations, relying instead on angels to do the will of god. Created out of light, angels can appear at any time. The foremost of angels is Jibril (Gabriel), assigned the task of delivering the Qur'ān to the Prophet Muhammad, whence the idea of an angel as messenger.[14]

One well-known example of the angel in the Hindi film is the character Imamsaab (A.K. Hangal) in the famous film, *Sholay* (Ramesh Sippy, 1975). The bandits who have been terrorizing the village of Ramgarh have killed the son of Imaamsaab, Ahmed, on his way to take up a new job. His donkey brings his body back to the village. The villagers gather and react to this in the presence of the film's heroes. One of them finally says that they can no longer bear the burden of the bandits' attacks. Imaamsaab responds:

Who cannot bear this burden, brother? Do you know what the greatest burden in the world is? The bier of his sons on his shoulders. There is no burden heavier than this. I, an old man, can bear this burden. And you? You cannot bear the burden of a problem. Brother, I do know one thing. A death of honour is better anywhere than a life of disgrace. I have lost a son. Yet I want the other two to remain right in the village. It is up to you. (*He hears the call to prayer from the mosque*). The time for my prayers has come. I will ask God today why he did not give me several sons to become martyrs (*shaheed*) for this village.

Here and in other films where these angels or messengers appear, they do pretty much the same thing.[15] They embody the *morality of the nation*, the *good sense* its people should always display but quite often do not, especially in a crisis. In this role, the Muslim contrasts rather sharply with the Hindu incarnation. As we have seen in *Jeet*, the incarnation is less concerned with morality. His focus is rather on directed force, right action at just the right time and place.

One example of a film where the hero is a Muslim is *Ghulam-e-Mustafa* (Parto Ghosh, 1999).[16] Its star, Nana Patekar (b. 1952), also made a patriotic film, *Tiranga* [Tricolour] (Mehul Kumar, 1992). According to the film's publicity, 'Ghulam-e-Mustafa is an attempt by its makers to help its countrymen to unite and treat each other's communities with love affection and respect.' Ghulam-e-Mustafa (Nana Patekar) is an orphan (*yatīm*) brought up (but not formally educated) by an underworld don (Paresh Rawal) known as Abba to become his accomplished henchman. After the opening scenes where we see Mustafa in secular settings in Mumbai, the camera cuts to a radically different location. From an aerial point of view we see Mustafa at a ruined mosque offering his prayers: he is an *orthodox Muslim* (*namāzī*) albeit a solitary one, more like a Sufi. A cell phone rings, his, and he answers it.

Arrangements have been made and we cut to the place where kidnappers are holding two men. Mustafa makes his grand entrance and makes it quite clear that he is no ordinary person. One of the kidnappers looks at him and asks: 'Mustafa?' and Mustafa answers, 'No. Ghulam-e-Mustafa.' The word *mustafā*, 'the chosen one', is an epithet of the Prophet. The word *ġulām*, 'slave', combined with the genitive e-mustafa means 'slave of the Prophet'. This is a term that could well be applied to one of Allah's angelic messengers, for they are all His slaves. The way Mustafa fights leaves little doubt that he is special.

Mustafa meets a young woman, Kavita (Raveena Tandon), a dancer. But she is mortally wounded in a murder attempt by Abba's rivals on Mustafa before the two can get married. At this point Mustafa, who is also human, undergoes a radical change. He renounces his 'profession' and swears to protect a family of orthodox Maharashtrian Brahmans which is threatened by the underworld and politicians. The reason? Dayanand Dixit is an honest civil servant. He has already impressed Mustafa with his incorruptibility. Overcome by despair after Kavita's death, Mustafa says God has punished him for his criminal acts in the past. Kavita has told him to do a good deed and seek forgiveness. So he pays the hospital bill for Dayanand's wife, Lakshmi, and arranges bail for Dayanand, who is falsely arrested. Dayanand says that he cannot seek out the angel (fariśtā) who paid for his wife's operation and paid his bail to get him out of prison.

Here we see the film positioning Mustafa as an angel or as a messenger. Indeed, at various points in the film we are encouraged to see Mustafa's life as a message of redemption in a corrupt and criminal world that threatens to ruin the good and bad alike. To help the distressed family, Mustafa makes a deal with the politician and Abba. He wins the by-election for the ruling party and decides to hand himself over to the police. However, the very existence of the underworld and the politicians is threatened if Mustafa goes behind bars. They decide to eliminate him, and Mustafa accepts the challenge. He in effect martyrs himself, both to save the family he has vowed to protect and to redeem himself. The final scene of the film takes place at Vidya's, his 'sister's', wedding. The police arrest him. He asks that he be allowed to witness Vidya's marriage before they take him away. Knowing he will die, he asks also to perform what will be his last prayer (namāz). A gunman shoots him in the back. As he dies he has a vision of the dead Kavita.

Ghulam begins his last prayers (*Ghulam-e-Mustafa*, Mumbai and London: Eros International Ltd.)

MARTYRDOM FOR THE NATION

'Sacrifice' (Hindi; *qurbānī*, Urdu) for the sake of others is central to the popular patriotism of film and song. It takes its most dramatic form in the shape of the 'hero as martyr' (*shahīd*), as we have already seen in *Jeet* and *Ghulam-e-Mustafa*. The martyr has a long and complex history, starting with early Christianity and continuing today with the suicide bomber.[17] The 'martyr' is a witness to the truth who is prepared to die for it. Offering 'witness' (*śahādat*) to God's truth and dying for it in a 'struggle' (*jihād*) is important for both Sunni and Shi'ite Muslims, but has a special role in the latter, where every imam of the faithful is considered a martyr. Sikhism appropriates this idea for its purposes.[18]

There are two kinds of martyrs in Indian films. The one most commonly thought of is the martyr who dies, in India's national theology, in order to liberate those in need or even the entire country. The second, more limited in scope, is the 'martyr to passionate love' (*śahīd-e-muhabbat*; *śahīd-e iśq*).[19] Amitabh Bachchan made the figure of the outsider who is willing to die for others [*Sholay* (Flames, 1975) and *Muqaddar Ka Sikandar* (Alexander of Destiny, 1978)] a commonplace of the 1970s and 1980s.[20]

The martyr, however, is also to be found in films with the explicit title, *Shaheed*.[21] Recently a spate of films about the most famous hero in the popular patriotism of north India and especially the Punjab, have appeared. That hero is not any of the political leaders one might expect. It is Bhagat Singh (1907–31), an atheist and socialist from a Sikh family.

At the age of fourteen, Bhagat Singh visited the site of the Jallian-wala Bagh Massacre of 1919.[22] He became a member of the youth organization Naujawan Bharat Sabha and met up with Chandrashekhar Azad and other young revolutionaries with whom he printed and handed out seditious handbills and newssheets. He is almost always shown in his hallmark trilby, wearing which he magically eluded the British authorities. The colonial government hanged him and his two companions, Sukhdev and Rajguru, for the murder of a British official on 23 March 1931 at the age of twenty-four.[23] He supposedly made the Urdu slogan *Inqilāb Zindābād* ('Long live the revolution'), famous, shouting it in front of British officials. The best of the recent films, *The Legend of Bhagat Singh* (Raj Kumar Santoshi, 2002) stars Ajay Devgan (b. 1967). The term for martyr used here and elsewhere to designate a martyr is *sarfaroś*.

Bhagat Singh is, of course, not the only martyr in the popular patriotic imagination. There is an excellent Punjabi film about another of these nationalist martyrs, Uddham Singh (1899–1940), executed in Pentonville Prison, London for the murder of Sir Michael O. Dwyer, who was the Lt. Governor of Punjab at the time of the Jallianwala Bagh Massacre.[24] People in north India and especially the Punjab enumerate many martyrs. Indeed, it seems that each region of the subcontinent has its martyrs drawn from the nationalist movement.

Four of the songs from *The Legend of Bhagat Singh* (*Music:* A.R. Rahman; *Lyrics:* Sameer) pull together much of my argument. They also show the importance of the march or procession as a practice leading to liberation both personal and national and of the emotions involved. I think these songs also show how popular patriotism can, and does, take possession of people's minds at least on certain occasions.

The first song *Desh Mere Desh* (*Singers:* A.R. Rahman, Sukhwinder Singh) is an excellent example of a patriotic song. The refrain proclaims: 'My country, my country, you are my life. My country, my country, you are my pride.' It shows India's martyrs in heroic poses, and it also describes the country. It represents India as a paradise on earth, a garden of delights. These include shots of the Taj Mahal, itself a garden of delights associated with a mausoleum, and of the field of grain divided into four like a quadripartite paradise garden. It also shows scenes of resistance to British tyranny and of the innumerable protest marches of the Naujawan Sabha and other nationalist organizations. One scene shows a play staged on the river. It depicts a fight between a Hindu and Muslim which Bhagat Singh stops.

The second song, *Sarfaroshi Ki Tamanna* 1 (*Singers:* Sonu Nigam, Hariharan) uses the lyrics of the poet Ramprasad Bismil, leader of the Kakori Rail Dacoity, and hung on 19 December 1927. Mohammed Rafi (1924–80) sang a version of this song in the earlier *Shaheed* (S. Ram Sharma, 1965; *Music:* Prem Dhawan). The famous and often-repeated verse is, 'The desire for martyrdom is now in our hearts. We have to see how much strength is in the arms of our murderers.' Bhagat and his companions sing this song in heroic mode (*vīr ras*), marching into the courtroom.

Divine rays of the nation shine on Bhagat Singh (*The Legend of Bhagat Singh*, Harrow, Middlesex: Tiptop Entertainment)

The second version of this song, '*Sarfaroshi Ki Tamanna* 2' (*Singer:* Sonu Nigam) shows the martyrs in jail. The men are all shown alone and experiencing despair (*ġam*). As Bhagat sings, their morale lifts and they slowly come together and embrace. The visual turning point here has the divine rays of the nation shine down on Bhagat Singh.

We also see the mothers of the men make offerings to Śiva, and children and adults marching in protest

The last song, *Mera Rang De Basanti* (*Singers:* Sonu Nigam and Man Mohan Waris), takes words from an anonymous song, 'Mother, dye my shroud yellow'. It shows the martyrs singing as they march to the gallows while their mothers anguish, and yet feel pride outside the prison walls. The men now experience the emotion opposite to the despair

Arrival at the gallows (*The Legend of Bhagat Singh*, Harrow, Middlesex: Tiptop Entertainment)

they had felt initially in prison, they experience exhilaration or ecstasy (*mastī*), the emotion a person feels when liberated from everyday life either in union with a lover or with God (as in the Sufi orders); or, in this instance, when united with the nation through martyrdom.

MARTYRDOM'S RISE

The idea of martyrdom seems to be drawn in the first instance from the violent, left-wing strand of Indian politics and this is obviously so in the case of martyrs such as Bhagat Singh and others like Netaji Subhash Chandra Bose (1897–1945), leader of the Indian National Army (INA).[25] Only here, it is put to work for the nation and not for an international class war. The history, however, is more complicated than this. Sikhism makes martyrdom a central component of its theology and it is clear that it has, in large part, drawn its notion of martyrdom (*śahādat*) from Shi'ite Islam.[26] So, once again we have here in India's unofficial civil religion, the nationalization of an element appropriated from the conventional religions.

More generally, the role in which the martyr for the nation appears most prominently in contemporary India is that of the *military* or *police hero*. Numerous films have been made about such figures. The most successful of these in both commercial and artistic terms have been *Border* (J.P. Dutta, 1997) starring Sunny Deol as a military commander and *Sarfarosh* (John Mathew Matthan, 1999) starring Aamir Khan as Assistant Commissioner of Police (ACP) (with Naseeruddin Shah).[27] It might seem odd that the ordinary people in a country whose leaders have promoted it as the home of nonviolence should take military figures or rogue policemen as their national heroes. This was not always so. Films made in the 1950s did promote nonviolence.[28]

The emergence of the military figure as the saviour of the Indian nation can, I believe, be traced back to an event and a film depicting it. The event was the India-China War of 1962.[29] The disillusionment with Nehru and his peaceful approach to international affairs was profound. The film that promoted the military hero, here the *jawan* (lit., 'young man') or ordinary foot soldier, at the expense of the naive politician was *Haqeeqat* (Reality, Chetan Anand, 1964), shot on location in Ladakh. It starred Dharmendra Deol (b. 1935), Balraj Sahni (1913–73), and Priya Rajvansh (d. 2000).[30] The song that concludes this black and white film, *Kar Chale Hum Fida Jaan-o-tan Saathiyon*, 'We have sacrificed our bodies and souls' [*Music*: Madan Mohan (1924–75); *Lyrics*: Kaifi Azmi (b. 1925)] uses 'realistic' shooting and incorporates newsreel footage. Note that the last verse calls the jawans, Rāms and Lakṣmaṇs who will not allow any Rāvaṇs (here the Chinese) to violate Sītā (here the nation and its women). The singer is Mohammed Rafi:

We have sacrificed our bodies and souls, companions. Now the nation, companions, is in your care.

Breathing stopped, the pulse froze solid, yet we stepped up our pace, we didn't let it slacken.

Our heads were cut off, we didn't let them be bowed. Though we died our swagger remained,

companions. Now the nation ...

The times for staying alive are many, but the time for giving one's life does not come everyday.

Beauty and love, he disgraces both, that youth who does bathe (himself) in blood. Tie (your) shroud to your head, companions. Now the nation .

Let not the way of sacrifices be deserted. You alone continue to decorate new convoys. The feast of victory comes after this feast.

Life and death continue to embrace one another. Today the bride has become the earth, companions. Now the nation ...

Draw a line on the ground with your blood. On this side (of the line) no Rāvaṇ gets to come.

You break your hand if your hand rises; nobody gets to touch the skirt of Sītā. You too are Rām, you alone are Lakṣmaṇ, companions. Now the nation .

PATRIOTIC FILMS

This war film was not the only response of the Bombay film industry. It emphasized the military hero and patriotism in films that were not represented as war or patriotic films. One of the heroes in the blockbuster of 1964, *Sangam*, Sunder (Raj Kapoor [1924–88]), also the director, plays an air force pilot. Dilip Kumar (b. 1922) starred in *Leader* (Ram Mukherjee, 1964). It opens with the official national song in Sanskrit, *Vande Mataram* composed by the Bengali writer, Bankim Chandra Chatterji (1838–94), whose novel *Ānandamaṭh* (1882) is written around the song, as the credits roll.[31] A patriotic speech and song soon follow. None of these films, however, was intended to be primarily a patriotic film.

One Hindi film star, Manoj Kumar (b. 1937), appeared in (and ghost-directed) a film that was the first explicitly patriotic film of the period—*Shaheed* (S. Ram Sharma, 1965). This black and white film was neither a historical film nor a social film in the conventional sense. It was a nationalist historical, a historical set in the British rather than the Mughal or post-Mughal period. It is notable not only for Kumar's portrayal of Bhagat Singh, but also for its explicitly patriotic songs. It is the direct ancestor of the shahīd films made in 2002. Manoj Kumar went on, following the moderate success of *Shaheed*,to direct and star in a series of patriotic films: *Upkaar* (1967), *Purab aur Pacchim* (1970), *Roti, Kapda aur Makaan* (1974), and *Kranti* (1981).

Lal Bahadur Shastri (1904–66), who succeeded Jawaharlal Nehru after his death in 1964, used the slogan *Jai Jawan, Jai Kisan* ('Victory to the soldier, Victory to the farmer') implicitly recognizing the failure of Nehru's pacifism and industrialism. The films Manoj Kumar made after *Shaheed*, set in the present, made use of this slogan. They featured a farmer named Bharat and military heroes, jawans, in secondary roles who represented the official post-Nehru patriotism.

After *Kranti*, Manoj Kumar was unable to gain success at the box office. He became a figure in the Bharatiya Janata Party (BJP) in the 1990s. Since then, others have made films the industry considered patriotic or nationalist. Mehul Kumar made a patriotic, antiterrorist film, *Tiranga* (Three Colours, 1992), and Vidhu Vinod Chopra revived the nationalist historical film with *1942 A Love Story* (1993). Patriotism became a more prominent theme in films made in and around 1997, the fiftieth year of India's Independence. Aamir Khan starred (with Naseeruddin Shah) in *Sarfarosh*, a film about Pakistani infiltration. *Lagaan* (Ashutosh Gowarikar, 2001) starring Aamir Khan, a story about a village's struggle against an oppressive impost (*lagān*) and featuring a cricket match between villagers and the British, is the most acclaimed nationalist historical film. *Mangal Pandey—The Rising* (Ketan Mehta, 2005) also stars Aamir Khan and retells the controversial story that is supposed to have sparked the so-called Indian Mutiny of 1857. Yet another film starring Khan, *Rang De Basanti—A Generation Awakes* (Rakeysh Omprakash Mehra, 2006) shows how present-day youth slowly get caught up in the revolutionary politics of the past. Two films made about the confrontation between the Pakistani and Indian military in Kargil in 1999, *LOC Kargil* (J.P. Dutta, 2003) and *Lakshya* (Farhan Akhtar, 2004) starring Amitabh Bachchan, Hrithik Roshan, and Preity Zinta have been much discussed.[32]

The true successor to Manoj Kumar as a maker of explicitly patriotic films, however, is Sunny (Ajit Singh) Deol (b. 1965), son of Dharmendra. Like Manoj Kumar, Sunny started out as a young lover but turned to action films and teamed up with director Rajkumar Santoshi to make *Ghayal* (1990) and, later, *Ghatak* (1997). The Deol–Santoshi partnership came unstuck over *Barsaat*. This film, supposed to be the platform for launching Sunny's younger brother, Bobby, did poorly at the box office and Sunny and Rajkumar parted company. This split figures in the making of *The Legend of Bhagat Singh*. Having reinvented himself as an action hero, Deol also made successful action films with other directors—*Tridev* (Rajiv Rai, 1989), *Narasimha* (N. Chandra, 1992), and *Jeet* (Raj Kanwar, 1997)—and a war film, *Border* (J.P. Dutta, 1997). All of these are entwined with the question of patriotism, but none of these are explicitly presented as nationalist or patriotic films. After several of his action films flopped, Sunny was reborn as a patriot. The venue for this was *Gadar: Ek Prem Katha* (Anil Sharma, 2001) which featured music by Uttam Singh, and was a Zee TV production. It is a nationalist historical film set in 1947, the year of Independence and the Partition. It tells the story of a truck driver, Tara Singh (Sunny Deol), a Sikh, who falls in love with a Muslim girl, Sakina (Amisha Patel), belonging to an aristocratic family. During the Punjab riots, Tara saves Sakina from an angry mob of Hindus and takes her home. After Partition, Tara and Sakina, now married with a son, are in India and her father (Amrish Puri) is in Pakistan. Arrangements are made for them to go to Pakistan, but only Sakina is allowed back. Eventually Tara gets into Pakistan and confronts Sakina's father. The film is noted for its 'authentic' and 'sensitive' portrayal of the 'communal' violence that occurred at the time of Partition, as well as Tara's response to Sakina's father. Some have criticized it, however, for its anti-Pakistani—the Pakistanis are almost all selfish and bigoted—attitude. Certainly, such a portrayal can be seen as playing into the hands of a political Hinduism which easily transfers this characterization from Pakistanis to Muslims.

Other films soon followed, *Indian* (N. Maharajan, 2001), *Maa Tujhe Salaam* (Tinu Verma, 2001), and *The Hero—Love Story of a Spy* (Anil Sharma, 2003). Deol was also involved in the making of a Bhagat Singh film, *23rd March 1931—Shaheed* (Guddu Dhanoa, 2002), starring Bobby. The other three films feature military and police heroes of the present day. It is here that one might expect to see a convergence with Hindutva. So it is worth looking at one of them.

POLITICAL HINDUISM?

Indian (N. Maharajan, 2001) is an admittedly patriotic and anti-terrorist film.[33] It is not, however, a war film. Its hero is a policeman and the enemies he has to fight are largely internal to the country. The emergence of the policeman as national hero is problematically to be attributed to *Zanjeer* (Prakash Mehra, 1973), the first film scripted by the team of Salim Khan and Javed Akhtar, which also happens to be the film which launched Amitabh Bachchan's career as a man willing to step outside the law in order to fight corruption and bring justice. I say this is a prob-lematic attribution because, unlike the military man who attains his goal *through* his occupation as fighter in the Hindi film, the policeman has to *renounce* his occupation or step outside it in order to achieve his heroic objective. So the police in the world of Mumbai films more often than not come across as the opposite of renouncers. They are quite ready to remain as policemen and take bribes, and adhere to a double standard. The rich who can corrupt them are treated as upstanding citizens while the poor are treated as enemies of the nation.

Indian opens with the Indian tricolour overlaid with the film title, first in Hindi, then in Urdu. It then shifts to a montage of newsreel footage of national events mixed with stills of national leaders (with a zoom shot of Bhagat Singh's picture) and the song *Watan Waalon* (*Music:* Anand Raaj Anand; *Lyrics:* Anand Bakshi [1920-2002]; *Singer:* Roop Kumar Rathod and Chorus) reminiscent of *Kar Chale* from *Haqeeqat*, while the credits scroll by. The opening verses of it urge: 'People of the nation, do not sell out the country. Do not sell its earth, its sky. Do not sell out the shrouds of the martyrs who gave their lives for the nation.' It then shifts to a mountain scene where a military spokesman announces Indian victory in the Kargil conflict in front of the troops.

Wasim Khan (Mukesh Rishi), a Pakistani terrorist, slashes at Indian troops held prisoner with his scimitar when they burst into song on hearing of India's victory. He says Pakistan may not be able to defeat India on the battlefield, but vows to fight in a new way. He will attack the heart (*dil*) and brain (*dimāġ*) of India, meaning he will deceive and provoke the people from inside its borders.

Cut to a meeting of the Research and Analysis Wing (RAW), India's foreign intelligence agency. Its head reveals that Wasim Khan, wanted in forty-eight countries, is now in Maharashtra. So he has asked Surya Pratap Singh (Raj Babbar), Director General of Police (DGP) in that state, to arrest him. Singh replies that this will not be easy because Wasim has friends and guardians in India. At this point, we in the audience might now be thinking that these 'friends and guardians' of the Pakistani terrorist in India, must be none other than their co-religionists—the Muslims of India.

A man who later turns out to be the son of Wasim's chief guardian in Maharashtra, enters a hotel to warn Wasim that the police are after him, only to discover that Wasim has a double. Wasim leaves in a car while the police arrest his double. On the street, the hero of the film, DCP Raj Shekhar Azad (Sunny Deol), appears from behind Wasim's double standing in the road before Wasim's oncoming auto. Resorting to the sort of trickery for which the incarnations of Viṣṇu are noted, Azad removes his sunglasses and, gun in holster at his side, approaches Wasim's car. Wasim shoots at him and hits his own double instead. After a car chase, Azad captures Wasim from a helicopter, a feat no mere human could perform. Later, Azad empties a theatre of people onto the street just as they pass by, causing the gangsters to give up their chase in confusion. Still later, Azad prevents a plot to kill a Muslim leader when he discovers an infiltrator among the security forces by using a fake command. Azad concludes this scene saying that the conspiracy to split Rām (Hindu India) and Rahīm (Muslim India) will never succeed. Then, when Wasim's Indian guardian tries to have Azad lynched by a mob, Azad plants his own men in the crowd and pretends to shoot them, causing the crowd to disperse in fear.

Azad's credentials as an incarnation are thus easily inferred. But we do not have to rely on inference alone. When Azad finds out that Surya Pratap Singh, his own father-in-law, is involved in protecting Wasim, he shoots him, to the tune of *Watan Waaloñ*. A Central Bureau of Investigation (CBI) inspector (Om Puri) who suspects Azad of this, meets with Azad and tells him he now knows Azad is guilty but says he has destroyed the evidence because Azad has slain him like Arjun slew the Kauravas. Arjun laid down his arms when confronting his own cousins. Krishna had to persuade him to kill them. Azad is Krishna and Arjun together, because he persuaded himself to kill his father-in-law.

Angels and martyrs also appear in the film. A restaurant owner (Shakti Kapoor), who displays the sign of Muslim orthodoxy, a bruise on the forehead (acquired from touching the head to the floor five times day), fulfils the role of a messenger angel, giving a short lecture on national morality. According to him, the main problem with India is corruption and greed, not fanaticism. Two of Azad's devoted young recruits, one a Muslim, Rahim, the other a Hindu, Pratap, commit suicide—martyrdom— to the strains of *Watan Waaloñ*.

Where is the patriotism or nationalism that makes the nation Hindu? Shankar Singhania (Danny Denzongpa), one of the ten top richest men in India, is implicated, by a man named Francis (by inference, a Goan Christian), in terrorist activities. He wants the land that belongs to a temple for development. The only scene in the film where we see a Hindu rite is here, on the occasion of Gaṇpati Pūjā, where Singhania pretends to be a devout worshiper.[34] It is this hypocritical Hindu and not a Muslim who is Wasim's guardian. The climax of the film consists of Azad's encounters with Wasim and Singhania. Azad fights with Wasim, to the tune of *Watan Waaloñ*. During this confrontation, Wasim has a vision of Azad as the epic hero, Arjun, clad in a dhoti and sacrificial thread, but also bearing a gun and holster.

Wasim amazed to see Arjun in epic clothes with gun and holster
(*Indian*, Mumbai and London: Eros International)

He shoots Wasim and says, 'We worship Gandhiji and Chandrashekhar Azad' (after whom he is apparently named). He adds that he is not just a police officer, he is an Indian. He does not need permission to kill an enemy of the country, which he equates with a raped mother.[35] Azad prevents panic that might be caused by a bomb by precipitating a bus drivers' strike. He then drives the bomb-rigged bus with Shankar in it into the sea, jumping out before it hits the water and explodes. The film ends with '*Watan Waaloñ*'.

All of the ideas I have presented as constituent of popular Indian patriotism are to be found in *Indian*—the incarnation of the nation drawn from Vaiṣṇava Hinduism, the angel or messenger of the nation's morality taken from Islam, and the idea of martyrdom appropriated directly from Sikhism and indirectly from Shi'ite Islam. At the beginning of the film we are positioned to suspect that Muslims in India are conspiring with the chief Pakistani terrorist against India, that is, Hindu India. The narrative of the film, however, clearly and systematically disabuses its spectators of this notion. The position of the little lectures that we receive in the film is that communalism is not in itself religious. Adhering to the line of older left-wing nationalists, these lectures want us to believe that communal conflicts are due to economic motives— private greed and public corruption. The film, thus, rejects the very idea of a political Hinduism in the form in which many of those associated with the politics of the BJP would have Indians practice it.

CONCLUSION

Popular patriotism in India consists of an unofficial civil religion that partly overlaps with the official civil religion and partly differs from it. The unofficial civil religion emphasizes sacrifice for the nation as the means to national prosperity and social justice. It is not opposed to the consumer society promised first by Nehruvian socialism and then by liberalization, but it is opposed to the greed of India's businessmen and the corruption of the nation's government officials often attributed to modern capitalism by socialists but more often than not attributed to India's traditional merchants or Westernized businessmen in films.

So far the unofficial and the official can be taken as concurring with one another. They go separate ways, however, over the question of secularism. The official secularism is legal and procedural and, as Hinduists are perennially fond of pointing out, inconsistent when it comes to Muslims (whose 'personal' law is retained). The unofficial civil religion is disinterested in this secularism. It does agree that none of the conventional religions of the subcontinent should be privileged over the others in the public life of the nation, but it rejects the proposition of secularization often implicit in some renderings of secularism. This is the idea that with increasing modernization, the conventional religions will or should diminish in importance and eventually disappear. The unofficial civil religion takes the position that the conventional religions are important for people, but that they remain a matter of familial and personal practice.

The main weakness of the secularist views is that they do not provide the nation with a way of life, a set of beliefs and practices to be followed.[36] The civil religion of the movies steps in to fill this void. The centrepiece of the way of life they represent is what I have called here a national theology. This national theology draws on the three main conventional religions of India. It is, hence composite, though I would not call it either eclectic or hybrid because the national theology has a coherence, a logic of its own. The incarnation or avatar from Vaiṣṇava Hinduism engages in just the right action, often through the use of trickery by drawing on the gap between appearance and reality (*māyā*). The angel/messenger taken from Islam embodies the morality of the Indian people, their good sense. Finally, and perhaps most importantly, the unofficial civil religion promotes a specific idea of sacrifice, that of martyrdom drawn from Sikhism (and indirectly from Shi'ite Islam). This idea and the language in which people have spoken it is largely Urdu rather than Hindi, as any analysis of the songs would show.

Similar ideas of patriotism, with different emphases, are also to be found in at least some of the regional films. Tamil films dubbed or 'reversioned' for the Hindi film market, are evidence for this. *Hindustani* (*Indian*, Shankar, 1996) is about a nationalist hero, Senapati (Kamal Hassan) who comes out of retirement to eliminate corruption. *Hey Ram* (Kamal Hassan, 2000) is about the religious riots involved in the Partition. It opens with the patriotic song Gandhi was supposed to like best, *Raghupati Raghava Raja Ram*. *Bombay* (Mani Ratnam, 1995) tells the story of a Hindu, Shekhar (Aravind Swamy) who falls in love and marries a Muslim woman, Shaila Bano (Manisha Koirala) despite the angry opposition of their parents. Their lives become entangled in riots after they move to Bombay.

Scholars are perhaps correct to see political Hinduism as posing a direct threat to the idea of a secular India. The difficulty is that the secular, post-Hindu India imagined by scholars and some Indian intellectuals has never existed. The advocates of Hinduization, however, also have difficulty. They may think that they are aiming at a soft target, the fragile or nonexistent secular India of Nehru. Their actual target, however, consists of the popular patriotism I have outlined above. The 'purification' of popular patriotism would prove a difficult task.

Let me end by asking what the status of these filmic representations of patriotism with respect to the life of the Indian nation are? I think it is important to distinguish between ideas and beliefs in talking about popular patriotism and the ideologies on offer by the major political parties. Ideas may have cognitive appeal to people, but unless they also have emotive appeal, they remain ideas. They do not become beliefs. I think it is also important not to reify ideas or beliefs either. What may be ideas in one setting for some people may be beliefs in another setting for other people. Hindutva, thus, may constitute a system of beliefs for members of the Rashtriya Swayamsevak Sangh (RSS) in Maharashtra but remain simply ideas for the bulk of the population. What I have tried to show is that the ideas of popular patriotism as represented in film and song have emotive as well as cognitive appeal to audiences, and that we should probably view these ideas as beliefs which a plurality of the population probably adheres to. People can, of course, change their beliefs, but this is not so easy as exchanging ideas.

NOTES AND REFERENCES

1. Interview with Prasun Sonwalkar, 'A Campaign That Lost Sheen', *The Hindu* (3 October 2004).

2. Philip Lutgendorf, *'Jai Santoshi Maa* Revisited: On Seeing a Hindu "Mythological"', in S. Brent Plate (ed.), *Representing Religion in World Cinema: Filmmaking, Myth-making, Culture Making* (New York: Palgrave Macmillan, 2003) analyses the last major film of this genre.

3. Arvind Rajagopal, *Politics After Television: Hindu Nationalism and the Reshaping of the Indian Public* (Cambridge: Cambridge University Press, 2001).

4. My idea of a national theology draws on 'political theology', the idea that modern political theories and institutions are a secularization, often unwitting, of older theologies. A legal and political theorist, Carl Schmitt is considered the problematic source of this idea. See George Schwab (ed.), *Political Theology: Four Chapters on the Concept of Sovereignty*, foreword Tracy B. Strong (Chicago: University of Chicago Press, [1934] 2005). Robert N. Bellah, 'Civil Religion in America', *Beyond Belief: Essays on Religion in a Post-traditional World* (New York: Harper & Row, 1970), pp. 168–89, reiterated a version of political theology under the rubric 'civil religion', attributed to Jean-Jacques Rousseau.

5. Far from being the unconscious resurgence of an age-old mythic tradition, this can be seen as a largely conscious reworking of theologies. One could point to parallels in Hollywood. See Joel W. Martin and Conrad E. Ostwalt, Jr. (eds), *Screening the Sacred: Religion, Myth, and Ideology in Popular American Film* (Boulder: Westview Press, 1995). See also, Philip French, 'Films of the Week', The *Guardian* (9 August 1998) for his discussion of Bruce Willis in *Armageddon* (Michael Bay, 1998) as a recent example.

6. There are popular 'street' editions of patriotic songs. One is *Rastriya Filmī Gīt* [National Film Songs] (New Delhi: Diamond Pocket Books, 1995). Another is Nareshchandra Chaturvedi (ed.), *Āzādī Ke Tarāne* [Songs of Freedom] (New Delhi: Diamond Pocket Books, 1986).

7. Some scholars include patriotism within nationalism, but then recuperate the older distinction by distinguishing a 'Western' from an 'Eastern' nationalism or a 'civic' from an 'ethnic' nationalism. See Liah Greenfield, *Nationalism: Five Roads to Modernity* (Cambridge, MA: Harvard University Press, 1992).

This is what I would characterize as the contemporary liberal view. Marxists, especially before Stalin reinvented a Mother Russia, were either hostile to nationalism altogether or saw it as transitional to a global class struggle.

8. Proponents of the official civil religion now favour *rāṣṭra* ('that ruled') because they consider the formerly more used term, *jāti* ('what is by birth'), used to mean caste, race, and tribe, as well as nation, as having divisive connotations.

9. The film, *Apna Ghar* (Ram Pava, 1960). The song also featured in *Yeh Gulistan Hamara* ['This rose garden of ours'] (Atma Ram, 1972; *Music:* S.D. Burman), a film in which Dev Anand patriotically quells tribal rebellion in the then North-East Frontier Agency (NEFA).

10. It stars Sanjay Dutt, Hrithik Roshan, and Preity Zinta (*Music:* Shankar, Ehsaan, and Loy; *Lyrics:* Sameer and Rahat Indori).

11. Gautam Kaul, *Cinema and the India Freedom Struggle* (New Delhi: Sterling, 1998), pp. 34–5. The only patriotic film funded by the Government of India was *Gandhi* (Richard Attenborough, 1983). Gandhi, of all nationalists, was the most opposed to film.

12. Geoffrey Parrinder, *Avatar and Reincarnation: The Divine in Human Form in the World's Religions* (Oxford: One World, 1997 [1970]), pp. 1991; Ronald Inden, 'Hindu Evil as Unconquered Lower Self', in *Text and Practice: Essays on South Asian History* (New Delhi: Oxford University Press, 2006), pp. 213–37; and Ronald Inden, 'Embodying God: From Imperial Progresses to National Progress in India', ibid., pp. 243–311.

13. The film is the sixteenth top grosser of all time unadjusted for inflation according to the website, www.bollywhat.com (accessed 22 July 2004). It is ranked twelfth for the 1990s by the website, www.ibosnetwork.com (accessed 22 July 2004).

14. D.B. MacDonald and W. Madelung, 'Malā'ika (A.) angels (Persian "angel" =*firishta*)', in *Encyclopaedia of Islam* (Leiden: E. J. Brill, 1960–) 6 (1991), pp. 216–19 and Shaykh Muhammad Hisham Kabbani, *Angels Unveiled: A Sufi Perspective* (Chicago: Kazi Publications, 1995).

15. The angel is not confined to older films or even to Muslims who embody national morality. *Kal Ho Naa No* [Tomorrow May Not Be] (Nikhil Advani, 2003) features a character Aman Mathur (Shah Rukh Khan). He is an angel who solves peoples' problems, constantly interfering in the affairs of a Punjabi family in New York that is partly Catholic. He extracts himself from a love affair by dying of cancer.

16. It opened on Diwali day, 31 October 1997, against *Dil To Pagal Hai*, the top film of the year. It did good business outside the metropolitan markets and ranked twenty-first for 1997 according to the website www.ibosnetwork.com (accessed 24 July 2004).

17. Farhad Khosrokhavar, *Les nouveaux martyrs d'Allah* (Paris: Flammarion, 2003 [2002]).

18. Louis E. Fenech, *Martyrdom in the Sikh Tradition* (New Delhi: Oxford University Press, 2000).

19. This martyrdom also has a Sufi connection where passionate love of God brings martyrdom. See Carl W. Ernst and Bruce B. Lawrence, *Sufi Martyrs of*

Love: The Chishti Order in South Asia and Beyond (London: Palgrave Macmillan, 2002).

20. *Qurbani* [Sacrifice] (Feroz Khan, 1980), and *Qayamat Se Qayamat Tak* [From Crisis to Crisis] (Mansoor Khan, 1988), are only a few of the many films where lovers are prepared to or actually die for their love.

21. The earliest of these, from 1948, was directed by Ramesh Saigal and starred Dilip Kumar as the martyr.

22. Vishwa Nath Datta, *Jallianwala Bagh Massacre* (Delhi: Pragati Publications and Indian Council of Historical Research, 2000).

23. Jyotsna Kamat, 'Amar Shaheed Bhagat Singh's Biography', www.bhagatsingh. com (accessed 27 June 2003).

24. *Shaheed Uddham Singh* (Chitrarth, 2001) starring Raj Babbar, Juhi Chawla, Shatrughan Sinha, Ranjit Gurkirtan, Gurdas Maan (Bhagat Singh), Amrish Puri; *Music* Jagjit Singh (available on DVD with English subtitles).

25. Leonard Gordon, *Brothers Against the Raj: A Biography of Indian Nationalists Sarat and Subhas Chandra Bose* (New York: Columbia University Press, 1990).

26. Louis E. Fennec, *Martyrdom in the Sikh Tradition* (Oxford: Oxford University Press, 2001).

27. *Border* was sixth top grossing film in the 1990s; *Sarfarosh* was forty-second. Source: www.ibosnetwork.com (accessed 17 June 2003).

28. *Mother India* (Mehboob Khan, 1957) did this from a loosely Nehruvian and Gandhian perspective. It also promoted national development through industrialization. See Gayatri Chatterjee, *Mother India* (London: British Film Institute, 2002), pp. 23–4, 72–4. *Naya Daur* (B.R. Chopra, 1957) is explicitly Gandhian in its rejection of machinery and support of his nonviolence.

29. Neville Maxwell, *India's China War* (New York: Pantheon, 1970), an unofficial account of the war, critical of Nehru's government, is also probably the most definitive.

30. Released on 1 January, it netted Rs 22,000,000. Its adjusted all-India net, according IBOS was Rs 442,820,496. It was the fourth most profitable film of 1964. Source: www.ibosnetwork.com (accessed 18 June 2003).

31. Sabyasachi Bhattacharya, *Vande Mātaram, the Biography of a Song* (New Delhi/ New York: Penguin Books, 2003) and Bankim Chatterji, *Ānandamaṭh, or The Sacred Brotherhood,* trans Julius Lipner (New York: Oxford University Press, 2005).

32. *LOC Kargil* flopped; *Lakshya* was the third highest grossing film for 2004. Source: www.ibosnetwork.com (accessed 23 February 2005).

33. Maharajan also wrote the screenplay. The dialogues, which are clever, were done by Sanjay S. Masoom.

34. The annual worship of Gaṇeś and accompanying festival was started by the Maharashtra nationalist, Bal Gangadhar 'Lokmanya' Tilak (1856–1920) in 1893. It is celebrated annually on *Gaṇeś-caturthī,* fourth day of the lunar month Bhādra (August–September). Like other festivals involving processions, it has been the occasion of communal clashes.

35. Chandrashekhar Azad, b. Tiwari (1906–1931) began his career in the Non-cooperation movement with Gandhi in 1921, then became head of the

Hindustan Republican Army. He shot himself in the head while surrounded by the police and under fire from them, on 27 February 1931. Source: www. indiansaga.info (accessed 24 July 2003). An old film *Chandrashekhar Azad* (Jagdish Gautam, 1963) and starring P. Jairaj, Nirupa Roy, Indira, Lila Misra, and Manju (*Music:* Sardul Kawatre) also exists. Sunny Deol went on to play the role himself in the Deol version of Bhagat Singh, *23rd March 1931—Shaheed* (Guddu Dhanoa, 2002; *Music:* Anand Raaj Anand; *Lyrics:* Dev Kohli) alongside his younger brother, Bobby, who played Bhagat Singh. Akhilendra Mishra plays Chandrashekhar Azad in Santoshi's version. Aamir Khan plays a modern character D.J. who plays Chandrashekhar Azad in *Rang De Basanti.*

36. Rajeev Bhargava, 'Is Secularism a Value in Itself?', in Imtiaz Ahmad, Partha S. Ghosh, and Helmut Reifeld (eds), *Pluralism and Equality: Values in Indian Society and Politics* (New Delhi: Sage Publications, 2000), pp. 101–12.

Contributors

MADHAV M. DESHPANDE was born in Pune, India. He received his B.A. (Sanskrit) from the Fergusson College in 1966, his M.A. (Sanskrit) from the University of Pune in 1968, and his Ph.D. in 1972 from the Department of Oriental Studies at the University of Pennsylvania. He has taught since 1972 at the University of Michigan in Ann Arbor, where he is now Professor of Sanskrit and linguistics. His publications include fifteen books and over a hundred research papers on the areas of Paninian linguistics, Sanskrit phonetics and syntax, editions of Vedic texts, sociolinguistics of Sanskrit and Prakrit languages, studies in Indian philosophy, and the history of intellectual traditions in India.

RONALD INDEN has recently retired from the departments of history and South Asian languages and civilizations at the University of Chicago, where he served on the faculty for over thirty-five years. He is currently investigating changes in class and national aspirations in India in the postcolonial period. His interests are wide-ranging, extending from indology, history, to anthropology and mass media. His early work, dating back to the 1960s, is on Bengali kinship, but he is more widely known for *Imagining India* (Oxford: Basil Blackwell, 1990; reprint with new preface, Indiana University Press, 2000). His other recent publications include the edited volume, *Querying the Medieval: Texts and History in South Asia* (London: Oxford University Press, 2000) and a collection of papers, *Texts and Practice: Essays on South Asian History* (New Delhi: Oxford University Press, 2006).

VINAY LAL was born in Delhi and educated at Johns Hopkins and the University of Chicago. He has been teaching history at UCLA since 1993, besides serving as Director of the University of California Education Abroad Program (India), 2007–09. His previous books include *Empire of Knowledge: Culture and Plurality in the Global Economy* (London: Pluto Press, 2002); *The History of History: Politics and Scholarship in Modern India* (New Delhi: Oxford University Press, 2003); *Of Cricket, Guinness and Gandhi: Essays on Indian History and Culture* (Delhi: Viking Penguin, 2005); *Introducing Hinduism* (London: Icon Books, 2005); and *The Other Indians: A Political and Cultural History of South Asians in America* (Delhi: HarperCollins, 2008). He has worked closely with Ashis Nandy over two decades and they have published three books together, including *The Future of Knowledge and Culture: A Dictionary for the 21ˢᵗ Century* (New Delhi: Viking Penguin, 2005) and *Fingerprinting Popular Culture: The Mythic and the Iconic in Indian Cinema* (New Delhi: Oxford University Press, 2006).

JULIUS J. LIPNER is of Indo-Czech extraction and he was born and brought up in India, mainly in Bengal. He has been teaching Hindu thought and tradition in the University of Cambridge for nearly three decades, and has lectured and published widely in his areas of expertise. He is at present head of the Faculty of Divinity at Cambridge and a Fellow of the British Academy. He is the author of several books, including *Hindus: Their Religious Beliefs and Practices* (London: Routledge, 1998); *Brahmabandhab Upadhyay: The Life and Thought of a Revolutionary* (New Delhi: Oxford University Press, 2001), and, most recently, *Ānandamaṭh* (New York: Oxford University Press, 2005).

ROBY RAJAN leads a double life: during the day he is Professor in the School of Business at the University of Wisconsin, Parkside (USA), at night, after having written for *Empirical Economics, Operations Research,* and the like, he dons more colorful clothes, writing fiery critiques of his profession and of the pretensions of modern knowledge for journals such as *The International Economic Review, Alternatives, Emergences, Futures,* and *Rethinking Marxism.* In a 2005 article in *Third World Resurgence,* he disputes both the liberal and Marxist accounts of the reasons for Kerala's unusually good 'quality-of-life indicators', arguing that both these accounts attempt to domesticate Narayana Guru's ethico-political intervention in Kerala society by reducing it to an instance of 'caste reform'. He has also authored, in the 'Dissenting Knowledges Pamphlet Series', *The Tyranny of Economics: Global Governance and the Dismal Science* (Penang, 2005).

J. REGHU is Assistant Editor at the State Institute of Encyclopedic Publications in Trivandrum, Kerala. He is a regular contributor to leading Malayalam journals such as *Mathrubhumi, Sameeksha, Malayalam, Kalakaumudi, Yoganadam,* and *Bhasaposhini.* The journal *Madhyamam* carried a series of his articles on the Sri Narayana movement spread over sixteen issues in 2005. He is also the author of a recent book in Malayalam titled, *Desarastravum Hinducolonialismavum* (Kottayam: Subject & Language Publishers, 2008) in which he explores the tensions between caste as autonomous community and its subsumption as a tertiary aspect of the national narrative.

PAULA RICHMAN is William H. Danforth Professor of South Asian Religions at Oberlin College in Ohio. Her monographs include *Women, Branch Stories, and Religious Rhetoric in a Tamil Buddhist Text* (Syracuse: Syracuse University Press) and *Extraordinary Child: Poems from a South Indian Devotional Genre* (Honolulu: University of Hawaii Press). She has edited two multi-authored works on the Ramayana tradition, including *Many Ramayanas: The Diversity of a Narrative Tradition* and *Questioning Ramayanas, A South Asian Tradition* (Berkeley and Los Angeles: University of California Press; New Delhi: Oxford University Press [Indian edition]). Recently, Indiana University Press published *Ramayana Stories in Modern South India,* an anthology of modern short stories and plays based on Ramayana incidents she compiled of translations from Tamil, Kannada, Telugu, and Malayalam.

JYOTIRMAYA SHARMA is Professor of political science at the University of Hyderabad. His recent publications include *Hindutva: Exploring the Idea of Hindu Nationalism* (New Delhi: Penguin Viking, 2003) and *Terrifying Vision: M.S. Golwalkar, the RSS and India* (New Delhi: Penguin Viking, 2007). His present work revolves around the thought of Coomaraswamy, Tagore, and Gandhi. He has held fellowships, teaching positions, and visiting professorships at a number of institutions, including the Centre for the Study of Developing Societies (Delhi), Indian Institute of Advanced Study (Shimla), and the universities of Baroda, Hull, Oxford, and Heidelberg. He held senior editorial positions at the *Times of India* and *The Hindu* during 1998–2006, and he is also a trained Hindustani classical musician.

AJAY SKARIA taught at the University of Virginia, Charlottesville, for several years before moving to the University of Minnesota, Minneapolis, where he is Associate Professor of history and global studies. He grew up in Gujarat and took his Ph.D. in Indian history from Cambridge University. He is a member of the Subaltern Studies Collective and co-editor of Volume 12 of *Subaltern Studies* (2005). His intellectual interests in the area of Indian history include histories of aboriginal groups, environmental history, modern politics, and the thought of Gandhi. He is now completing a book on Gandhi, and he has previously published *Hybrid Histories: Forests, Frontiers and Wildness in Western India* (Delhi: Oxford University Press, 1999).

JOANNE PUNZO WAGHORNE earned her Ph.D. from the University of Chicago and she is presently Professor of religion at Syracuse University. She currently works on issues of changing religious organizations, practices, and self-understanding in the present era of mass communication, urbanization, globalization, and transnational migration. Her past publications contextualized these issues in contemporary urban India and in the Hindu diaspora. Her fieldwork in India has been supported by fellowships from the National Endowment for the Humanities, Fulbright Foundation, and the American Institute of Indian Studies. Her latest book is *Diaspora of the Gods: Modern Hindu Temples in an Urban Middle-Class World* (Oxford and New York: Oxford University Press, 2004).

Index